The Nine Hundred

ALSO BY HEATHER DUNE MACADAM

Rena's Promise: A Story of Sisters in Auschwitz
The Weeping Buddha

The Nine Hundred

The Extraordinary Young Women of the First Official Transport to Auschwitz

HEATHER DUNE MACADAM

HODDER &
STOUGHTON

First published in Great Britain in 2020 by Hodder & Stoughton
An Hachette UK company

1

Copyright © Heather Dune Macadam 2020

A CIP catalogue record for this title is available from the British Library

Hardback ISBN 9781529329315
Trade Paperback ISBN 9781529329322
eBook ISBN 9781529329339

Printed and bound in Great Britain by Clays Ltd, Elcograf S.p.A.

Hodder & Stoughton policy is to use papers that are natural, renewable
and recyclable products and made from wood grown in sustainable
forests. The logging and manufacturing processes are expected to
conform to the environmental regulations of the country of origin.

Hodder & Stoughton Ltd
Carmelite House
50 Victoria Embankment
London EC4Y 0DZ

www.hodder.co.uk

for Edith

in memory of
Lea
&
Adela

Contents

For most of history, Anonymous was a woman.
                        —VIRGINIA WOOLF

The measure of any society is how it treats its women and girls.
                        —MICHELLE OBAMA

Woman must write her self: must write about women and bring women to writing...Woman must put herself into the text—as into the world and into history...
                        —HÉLÈNE CIXOUS, "The
                        Laugh of the Medusa"

Foreword

BY CAROLINE MOOREHEAD

No ONE KNOWS FOR CERTAIN, or will ever know, the precise number of people who were transported to Auschwitz between 1941 and 1944, and who died there, though most scholars accept a figure of one million. But Heather Dune Macadam does know exactly how many women from Slovakia were put on the first convoy that reached the camp on March 26, 1942. She also knows, through meticulous research in archives and from interviews with survivors, that the almost one thousand young Jewish women, some no older than fifteen, were rounded up across Slovakia in the spring of 1942 and told that they were being sent to do government work service in newly occupied Poland, and that they would be away no more than a few months. Very few returned.

Basing her research on lists held in Yad Vashem in Israel, on testimonies in the USC Shoah Foundation's Visual Archives and the Slovak National Archives, and tracing the few women still alive today, as well as talking to their relatives and descendants, Macadam has managed to re-create not only the backgrounds of the women on the first convoy but also their day-to-day lives—and deaths—during their years in Auschwitz. Her task was made harder, and her findings more impressive, by the loss of records and the different names and nicknames used, as well as their varied spellings, and by the length of time that has elapsed since the Second World War. Writing about the Holocaust and the death camps is not, as she rightly says, easy. The way she has chosen to do it, using a novelist's license to re-imagine scenes and re-create conversations, lends immediacy to her text.

IT WAS ONLY in the late winter of 1940–41 that IG Farben settled on Auschwitz and its surroundings, conveniently close to a railway junction and to a number of mines and with plentiful supplies of water, for the construction of a major new plant in which to make artificial rubber and synthetic gasoline. Auschwitz was also given a mandate to play a role in the "Final Solution of the Jewish question," a place where, alongside labor allocations, prisoners could be killed rapidly and their bodies as rapidly disposed of. When, in September, a first experiment using prussic acid, or Zyklon B, proved effective in the gassing of 850 inmates, Rudolf Höss, the camp's first commandant, saw in it an answer to the "Jewish problem." Since camp physicians assured him that the gas was "bloodless," he concluded that it would spare his men the trauma of witnessing unpleasant sights.

First, however, the camp needed to be built. An architect, Dr. Hans Stosberg, was asked to draw up plans. At the Wannsee Conference on January 20, 1942, the Reich Main Security Office estimated that occupied Europe would yield a total of just under eleven million Jews. As Reinhard Heydrich, second in the SS hierarchy to Heinrich Himmler, put it, they should be "put to work in a suitable way within the framework of the Final Solution." Those too frail, too young, or too old to work were to be killed straight away. The stronger would work and were to be killed in due course since "this natural elite, if released, must be viewed as the potential germ cell of a new Jewish order."

Slovakia was the first satellite state to become a deportation country. For over a thousand years part of the kingdom of Hungary, and since the end of the First World War part of Czechoslovakia, it had become an independent country only in 1939, under German protection, ceding much of its autonomy in exchange for economic assistance. Jozef Tiso, a Catholic priest, became president, banned opposition parties, imposed censorship, formed a nationalist guard, and fanned antisemitism, which had been growing since the arrival of waves of Jewish refugees fleeing Austria after the Anschluss. A census put the number of Jews at 89,000, or 3.4 percent of the population.

The order for unmarried Jewish women between the ages of sixteen and thirty-six to register and bring their belongings to a gathering point was not initially viewed as alarming, though a few prescient families made desperate attempts to hide their daughters. Indeed, some of the girls found the idea of going to work abroad exciting, particularly when they were assured that they would soon be home. Their innocence made the shock of arrival at the gates of Auschwitz more brutal, and there was no one there to prepare them for the horrors to come.

That same day, 999 German women arrived from Ravensbruck, which was already full with 5,000 prisoners and could take no more. Having been selected before leaving as suitable functionaries, they oversaw the young Jewish women's work of dismantling buildings, clearing the land, digging, and transporting earth and materials, as well as in agriculture and cattle raising, thereby freeing the men already at Auschwitz to work on the heavier tasks of expanding the camp. Coming from large and loving families, accustomed to gentle manners and comfortable living, the Slovakian women found themselves shouted at, stripped naked, shaved, subject to interminable roll calls in the freezing dawn, forced to walk barefoot in mud, fighting for rations, subject to arbitrary punishments, worked to exhaustion and often to death. They were hungry, sick, terrified. The female guards, from Ravensbruck, were later admitted by Höss to have "far surpassed their male equivalents in toughness, squalor, vindictiveness and depravity." By the end of 1942, two thirds of the women on the first convoy were dead.

And Auschwitz itself kept growing. Jews from all over occupied Europe, from France and Belgium, Greece and Yugoslavia, Norway and later from Hungary, poured in, soon arriving at the rate of some three trains every two days, each train consisting of 50 freight cars containing more than 80 prisoners each. By June 1943, four crematoria were up and running, able to burn 4,736 corpses per day. Most of the new arrivals, whole families with babies and small children, went straight to the gas ovens.

The surviving Slovakian women, their bodies and minds grown stronger, devised strategies to stay alive, volunteering for the nastiest jobs, or finding safety in sewing or farming details or in the camp offices, becoming adept at escaping the daily extermination of the weakest, those who fell ill or who had become too emaciated for useful work. It was, notes Macadam, "a survival seesaw." The luckier found occupation in "Canada," the ironical prison term for the property plundered by the Nazis from the arriving Jews who had been instructed to bring with them from home between 66 and 100 pounds of things they thought they might need. Blankets, coats, spectacles, crockery, medical instruments, sewing machines, shoes, wristwatches, furniture overflowed across an extensive network of depots from where teams of the more fortunate or canny men and women inmates, working in continuous shifts, prepared shipments to put on the trains back to Germany. It was later estimated that at least two crates, weighing a thousand kilos each and containing valuables, were shipped back to Berlin every week.

For a long time, the Slovakian women's families at home had no idea where their daughters had gone. The few postcards that arrived, with cryptic references to long-dead relations, were puzzling and often so peculiar that many parents were able to persuade themselves that their daughters were safe and being cared for. But as the months passed, so fear spread, and it grew worse as fresh roundups took whole families away. One of the most poignant moments in Macadam's book is the arrival of family members in Auschwitz, greeted with horror by the surviving women, only too aware of the fate that awaited their parents and siblings.

Much has been written about the experience of Auschwitz, the battle for survival, the typhus, the gassings, the ever-worsening conditions, the starvation and brutality, and Macadam does not shy away from the horror. Books such as this one are essential: they remind modern readers of events that should never be forgotten.

Her book is good, too, on the background to the Slovakian deportations, on the life of the Jewish communities before the war, the buildup of Jewish persecution, and on the innocence of the families as they prepared their daughters for deportation. She writes just as evocatively on the sadness of the few who survived and returned home to find their parents dead, their shops boarded up, their houses and possessions grabbed by neighbors. Of the Slovakian prewar Jewish population, 70,000 people—over 80 percent—were dead and the postwar one-party regime banned all discussion of the Holocaust. Those on the first transport had left home as girls. Three and a half years later they came back as women, old beyond their years, who had seen, suffered, endured too much. Just surviving made them suspect: what had they done, what moral compromises had they made, not to have died with their friends?

THERE IS AN IMAGE at the end of this fine book which stays long in the mind. One of the surviving young women, Linda, having escaped Auschwitz and the death marches that took the lives of many survivors, having crossed countries in chaos and devastated by the war, at constant risk of being raped, finds herself at last on a train bound for home. The carriages are full to over-flowing with refugees, so she climbs on to the roof and it is there, perched high on the slowly moving train, that she looks out across a landscape which is not full of barbed wire or watchtowers, or guards with guns. She is, she realizes, free; it is spring, and the trees are turning green.

Author's Note

"IT IS TOO LITTLE, too late," Ruzena Gräber Knieža says in German. The phone line crackles. My husband, who is translating for me, shrugs. At the time, Ruzena was the only survivor I had found who was still alive who had been on the first transport to Auschwitz; her prisoner number was #1649. A few months earlier, she had been willing to be interviewed for a documentary I wanted to produce on the first girls in Auschwitz; however, my own health prevented me from flying to Switzerland to interview her. Now she is the one who is ill.

I try to explain that my main interest is speaking to her about Slovakia and how she and the other girls were collected and betrayed by their government. She sighs and says, "I don't want to think about Auschwitz before I die." At ninety-two years of age, can we blame her?

I send her a thank-you card, and then locate her testimony on the USC Shoah Visual Archive. It is in German. We can translate it, but the Shoah archive did not ask the questions I wanted to ask. Questions that have arisen since I met and worked with Rena Kornreich Gelissen, a survivor from the first transport, in 1992, over twenty-five years ago. Since I wrote *Rena's Promise*, family members of women who were on the first transport have contacted me with more stories about their cous-

ins, aunts, mothers, and grandmothers, and with that information, more questions arose. I have filmed and recorded
interviews with these families, but without a living survivor willing to speak with me—and a family who would let me speak
with her—those questions were never going to be answered. I
understand the desire to protect these elderly women; if you survived three years in Auschwitz and the death camps and lived
into your nineties, why should you have to think about that hell?
I do not want to hurt anyone, especially these amazing women,
by asking painful questions that raise the specters of the past.

A year after my conversation with Ruzena, I sent an email
out to second-generation (2G) families and asked if anyone
wanted to retrace their mother's journey to Auschwitz from Slovakia on the 75th anniversary of the first transport. Quite a few
people responded with interest, but in the end it was a small,
intimate group of three families: Erna and Fela Dranger's sons
from Israel (Avi and Akiva); Ida Eigerman Newman's family
from America (Tammy and Sharon, and Tammy's children:
Daniella and Jonathan) and Marta F. Gregor's daughter (Orna
from Australia). Then, a few weeks before we were set to meet,
I learned that ninety-two-year-old Edith Friedman Grosman
(#1970) was going to be the guest of honor at the 75th-
anniversary ceremonies. A few days later, Edith and I were
speaking via FaceTime. We clicked immediately and she told
me she would be happy to meet me and my camera crew in Slovakia. Two weeks later, we were sitting together in an early
Soviet bloc–style hotel room with dingy white walls and hideous décor, and I was asking her the questions I had not
known to ask Rena Kornreich (#1716) twenty-five years earlier.

Like Rena, Edith is vibrant, quick-witted and sharp. A little
bird of a woman who lights up the room. Our time together in
Slovakia was a whirlwind that took us to the barracks where she
and the other girls were held and to the train station from which
they were deported. At the ceremonies, we met the president

and prime minister of Slovakia, the Israeli ambassador to Slovakia, and children of other survivors. In a powerful homage of tears and hugs, the second-generation group I was traveling with bonded with Slovak second-generation families. At the end of our week, my husband told me, "This is not just a documentary. You have to write a book."

Writing about Auschwitz is not easy. It is not the sort of project one takes on lightly, but with Edith beside me, I was willing to try. This book would not be a memoir, though. It would be about all of them, or as many as I could find information on and fit into this complex history. In Canada, I found another survivor, Ella Rutman (#1950), and I flew to Toronto to bring the two survivors together. Edith and Ella remembered each other, but even at their advanced ages they were wary. As they spoke in Slovak, Edith cast a pained glance at me. This was not the warm bond I had imagined—Edith had not liked Ella when they were in Auschwitz, I realized. The meeting was awkward and distant until the two old women began looking through a magnifying glass at the numbers on their left forearms.

"I can't see my number anymore, it is so faded," Edith said.

The memories are fading as well. But the truth is there, if you know where to find it. Looking at old photos with Edith one day, I noticed Ruzena Gräber Knieža's face.

"Did you know Ruzena?" I asked.

"Of course!" Edith answered, as if this were the most obvious question in the world. "We were in class together and good friends with Ruzena and her husband, Emil Knieža, after the war. He was a writer like my husband. We used to visit them in Switzerland."

I had come full circle.

MANY OF THESE WOMEN knew each other before Auschwitz, either from their hometowns or villages, schools or synagogues; however, in the USC Shoah Archive testimonies, it is rare that anyone mentions a girl's maiden name. Sometimes, a survivor mentions a girl by her nickname or gives a physical description of a friend, so it can be hard to confirm if survivors are speaking about someone from the first transport. Margie Becker's (#1955) testimony is one of those rarities where the full names of the girls she and Edith grew up with are almost always mentioned, and because of the photograph of their class, Edith has been able to identify most of those girls. It had never even occurred to me to ask Edith if she knew Ruzena before I saw them together in their class photo, because Ruzena's name on the list of deportees lists her as being from a different town. I didn't know she had lived in Humenné when she was a young girl. If only I had started this journey when they were all still alive.

As I am wrapping up the final edits on this book, my email pings at me:

> My grandmother was on the first transport. I remember the stories she told us. She wrote a book about the deportation, but she later threw it away, saying no one would believe her. The first page of her written testimony survived, and I have it with me. Her name was Kornelia (Nicha) Gelbova, of the Slovakian town "Humenné." She was born in 1918.

Seconds later, I have opened an Excel file I created that has every girl's name, hometown and age in it, and Kornelia Gelbova's name is in front of me. She is number 232 on the original list archived at Yad Vashem in Jerusalem. Even more extraordinary is that her sister is mentioned in Ruzena Gräber Knieža's testimony. They were in Ravensbrück together. Both girls are on the same page of the list as three girls you are about to get to know very well: Edith and Lea Friedman, and their friend Adela Gross. And on that very same page are two girls some of you already know, Rena Kornreich and Erna Dranger.

One of my biggest concerns in writing this book is accuracy. I worry constantly about getting the dates and chronology correct, and making sure the narratives have been accurately chronicled. Edith assures me that I am "never going to get it all right. No one can get it all correct. It is too big. So you don't have the date, so what? It happened. That is enough."

I can only hope it is.

This story has multiple narratives. The core of this narrative comes from my interviews with witnesses, survivors, and families, and USC Shoah Archive testimonies. Memoirs, Holocaust literature and historical documents have been used to further elaborate on those personal stories, the atmosphere and politics of the time. My goal is to build as complete a picture as I can of the girls and young women of the first "official" Jewish transport to Auschwitz. One of the devices I have used to accomplish this is dramatic license. Where you find dialogue in quotes, you can be sure that those are direct quotes from interviews with survivors or witnesses who are reporting conversations they had or overheard. In other cases, to more fully illustrate or complete some scenes, I have used em-dashes to indicate dialogue I created; I only do this when conversations or arguments were mentioned in a testimony but *not* elaborated upon.

I am deeply grateful to Edith Grosman and her family, as well as the Gross, Gelissen, and Brandel families, who accepted me into their nucleus and have treated me as an honorary member. "You are like a cousin of ours," Edith told me at her ninety-fourth birthday party. Around her were her son, daughter-in-law, granddaughters, a great-grandchild, and another great-grandchild on the way. It is a great honor and privilege to be part of these women's histories, their champion and their chronicler. They were teenagers when they were sent to Auschwitz. Only a few ever came home. How they survived is a tribute to women and girls all over the world. This is their story.

Principal Characters on First Transport

The number of Ediths and Magdas, Friedmans and Neu-manns on the first transport necessitated that I create names to identify our young women in a unique fashion. That often meant using a version of their given names. Our primary characters are referred to by their real names or the name they reported on the transport list. (For some reason, girls often gave nicknames rather than the names they normally went by— my first choice in naming is therefore the name given on the list.) For the many duplicate names, another version of that name may be used (e.g., Margaret becomes Peggy). If a name is repeated more than twice, the last name or some alternative is used. That is the case with the many Magdas and Ediths I had to contend with. I hope families understand this need for clarity in the narrative. It is not out of disrespect that names were changed, but out of the hope that readers can identify— and identify *with*—these girls and women clearly.

Please also note: In the Slovak language *ova* is the equivalent of Miss or Mrs. I chose not to use *ova* with the names of the deportees because some of them were Polish and would not have used that syntax, and the USC Shoah Foundation does not use *ova* in its archives.

WOMEN ON FIRST TRANSPORT FROM SLOVAKIA, BY REGION OR TOWN OF ORIGIN

Humenné

Edith Friedman, #1970

Lea Friedman, Edith's sister, #1969

Helena Citron, #1971

Irena Fein, #1564

Margie (Margita) Becker, #1955

Rena Kornreich (originally from Tylicz, Poland), #1716

Erna Dranger (originally from Tylicz, Poland), #1718

Dina Dranger (originally from Tylicz, Poland), #1528

Sara Bleich (originally from Krynica, Poland), #1966

Ria Hans, #1980

Maya (Magda) Hans, # unknown

Adela Gross, # unknown

Zena Haber, # unknown

Debora Gross, not deported

Zuzana Sermer, not deported

Ruzinka Citron Grauber, # unknown

Michalovce

Regina Schwartz (with her sisters Celia, Mimi, and Helena), #1064

Alice Icovic, #1221

Poprad Region

Martha Mangel, #1741

Eta Zimmerspitz, #1756

Fanny Zimmerspitz, #1755

Piri Rand-Slonovic, #1342
Rose (Edith) Grauber, #1371

Prešov

Magda Amster, #unknown
Magduska (Magda) Hartmann, #unknown
Nusi (Olga or Olinka) Hartmann, #unknown
Ida Eigerman (originally from Nowy Sącz, Po-
    land), #1930
Edie (Edith) Friedman, #1949★
Ella Friedman, #1950★
Elena Zuckermenn, #1735
Kato (Katarina) Danzinger (mentioned in
    Hertzka letters), #1843
Linda (Libusha) Reich, #1173
Joan Rosner, #1188
Matilda Friedman, #1890★
Marta F. Friedman, #1796★

Stropkov Region

Peggy (Margaret) Friedman, #1019★
Bertha Berkowitz, #1048
Ruzena Gräber Knieža, #1649

**WOMEN ON SECOND TRANSPORT FROM
SLOVAKIA**

Dr. Manci (Manca) Schwalbova, #2675
Madge (Magda) Hellinger, #2318
Danka Kornreich, #2775

★ No relation to Edith and Lea Friedman

Part One

Map of Slovakia, 1942, showing the wartime borders and some of the towns from which the first Jewish women were deported to Auschwitz. The town of Ružomberok is identified because it was bombed by the Germans in 1944. Many Humenné families died in the explosion.
© HEATHER DUNE MACADAM; DRAWN BY VARVARA VEDUKHINA.

Chapter One

It's a sad business, even worse perhaps than the stars
they have branded us with...
because it's going to hit our children this time.
—LADISLAV GROSMAN, *The Bride*

FEBRUARY 28, 1942

THE RUMOR STARTED as rumors do. There was just a hunch. A sick feeling in the stomach. But it was still just a rumor. What more could they do to Jews? Even the weather seemed against them. It was the worst winter on record. Drifts higher than people's heads. If the government had had any practical sense, it would have made a proclamation that forced short folks to stay inside for fear of disappearing in all that snow. All the shoveling was taking its toll on backsides. Sidewalks had become instant playgrounds for children who didn't have sleds but could slide down drifts on their rear ends. Sledding was the new national pastime—that, and slipping on the ice.

Every blizzard was followed by subzero temperatures and gusts of wind from the Tatra Mountains. Slicing through thin coats and thick, it was impartial and pitiless to rich and poor

3

alike. The wind could find its way between the seams of even the best-sewn garments and nick flesh with biting cruelness. Lips and hands were cracked and chapped. Leftover goose fat was smeared inside nostrils to prevent nosebleeds. As cold drafts sneaked through the cracks of windows and under doors, tired parents welcomed tired neighbors to sit on stools and fret together about the rumor in front of a fire, though many worried in front of cold hearths—even firewood was hard to come by. Some Jewish families barely had food. It was bad for everyone, worse for some.

Flames of doubt and uncertainty were quenched by reason. If the rumor was true, the most reasonable said, and the government did take girls, they wouldn't take them far away. And if they did, it would only be for a little while. Only for the spring—when and if spring ever arrived. *If*, that is, the rumor was true.

The *if* was so big no one dared to say it, just in case the very word would curse them with its reality. It simply had to be a rumor. Why would anyone want to take teenage girls?

THE SNOW BEGAN FALLING as Jewish mothers all over Eastern Europe prepared the Sabbath candles. In the Friedman home, Emmanuel Friedman came in through the front door clapping and singing, "Shabbat Shalom! Shabbat Shalom! Shalom! Shalom! Shalom!" Clapping and singing, the children joined their father. Then the family gathered around the Sabbath table to watch as their mother lit the Sabbath candles. After circling her hands over the flames three times, she brought the light toward her heart—for it is a woman's place to bring light into the home—placed her hands over her eyes and murmured the Sabbath blessing:

> *Barukh ata Adonai Eloheinu Melekh ha-olam, asher kid'shanu b'mitzvotav v'tzivanu l'hadlik ner, l'hadlik ner shel Shabbat.* Blessed are You, Lord, our God,

King of the universe, who has sanctified us with His
commandments and commanded us to light Shabbat candle[s].

Edith and her sister Lea watched in reverent adoration as
their mother prayed silently, blinked three times, and then
opened her eyes. "Good Shabbes!" Her daughters hugged her,
and she blessed them each with a kiss in order of age, eldest to
youngest, but she bestowed a little longer kiss on the brows of
her teenagers Lea and Edith. There had been other rumors that
never came to fruition, she told herself, hugging her girls close
to her heart. Her secret prayer to God that night was that this
rumor, too, would be false.

Outside, thunder rolled like a great drum through the sky.
Lightning flashed. Snow fell in sheets. No one could remember
how many years it had been since there was a storm like this.

By Shabbat morning, the blizzard had dumped over a foot
of snow, and by midday, it was thigh high. As usual, a few stalwart individuals started shoveling, figuring it was better to
get the work half done and do it twice than to wait and have
to shovel once but twice as hard. The tobacco shop was not
only partially cleared, it was open. Weather never stopped a
serious smoker.

It was unusual for the town crier to make announcements
on Saturdays, even rarer than thunder in a snowstorm. Normally, proclamations were made during Friday or Monday
market. But in the afternoon, out in front of town halls all over
eastern Slovakia, drums started beating and, despite the blizzard,
a few gentiles out on the street stopped to listen. The wind was
up and the snow was deep, muffling the drum's call to attention.
No one in the Jewish neighborhood, across the low banks of a
small river meandering along the south edge of town, heard it.
The weather—for while there was always weather somewhere,
today there was just more than usual—wasn't helping.

Among the smattering of people gathered round the town crier stood twenty-one-year-old Ladislav Grosman, who for reasons known only to himself was in the square instead of at the synagogue or home with his family. Dark-eyed, open-faced, Ladislav was more likely to generate a smile than a frown, and laughter than tears. A poet at heart, he may have been taking a stroll after the family repast, appreciating the trackless white carpet across the square, wincing at the cold sting of snow pelting his face. Perhaps he just needed a smoke. Whatever the reason, when the town crier began banging his drum, Ladislav hurried with the few others who were out traipsing through the snow to hear the latest news.

Normally, the town crier would wait for a crowd to arrive before he began his announcement. Not today. He began at once so he could get out of the damn weather that was wetting his collar and freezing his neck. The flakes falling upon the heads of gentiles and Jews alike were large and wet now, a sure sign the storm was ending.

For some, it was about to begin.

Over the din of the storm, the town crier cried, "All Jewish girls of sixteen years and over. Unmarried girls [are] ordered to come to the appointed registration office; details of the medical inspection and the purpose of the whole business [to] be officially notified in due course." There was almost no one about to hear. It was a blizzard after all. Just a few ardent smokers, but the men who did hear it turned to their neighbors to say, I told you so.

Not having any more information about dates or times or places to add, the town crier appended the announcement with his own verbal signature, a kind of Bugs Bunny sign-off, and one last roll of his drum: "And that's the lot, the whole caboose, the dope the public is required to take notice of, full stop, *ende*, finish, *fin*, off home with the lot of you in this ruddy weather you wouldn't put a dog out in..."

There were no more ifs, ands, or buts—the rumor was true. And by the next morning, even with the snow piled high against their doors, everyone knew it. The latest proclamation fell on the heads of the Jewish community as heavily as icicles falling from the rooftops but far more dangerous.

WHEN IT CAME TO DRACONIAN MEASURES against its Jews, the Slovak government seemed to be trying to surpass the Germans. Young thugs, who had joined Slovakia's fascist, right-wing Hlinka Guard, bullied and beat up Jewish boys and men wearing the mandatory armbands, which had now become yellow stars. Gravestones were toppled or smashed, shops were defaced with anti-Jewish slogans. In the larger cities, there were bloodcurdling, nationalistic songs, punctuated by a rhythm section of stone throwing, a cymbal section of glass shattering. Newspaper kiosks served up *Stuermer* (Striker), the propagandist newspaper that fed ignorance and racist ideologies while publishing defamatory caricatures of hook-nosed Jews raping Slovak virgins, cutting children's throats and collecting their blood for the baking of matzo, straddling the Earth as if the globe were a horse to ride and conquer, while heroic German soldiers fought the devilish Jew—humanity's evil fiend.

One woman in the market even asked Edith, "Where are your horns?" When Edith showed her she didn't have any, the woman was shocked. How could anyone be so stupid as to think Jews had horns, made matzos with children's blood, or killed God? Jews invented God, for God's sake!

How could anyone actually believe what the propagandist newspapers said?

In September 1941, the Slovak government devised a Jewish Codex, laws and regulations that began to be implemented with increasing frequency throughout the fall, until it had seemed like every day the town crier was making another pronouncement against Slovak Jewry. One day it was:

We hereby make it common knowledge that the Jews: must register themselves and every member of their family at the mayor's office in the next twenty-four hours, with a list of all their real estate possessions.

The next day:

Jews must present their bankbooks from local as well as from foreign banks and are henceforth forbidden to reside on any main street and must vacate main street abodes within seven days.

A week later:

Jews must wear a yellow star on all their clothing 24 x 24 cm.

Jews may not travel interstate and for local travel must have a written permit by the Hlinka Guard, costing one hundred crowns. They may obtain it only if the Hlinka Guard accepts their request as being a valid one.

But what Jew had one hundred crowns, and what Jew knew a Hlinka Guard who would validate their request?

Jews must deposit all their jewelry within twenty-four hours at the head office of the Hlinka Guard.

Jews cannot have pets—not even a cat!—cannot have radios and cameras, so as not to become spreaders of lies from the BBC.

Jews must deposit their fur coats at the Hlinka Guard headquarters

Jews must turn in their motorcycles, cars, and trucks.

Jews will not be admitted to any hospital and will not
be eligible to receive operations.

Jews may no longer enter any high school, nor demand any reports from the various state authorities.

Edith still shakes her head at the laws that stunted her education. "My siblings had school still, to grade five. When they
finished, the law said they had to go to school till age fourteen."
So they had to repeat the fifth grade, three times! Meanwhile,
Edith and Lea fell in the difficult spot of already being over
fourteen, and despite their yearning for knowledge and their
quick minds, Jews were not allowed to finish high school.
Then another law passed.

Jews may not enter any public parks.

And another:

Jews may not employ any Aryans, nor socialize with
any Aryans, visit any theaters, pictures or cultural
festivities, congregate in bigger numbers than five.
No Jew is permitted to be on the street after twenty-
one hundred hours.

No one could have predicted the Aryanization of Jewish
businesses, which allowed gentiles to legally take over Jewish
businesses, and "all business practices to enable the fastest pos-
sible transfer of said business into the Aryantor's sole hands."
No compensation was paid to the Jewish business owner.
"The only thing permitted to Jews was to commit suicide,"
Ivan Rauchwerger's mother said.
And now they wanted their girls?

It didn't make any sense. Why would anyone want to take teenage girls for work? Teenagers are lazy and argumentative. And girls? Girls are the worst! They giggle one second and burst into tears the next. They get cramps and get cranky. They are more worried about their hair and fingernails than doing a proper day's work. Just look at the floor in the kitchen, after Priska was supposed to have swept it! Just look at the dishes that still have kugel stuck on the side because the scrubber was looking out the window at Jacob, the rabbi's son, instead of at the dishes. Without their mothers teaching them how to clean and take pride in their labors, most girls would never do a lick of work! What teenager likes to work?

And yet, the world revolves because of girls. When they are sweet and kind, they are the sweetest and kindest. When they take your arm in theirs, you feel the most loved and valued creature in the universe; even the stars stop revolving in the heavens to say, "Look at that!" We depend on girls for their brightness, their effervescence, their hope. Their innocence.

That was why it had been so hard to believe the rumor circulating through the towns and villages of Slovakia—the rumor that was about to become a law. Why would anyone want teenage girls to go do government work service? Why not take boys? It was a sad business, everyone said.

Chapter Two

Where there is a Slovak, there is song.
— TRADITIONAL SLOVAKIAN SAYING

THE FRIEDMANS AT HOME sounded like a Jewish von Trapp family in a Slovak *Sound of Music*. Edith and Lea always sang their way through the morning chores, so the day was beautiful no matter what the weather. And who needed a radio with voices like theirs?

Hanna Friedman listened to her daughters sing and worried at the silence that would descend upon her home if her teenagers were sent away by the government. Who else could warble in the tones of Edith's melodic lark or Lea's throaty sparrow? Unaware of their mother's sentimental ear, the girls harmonized their way through the breakfast dishes, the sweeping and mopping of the kitchen floor, and finally opening the front door to let in a blast of fresh, cold air. Down the street, children could already be heard shouting and laughing in the snow. Mrs. Friedman snapped the eiderdowns free of dust and sleep, then folded the duvets back to the foot of the bed so the mattresses could air.

Outside, the world was a marvel of white. Rainbows sparkled in the snow, formed by prisms of icicles dangling off the edge of rooftops. Black tree branches were laced with a fairy dusting of snow. A pale sun cracked through thinning clouds as a southeasterly wind swept streaks of white across an even paler sky.

On a typical market day, Edith and Lea would head to the town center carrying a basket between them and do the shopping for Babi, their grandmother. They would see their friends and neighbors, catch up on the latest gossip, and read the signs posted on the notice board and around the square. On a typical market day...but today was anything but typical. First, market would probably be sparingly attended, as farmers were still digging out. When the farmers did arrive, it would be with sleighs and sleds of produce and the spare offerings would be frozen from the journey. But that was winter for you. Still, that was not why today was unlike other days. Today, everyone was heading to the market to see if the town crier had any addenda to Saturday's proclamation, which almost no one had heard but everyone was now forced to believe.

The girls did not know anything yet. Not yet. And after being snowed in for over twenty-four hours, Edith and Lea were probably anxious to see their friends. Hurrying out the door ahead of their mother, they swung Babi's basket between them.

As the girls crunched through the crust of fresh fallen snow and headed toward town, they might have heard doors up and down the street opening and shutting as young men and women, eager to get outside, bundled their way across the drifts and barely cleared sidewalks. There had been only the faintest hint of overheard whispers, and the only way to find out what was really going on was to sleuth out the truth. To that end, one of Lea's best friends might have called out their names. With a knit hat over her strawberry-blond hair, Anna Herskovic might have raced to join the Friedman sisters on this atypical market day.

Anna Herskovic was a cheerful, chatty girl with big brown eyes and pale skin. A beautiful girl, among beautiful girls. Before the world turned against them, Anna and Lea had loved to frequent the cinema together. Real movie buffs, they always saved their money to catch the latest feature, that is until movie theaters became one of the many places where Jews were forbidden.

Along the narrow banks of the Laborec River, branches of birch trees were cut and dressed with colorful glass bottles to capture the tree sap as it rose with the temperature. With the latest cold snap, the bottles would have barely any clear liquid at the bottom. But warmer days were coming, and the bottles tinkled in the wind like chimes, pending the flow of sweet tonic that drips from birch trees in spring.

On either side of the railroad tracks, post-blizzard forts might have been built in the snow so little boys could lob snowballs at each other in a microcosmic war that echoed the one in Europe, though both sides here were likely soon to celebrate armistice by sledding together. Arming themselves, girls patted snow into their mittens and threatened errant lads daring to target them. Older girls, like Edith and Lea, could traipse across the small bridge into town unscathed. Veering to the left, they took a quick detour to Štefánikova Street where their friends Debora and Adela Gross lived.

Štefánikova Street was fondly referred to as Gross Street by the townsfolk because eleven of the houses on the street were filled with the children and grandchildren of the wealthy lumber merchant Chaim Gross. Even Ladislav Grosman and his family, who were no direct relation, lived on Gross Street.

If Ladislav and his brother, Martin, had been shoveling sidewalks when the girls arrived, they would certainly have greeted the young women, though Ladislav probably paid little attention to the teenage waif Edith. Over the weekend, the Gross family had lost no time in making sure that Martin and

Adela Gross, circa 1940.
PHOTO COURTESY LOU GROSS.

Lou Gross, circa 1941.
PHOTO COURTESY LOU GROSS.

Debora were formally engaged. As Debora and Adela met the Friedman sisters and Anna Herskovic, news of Debora's upcoming nuptials would have been the latest gossip.

Did the nineteen-year-olds jump into the kind of conversation only girls who haven't spoken to each other in twenty-four hours can have? Add to that Debora's wedding, and we can imagine excited hugging and mazel-tovs. "Debora would have her grandfather's family exception and Martin's," Edith recalls. "Double protection" from the proclamation. Besides the government only wanted unmarried girls. Did Lea wonder if she should get a quick husband, or did it seem ludicrous to bother? It must have felt strange to celebrate good news served up as an aperitif to bad.

Edith and Adela were not as close friends as their sisters. At seventeen, Edith had not been in the same class with Adela at school, and that one-year age difference between them created a divide that teenagers can find difficult to cross. Adela's perfectly oval face and full lips peeked out from under a mass of spiraling red curls at Edith's more delicate features. Marriage was a long way off for the teens, who had yet to blossom into womanhood.

Irena Fein had worked as an assistant at the recently Aryanized photography studio in town. A pensive and bookish girl,

Irena was also dedicated to the photography profession and very likely honed her skills by taking pictures of her friends. Adela seems to have had the confidence of a movie star and would have made the perfect subject with her auburn tresses and ivory skin. Was it Irena Fein who took the photographs of Adela smiling coyly up at Irena's Leica, just a year before the Jewish Codex made it illegal for Jews to own cameras?

Inside the Gross family home, Adela's three-year-old cousin Lou was the odd man out. Romping through the snow toward his older cousins, he begged the girls to play with him. The girls may have laughed and hugged him, but their plans did not include babysitting. It may not have been a typical market day but it was a day for market. They had plans.

In danger of being left with nothing but his rocking horse to play with, Lou would scamper after the older girls on his stubby little legs, calling out the sweetest form of his cousin's names—Adelinka! Dutzi!—and sticking out his lower lip in a dramatic but wasted pout.

—*Ljako!* His nanny used the family's own endearment and hauled the toddler back inside, to bundle him up like a marshmallow before returning him to the outside.

NOT ALL OF THE YOUNG WOMEN making their way to the center of Humenné for market that day were Slovak. After the German invasion of Poland in 1939, many Polish Jews had sent their daughters to the relative safety of Slovakia, where Jews still had some rights and Jewish girls did not face the threat of rape.

Dina and Erna Dranger were first cousins from what had once been a sleepy village on the border of Poland called Tylicz, which had become a strategic border town filled with German soldiers immediately after the invasion. Their best friend, Rena Kornreich, had escaped to Slovakia first. The Drangers had followed. Both Rena and Erna had younger sisters living and working in Bratislava, the capital of Slovakia. There was at least one other Polish refugee in Humenné; Sara Bleich grew up a few kilometers away in the spa town of Krynica, where today you can still "take the waters" and find many different types of mineral water gushing from the mountain springs. They must have all known one another.

We can imagine Erna and Dina walking arm in arm down Štefánikova Street toward the market that day, talking excitedly about their friend Rena's upcoming nuptials. Rena needed to find a nightgown for her wedding night, which probably elicited all manner of blushing and giggling from the young women. With Passover just a few weeks away, they were also eager to send dried fruits and nuts home to their parents, whom they had not seen in over a year.

A few years older than the Friedman sisters, the Polish girls would not have moved in the same social circles. Ensconced in the Jewish community of Humenné, the Friedman girls were from a well-respected local family, while the Polish refugees worked as nannies for well-to-do families with small children. However, passing the Gross family's home and seeing the others outside, the Polish girls would have waved or said hello. Adela's mass of freckles and waves of red hair were as hard to miss as her smile, and they would have recognized each other from sitting upstairs in the women's section of the synagogue. Even though the Gross sisters came from an extremely wealthy family, they never treated others as inferior. They were dedicated to living in a kind world, a moral world, a world that helped those less fortunate and in need.

THE WORD *humenné* comes from the Slavic word "backyard." Never had a town been more aptly named. "We were a big family," Edith says of the town. "Everyone knew each other. Everyone!"

Once an important town on the trade route between the kingdoms of Poland and Hungary, Humenné had been an important cultural hub for the arts, known for its crafts, fairs, and market. Marble lion sculptures twitched their stone tails above the wrought-iron gate of the mansion at the end of the square, though "square" is not the right word for the long, rectangular avenue that served as the town center. Main Street was unpaved; horse-drawn rollers made of logs and chain smoothed the dirt and gravel. Lined with saplings on one side and the town's shops on the other, the square was the central meeting place for Jews and gentiles. This was a one-car town, with one taxi driver.

Along the edge of the square, in front of towering snowdrifts, a few stalwart vendors and farmers would have set up their stalls. The wind nipped the ungloved hands of a gentile butcher winding his last sausage links together. Wheels of cheese were covered with cheesecloth to protect them from the cold. There were no green vegetables yet, just potatoes, rutabagas, a few parsnips. The Slovak military police—the Hlinka Guard— stomped through the windswept crests as if patrolling snow mounds was part of their duty. Booted, belted, and buttoned up against the winds off the Low Tatras and Carpathian Mountains, the young Hlinka Guardists tried to look intimidating in their black woolen coats and jodhpurs. Barely old enough to shave, they did not intimidate Adela or the other girls. Why should they be frightened? They had grown up together. And boys always like to play soldier. Still, it seemed odd that when the girls said hello, their old school chums chose to ignore or glare at them.

The world was small in this corner. It was impossible not to greet one's neighbors, but in the past year, those greetings had become stiffer and warier, whispered instead of shouted. Then, "all of the sudden, gentiles stopped speaking to us," Edith says. "They even didn't answer when my mother greeted them!" How could neighbors be so rude to one another? But everyone was just that bit more on edge.

On a typical market day, Edith and Lea would have entered the marketplace amid the familiar staccato of shopkeepers hawking wares and the animated melody of shoppers bartering without a care in the world. This was anything but a typical market day, though. The Friedman girls and their friends may have laughed freely in the open air, but they were blissfully unaware of wistful glances, a stray tear snagged by the wind, an older policeman watching them for a tender moment, confused by his own sentiment.

Once the afternoon market was open to Jews, Edith's mother would have arrived with Irena Fein's mother and Mrs. Fein's sister-in-law, the local midwife who had delivered Edith, Lea, and probably the whole Gross brood into the world. They would have seen Mrs. Becker with her teenage daughter, Margie. Margie had a sharp wit and had acted in several of the Beth Jacob theatrical plays with Edith and Lea. Margie's family also owned the shop on the corner near the Friedmans' home.

Despite living around the corner from the Becker family and their shop, the Friedmans were not close friends with them, because, as young men, Emmanuel Friedman and Kalman Becker had vied for the love of the same woman. "My mother was not only very beautiful," Edith says, "she was the most clever woman in the city." Emmanuel Friedman won her heart and they were married. Afterwards, Margie's father refused even to speak to Edith's father, except "when they went to the Shul for *Kol Nidre.* Then they wished each other all the best for a good year, a healthy year, a happy year, a year of richness. The rest of the year, they wouldn't speak." Edith chuckles.

This was a real community. People fell out and made up, some had strict religious principles, some had lax. It didn't matter. In the market, everyone knew everyone else. Mrs. Friedman would have greeted Mrs. Rifka Citron—a strict and committed Zionist—as they picked over a pitiful selection of end-of-season potatoes. The Citrons were poor and they had a large family. They had children almost in their thirties as well as in their teens. Their dashing son Aron and gorgeous daughter, Helena, could have been Hollywood movie stars, especially if you heard them sing. Helena's sister, Ruzinka, had recently returned from Palestine with her daughter, Aviva. Scampering after her aunt, Helena's four-year-old niece brought smiles from Jew and gentile alike. A tiny towhead with a mass of curls, Aviva was lighter skinned than most Aryans.

"Hitler wouldn't know what to do with this one," Edith's mother joked.

"There must have been a shiksa in the woodpile" was another Jewish joke.

Mrs. Friedman smiled at Helena, who had real dramatic flair and often performed with Margie Becker, Edith and Lea in the annual theatrical productions organized by the Beth Jacob school, back before the Codex changed everything.

Despite themselves, the young Hlinka Guards watched the girls as they moved across the square. The opposite of her niece, Helena had thick, dark hair and full cheeks. In the full bloom of womanhood, she didn't need to flirt with boys to torture them. All she needed to do was stand there. The other local beauty, Adela Gross, was more likely to smile bashfully and drop her eyes to the ground when a boy caught her attention.

Somewhere between the bread cart and the kosher butcher, Edith might have seen one of her former classmates, Zena Haber, with Margie Becker. It was good to catch up with her friends, but their conversation was cut short when they noticed the pasting of posters on the sides of buildings and the town crier moving to the bandstand. The crier's drum thrummed the air, quelling the hustle and bustle of the Jewish market. Shopkeepers and customers stopped their haggling. Would there be further explanation about the bulletin slipped under the cover of the snowstorm? With a proper crowd now attentive to his voice, the town crier read the latest proclamation, now posted with a smear of glue to secure it against the cold wind and printed in black and white for all to see. Of course, for those who could not read, he read it out loud. Twice.

Voices shrilled with shock. Anyone who could not believe the news before now came racing, as the town crier's aria carried over the earmuffs and hats of the crowd, announcing once more and for certain that all unmarried girls between the ages of sixteen and thirty-six had to register at the high school for a health examination on March 20 and commit to three months of government work service. Oh! And each girl should bring no more than forty kilos of her belongings.

That was less than two weeks away.

Voices erupted. Everyone—the rabbi, the priest, the tobacconist, farmers, customers, unmarried girls—began speaking at once, questioning the crier, the police, the guards, and each other.

—What kind of work? What if they get married in the next two weeks? Where are they going? How should they dress? What should they bring?

It was a cacophony of muddled speculation mingled with outrage and worry. This ordinance had nothing to do with pets or jewelry or shopping. It made no sense. Why would the government want their girls? Lea slipped her arm around Edith. Margie Becker looked up at Zena Haber and shrugged. What else could they do? Helena Citron stopped playing with Aviva and looked over at her married elder sister, Ruzinka. Adela and Debora Gross clasped hands.

THE LARGEST AND WEALTHIEST TOWN in the eastern region of Slovakia is Prešov, just seventy kilometers west of where the Friedman girls and their friends were standing, gobsmacked by the announcement that would change their young lives. With the largest Jewish population in the region dating back to the early 1600s, Prešov was home to the Great Synagogue, near the town center. The building was deceptively austere on the outside but rivaled the city's Gothic cathedral, the Roman Catholic

Magda Amster in Presov, circa 1940.
PHOTO COURTESY BENJAMIN GREENMAN FAMILY.

church of St. Michuláša, in size. Amid silver firs and European black pines, the cathedral's spires punctured the sky above the city square next to a fountain that commemorated the day Jews were allowed to live within the city walls, over one hundred years earlier. A gift from Marcus Holländer, the first Jew to settle within the city gates, the Neptune Fountain had been given a place of honor and had become a popular meeting place for young Jews and gentiles. No more. Once, sixteen-year-old Magda Amster had loved to sit in reverie by the flowing waters of the fountain where she could meet her best friend, Sara Shpira. Now, the park and even the city center were off-limits to Jews, and Magda's best friend had moved to Palestine.

TODAY, AT THE TOP of Hlavná Street, which is still the main artery into the city square, there is a busy intersection of four-lane traffic and a complicated array of traffic lights. In the 1940s, this corner was the site of the marketplace, where horses pulling sleds or carts for the vendors trotted past Jews and gentiles alike. Trying to find some remnant of the past, the daughter of Marta F. points to the busy roadway. Now there is a crosswalk instead of the house where her mother once lived with her large extended family. In a faded black-and-white photo, Marta F., age thirteen or fourteen, stands in the snow looking up a narrow alleyway. It looks strikingly similar to today's Okružná Street, which still leads to the Jewish center of Prešov. Smiling shyly at the camera, Marta is wearing her Sabbath best and looks as if she might be heading to synagogue.

It is confusing to meander the streets of Prešov's old Jewish section today. A dilapidated wall, tagged by Slovak graffiti artists, has four rows of barbed wire secured to rusted metal posts along the top edge. Inside the enclosure, there appear to be mostly derelict buildings with peeling paint and wired-up windows. It is hard to imagine that this complex once embraced three synagogues, a children's school, a "playing field for children," a kosher butcher, and a bathhouse. As the daughters of Marta F. and Ida Eigerman wander the courtyard, we find the synagogue's caretaker's house and knock on his door. A solidly built, gentle-faced man answers the door. Peter Chudý has deep sorrowful eyes and speaks very little English. Orna explains in rudimentary Slovakian that their mothers were from Prešov and on the first transport.

"So was mine!" he blurts. Moments later we are in his home and looking at a photograph of Klara Lustbader, with her hair in braids and wearing a school uniform. The picture is from a class photo with Magda Amster.

Moments later Chudý has granted us private access to the Great Synagogue—concrete proof of a vital Jewish community that once lived and worshipped in Prešov. Inside, this large two-story building, with its two towers, is breathtakingly beautiful. Under a powder blue vaulted ceiling with an intricately painted border of geometrical and abstract Moorish designs, an elaborate brass candelabra hangs. Ornate starbursts and gold Jewish stars look down on worshippers sitting in the women's balcony. On the main floor, the men prayed before an elegant two-story *Aron Hakodesh* or Torah Ark.

This is the oldest Jewish museum in the country, and tourists who visit the Great Synagogue can find display cases from the

Bárkány Collection, artifacts of the medieval Jewish diaspora, upstairs in the women's section. This is where Giora Shpira stood at the *Bimah* (Sacral Desk) and read the Torah for his bar mitzvah, where Orna Tuckman's mother, Marta, may have worshipped in the women's balcony alongside Ida Eigerman and Gizzy Glattstein, Joan Rosner, Magda Amster and about 225 other young women about to be deported from Prešov.

There is also a book listing the names of Prešov families who did not survive the Holocaust. Looking through the pages, Orna Tuckman stands with her face reflected in the glass case below the Jewish star. "This makes it real," she says when she finds her grandparents' names and attempts to squeeze back the tears. "They existed."

BEING FROM AN UPPER-CLASS FAMILY, Magda Amster was not the kind of girl who had to do the food shopping on market days. Market day was still a vital social occasion, though, and after the blizzard, everyone would have been a little stir-crazy and anxious to get outside. Disarmingly happy, her delicate cheeks pale pink from the cold and her long neck swathed in a handknitted scarf, Magda Amster headed down the hill from her home to meet up with Klara Lustbader and a few other girls she had known at school.

Now that no Jew over the age of fourteen could attend school, market day was one of the few occasions that boys and girls could meet each other without too many adults chaperoning their conversations. Giora Shpira, the fourteen-year-old brother of Magda's best friend, Sara, was a scholarly lad who enjoyed Magda's company because she treated him like a kid brother. Giora's black-rimmed glasses circled bright, intelligent eyes, but without the structure of formal education anymore, Giora and his younger brother, Schmuel, spent much of their time studying at home or doing odd jobs, trying to avoid mischief. The boys knew how smart each girl was and which studies she excelled at. They knew their families and siblings, and had grown up playing tag with these girls now hurrying toward adulthood.

In the Jewish square outside the Great Synagogue, Neolog (or reform Jews) and Orthodox men, plus Hasidim, who should have been making their way slowly across the icy cobbles to begin *Minchah* (afternoon prayers), were conversing about the rumor. There had been no formal announcement in Prešov, yet. And while news travels fast, it did not travel so fast that one town knew what was happening in another on the same day. In eastern Slovakia, news was dependent on town criers.

Not far from the town center, the Jewish section of Prešov was in a slight dell, protected from the mountain wind. A few junior members of the Great Synagogue had already headed toward the town hall to see if there would be any announcements. Giora and Schmuel had the same idea, and passed the men hurrying toward the square.

It was hard to believe that just a few months earlier, Giora had been bar mitzvahed in the grand, two-story edifice and had celebrated his coming of age at Magda Amster's home with forty of his best friends and schoolmates—girls and boys. The Amster family was always generous, and the bond between Giora's parents and Magda's was all the more devoted because of their daughters' close friendship. Now, these same girls were being threatened by the rumor of government service. Giora felt both protective and alarmed as he and his brother hurried toward Hlavná Street, past Gizzy Glattstein's corset shop where a Polish refugee, Ida Eigerman, had found employment.

Having fled Poland in 1940, Ida had left her family behind in the town of Nowy Sącz, where there was now a ghetto. Ida had first hidden near the Polish border, in Bardejov. There she lived with her uncle and worked in his kosher butcher shop. On Kláštorská Street, across from the kosher butcher, was the Bikur Cholim synagogue. In the women's gallery upstairs, Ida probably sat near Rena Kornreich, who was hiding at her own uncle's home around the corner. The two Polish refugees certainly knew each other before Rena moved to Humenné. Ida Eigerman had apple cheeks and smooth black hair that she curled back off her forehead. Her days were spent measuring the middle-class and upper-class Jewish women of Prešov for girdles and other undergarments.

Past the corset shop, down the hill toward the cathedral where the statue of Neptune stood, Magda Amster may have been pondering her young life on the edge of the city square— where Jews were no longer allowed. She missed going to school, missed having a cat. Most of all, she missed Giora Shpira's sister, Sara. Sara had been so determined to go to Palestine that she went on a hunger strike when her father refused to let her leave. Magda didn't have the chutzpah to starve herself or defy her own father's wishes and had been left behind. Magda's elder sister and brother had already left for Palestine, and Magda understood that her father wanted at least one daughter to stay home—as the youngest, she understood that was her duty. Still, she pined for the company of her best friend and siblings. In a few years when she was older, her father had promised, she could visit Palestine. But a few years is a lifetime to a teenager. The wind whipped her face and made her eyes tear. The only reason to smile was the sight of her friends Giora and Schmuel racing down the hill toward her, waving a letter. The wind tried to snatch the thin sheets as they passed the missive into Magda's gloved hands, but she held on tightly to Sara's latest letter home:

> It's simply beautiful to live. The world is so perfect. Quiet in its happiness, in which it rejoices and with which it enriches so much. I gain satisfaction in my work, and every limb sings its songs. After a few days of rain, the skies are happy again, blue

and deep, above the gray houses. Suddenly, there
are vegetables, flowers of every color, and maiden-
hair ferns appear among the rocks. Everything is
refreshed, satisfied, spring-like, and I am also
happy and I love to be alive!

It was a moment of reverie shattered by the drumbeat of
Prešov's town crier, announcing the same news that Edith and
her friends were hearing in Humenné. Members of the Prešov
Jewish community hurried back to the synagogue to report to
the elders as the teenagers pressed through the crowd to read
the notice being slapped up on the side of town hall and slath-
ered with glue. All over Slovakia, the same notices were being
posted and simultaneously heralded by town criers clanging
brass bells or banging drums. The only variable between communities was where the girls should go: firehouse, school,
mayor's office, bus stop. The rest of the news was the same:

> All unmarried girls between the ages of sixteen and
> thirty-six must register…on March 20 for a health
> examination in order to commit to three months of
> government work service. Each girl should bring no
> more than forty kilos of her belongings to the school
> on the day of registration.

"Why take girls?" Giora Shpira asked.
It was a question he would ask for the rest of his life.

Chapter Three

Why does Herodotus begin his great description of the world with what is, according to the Persian sages, a trivial matter of tit-for-tat kidnappings of young women?

—RYSZARD KAPUŚCIŃSKI

FRIDAY, MARCH 13, 1942

THE DOUR, GRAY, COLUMNED BUILDING of the Department of Finance sat on the corner opposite of one of Bratislava's most beautiful buildings. Erected in 1890, the art nouveau edifice, designed by the Austrian architect Josef Rittner, housed the Ministry of the Interior under President Jozef Tiso in the 1940s. Originally meant to serve the Austro-Hungarian Empire's army, it was where the wheels of the National Slovak Party's government turned. Looking out over the banks of the Danube, decorated with ancient Roman helmets on the four corners of its many domes and arches, it was a tribute to the empire's rich and ornate past. The Department of Finance was housed in a more minimalist structure, with a dash of 1920s deco. Sandwiched between these two incongruous structures, the Franz Joseph Bridge stretched across the Danube.

Today, you can still see fishermen sitting along the banks next to small fires smoldering in the river's fog, while trolleys jangle past on the streets above. Some things have changed. The Department of Finance is now the Ministry of the Interior. There is a shopping mall down the street and a four-lane highway. But the same wide stairway leads up to thirty-foot-high wood-hewn doors with brass knobs the size of a giant's paw. Inside, just to the right of the marble foyer, a *paternoster* elevator has moved on its continuous conveyor belt of bureaucratic efficiency since it was installed in the 1940s. This doorless elevator never pauses its incessant cycle of moving cubicles. Like the "Our Father" prayer it was named for, it moves as seamlessly as rosary beads in one's hand. Not that it helps to pray before you get in. People have lost lives and limbs in these human filing cabinets, but it was the conveyance of the time. And this paternoster is one of the few of its kind remaining in Europe.

Minister of Transportation and Chief of the Jewish Department Dr. Gejza Konka would have mastered the technique of stepping onto the rising shelf as it moved past, and been used to the sound of wood creaking, objecting to his weight as it carried him upstairs to where the Minister of Finance was busily calculating the costs of rehoming Jews.

As Chief of the Jewish Department, a department he helped create with the fascist Minister of the Interior Alexander Mach in the summer of 1941, Konka was responsible not only for devising the plan that would deport the girls, but for organizing the transports with the railway. Since financing and cost-effectiveness was not his department and since there were costs that needed to be considered (food, lodging, guards, fuel), he would have made frequent visits to the Minister of Finance. The Slovak government was paying the Nazis 500 *reichsmark* (the equivalent of $200 U.S. today) to "rehome" their Jews in Poland. The euphemism for "rehoming," defined at the Wannsee Conference, was "evacuate." The meaning of both terms was the same. In fact, on an order for Zyklon B (the gas used to execute Jews and other "undesirables"), the actual terminology used to request five tons of the gas was "materials for Jewish resettlement."

In 1941, after the Slovaks had agreed to German demands to send twenty thousand Slovak workers, Izidor Koso, head of President Tiso and Interior Minister Mach's chancelleries, suggested that the Germans take Jews instead. The scheme to collect twenty thousand able-bodied "persons" between the ages of eighteen and thirty-six to construct buildings for Jews who would be "permanently resettled" in Poland originally began in 1941. However, knowing they couldn't supply the Germans with the numbers required, Koso lowered the age to sixteen. That the first five thousand of those able-bodied persons should all be young women was never stipulated in any of the paperwork. It was at the Wannsee Conference, held on January 20, 1942, that "an organizational task unparalleled in history" was clearly outlined by the Deputy/Acting Reich-Protector, SS Reinhard Heydrich, and his then assistant, Adolf Eichmann. In a dramatization of the partial transcripts taken during the Wannsee Conference, *Schutzstaffel* (SS) men and politicians sit around a large oak table discussing the destruction of European Jewry, outlining the Final Solution with a callous lack of emotion. Among the euphemisms bandied about was the "opportunity" the Jews were being given to "work"—that is, be worked—to death. It was for this "opportunity" that Edith and her friends were about to register.

The meetings leading up to the fateful decision to deport unmarried Jewish girls were probably conducted behind closed doors and without a stenographer. Who instigated this idea? Did it come from Adolf Hitler and Hermann Goering, or Heinrich Himmler? All we can be sure of is that the usual suspects devising the plan in Slovakia would have included SS Captain Dieter Wisliceny; Alexander Mach, former head of the Hlinka

Guard and now Minister of the Interior; Prime Minister Vojtech Tuka; Izidor Koso; and others. We do not find Dr. Gejza Konka among this eminent group of fascists. A steely-faced, bald headed man with hard eyes, Konka does not appear to be in any of the group photographs taken during this period, nor is he regularly written about. But his name slips in and out of the historic record and appears on enough documents to make him an important question mark.

Everyone in attendance at these closed-door meetings would have agreed that the Aryanization of Slovakia was of paramount importance, but there were a few obstacles standing in the Slovak National Party's way: the law and the Vatican.

First and foremost, it was illegal to deport Jewish citizens because they were still considered citizens. The Slovak assembly needed to pass legislation making it legal, but a bill had not yet been brought up for debate. The announcement was for girls to report for duty. They were not being deported; they were being given the "opportunity" to work for the government. Of course, none of the men concocting this covert plan were overly concerned about the rule of law. For Alexander Mach, the vote was a mere formality. By the time the measure was finally passed, more than five thousand girls and a few thousand young men would already be in Auschwitz. There was a reason the Slovak government was referred to as a "puppet state" of Germany's Third Reich.

While changing the law was a hindrance, the Vatican's objection to the deportation of Jews was far more problematic. Much to the dismay of both the Slovak and German governments, the plan to send Jews to work camps had been leaked in November 1941. In direct response, Pope Pius XII immediately dispatched an emissary, Luigi Maglione, to meet with Slovak ministers and deliver the Holy See's message that the Jewish citizens of Slovakia should not be forced into work camps, because "it is unchristian."

To go against the Holy See was indeed serious. Many of the ministers were devout Catholics. However, the Vatican had not come out fervently against the Jewish Codex, so the masterminds behind the relocation of Jews were not overly concerned. In addition, Slovakia's president was a priest as well as a fascist. How serious could the Vatican be if it did not publically reprimand President Tiso?

Prime Minister Tuka maintained a characteristically pained expression behind the round-rimmed glasses that made him look perpetually surprised (or as though he suffered from intestinal gas), while the fiendishly handsome Alexander Mach seethed. How dare the Vatican challenge them! Christian ethics were of no concern to the Slovak People's Party. Their president was a mediator between man and God, not Jews and God. The country's president-priest didn't like Jews. Protocols hampered efficiency.

The Vatican shook its finger and insisted that caveats be included for Jews who converted and were baptized. Those who provided important work to the state of Slovakia, like factory owners, farmers, and mechanics, should also be exempt from "rehoming." So-called Christian charity did not include poor Jews.

Sending the Jews to work camps was supposed to save the Slovak government money, a theory based on the double-edged sword of propaganda, since the government claimed that their poverty made Jews a state burden—even as they insisted that Jews were getting rich off the back of poor gentiles. The paradox was ignored. Economists outside of the government, who had already disproved this cost-saving theory, were also discounted. Alexander Mach had his own economist, Augustín Morávek, chairman of the Central Economic Office, manipulate the numbers by conveniently overlooking a full cost analysis, which should have included not only the collection and transportation of the Jews to work camps but also the care of the laborers. What if workers fell ill? Workers needed to be fed, didn't they? At least girls did not eat that much.

OF COURSE, THE FINAL ECONOMIC BETRAYAL was that Mach and his cronies had approached the RSHA (the Reich Main Security Office) about taking Slovak Jews in June 1941. Then, in March 1942, Prime Minister Tuka told the Slovak Assembly that "representatives of the German Government have declared their willingness to take all the Jews." The cost for "resettlement" would be 500 *reichsmark* per Jew. The Germans weren't paying for their slave labor; they were forcing the Slovaks to pay them to take Jewish slave labor. One wonders if the cost paid per Jew was a line item included in the total budget?

The Department of Transportation, headed by Dr. Gejza Konka, must have agonized over every detail, right down to the kind of carriages that would transport one thousand "persons" across difficult terrain with hairpin mountain turns. Cattle cars would be the most cost-effective; the Germans had already measured cattle cars and estimated that twice as many people as horses or cattle could fit inside. To move a thousand people would require at least twenty cars linked together. This wasn't just a train—it *was* a transport.

It was a Herculean task. Not only would the railway need to commandeer cattle cars, but they would need buses to shuttle "persons" from far-flung villages to central holding places large enough to keep the laborers until an adequate number had accumulated to make their transportation to the work camps cost-effective. They also needed a train station that could store at least twenty cargo cars off the active line. In the eastern region of Slovakia, that station was Poprad, a small town where the train line from the southeast and northeast could be switched without suspending regular rail services. Konka also needed a place to hold people. Poprad had a two-story army barracks that was securely fenced. Problem solved.

TODAY, THERE ARE battered old rails overgrown with grass and peeking out from the brambles that run just to one side of the active tracks in Poprad. Not half a meter from the barracks where the girls were first held, this unused line leads to a storage area, where rusting cars are kept off the main line. In the distance the whitecapped mountains of the High Tatras punctuate the sky.

Making sure the first transports hailed from a rural location was probably planned. For one thing, it would attract less attention if there were mistakes. For another, if there was an outcry or rioting, the Hlinka Guard could handle the resistance without too much publicity. The government didn't want to alarm anyone. Since the Slovak assembly had not yet passed a law making the deportation of Jews legal, everything had to appear as normal as possible. Of course, they weren't officially deporting anyone. Government documents referred to the girls as "contract" laborers.

So WHEN DID YOUNG, UNMARRIED WOMEN become the target population? Who suggested it? There seems to be no one man to blame, but it was certainly men who made the decision. Did they laugh when they invented the official reason for the first transport: to provide a workforce to "build housing" for more Jewish laborers? Who brings 999 girls to work on a construction site? At some point, the news was leaked that the girls were going to work in a "shoe factory." At that time, Slovakia was one of the largest shoe manufacturers in the world and the T. & A. Bat'a Shoe Company was a major employer in Slovakia. In fact, there would be a shoe factory associated with Auschwitz-Birkenau, and while none of the 999 (that I know of) worked there, evidently it was owned by Jan Antonín Bat'a. The idea of their daughters going to work in a shoe factory placated many of the worried masses. But it was a sleight-of-hand trick, and the government was playing with a stacked deck.

Implementation was the next phase of the inevitable. The Germans had already discerned that the best way to deport hundreds of people was in cars previously used for livestock transport. Konka and his colleagues concurred. Did any of them consider how cold and drafty the cattle cars would be for young women wearing dresses and skirts, especially going through the Tatra and Carpathian Mountains in March? Who came up with the idea of registering the girls on the Sabbath? Or of tossing two buckets into each car, one with drinking water, the other empty, to use as a latrine? Did any of the men consider that some of the girls might have their periods? Of course not! This was psychological warfare, soon to metastasize into genocide. The logistics of the transports were vast, but when it came down to their actual implementation and ap-proval, did any of the men think about their own daughters? Sisters? Cousins? Did any of them stop and think: This isn't turning out like I thought it would. This is uglier. Messier. This is girls.

THERE WERE NO PATERNOSTERS in the Ministry of the Interior; the building was too old for elevators, so Dr. Gejza Konka had to climb stairs to reach his office. In an oak-paneled room, he would have buzzed his secretary to bring in the latest doc-uments requiring his signature. Freshly typed on tissue-thin onionskin paper, sandwiched between leaves of carbon for trip-licate copies, the orders arrived on his desk for final approval.

Ignoring the fact that the "persons" to be deported were ac-tually women, and young, unmarried women at that, he checked the documents for typographical errors:

> Bratislava-Patrónka, Lemec railroad station, with the capacity of 1,000 persons
> Sereď: Sereď labor camp for Jews, Sereď railroad station on the River Váh, with the capacity of 3,000 persons
> Nováky: Jews camp, Nováky railroad station, with the capacity of 4,000 persons

Poprad: Poprad railroad station, for 1,500 persons
Žilina: Žilina railroad station, for 2,500 persons

Originally, the Slovaks planned to remove five thousand Jewish girls in just five days—a monumental task that even the Nazis had not accomplished yet. The document Konka was about to sign was even more daring, confirming the illegal deportation of twelve thousand "persons." As he prepared to sign the document, did he worry about the Vatican's opinion? He would have been quite sure of the Jewish question a few months before, but now that it was *his* name on the document, did any moral qualms prick his conscience? If he didn't care about the Pope's view on the matter, did he care about God's?

Department 14—the Jewish Department—had just two weeks to wrap up the final details and begin the largest deportation of human beings in history. But then, the Almighty had created the heavens and the earth in seven days. Nothing was impossible.

Beyond the window of his office, a fog rose up off the frozen Danube. As he raised his pen over the paper he was about to sign, Konka probably believed his career trajectory was right on course. Pressing the nib of his fountain pen to the paper, he scribbled, *in the name of the Minister Dr. Konka*—and sealed the fates of thousands of young women.

Although that signature alone secures his place in the annals of infamy, within weeks Konka all but disappeared from the historical record, and he was replaced as Chief of the Jewish Department by his second, the notorious Anton Vašek. A self-satisfied, overweight, and corrupt bureaucrat who would be known as "King of the Jews," Vašek delighted in accepting bribes, selling exceptions to the highest bidders, and withholding exceptions from Slovak Jews who did not pay him enough money. Meanwhile, except for his signature, Konka would virtually vanish a few weeks after the first transport made history, much like the thousands of teenage girls he deported.

Chapter Four

What could they possibly want with them?
They're nothing but children, most of them.
—LADISLAV GROSMAN, *The Bride*

EMMANUEL FRIEDMAN WAS PROUD of his daughters' intelligence, and he wanted them to become educated professionals—Lea a lawyer, Edith a doctor—so that they could be in control of their own lives. The men he usually prayed with adhered to the ancient Talmud instructions that women should stay at home and work as mothers and chided him for wanting to educate his daughters. Emmanuel, who was passionate about women's God-given right to education, promptly changed synagogues and found a more liberal place of worship. It was the Jewish Codex against education that forced Edith and Lea to give up their dreams of having professional careers. Another young woman, Manci Schwalbova, had studied for years to become a physician and only had one more exam to finish before becoming a doctor. Then the codex passed. Manci wasn't allowed to take the final test.

Emmanuel and Hanna Friedman were concerned that their daughters would not even be allowed to finish high school. How would they ever succeed if they couldn't even get high school diplomas? And now they were supposed to work for the very government that had taken away their right to education?

THE ONLY GOOD NEWS was that the government promised exemptions for families whose businesses were economically essential to the government and the war effort, and the Friedmans were supposed to be among them. There were a few other lucky families. Chaim Gross's granddaughters, Adela and Debora, were supposed to be exempt, as well. When the Gross family decided that Debora was old enough to marry Martin Grosman, they hoped to secure a double exception for her through her husband, as well as her grandfather. At eighteen years old, Adela did not have that double security.

Despite her inordinate beauty, Helena Citron was still not married, and the family was not wealthy. There would be no exception for the Citrons. Unless Helena got married immediately, she was going to have to work for the government. Her elder sister, Ruzinka Grauber, was married and had a child; Ruzinka would be safe.

Hanna Friedman wrung her apron and furrowed her brow. The exceptions were a welcome relief for families important to the government, but Hanna's neighbors also had daughters. What about Edith and Lea's friends? Zena Haber, Margie Becker, the strawberry-blond Anna Herskovic, a delicate girl, not made for factory or farmwork. And what about sweet-natured, pudgy-faced Annou Moskovic, who always found an excuse to stop by the Friedman home on bread-making day? Annou loved Mrs. Friedman's bread. Would Irena Fein be exempt since she worked in the photography store and helped her family with her extra income? Why couldn't everyone stay and work for the government from home? Hanna fretted and fumed as her daughters cleaned up after dinner. She would have to prepare a little more dough than usual on bread day to make an extra braided loaf for Annou.

Sitting by the hearth in the "white room," Emmanuel looked at his wife's worried face. There was no question that their daughters were "ripe to go" to work.

"Lea already has papers for traveling to Hungary," Hanna reminded her husband. "Let them stay there, where it is a little bit quieter. Once Lea is there, Edith can sneak across the border and join her. It is better for them to go away than go to work."

Emmanuel did not approve of shirking the legal mandates being imposed by the government. "It's a law," he told his wife.

"It's a bad law."

"But it's a law." And a Jew breaking a law was simply not the same as a gentile breaking one. He feared the repercussions.

The debate the Friedmans were having was a microcosm of the dilemmas facing Jewish parents all over Slovakia. The snow, no longer trackless and white, had grown gray and dirty. Pines now heavy with ice were forced to bend and break in an unforgiving wind. Sastrugi shaped the landscape. Snow snakes undulated across the frozen ground. Great thunderheads slipped across the night sky and over the Hungarian border, heading toward the Eastern Front.

No Jew slept well that week.

IN PREŠOV, ADOLF AMSTER had been assured that, as an important business owner, he would get exceptions for his family—and his youngest daughter, Magda, would be safe. The Hartmanns, who ran an essential dairy farm, were also supposed to be exempt. To hear some people talk, it seemed everyone would have an exception. Factory owners, skilled tradesmen, farmers—any family who had a business that was economically viable and important to the Slovak government would be permitted to keep their daughters at home.

The documents authorizing the exceptions were not small, and secretaries at the ministry in Bratislava must have diligently typed up many. But the process was anything but simple, and government bureaucracy, never that efficient, now became even more sluggish. As news of the compulsory work service reached Rome, the Vatican sent another representative that March to intercede on behalf of the Jews. To counter the pressure from the Vatican, Eichmann sent his right-hand man and "specialist and adviser in Jewish affairs," the slightly chubby SS Dieter Wisliceny, to Bratislava to help ensure that the first "official" Jewish transport went off without a hitch. Wisliceny consulted with Konka on the difficult issues of implementing the deportation of the first one thousand girls, but Konka was certain his "grandiose" plan to remove five thousand girls in five days was achievable.

Unaware of the political chaos being caused by the exceptions, Jewish parents trusted the government to deliver the promised paperwork before their daughters had to report for work. Every day, Hanna Friedman anxiously awaited the postal delivery. Grabbing her daughters and hugging them spontaneously, she would stroke Lea's hair, pat Edith's cheek, sing songs with them as they did their chores. Chaim Gross had his staff work the phone lines to the Ministry of the Interior. Debora's marriage was moved up. Since she had also suffered from juvenile rheumatoid arthritis, she would definitely be excused from work. But what about his other granddaughter, Adela?

The mayor of Humenné offered assurances to his vital Jewish families, but without the official documentation from the ministry, his assertions were meaningless. Emmanuel Friedman had known the men working in the regional government for years, but they were just as confused about the exceptions as he was. No one knew when they were supposed to arrive. The only thing definite was the stern warning that was repeated

Okres: Humenné

Číslo listu: 14

1 Radné číslo	2 Meno Priezvisko	3 Deň, mesiac a rok narodenia	4 Bydlisko	5 Poznámka
1.	Deutschová Priška	1.10. 1918	Humenné, UL.HG 47 ✓	
2.	Davidovičová Margita	23.3. 1923	" Vyšný Majer	
3.	Ehrenbergová Hena	19.6. 1925	" Štefanikova 29 ✓	
4.	Ehrehbergová Helena	13.12. 1922	" Štefanikova 1	
5.	Eichlerová Edita	12.7. 1922	" UL.HG.46 ✓	
6.	Engelmanová Edita	21.10. 1918	" Hviezdoslavova 860	
7.	Engelmanova IRena	14.6. 1920	" "	
8-	Erlichová Dorota	4.7. 1921	" Ružová 380 ✓	
9.	Feinová Janka	23.6. 1907	" Hlinkova 77	
10.	Friedmanová Róza	27.10. 1925	" Hlinkova 134 ✓	
11.	Friedmanová Ružena	9.9. 1923	" Hlinkova 117	
12.	Friedmanová Sara	26.6. 1925	" Hlinkova 117	
13.	Findglingová Serena	20.5. 1922	" UL.HG.46 ✓	
14.	Friedmanová Margita	24.12. 1920	" Hlinkova 86	
15.	Friedmanová Lea	2.7. 1922	" Hlinkova 86 ✓	
16.	Friedmanová Edita	11.7. 1924	" Hlinkova 86 ✓	
17.	Friedrichová Anna	28.9. 1909	" Hlinkova 19	
18.	Friedrichová Ružena	21.8. 1911	" Hlinkova 19	
19.	Friedrichová Ida	7.10. 1914	" Hlinkova 19 ✓	
20.	Fuchsová Margita	6.6. 1908	" Hlinkova 69	

The town of Humenné's List of Girls, with their birth dates and street addresses.
Lea and Edith are numbers 15 and 16. Checks imply that they were registered.
PHOTO COURTESY JURAJ LEVICKY.

all over the town: If a girl's name is on the list and she does not show up to register, she will be arrested.

There was a list of names?

There was, indeed.

WHEN GERMANY ANNEXED SLOVAKIA, Jewish councils convened, ostensibly to advocate for their communities. In reality, these councils held no power or responsibility aside from collecting information about the local Jewish population. These censuses seemed like harmless bureaucratic paperwork initially, but the data was being harvested for far more reprehensible reasons and would eventually enable the Hlinka Guard to mobilize against Slovak Jewry. This was a 1940s-style computer hack implemented by the government. Regional lists were alphabetical and included birth dates and street addresses. All the police had to do was show up at a house or apartment on the list and arrest the missing girl—unless her name had been formally crossed off the list.

On the morning of March 20, 1942, Brody Sloboda came out of his apartment at the same time as a gentile civil servant neighbor.

"It's a bad day to be a Jew," the man said to Brody.

"Why's that?" Brody asked.

"You see this?" He showed Brody a list of girl's names. "They are taking Jewish girls to work camps today."

At the top of the list was the name of one of Brody's cousins, Judita Hassova.

"Do me a favor," Brody said. "Scratch out that name?"

The man took his pencil and drew a line through her name.

Seventy-five years later, Judita's son, Ivan Sloboda, still wonders if his mother was the reason there were only 999 girls. "Maybe my mother was number one thousand?"

But there may have been a much more sinister reason for the numerical configuration of 999.

Chapter Five

The Tet: ʊ
9: represents hidden, inverted beneficence.

OBSESSED WITH OCCULT MYSTICISM, the leaders of the Third Reich were not beyond using whatever practices they could to secure victory. Himmler was an avid astrologer; Goebbels was fascinated by Nostradamus and shared his interpretation of the predictions with Hitler, who was "very interested." By the 1940s, the Reich included "scientific" astrologers, parapsychics, and a virtual Nostradamus division, busily interpreting the prophecies to foretell the fall of France and the whole of Europe. "Caution! Show nobody Nostradamus," Goebbels warned his confidants. It is interesting to note that Nostradamus uses the number 999: "At the judgment, although there be 999 who condemn a man, he shall be saved if one plead for him." There would be no one to plead for our 999 girls.

Hitler's use of pagan mythology to manipulate the masses is well documented, and the more "cosmobiologists" supported Nazi ideology, the more convinced leaders became that "whoever gets in touch with it puts magic in motion." Himmler deemed astrology to be "scientifically justified and completely accurate," so it is no wonder that he had his own personal astrologer, Wilhelm Wulff, upon whom he became so dependent that by 1944 he was using the stars to chart military decisions and strategies. In the last days of the Reich, the head of SS foreign intelligence would turn to Wulff "just to find out what Himmler—by then the second most powerful figure in the Reich—might do next."

The practice of numerology dates back to the ancient Greeks and the mathematician Pythagoras, and even further back to Babylon and its Chaldean system. Astrologers often use numerology, and given the Nazis' amalgam of Nostradamus, pagan mythology, and astrology, one has to wonder if any or all of these practices influenced the use of the number 999, because the first women's transport to Auschwitz was personally ordered by Himmler himself.

On March 3, 1942, Himmler visited Ravensbrück in order to discuss the new directive that had come out of the Wannsee Conference—the creation of extermination camps for Jews—with Max Koegel, the commandant of Ravensbrück. Why bring Koegel into this conversation? Ravensbrück was the only German concentration camp for women, and while we have no concrete proof that the directive was supposed to target young women first, Himmler already knew, or had decided himself, that the first transports from Slovakia would be made up of young women. The problem was that Ravensbrück already had about five thousand female prisoners and was not large enough to hold more. A new women's camp needed to be created. In Auschwitz.

Apprised of Himmler's plan, the commandant of Auschwitz, Rudolph Höss, ordered Blocks 5–10 to be emptied of male prisoners. Formerly, those blocks had housed over twenty thousand Russian prisoners of war (POWs), most of whom had died or been killed by March 1942. The nine hundred Russian POWs still alive were relocated to the Polish cavalry's former stables, five kilometers away. All that needed to be done now was to build a dividing fence between the men's and women's camps and find a female overseer.

Forty-two-year-old SS woman Johanna Langefeld was the perfect choice. Having worked in Ravensbrück since 1939, Langefeld had a long-standing working relationship with Himmler, and he knew he could depend on her organizational skills to create the new women's camp. She believed prisoner reform meant corporal punishment of the type that today would be classified as torture, but she was a tough advocate for the prisoners who worked under her when she liked them. The new policies put in place by the Wannsee Conference and Himmler were no secret among members of the SS; as the overseer of the new women's camp in Poland, Langefeld had to have been aware that the Jewish women under her control would be used as slave labor until they were no longer fit to work, at which point they would be killed. While this policy was counter to her religious beliefs, she was no Jew lover, and the transfer to Auschwitz was a welcome promotion. Often at loggerheads with Max Koegel, the commandant of Ravensbrück, she was finally going be responsible for an entire women's camp and be able to prove herself to Himmler. At least, that is what she hoped.

There seems to be only one known photograph of Langefeld. She is walking behind Himmler and three other Gestapo officers along the barbed-wire fences of what is most likely Ravensbrück. Himmler strides ahead of the others, carrying his gloves in one hand. There is snow on the ground, and behind the goliaths of the Gestapo, Langefeld appears dwarfed. She wears a narrow cap; her graying hair is pulled back tightly in a knot. Her overcoat is plain, undecorated by stripes and buttoned up to the collar. Her middle-aged chin wattle droops beneath a severe mouth and drawn face, making her look like a sour, aging matron.

Auschwitz was about to age her even more. With just three weeks before she would receive the first official transport of Jews, there was a lot of work to do. Himmler ordered her to select SS women, as well as 999 Ravensbrück prisoners, to work as *kapos*.

Why not just take one thousand women? Was the number 999 coincidental? Did Himmler do anything by accident?

Traditionally, numerology and astrology are thought to be "wisdom tools" that help create order in a chaotic universe. Each number is given a specific meaning and power, but when a number is tripled, the intention of that number is supposed to increase to the third power. So creating a numerical triplet might serve an intended purpose.

In the Pythagorean system, numbers represent cycles. The number one is the initiation number. The number nine is the point of culmination. Completion. Placing three nines together signals a decisive ending point, while the numbers ten and one thousand, which follow 9 and 999, respectively, represent a new starting point—a millennium. If nine is a shadow number,* a numerologist would look at the intention behind the use of the number. In the case of the Holocaust, three nines would indicate a clear desire to end something. Nine also has its own mystical mathematics because numbers that are divisible by nine always reduce to or culminate in their source number: nine.

$9 + 9 + 9 = 27$; add $2 + 7 = 9$

Using dates, Pythagorean numerologists break down the digits for month, day, year into single digits, and then add numbers together until the sum is a single digit. Using this system, the date March 26, 1942, also equals a nine: $0 + 3 + 2 + 6 + 1 + 9 + 4 + 2 = 27 = 2 + 7 = 9$.

---

* A shadow number implies it has negative connotations, astrologer and numerologist Molly McCord explains.

In addition, using the Pythagorean system, every letter has a numerical value; Heinrich works out to a 9, as do Luitpold and Himmler. His birth date, October [10] 7, 1900, was also a nine. Was Himmler using the sequence of numbers from his name and birth date for the official beginning of the Final Solution in an attempt to stack an occult deck of cards against the Jews? In Himmler's mind the power of the numbers and the astrological charts for these events would assure the Final Solution's success. And the Jewish question would be decided. Completely.

It is hard to single out what Himmler might have believed without hard evidence in his diaries, but the fact is that the number of girls arriving in Auschwitz on the first transport was not the 1,500 "people" originally documented in the memo that Konka signed on March 13, 1942. Instead it would be 999—the exact same number that Himmler ordered ten days earlier at Ravensbrück.

Here we must examine the astrology behind the date the girls arrived. A dedicated devotee of astrology, Himmler had been having astrological charts done since 1928. His own chart is considered astrologically "extraordinary," Molly McCord, an astrologer and numerologist, tells me. I haven't told her whose chart I have asked her to do, so initially she had no idea that the birth date was for one of Hitler's most notorious SS officers. "Rare aspects reveal an individual who has a keen mind, will do great things in the world, wield great power, and be a great leader," she explains. I suppose to Nazis, he did do great things. As he moved through the ranks of the SS, Himmler's ruthless lust for power made him a tough adversary and political opponent. This was a man who excelled at mind games and mental manipulation, a man always looking for the checkmate move while scheming behind the scenes to better his position and shift power in his direction.

The four elements that dictate a chart include air (intellect), fire (energy), earth (groundedness) and water (emotion). "This chart reveals a self-involved individual who is personally driven by his own interests and a desire to be number one," McCord continues. "His moon, at zero degrees Aries, shows someone who has no compassion and little empathy for humanity."

Of course, it is possible that the implications of the number 999 were particular to Himmler's personal mix-and-match theory. This is not as far-fetched as it sounds. Goebbels was known for interpreting Nostradamus to suit his agenda. If there is any numerological meaning behind 999, that kind of cold calculation is indicative of the game Himmler was playing on the chessboard of the Final Solution. Women were his pawns. If the 999 Ravensbrück kapos were his first move, were the 999 Jewish girls supposed to be his second? And did he purposely make the moves on dates when he was told the stars were best aligned with his chart for ultimate success?

According to historical astrologer Robert Wilkinson, the transport's date and time had a number of factors indicating it was a "fork in the road of destiny." "In astrology," he explains to me, "the septile series represents points where decisions must be made that determine the future 'destiny' of whatever is happening, an 'irrevocable, absolute destiny.'" However Himmler manipulated the signs or had them interpreted, it is unlikely he pulled the dates March 20 and 26 haphazardly out of a hat any more than he decided to pick only 999 prisoners from Ravensbrück instead of one thousand. He was too much of a control freak to do that and, like others in the upper echelon of the Reich, would have wanted the edge he believed astrology could give him.

On the evening that the train left the station in Poprad, the planets were aligned in a complicated trine with the date of Himmler's visit to Ravensbrück and the date in July 1941 when Goering "called for the complete annihilation for Europe's Jewish population." It was Goering's demand that set the wheels in motion for the Wannsee Conference to formulate the Final

Solution, and the rapid implementation a few weeks later that would result in the deportation of our girls.

Dates and times are crucial elements in astrological charts. We know that the train left the station at 20:20 hours, which Wilkinson notes aligned with Himmler's original visit to Ravensbrück. The next morning, when both transports of women—the kapos and our Jewish girls—arrived in Auschwitz, Mars was in Gemini, which corresponded with the lunar eclipse of March 3, 1942—the date Himmler was in Ravensbrück commandeering the 999 kapos to work in Auschwitz. That lunar eclipse had what is known as a Mutable T-square, which is considered to be quite powerful and thought to create "focused conflict." Driven by Mars, this Mutable T-square created a Grand Mutable Cross, which constitutes a "severe fracturing." Pulling in "contrary directions, it can be very destructive." And it would be.

Finally, there is a correlation to the town criers' announcements a few weeks earlier. On March 20, at precisely eight o'clock in the morning, when the girls had to register for work and have their health exam, the sun was in Himmler's moon, which was in Aries. The first sign in the zodiac, Aries—the god of war and aggression—is known for power and initiation. That means it was an excellent moment for Himmler to initiate a plan of action. This was war, and with the stars on his side, Himmler attacked—he attacked young, Jewish women.

Chapter Six

It's not my parents fault, they didn't know it was my destiny.

—ROSE #1371 (EDITH GOLDMAN)

IT WAS THE CHIEF of the Jewish Department, Gejza Konka, who came up with the idea that individual deportation orders should be delivered with very little notice so no one would have time to escape or hide. Of course, the announcement for the first transports had been posted two weeks in advance, so Konka must have decided to revise that idea when they did not meet the intended quotas. Under his successor's tenure, deportations would sometimes be executed within hours. Families living in villages of fewer than twenty people had little idea what was happening in the cities. News of the girls' work orders had not yet made it into the most rural communities. No one in those tiny hamlets even knew about applying for exemptions—not that they were rich enough to buy one, or important enough to be considered.

Despite assurances from the mayor of Humenné that the exceptions for the Friedman girls and other supposedly important local families were forthcoming, the paperwork had still not arrived. For law-abiding citizens, breaking the law is never an easy decision, and so, on the morning of March 20, most families took their daughters to the reporting centers as ordered. The Friedman girls were among those who complied with the ordinance. There was supposed to be a luggage allowance of up to forty kilos, but "we didn't have forty kilos to take with us," Edith says. She and her sister folded their best clothes—a sweater, a skirt, some warm leggings—because that's what you pack when you are going away, your best clothes. Their mother wrapped her homemade bread into cloth and placed a loaf into Lea's valise. Putting on a good face, they convinced themselves that they were doing their duty for their country, Lea kissed her mother first, then Edith. When they left the house, it was without any doubt that they would be back in a few hours.

The idea of leaving their parents and families for three months was frightening for many of the young women raised in devout and protective homes. Giora Shpira remembers his and Magda's mothers washing their daughters' hair with rainwater so the girls long tresses would be soft and clean. These were girls who were doted on, who could do no wrong. Their parents would do anything for them.

Some girls thought they were going on an adventure. Margie Becker confesses that deciding to leave her family to "work in the shoe factory" was the first time that she had ever seriously disobeyed her mother. "My mother said, 'You don't have to go.' I wanted to go with my friends. Friends are very important at that point. So I didn't want to be left behind." The same was true of Adela and her friend Gizzy. They were not afraid of work and thought of it as a chance to prove to the Slovaks and Germans how wrong they were about Jews. They were going to show them how strong Slovak Jewish girls really were.

Piri, Eta, Rena, Fanny, Olga, Marta, Ida, and hundreds of other young women all over Slovakia stood before mirrors or reflecting glass, brushed their hair, and assured themselves: everything will be okay, you will return home in a few months, and then you will get married, then you will finish high school, then you will start your life...

Why should anyone doubt what they had been told?

"To REGISTER" IMPLIES the official signing up for duty but not necessarily immediate activation, so the girls went to register believing they would return home for Shabbat. That was the trap that Konka had carefully laid—surprise was paramount.

Memories about the actual registration vary from community to community. The one constant is that the atmosphere in the buildings where the girls registered was surreal and strange. In Humenné, the building was a school; in Prešov, the firehouse; the town hall was used in Bardejov. Unsure of what to expect but confident they were doing the right thing, some parents did not even escort their daughters to the reporting centers. If they did, they were forced to wait outside in the March drizzle that was melting the last remnants of February's snowstorm.

Girls from neighboring villages arrived in horse-drawn carts or on foot, their boots crusted with snow and mud. Accompanied by brothers or parents, they had left early in the morning to get into town on time. Like the town girls, they were wearing their Sabbath best. Not all of these girls from the outlying communities were strangers; many were related. Many rural families willingly delivered their daughters, grateful for the opportunity the girls were being given to support already impoverished families.

Town girls who had dawdled at home now hurried to the call-up place. Mothers up and down the streets of Humenné waved: there was Klary Atles (the well-to-do rabbi's daughter); gangly Zena Haber; gorgeous Helena Citron; rambunctious Margie Becker; statuesque Ria Hans and her little sister, Maya, with the frizzy hair; Lea's friends, Anna Herskovic and Annou Moskovic with her extra loaf of Mrs. Friedman's bread. Joining Edith and Lea, girls they had known all of their lives made their way across the train tracks and up the street to the old school building.

A local policeman stood at the door, instructing parents to remain outside and wait. The girls organized themselves into a single file and headed into the school, where they had not been allowed to study for over a year. The officer would have known most of the girls since they were toddlers tagging each other around their mothers' skirts. After all, everyone knew everyone in Humenné. Did he know anything more? If he did, he did not let on. The blinds were pulled down over the windows so no one could see in.

We can imagine them obediently entering the building: strawberry-blond Anna Herskovic, next to the raven-haired Helena Citron, next to redheaded Adela Gross. Their hair is brushed and glossy, curls tumbling out from beneath winter hats. Adela looked a little lost without her older sister. Edith looked warily around but stayed close to her own sister's side. The only time Edith had ever been away from home was to visit her uncle in Stropkov, and the thought of leaving home for a few months filled her with trepidation. At least she would be with her sister and their friends.

"We are strong and young. This will be nothing," one of Adela's friends boasted, her youthful bluster encouraging the others to be optimistic.

The girls whispered together as the line inched forward to two long desks, where names were given and well-prepared excuses were blurted out. The richer girls spoke proprietarily—they had been promised exceptions and should be excused from work. At any moment, their parents might come running down the road waving the papers that would spring them from this mandatory physical labor. Confident that they would be treated with respect because of their families' standing in the community, these richer girls hid any doubts and concerns beneath a veneer of bravado. The poorer girls bowed to their fate or pleaded for release by handing the officials a piece of paper acknowledging their status as bread-winners in their families. Not one of the civilian officials responded to these hardship pleas or paid any mind to the social rank of the rich girls' fathers.

If anyone was confident enough to say something about the exemptions, it would be the girl from the wealthiest Jewish family in Humenné. Proudly, Adela Gross looked down at the intimidating men, the arch of her eyebrows a silent query, and informed them that her grandfather was Chaim Gross, the prominent lumber tycoon. An exception had been promised from President Tiso himself. They looked right through her.

—Next!

There is a look that men have when they don't want to be bothered by a women, a look so dismissive that she feels at once disregarded and invisible. That was the look the girls received now. For many, it was the first time they had faced such dehumanization.

Edith noticed that at the long table next to the civilian officials, there were several Hlinka Guards and an SS man. This surprised her. What did the SS have to do with them?

It was a good question. If they had known, their parents, neighbors, and community might have resisted more. But they didn't know, and while smart girls like Edith noticed and wondered, they knew better than to ask. No one would have responded, anyway. Who answers questions asked by girls?

As their names were checked off the list, they were asked about their professions: seamstress, domestic help, milliner, factory worker. Teenagers still living with their parents were listed as "domestics." At no point was "child" written down as a vocation.

With more than a hundred girls now in the building, they were told to take off their clothes so a doctor could give them a physical exam. The girls froze at the order. Not one of them had ever undressed in front of a man before. The officials seemed delighted by the utter terror in the girls' eyes. The men yelled at them to undress. Reluctantly, slowly, Edith and her friends began to unbutton and unzip their outer blouses and skirts.

Margie Becker had worn two coats, a lighter gray one and her best beige coat underneath, to keep her warm. She looked very stylish, but no less than the other well-to-do girls of Humenné. Folding her beautiful blue dress carefully, she hesitated at the thought of placing it on the floor, which was dirty with slush from the outdoors. Other girls hesitated as well, and looked for a way to hang their clothes properly on wall hooks.

—This is a physical exam! Remove everything! one of the officials bellowed.

Standing in their panties and bras, they wrapped their narrow arms around their waists and breasts and shivered.

"We were so ashamed to be standing there in front of men without our clothes on," Edith remembers. A gentile doctor walked up and down the rows scanning their budding figures.

"Open!" he shouted, peering inside their mouths. "Stick out your tongue!" He looked at their tongues.

Ediths scoffs at the memory. "It was not a physical."

"The call-up was the chance for cheap and lewd enjoyment of girls stripped naked by official decree," Ladislav Grosman wrote years later.

"If they want to see a girl's breast, they made her remove her bra," Edith confirms. "They weren't interested in mine."

Behind the doctor, a clerk flipped back and forth through the pages of his list, checking Citron on one page. Gross on another. Check. He was supposed to write down health notes, but "the whole examination was a lie." Whether they were healthy or not didn't matter. The officials needed only to appear as if they cared; they did not actually need to care.

"How are you feeling?" the clerk asked Edith.

"I am often dizzy."

"Every month?" he sneered.

She felt more like a farm animal than a human being. Huddled together like a flock of lost lambs, the girls shuddered under the stares of the men. Why weren't there any matrons from the school to protect them from the ogling eyes of the officials? Why weren't their parents there? The only comfort they had was that it was almost Shabbat, and in a few hours it would all be over and they would be released into their mothers' arms and the light of her candles and blessings. All Edith wanted was to hear her father sing "Shabbat Shalom" and feel his strong, comforting embrace.

Outside on the sidewalk, parents stomped their feet to shake the numbness from their toes. It had been a few hours now and all of the Jews in town, and half the gentiles, were milling around the school in various states of confusion and distress. What had been gossip was now reality, and there were still questions to be asked. What were they doing to their girls? Why was it taking so long? They hadn't even broken for lunch!

Voices of dissent rose outside the schoolhouse:

—What is happening to our girls?

—They are going to work.

—What kind of work?

—I heard a shoe factory.

—It can't be just one factory.

—For how long?

—Three months.

—Where is this factory?

No one knew the answer.

INSIDE, THE FRIEDMAN GIRLS STOOD next to girls they had known all their lives. Some were Lea's friends, some were Edith's. Everyone knew everyone from the marketplace, from synagogue, from splashing in the river on a hot day. There were also over a hundred girls they did not know well, who had come from the provinces. Under the lascivious gaze of the men, the girls began to share a new, unspoken kinship. Pale, anxious faces mirrored one another. Class no longer divided them. They were equals in fear.

Among the Polish refugees, Rena had left her suitcase at the house where she worked as a nanny. "Someone will take you to pick it up," the policeman told her. Erna's cousin Dina had decided to hide, but at some point in the afternoon, she came stumbling into the school escorted by the Hlinka Guard; her face was flushed with humiliation, her hair disheveled. She had been found and arrested.

The slow trudge of time made the teenagers impatient and irritable. Then the government's gears began to crank. They were in it now. Dressing. Moving. The authorities—all men— were shouting.

—Get your things!

—Get in line!

—Move out!

Startled, not only by the instructions but by the gruffness of the orders, the girls bumped into each other as they dressed again and headed toward an open door. Surrounded by armed guards, they stepped into the gloaming.

From the front of the school, someone yelled that the girls were leaving through the emergency rear exit. The crowd hurried down the side street. Some parents ran home to get supper ready for their daughters, sure they were famished and would be home soon. Others ran after the column of girls shouting their names. Questions tumbled out into the impassive air: Where were they taking them? When were they coming back?

Margie Becker knew one of the Hlinka Guards quite well and asked him if she could go home to say good-bye to her mother. He slipped her out of the line and escorted her down the street. Standing next to one of their neighbors, "who was a relative also," Margie's mother held onto the window curtain, wringing it in her hands. She didn't want to cry in front of the Hlinka Guard member, even though she had known him since he was a boy. Why was he, of all people, taking her daughter, his childhood friend, away? Tears streamed down her face as she whispered to her daughter, I won't "give him the satisfaction of crying…" Slipping Margie some food for Shabbat, "fresh challah and some hamburgers," she kissed her daughter good-bye. It was the last kosher food Margie would eat for three years. It was also the last time she would ever see her mother.

Returning to the column of girls, Margie dragged her luggage with her friends. Down Main Street. Past Gross Street. Suitcases bumped against shins and scraped ankles, handles dug into palms. Edith's weighed almost as much as she did. Her siblings always joked that a strong wind could blow her away. Her sister's hand reached down for the handle and shared the burden. Tears stung Edith's eyes. Something was wrong. She could feel it in her bones, but it was too late to run or hide. Looking for assurance from the adults in the crowd, she heard only woe.

The news that the girls were being taken directly to the train station spread through town instantly, and the entire population of Humenné rushed down Ševčenkova Street to reach the yellow and red stucco train station before it was too late.

Being surrounded by the Hlinka Guard, with their hard faces, black uniforms, and guns, made the youngest begin to cry. Guards pushed back mothers who tried to break through to hug their daughters. Edith frantically searched the growing throng for her parents. Saw them. Cried more. Anxious voices called out. Brothers to sisters. Mothers and fathers. Aunts and uncles. Cousins, grandparents, friends. Names rose into the cold air, mingled with prayers. How many girls were there? More than two hundred. How many tears? Too many to count.

"We were so afraid of what might happen, we could not think," Edith remembers. "All around us girls were weeping."

Lamentations. Weeping and waving. Waving and weeping. A strong March wind blew down from the mountains. Lea grabbed her sister's hand lest Edith be carried away with the rotting leaves and sorrow.

At the station, a passenger train was idling. Forced onto the platform, the girls hauled their luggage up the metal stairs of the carriages and clambered aboard. Crowding to the windows, they waved good-bye to their parents and families. Lou Gross was too small to remember going to the train station and waving good-bye to Adela, but her sister and the rest of the family chased the air with their hands.

"When next you see me, I will be a married woman!" Debora shouted. "I'll miss you, Adela! Lea! Anna!"

Through the open the windows of the train, girls leaned out and shouted back to their families. —Don't worry! I'll be home soon! I love you!

From over the heads of neighbors and relatives and the whole of Humenné, Edith heard her mother's voice, "About Lea, I'm not so worried, she is strong, but Edith…she is like nothing."

The train whistle blew. The carriages shifted forward. As Humenné faded in the distance, Margie Becker tried to lighten the mood, and others joined her. Klary Atles, who was older, gave everyone a pep talk; she reminded the older girls to help the younger ones because they all needed to be grown-ups now. Then Gizzy Ziegler teased Adela. Someone burst into song. Helena, who had a lush soprano, joined in. With the resilience of youthful optimism, the girls revived their sense of adventure. They were going into the world. They were together. They were being asked to do something for their government. They were adults now. Soon, everyone began to feel more excited and positive about the unknown. Even the idea of traveling on Shabbat, which was against Jewish tradition, added to their sense of maturity. In the spirit of the holy day, Margie and others shared the food their mothers had packed for them with their friends and girls who had nothing and hadn't eaten all day.

As the train rounded a bend in the tracks, the highest mountain peaks east of the Swiss Alps rose in the distance. Magnificent white crags glinted under the setting sun. Girls leaned out the windows and shouted that they could see Gerlachovský Peak!

Some of the peasant girls had never even seen the High Tatras before. Filled with patriotic idealism and a sense of purpose, they began to sing the Slovak national anthem. Edith's and Lea's voices lofted over the rumble of the engine.

> *There is lightning over the High Tatras*
> *Thunderclaps wildly beat*
> *Let us stop them, brothers*
> *For all that, they will disappear*
>
> *The Slovaks will revive*
> *That Slovakia of ours has been fast asleep so far*
> *But the thunder's lightning*
> *Is rousing the land to wake up.*

It was almost dark when the train shuddered to a stop at Poprad Station. Disembarking with their suitcases and buoyant cheerfulness, the girls were met by black-coated Hlinka Guard members wielding riding crops. These were not the boys they had known as children. These were stony-faced, violent men yelling at them to march and lashing their backs and behinds with whips. The same jagged peaks of the High Tatras that had filled their hearts with song and patriotism now looked cold and threatening. Everything strange got stranger. An empty two-story army barracks awaited them. Forlorn and tired, Edith thought, At least now we will be informed and know what to expect. But there was no welcoming committee, no matron, no organization at all. The girls wandered into the massive building, confused about where they were supposed to sleep. When no one told them, they found corners and haphazardly hung hammocks to curl up in. As darkness descended, the empty building echoed with the sound of girls sobbing themselves to sleep.

Chapter Seven

Women are the bearers of life and light to the world.
                                                  —THE KABBALAH

SHABBAT—SATURDAY, MARCH 21, 1942

WHEN ELSE BUT ON SHABBAT would young, unmarried, well-brought-up young Jewish women be sure to be at home? Setting registration on the day before Shabbat assured authorities that anyone trying to shirk the government call-up and avoid the opportunity to work by hiding could be easily picked up in the morning in her parents' home.

Hiding created its own uncertainties, but there were few other options, especially for teenagers. In order to save them from the unmarried status that made them immediately vulnerable, some families had spent the weeks after the initial announcement trying to get their daughters married off. Other families sent their daughters to relatives in neighboring Hungary. Families who were promised government exceptions did not think any of those drastic actions were necessary. But when the exceptions didn't arrive, these families had only two choices: obey the law and surrender their daughters, or disobey the law and hide them. The Gross and Friedman families obeyed the law. The Amsters did not.

In the early hours of March 21, the local police showed up at Adolf Amster's villa with the Hlinka Guards. A knock on the door that early in the morning meant only one thing. Magda's mother rushed to her daughter's bedroom and sent Magda straight into "a hiding place under the roof" of their large home. Wiping the sleep from his eyes, Mr. Amster answered the door as innocently as possible. His reception was not pleasant.

Giora Shpira remembers seeing his former classmates, now Hlinka Guards, collecting their friends—classmates arresting classmates. So it is likely that Adolf Amster opened the door that morning and found the same young men who had once been the pimply-faced boys who knew his daughter, standing in front of him with guns drawn. He told them that the government had promised the Amster family exceptions, so they needn't have bothered to come. Puffed up with the power of their black garb, the boys dragged him out into the street, raised their batons, and beat him.

Was it because Mr. Amster was considered a wealthy Jew that they wanted to lash out at him and degrade him publicly? Neighbors came outside and watched in horror. Bloodied and bruised, Mr. Amster pleaded for the young men to stop. He was not too rich or important to beg.

The boy guards yelled at Mr. Amster.

—What daughter lets her father get beaten to death? If Magda truly cared for her father, she would save you! What kind of daughter is she to let you suffer so much?

The trap was laid with the bait of love. To hear her father being viciously pummeled was more than Magda could bear. The gentle-faced wisp of a girl stepped into the street. Her father held her in his arms and begged the guards to let her stay. He had no other daughter. They needed her at home. What about his own service to the government?

The guards guffawed and taunted the Amsters. Whisking the delicate young Magda away, they forced her down the snowy street to join other girls who had thought they could hide. Good girls were so easy to find!

A FEW KILOMETERS away, in a community outside of Prešov, the Hlinka Guard arrived at the Rosner family home and gave their daughter, Joan, two hours to pack. Together with twenty-three other girls from Šarišské Lúky, she was "crammed like sardines into a pickup truck," driven into town and dropped at the firehouse, where their names were checked off. By now it was about ten in the morning and over two hundred other young women were being processed at the firehouse.

Despite the early hour, Giora Shpira and his brother had heard about the confrontation at the Amsters' house and

Giora Shpira (Amir), then and now. PHOTO COURTESY GIORA AMIR.

waited outside the firehouse to see what would happen next. When the girls were suddenly marched out onto the road, the boys ran after the column of girls, calling Magda's and Klara's names as they stumbled through the streets. Because it was early Sabbath morning, some members of the Jewish community were not yet aware that the girls were being treated as if they were common criminals, and bereft of one last caress or kiss from their families marched to the train station. The image of these distraught and confused young women haunts Giora still. "The worst disaster of all was when they caught the girls and rounded them up...It was the prototype of all of the evil that would follow."

Seeing their daughters board a passenger train bolstered the illusion that the newest proclamation truly was nothing more than government service and may have alleviated the anxieties Jewish parents felt as their daughters were taken. In the morning light, the girls opened the windows and leaned out to blow kisses to their family and catch return kisses on the wind. They shouted to their parents, if their parents were there. Prayers were offered. Few were granted.

For Ida Eigerman, there was no one but her aunt to wave good-bye to. She wondered how her parents were faring in Poland; if she had known, she might have fled the station. In fact, in a few days time, back in her hometown of Nowy Sącz, elderly Jews, along with Jewish and gentile business owners, would be taken to the Jewish graveyard and gunned down. Among the murdered were, most likely, Ida's parents as well as Rena Kornreich's parents from Tylicz.

Orna Tuckman's future mother, Marta F., had a large family that stood waving to her. Next to her in the same compartment were her good friends: Minka, Margita, and another Marta. In their early twenties, these young women felt differently than the teenagers, who were being separated from their mothers and fathers for the first time. Many of these young women had jobs and lives outside their immediate families. Leaving home to work for three months of government service was going to make their families' lives more difficult because they were working girls and brought in needed income. Postponing their own young lives, they worried about their futures. How could a young woman fall in love and get married if she was doing government service for three months? What young man would wait for a young woman who was no longer available for long walks and sweet murmurings? Were there many nice Jewish men working at the shoe factory?

Chapter Eight

Sexism is like racism. It's very dehumanizing.
— WILMA MANKILLER, Chief of the
Cherokee Nation, Western Band

IN THE POPRAD BARRACKS, EDITH and Lea woke to a world transformed. There was no breakfast, no singing, no mother. Edith's eyelids were stuck together from tumult, tears, and sleeplessness. To make matters worse, she had gotten her period. As she and Lea wandered down the hallways, they could hear girls' voices in hollow rooms and footsteps echoing inside the vast empty barrack.

Shock has prevented many survivors from remembering details about their time in the Poprad barracks. Margie Becker recalls working in the kitchen peeling potatoes and slipping food to one of her friends, but "felt so sorry that I gave her the unkosher food." Commandeered to cook stewed cabbage for the afternoon meal, the girls in the kitchen were also instructed to cut precisely 150 grams of bread—the size of a clenched fist—for each girl.

Others were ordered to clean the barracks. Edith and Lea held back tears as they worked on their hands and knees scrubbing floors and walls. "No one told us what we were doing there," Edith says. "They gave us rags and mops and told us to clean the barracks. So we cleaned. We wondered, is this it? Was this the work we were supposed to do? That's not so bad, but it seemed strange to bring a couple hundred girls to clean some barracks. Why so many? We knew nothing."

And then 224 girls from Prešov arrived at the barracks. Seventy-four of them were teenagers, including Magda Amster.

"You know," Edith says, "the feelings are very hard to explain, because a seventeen-year-old girl, if she's not completely stupid, is a lot more optimistic of the future than an older person. With all the fear and all the insecurity, our optimism was there." She and the other girls looked at what they were being told to do and figured, "Maybe it is only really for work. Maybe it is only for something special. Maybe it is for work that is not so hard or horrible. We didn't know. How could we? No one knew about Auschwitz then. It didn't exist yet!"

Among the group of young women from Prešov were two middle-aged women. Fanny Grossmann and Etela Wildfeur were both forty-five, and while we can't be sure, it seems possible that they joined eighteen-year-old Ruzena Grossmann and nineteen-year-old Marta Wildfeur, who may have been their teenage daughters.

The government had been clear in its stipulation that only young, unmarried women were expected to register for work. So what were Fanny and Etela and, by the end of the week, twenty-seven other middle-aged women doing on the first transport? They did not come from one single community. Seven of these women came from Prešov, four were from Edith's hometown of Humenné, three came from Levoča, and one arrived on the bus from Stropkov.

Perhaps some of these women had planned to go together, but there is no way to know if they organized themselves ahead of time as an act of resistance—going in place of their daughters or niece—or of solidarity, refusing to let the girls go alone and unprotected. Perhaps the middle-aged women were unmarried and unrelated to the younger women and girls. We simply do not know. What is striking about these older women is that they are there. They are listed and accounted for, and they may represent a small act of rebellion that could have been perpetrated only by women. Men could not volunteer to replace their daughters or sisters. Only women. And when these women showed up at the trains and bus stations with their suitcases, they were not turned away.

The question has to be asked: If they were not on the original roundup list, did they register under the names of the daughters or family members they wanted to replace? Or did they give their own names and simply volunteer to go in place of the younger women? Whatever the case, by the time the list was typed and the quota had been made, no one was turned away.

So these God-fearing, religious women stood before the Hlinka Guard members...and stated their names and ages for the record: Eta Galatin, age forty; Margita Gluck, age forty-five; Lenka Neumann, age forty-two; Fanny, Paula, Ilona, Rezi...At fifty-eight years of age, Etela Jager was the oldest, and truly alone—she was the only woman on the transport bearing her family name and she came from a village that no longer even appears on a map. What was she doing there? Perhaps she was going in place of her granddaughter.

Whether they were resisting the government orders or going in solidarity with their daughters, we cannot know. Their silent courage speaks to the spirit of women, and it is a feat that has never been recognized. None of these women survived.

The first transport incited another, much better documented, act of resistance. In the border town of Bardejov, three hundred girls were supposed to report on March 20 and stay overnight in the town's Jewish school. However, on March 19, Rabbi Levi went to Dr. Grosswirth and Dr. Moshe Atlas with a risky idea. He asked the doctors to inject some of the girls with a double dose of the vaccine against typhus so that by morning they would be feverish. The doctors did so, and in the morning they declared that there was a typhus epidemic. The local authorities placed the entire Jewish section of Bardejov under quarantine, and every girl living inside the town perimeter was immediately excluded from reporting for "work." They were not even allowed to enter the school.

On Saturday morning, after spending the night in the school, about two hundred girls from the surrounding region were taken by passenger train to Poprad. But not a single girl was from Bardejov itself.

Konka still had a quota of girls to deliver and a target of five thousand in the space of a week, which may explain why town criers were suddenly making announcements in smaller towns. "Town criers were not always prompt," Edith says. "They went around to villages and banged on their drums, but there were lots of villages to go to, so it could often take days for news to arrive." Two weeks had passed since the first announcement though. With Bardejov coming up short, Konka and his cronies would have to look elsewhere for deportable young, unmarried women.

SUNDAY, MARCH 22, 1942

While families in the larger towns like Humenné and Prešov had had time to prepare or perhaps escape, girls in smaller towns had almost zero warning, a method that would prove to be highly effective. Over half of the population in the town of Stropkov was Jewish. They had a synagogue and yeshiva, and while poverty was rife in rural communities, Stropkov had an active marketplace and its own rabbi. In the surrounding valleys tiny villages were often made up of only one or two Jewish families.

Peggy knew literally everyone in Kolbovce, the village where she had grown up—she was related to them, after all. Her protective elder brothers returned unhappily from work that Sunday afternoon to inform the family that the town crier had been banging on his drum, and Peggy was supposed to report for government service the next day. The good news was that the work she did would benefit the family, her brothers assured their parents. If the family could receive a stipend from her service, it would be appreciated. Times were rough, and even rougher for Jewish families, who needed every little bit of help they could get.

That evening, after Peggy packed her things, did she pause to study her face in the mirror and think how grown-up she suddenly looked? Did she try smoothing her thick black hair by rolling it with socks, so she would look more sophisticated? She had never gone away on her own before, but the idea of supporting her family felt very adult and responsible. Like most teenagers, she thought growing up was exciting and something to be rushed into. Sighing with anticipation, Peggy figured she was going to have an adventure of her own. She couldn't wait.

THAT SAME SUNDAY, in another small village outside of Stropkov, the Berkowitz daughters were already hiding when a local policeman came by with a list in his hands. Bertha's mother claimed the girls had gone to visit relatives, but he had heard that excuse enough already and threatened to take Mr. Berkowitz if at least one of the girls didn't come with him.

Bertha's mother and father asked where the girls were going. They wanted to know what they would be doing—what parent wouldn't?

When the policeman said, "a shoe factory," they decided that didn't sound so bad.

Mrs. Berkowitz called her sixteen-year-old daughter, Bertha, to come out from her hiding place. Her younger daughter, Fany, remained in hiding.

Sisters Lea and Edith Friedman were two years apart in age.

"It was a holiday, probably Passover," Edith says. "They look about fourteen, so it was about 1936." The girls were friends, but Edith does not remember all their names. *From left to right:* an unidentified girl, Anna Herskovicova, another unidentified girl, Lea Friedman, and Debora Gross (Adela's sister).

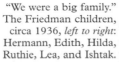

"We were a big family." The Friedman children, circa 1936, *left to right*: Hermann, Edith, Hilda, Ruthie, Lea, and Ishtak.

Magduska Hartmann's cousins included her best friend and eldest cousin, Nusi, also known as Olga (*far right*). Also shown are Nusi's siblings—Andrew (*front*), Bianca (*far left*), and Valika (*back row, center*). Olga, Valika, and their parents did not survive.

Magduska Hartmann grew up on the family farm with her cousins and brother, Eugene.

Annou Moskovic (*left*) grew up down the street from Edith and Lea Friedman, and loved to visit their house on bread-making day. Zuzana Semerova (*right*) was one of Annou's and Edith's friends. She went into hiding and worked with partisans who resisted the Hlinka and Nazi regimes.

Maya (Magda) Hans was the younger sister of Ria Hans. Ria was forced to make a heartbreaking decision to protect Magda from being murdered by the SS.

This photo was sent to family in America. We know nothing about Rozalia and Therezia Ziegler (*back row*) except that they were on the first transport and no one in their immediate family survived.

The redheaded Adela Gross. It took her family seventy years to discover what happened to Adela in Auschwitz.

Lea Friedman (*left*) and Anna Herskovicova loved to go to the movies together.

This photograph was taken at a private school for girls in Prešov, probably in 1938. The second girl in the back row is Klara Lustbader. In the front row, sitting at far right is Giora Shpira's friend, Magda Amster. The other girls are unidentified, but many would have been on first transport.

On December 6, 1945, the Banders, part of the Ukrainian Insurgent Army, brutally shot fifteen young Jews in Kolbasovo, Slovakia. Among those murdered was Gizzy Grummerova (*center*) from the first transport. Irena Fein is at left in this prewar photo.

Women of Humenné

Irena Fein (#1564; Ferencik), wanted to be a photographer when she grew up. She was good friends with Adela and Debora Gross, Margie Becker, and Lea and Edith.

On their way to Palestine in November 1945, Helena Citron (#1971; Tsiporah Tehori) and her sister, Ruzinka Grauber (Ornstein), traveled through Rome, where they posed for this photo with Italian soldiers.

Edith (#1970; far left), stands with arms folded. Sitting next to her is Margie Becker (#1019). To the right of the teacher, in white, is Lea wearing a veil. The girls were part of the cast in the annual Beth Jacob School theatrical production in Humenné, circa 1940.

Ria Hans (#1980; Elias), spent six months in a standing cell in Block 11, the Block of Death, for the crime of trying to save a fellow prisoner.

Edith's school class. Of the nine Jewish girls in school, only three survived. *Back row, left to right*: Edith is second from left; Zena Haber is the tall girl in the middle; Lenka Treil is second from right. *Middle row: second from left*: Margita Anis; Zuzana Sermer on far right; next to her is Eicherl. *Front row*: far left is Srulovic; Ruzena Boruchovic in polka-dot dress; next to teacher on right, Irena Greenberger. (The rest of the girls are gentiles.)

Polish Women

The girls from Tylicz used to hike seven kilometers to the town of Krynica to collect water from the mineral springs there. *Left to right*: Danka Kornreich, Dina Dranger, Bear, Rena Kornreich (circa 1938).

This photo was taken on the farm where Dina Dranger (#1528; Vajda), lived in Provence after the war. Her cousins were Erna and Fela Dranger.

Rena promised their mother she would take care of her little sister. Danka and Rena Kornreich (#2775 and #1716; Brandel and Gelissen), in Holland, a few months after liberation.

Ida Eigerman (#1930; Newman), was from Nowy Sacz and worked in the sorting detail known as "Canada."

Erna Dranger (#1718; Koren) was Rena Kornreich's best friend growing up in Tylicz.

Sara Bleich (#1966; Glancszpigel) grew up in the spa town of Krynica. She emigrated to Argentina after the war. Her granddaughter wrote, "I never saw her smiling like that. I'm not sure she was ever that girl. This is our way to honor her."

Fela Dranger (#6030; Ischari) had several breakdowns after the war.

Magda Moskovic (#1297; Bittermanová)
returned and settled in Slovakia after the war.

Joan Rosner (#1188;
Weintraub) was one
of the Jewish
hostages released as
part of Count
Bernadotte Folke's
negotiations with
Reichsführer
Heinrich Himmler.

Klara Lustbader
(#1808; Chudy)
lived near the
Great Synagogue
in Prešov
after the war.

Matilda Friedman
(#1890; Hrabovecká)
wrote the book
*Ruka s Vytetovanym
Cislom* (Arm with
a Tattooed Number).

Ruzena Gräber
Knieža (#1649;
shown here,
postwar, with
her husband,
author Emil
Knieža) went
to school
with Edith
in Humenné.

Perel Kaufman (#1461; Fridman) was subjected
to medical tests by Dr. Mengele, who injected
her with malaria and other illnesses.

Women of Prešov

Magda Friedman (#1087; Ziegler) was first cousin to Ella and Edie Friedman

This photo, taken in their hometown, Kapušany, shows (*left to right*) Edie Friedman (#1749; Valo), Ella Friedman (#1750; Rutman), and others, circa 1938.

Minka Friedman (#1174; Weiss) was close friends with Marta F. (#1796; Gregor).

Klára Herz (#1354; Baumöhlava) was in Bergen-Belsen with Bertha Berkowitz and was friends with Klara Lustbader after the war.

Kato (Katarina) Danzinger (#1843; Prinz) with her husband and their daughter, postwar.

Marta F. (#1796; Gregor) was subjected to experimentation and made sterile. Her daughter, Orna Tuckman, was adopted.

Linda Reich (#1173; Breder) lost her parents, sister, and three brothers (one of them her twin) to the gas chambers in Auschwitz.

Matzo making with the Berkowitz family and friends, Pesach, 1940.
Only two people in this photo survived. Far left, standing in a white apron
is Peshy Steiner, Bertha's best friend; behind Peshy is Bertha (#1048).
The next four standing are an unidentified young woman, then two of
Bertha's sisters, Lily and Magda, and Peshy's sister in a white apron holding
a roller. In front of the young women are Bertha's mother, dressed in black,
and Peshy's mother, beside her. Sitting and holding the large bowl is Bertha's
brother, Volvi. The only other survivor besides Bertha is Herschel Einhorn,
standing at far right in the middle row with a cap on and a cocky smile.
Bertha's surviving only sister, Fany, and brother, Emil, are not in this photo.

Peggy Friedman (#1019;
Kulik) is the young girl,
sitting front and center,
in this photo taken circa
1935. None of her
family survived.

The wedding of Regina Tannenbaum
(#1397; Wald) was the first Jewish marriage
in her hometown after the war.

The Kleinman family in Breznica, Slovakia,
circa 1935. *Back row, left to right*: Ruzena
(#1033; Guttmann), who walked with Peggy
Kulik on their way to the first
transport and remained her friend after the
war. Next to Ruzena are her siblings Josef,
Tonci Berkovic, Max, Malvina, and Adolf.
Front row: their parents, Aron and Ester.
Adolf and another brother, Irving
(not pictured), survived.

"Don't worry," her mother assured Bertha, "I'll go with you to the registration."

Together they packed a few of Bertha's things into a satchel while the policemen waited. As Bertha stepped into the center of their home, her father motioned for her to sit on a stool. Tears streamed down his face as he placed his hands on her head and prayed: "God is going to help you. You will be home soon." It was the first time she had ever seen her father cry. They were the last words he ever spoke to her.

As they were leaving, Bertha's mother called back to her sons. "Don't forget to take down the laundry!" Frozen on the line, the shirts and socks jerked in the wind, waving an awkward good-bye.

Mrs. Berkowitz and the policeman escorted Bertha and her best friend, Peshy Steiner, to the larger town of Kapišová, where they were told to sleep for the night. A bus would pick the girls up in the morning. Bertha and Peshy spent the night in a friend's home with other girls who had come from the surrounding villages with their mothers or fathers. While the teenagers slept on the floor, tense voices full of dread worried their dreams. "I did not sleep very well," Bertha says. "My mother didn't sleep at all. She aged ten years in one night."

ON MONDAY MORNING, a policeman showed up at Peggy's house. Her mother packed sandwiches and some sweets for the two-hour walk to town, and Peggy hugged her brothers and parents good-bye. Wrapped warmly, a scarf around her neck and shoulders, she waved and headed off on her adventure.

The only way out of the valley was along a dirt road between the mountains. Snow clung to the hills, and the ground was hard and frozen. A lemony sun crested the mountains as the morning shadows receded toward the forests.

At the next village, Brusnica, twenty-one-year-old Anna Judova joined Peggy. The girls had grown up in the farmlands of

Slovakia among gentile neighbors with very little thought or care about the wider world. Peggy's eager face wore a broad smile as they headed down the road, her mass of dark hair pinned back under a hat to keep her ears warm. An hour later, their police escort stopped to pick up Ruzena Kleinman. The three girls swung their bags and chatted buoyantly in the brisk morning air.

Forty other young women were standing at the bus stop in Stropkov when Peggy, Ruzena, and Anna arrived. Amid a din of young voices, the girls chitchatted about the mystery of their government jobs. Like Bertha, some of them had been told they would be working in a shoe factory; others had been told they would be working on farms. The bus driver was affable and smiled at the girls, but all he knew was that they were going to Poprad. With Passover just a week away, the girls immediately began to wonder if maybe they would be allowed to come home for Seder. Poprad was only a few hours away, after all.

Peshy Steiner was like a daughter to Mrs. Berkowitz, and as the others were boarding the bus, Bertha's mother looked at Peshy's beautiful face and took her hand. The other girls they had walked with stood by her. "Promise me you will look after each other," she told them. "And remember Bertha is the baby of you. Take care of her, like you would your little sisters."

In an instant, they were bound by their vow and formed a sorority among themselves. As Bertha kissed her mother goodbye, she felt something change deep inside her. At that moment, she says, "I became very grown up."

The engine on the bus coughed, then sputtered. The smell of petrol stung their noses as black smoke puffed out of a rusty exhaust. There was a great deal of chatter and excitement; most of the girls were anything but sad. "Nobody thought it was the last time they would see their parents. We were going away for a little while and would be back soon," Bertha recalls.

"We were laughing and singing," Peggy says. "It was an adventure. The bus driver was very nice, and we had sandwiches that our mothers had packed for us. It was like a picnic!" Even the bus driver joked with them.

About two hours into their journey, the scenery outside began to change as the High Tatra Mountains came into view with their dragon-toothed peaks bedecked in winter white, majestic against an ice blue sky. Like the girls from Humenné before them, these young women were filled with such a sense of patriotic pride at the sight of the High Tatras that as the bus rounded the bend in the road and revealed what they thought was their final destination, they burst into song.

Pulling up at the barracks in Poprad, the driver opened the door to the bus and the enthusiastic girls tumbled out. Looking quizzically around the compound, they smiled at the men in black uniforms stepping toward them, whips in hand.

"The moment we got off the bus, everything changed," Peggy recalls. "There were guards yelling at us. Whipping us." Being pushed and shoved around by men, who were rude and gruff, the girls stopped short and looked at the bus driver for help. What was this? What was happening?

The driver looked as shocked as his passengers.

The girls' confusion was compounded by the incongruity of their situation. Their lighthearted mood of hope and eager compliance collapsed.

Outside the windows of the barracks, the day shifted to night. The sandwiches they had eaten on the bus were gone. Their mothers hadn't packed more than lunch, thinking that their daughters would be fed supper. Inside the barracks, there was no meal prepared for the new arrivals. Edith and the others had already eaten their Monday allotments, 150 grams of potatoes each. The robust country girls from Stropkov met the hollow-eyed girls who had been in the barracks for two days, whose faces were distorted by shock and hunger. Since the girls from Humenné had arrived on Friday, they had been fed no more than 150 grams of millet, cabbage, legumes or kasha each day, along with their allotment of one piece of bread. It was hard to believe that a few days earlier, those same girls had also been singing patriotic songs on their way to Poprad. No one was singing now.

SIXTEEN-YEAR-OLD Ivan Rauchwerger arrived with two of his friends to check on the girls from his town of Spišská Nová Ves, about twenty-four kilometers from Poprad. Ivan had been staggered by the announcement that the girl he was in love with, and so many of the girls he had gone to school with, were being rounded up for government service. Why not call young Jewish men, who were stronger and more fit for work? Why not call him?

Like everyone in the Jewish community, Ivan's family was dismayed by the abrupt government requisition. "The country

Ivan Rauchwerger as a young man. PHOTO COURTESY IVAN JARNY.

had not turned a complete blind eye to what was happening," he remembers. "Many gentile business owners contacted bishops in Bratislava and asked them to intercede with President Tiso on behalf of their Jewish friends, as this deportation of single, young girls was in contrast to everything the Christian religion teaches, especially 'Love your neighbor.'"

That Monday, Ivan's mother, Eugenie, insisted he go check on their neighbors who had been taken. One of Ivan's friends borrowed his uncle's car and, together with Ivan and a couple of other friends, drove to the barracks in Poprad. Less than half a block away from the railway tracks, the two-story building would have been easy to spot from the main road. Despite a fence around the grounds and guards at the entrance, Ivan and his friends were able to talk their way inside. Immediately, they were surrounded by panicked and frightened girls. "Their cheeks were streaked with mascara, and they begged my friends and me to bring food and medicine. It was horrible to see them so distraught. They were desperate."

"We were crying the whole time," Edith says. "What will happen to us? What are we doing here? The guards didn't tell us anything."

By the next day, when more men arrived to check on their sisters and cousins, the guards stopped allowing anyone inside the compound. Joan Rosner's brother Luddy tried and tried to see his sister, to no avail. Emil Knieža was able to borrow an army uniform from a gentile friend and was allowed to visit his young wife, Ruzena Gräber, whom Edith knew from school. Ruzena had argued for her freedom, and as a married woman she should have been exempt, but officials did not concern themselves with specifics. Winding their fingers through the chain-link fence, Ruzena and Emil had a desperate conversation.

—They are taking you to Poland, he warned.

Neither of them knew what that meant.

The girls in the barracks seethed with unrest and impatience. It seemed like they were waiting for something. But what? Meanwhile, buses from other far-flung towns kept arriving.

THE HARTMANN FARM was run by two cousins who were as close as brothers. Renting the spacious farmhouse and the attached farmland from an aristocratic Hungarian woman, Bela and Dula Hartmann shared everything. The house had two wings, so each family had its own kitchen and bedrooms, conjoined by a communal family room, where the children would gather at night to sing songs, play games, or read quietly by candlelight. There was no electricity or indoor plumbing, but that was neither unusual nor considered a hardship.

Six children filled the gables of the Hartmann home. Bela's daughter, Magduska, was a dark-haired, somber child with a Mona Lisa smile. Bela's wife had contracted multiple sclerosis when the children were young. Before the war, before the Jewish Codex was implemented, gentile women had cared for her, but when it became illegal for gentiles to work for Jews, Magduska became her mother's primary caregiver. It was hard work. Cleaning and bathing her mother, helping her eat and use the toilet, made Magduska an overly responsible teenager, which may explain the somber way she had of looking right through you with her piercing brown eyes. Eugene, Magduska's brother, was an equally responsible lad of fifteen who worked in the fields with his father.

Their cousin Olga had lighter burdens to carry on her side of the house, but as the eldest of Dula's children, she was in charge of her younger siblings, Bianca, Valerie, and Andrew (Bundi), the baby of the family, who was always scampering off to the orchard to climb trees and pick cherries. A jolly girl of sixteen, Nusi (as everyone in the family called her) doted on her older cousin, Magduska. Nusi's pancake-round cheeks and wide-open smile contrasted with her cousin's darker complexion and more wistful face. Nusi always looked like she had a joke to tell, Magduska a secret, but despite their differences, the girls were close as sisters. They had been in diapers together and had helped on the family farm since they were old enough to gather eggs from the chickens.

Roškoviany, a farming community, had just three Jewish families amid its six hundred rural residents. There was no outward anti-Semitism among the farmers, who depended on each other for support during harvest and hard times. Both Eugene and Andrew played with gentile and Jewish children and had good friends from both faiths.

The Hartmann brothers' prominent farm employed locals in the dairy and in the fields, where wheat, corn, oats, and hay were grown. They had flocks of sheep that were milked for cheese, as well as orchards with pear, apple, and cherry trees.

The nearest town was about three kilometers away, in Lipany, which had a small synagogue, where the Hartmanns worshipped. Because there had been very little warning in the rural villages, the Hartmanns had only the vaguest idea about the new work order. Nusi's little sister Bianca was almost fifteen, so as a precaution, Dula had sent her to a gentile friend's house for a sleepover. Like the Friedman family, the Hartmanns didn't want to break the law. Nusi was at home when the local policeman came to collect the girls.

Watching his sister pack, Andrew says it was "as if she was going to summer camp." She packed a canteen of water, a drinking cup that telescoped so she could fold it and place it in her pocket, her toothbrush and toothpaste, and a pencil and paper so she could write home. Sensible work shoes. Her best coat. Mittens. Scarf. Hat. Pajamas. One change of clothes.

Magduska did not pack anything. The policeman, who knew the family well and understood she was her mother's caregiver, said, "Oh, we are just taking her to the next city. I'm sure they will release her." All Bela had to do was explain the family situation.

"Then that is what we'll do." Bela got his coat. Magduska kissed her mother, ruffled her brother's hair, and said, "See you later."

It was "very nonchalant," Eugene says. "She was just going to the next town." No one was worried. She would be back in no time.

Accompanying the policeman with his daughter and niece, Bela found seventeen other girls had also been collected. All of the girls knew one another, but Ellie and Kornelia Mandel were good friends. Bela was relieved that Nusi knew some of the other teenagers, especially since Magduska would not be joining them. As Nusi went to speak to the Mandel sisters, he took Magduska by the hand, marched straight up to the official checking names off a list, and explained the important duties his daughter performed as a caregiver for her mother.

A PENCIL-PUSHING BUREAUCRAT gave Mr. Hartmann an incredulous look. "We're not taking the mother. We are taking the daughter."

"You can't do that!" Bela explained. "We run an important farm that feeds the troops, and my son is in the fields working. Her mother is bedridden."

"That is not our problem."

"Please. Magduska is a necessary part of our farm. I can't care for the dairy and my wife at the same time. How can we milk cows and sheep, plant the oats and wheat, and care for an invalid? We depend on Magduska."

"Then you will have to find someone else to depend on. This one has to report for government service for three months."

Magduska's calm veneer shattered. Her deep dark eyes filled with tears. What would they do without her? She hadn't even said good-bye.

Nusi and the Mandel sisters tried to comfort her. Bela wrapped his huge arms around his only daughter and pulled her into his embrace. He told the girls to write as soon as they could so the family knew they were safe. As soon as they had her address, he promised to send clothes and some money, so she could buy what she needed once they got to the factory. He asked Ellie and Kornelia to keep in touch, too.

He told them to take care of each other, and remember that God was with them. The time would pass so quickly that before they knew it, they would all be celebrating Rosh Hashanah together.

Their smiles blossomed under his assurance and courage. As he blessed his daughter's eyes and brow with kisses, did he think to himself, the next time I see her she will be seventeen?

There was no bus to board this time. This was the final group of girls to be collected, and almost forty young women were wedged in the back of a truck along with their luggage. Bela helped his daughter and niece up onto the flatbed and kissed them both good-bye. It was a little over one hundred kilometers to Poprad. The girls hunkered down below the sides of the truck to keep out of the wind.

Among those shivering in the truck bed was eighteen-year-old Linda Reich, who had been "sitting comfortably at home with my family when the Hlinka Guard banged on the door, just after supper."

Bewildered by the interruption of an otherwise quiet evening, neither Linda nor her parents understood what was going on, "but the Hlinka Guard told us 'We are taking you to work in Germany so you can help your families who are left behind, and support them.'"

She was young and said, "Oh, that would be wonderful, because already it was horrible."

The Reich family had no money for food and no fuel to heat the house. Her brothers were working as farm laborers, but there was very little food for Jews, and the winter had been hard. Like most of the other girls in the back of the truck, Linda thought the least she could do was help her family.

"We can send money home to help them," she told the others.

Magduska and Nusi kept silent—money and food were not things their families lacked. In the dark, the girls bounced against each other in the back of the old truck as it banged into potholes along the unpaved highway, rattling its way toward Poprad. It was after midnight when they arrived.

WEDNESDAY, MARCH 24, 1942

At this point in our story, we have to imagine what happened next, because the only proof we have of the incident is on paper—a list of the names of every girl on the transport, dated March 24, 1942. The document itself sits in the archives of Yad Vashem in Jerusalem. Yellowed by age, the corners of the pages curled by time, the sheaves are so delicate that you must wear white cotton gloves when touching them. Here are their names. Children of survivors can find their mothers' names; families of nonsurvivors can find the names of lost aunts, sisters, cousins.

Memories about the barracks and "Camp" Poprad are hazy at best. Some girls do not even remember being there. The shock of being ripped from their homes, forced to sleep on the floor or in hammocks, fed starvation rations, and watched by military police simply did not register in the catalog of horrors that were to come. Their stay in the barracks is lost time, one of the least-recalled incidents in the testimonies, and the actual event of the typing of their names has slipped into the fog of that oblivion. No survivor I have spoken with remembers it.

Perhaps the list was organized before a supper of beans was doled out, or perhaps it was earlier in the day when the girls were forced to line up in what was fast becoming military drill. Perhaps it was compiled from lists typed in Prešov, Bardejov, and Humenné, handwritten in Stropkov. We do not know for sure. The list is a vitally important item, though, for without this list, we would not know the names of the girls on the first transport and they would, indeed, have disappeared from history forever. Whether they stepped up to a table and reported their names in Poprad or the list was compiled from lists made when they first registered in their hometowns, the information was gathered and typed into one thirty-four-page document on March 24, 1942. It had to have been typed after the arrival of the last group of girls, among whom were Magduska and Nusi Hartmann and Linda Reich.

Imagine a table with a black metal Erika or perhaps a Mercedes typewriter. The typist sits straight-backed and alert beside a stack of blank sheets of paper on the left, finished pages facedown on the right. With the first clack of the keys, the typist numbers the first page, *1*, then types, *Soznam darujúcich zmlúv.*

Here we must pause and consider the phrase *Soznam darujúcich zmlúv*, which translates to "List of Donation Contracts." The Slovaks did not want anyone to know that they were using slave laborers, so the official line was that the girls were contract volunteers, "donating" their time to work for the government. In this way the Slovak government was able to skirt the illegality of deporting its Jews.

Below this line is typed *Tábor Poprad*—Camp Poprad, in English.

Setting the tabs on the typewriter's carriage, the typist labels the columns at the top of the page and then underlines the headings with a series of dashes that have the smallest gaps between them. It is all very efficient and organized.

"Number of person." TAB.

"Last name, First." TAB.

"Birth year." TAB.

"Town." TAB.

Now the typist is ready.

At first, there seems to be some organizational pattern. The first girl, Zlata Kaufmannova, is from Malcov, followed by two sisters from the town of Beloveža, which is just a few kilometers away. Most of the girls on the first page are from towns within twenty or thirty kilometers of each other, not far from the Polish border; towns near Bardejov and its typhus epidemic hoax. In the following pages, incongruities begin to creep in. Sometimes friends and cousins are next to each other on the list; sometimes they are not. There are whole pages of girls from the towns of Humenné or Prešov, and then a stray girl from a village that is hours away appears in the mix. Linda Reich, who had only just arrived, is number 582, in the middle of the list. So we know it was not numbered by order of collection. Order is implied, but it was not strictly adhered to, which explains why Dina Dranger is not next to her cousin, Erna. However, Adela is next to Edith and Lea.

By page eight, the typist had already recorded more than two hundred names.

Slightly askew, the page looks as if the carbons caused the paper to slip as the typist hurriedly fed the paper into the roller, typed the page number, hit the return bar, tabbed over a few indents, and hit the keys: *T-á-b-o-r-space bar-space bar-P-O-P-R-A-D, back up and underline:* _ _ _ _ _ _ _ _ _ _ _ _ _ _ _ _ _

Near the top of the page, number 211, is Lea's friend, Anna Herskovic, the strawberry-blonde with soft curls and worried eyes. After her come two of our Polish refugees in a scene that must have gone something like this:

—Last Name?

—D-r-a-n-g-e-r-o-v-a.

—First?

—E-t-e-l-a.

Why did Erna say Etela? Her friends called her Erna. Was she confused or using a pseudonym? We do not know.

—Year? What year were you born?

—1-9-2-0.

—Town? The scribe hits the tab key.

—Humenné.

The typist presses the shift and hits the number two to create an accent mark, but the keys jam and the number 2 appears instead. The typist doesn't seem to care.

—Next!

Erna Dranger moves aside.

Rena steps up and emulates her best friend by giving her nickname:

—Rifka Kornreich.

The typist gets the shift to work this time, and when Rena says she came from Humenné, neat accent marks appear before the roller clicks the paper down one more line.

Next line. Next number.

The page rolls up.

Next line. Next number.

When Lea steps up to the table, she is 236. Edith is 237. Adela Gross is 238.

The typist pulls the finished page out of the typewriter with a flourish and places it in two neat stacks—one of originals and one of carbon copies. Takes two fresh sheets, secures the carbon between them, places the paper edge against the roller, turns the knob so the paper catches nice and straight, then slaps the return bar and types the page number: 9.

Slaps again.

T-á-b-o-r-space-space-P-O-P-R-A-D. Pushes the carriage back to the left to carefully underline the heading: _ _ _ _ _ _ _ _ _ _ _ _ _ _ _

2-3-9-.-space-B-e-r-k-o-v-i-c-o-v-a-space-J-o-l-a-n-a-space-space-1-9-2-5 . . .

It will take hours.

The substance of every page is almost identical, but the title "Camp Poprad" is sometimes centered and sometimes tabbed too far to the right, which speaks to the immediate pressure of typing quickly, as if the girls in line stepped up and stated their names, birth years, towns... If the list had been typed in a quiet office, formatting would probably have been more consistent, fewer mistakes would have been made, and corrections of those mistakes would probably not have been made by hand.

At some point, the ink ribbon must have been replaced because the ink impressions get thinner and lighter, then are suddenly black and sharp again. It is also possible that a second typewriter and typist were used. Some pages are missing the title, and the keystrokes are slightly more askew on some pages than on others.

Mistakes become more frequent as the list lengthens and fatigue sets in. The numbers 377 and 595 are completely missing, which means there were actually 997 girls on the transport, not 999. By pages sixteen and seventeen, a pen has been used to correct a mistyped name, replacing *hp* with *ph*, and the name of a town has been erased and replaced with a quote mark, signifying that it should repeat the line above. Bleary-eyed and sore-fingered, on page twenty-six, the typist misnumbers almost the entire page, going from 754 to 765. After pulling the sheet of paper out and typing 790 at the top of the next page, someone must have seen the error. A black pen scratches over the numbers, correcting: *755. 756. 757.* to the bottom. An *8* is typed over the *9* at the top of the next page. The human line begins moving again: *780. 781. 782.* On page thirty, the Hartmann cousins Magduska and Nusi (who gives her name as Olga) are together, the only representatives of their tiny village of Rožkovany. A few names later, the Guttmanova sisters get confused with the Birnova sisters, and the typist has to back up and cross out the last name and retype

Birnova. Was the order so important that the girls couldn't be shifted in line?

Finally, the last page is rolled into the typewriter and the last two girls give their information: nineteen-year-old Hermina Neuwirth and her twenty-five-year-old sister, Giza, from Strop-kov. It must have been late afternoon when the final number was typed, incorrectly: *9-9-9*.

Chapter Nine

History has failed almost everybody who is ordinary.

—Min Jin Lee

POPRAD, THURSDAY, MARCH 25, 1942

The telegram from Konka's office addressing the issue of "preliminary liberation from work" for Jews under amendment §255 was sent "to all district governors, chief police officers, and directors in Bratislava and Prešov, into their own hands" and marked as "Confidential and Urgent." Among the girls that amendment could have saved were Edith and Lea, Adela Gross, Magda Amster, and Magduska and Olga Hartmann.

> It is probable, that Jews who have asked for an exception within the meaning of provision were *allowed* to work [emphasis added] and were included into the lists.

> In such cases, the governors know about them, as these requests were sent through the offices or were

86

sent through the office of the President in order to be scrutinized.

I am asking the officers (presidents) not to call up these Jews and to remove them from the lists as persons added to the lists by mistakes.

To the guard!

On behalf of the Minister:
Dr. Konka

One cannot help but appreciate the understatement of being "allowed to work." It is also clear from the telegram that President Tiso had not yet approved anyone for work exemptions. The regional lists of important workers, as defined under §255, may have been submitted by mayors and governors of the various regions in the country. They may have been sent to the government in Bratislava, but there the process had slowed as President Tiso decided who should be "allowed to work." So the mayor of Humenné, who had told Mr. Friedman that his daughters had to report for duty because that was what the law stated, was now being told the exact opposite: They should be removed from the lists.

But the list had already been typed. The girls were about to be deported.

At first, there was only one response to Konka's telegram, the District Branch for the Jewish Center in the town of Levoča sent a telegram to Konka requesting that three of its female residents be released. These were girls Ivan Rauchwerger knew.

The date on the telegram is smeared, almost illegible after seventy-five years. Strips of wrinkled ticker tape are pasted onto a rectangular sheet of paper, itself brittle with age. The stamps are torn.

dept. 14 [sic]

Levoča

Magdalena Braunova born March 28 1926 was taken to Poprad to fulfill her work duty after turning 16 years

Hermina Jakubovicova born August 14 1921 was during female presentation on February 26 1942 recognized as unable to work; in spite of it, she was taken to Poprad camp on 23. 3. 1942

Lenka Szenesova (born Singerova) as a married person was also taken to Poprad and the mentioned three persons were by mistake taken to fulfill their work duty and therefore we ask you to make an edit and send them home.

District branch of the Jewish Center Levoča

Then, a flurry of telegrams from desperate Jews began arriving at the ministry.

In Poprad some very different preparations were being made. For supper that Thursday, the girls from Levoča (fifteen-year-old Magdalena, disabled Hermina, and already-married Lenka) were standing in line for something that was called "goulash" although it looked more like garbage. It contained, per dietary instructions, their allotment of 100 grams of meat for the week—less than a can of cat food. It would be the last real meal they would eat for the next three years. If they survived the next three years.

In the afternoon, the guards shouted for everyone to gather their things and line up outside. There was an odd sense of relief. After the constant stress of the unknown, the impending sense of doom, and days waiting in the barracks, the girls were going somewhere. Impatient to get moving and do something different, they packed up their few things and chatted among themselves, guessing, always guessing: Were they going to the factory now? Were they going to start work soon? Would someone feed them more at the factory?

Organizing one thousand people to do anything rarely runs smoothly. There was shouting among the girls. Sisters and cousins hurried each other. Chaos.

No one had brought all that much. Most of the young women were still wearing what they had worn the day they left home. Woolen dress suits, sensible shoes, woolen leggings, maybe stockings on the town girls. Village girls wore longer skirts and hand-knit sweaters. Everything from fashionable hats to babushka-length scarves covered their heads.

EARLIER IN THE DAY, at least two Jewish physicians had reported for duty in Poprad after being ordered to accompany a trainload of girls. There were supposed to be seven Jewish doctors in all on the transport. When Dr. Weiszlovitz arrived, he was told his services were no longer needed and he was excused. The reason the authorities gave him was that there were more than enough doctors for the transport. In fact, there was only one—Dr. Izak Kaufmann. Evidently, one medical practitioner was enough for 999 young women.

There is some confusion about Dr. Kaufmann's presence on the transport. Some believe that Dr. Kaufmann took the place of the last girl on the list, twenty-five-year-old Giza Neuwirth, but this does not concur with Yad Vashem records. His presence could not have been covert in the barracks; no one would have forgotten a man's presence among the girls, let alone a doctor's, yet not one survivor ever mentions a doctor in the barracks. Certainly, Edith never saw him. And when our young witness, Ivan Rauchwerger, drove to Poprad to check on his girlfriend, he was asked to bring some of the girls' medications back with him. If a doctor had been available in the barracks, why would girls have asked for their medications?

Dr. Kaufmann was conscripted as part of the authorities' ruse, and like Dr. Weiszlovits he must have arrived on the day of departure. His name is not to be found anywhere on the list of 999 girl's names, typed on March 24, 1942. It is found only at the bottom of a separate list of ninety-nine of the girls' names. Next to his name, it states that he was the only doctor for one thousand "people."

HOW LONG DOES IT TAKE to load almost one thousand women onto a train of cattle cars? Was it still daylight when the last of them stepped outside to breathe the brisk mountain air and send a prayer up to God, thankful that they were free of the horrible barracks?

That moment of respite faded as the guards shouted at them to march to the railway tracks outside of the barracks.

It was the longest line of cars Edith had ever seen. Even cattle market trains were shorter. The size filled the girls with trepidation. "We didn't think that these were for us," Linda Reich says. Then the Hlinka Guard opened the doors to the cattle cars and ordered the girls to get inside.

Who in their right mind would willingly board a freight train like this? There were no ramps. Ramps were used for cattle, but not for human beings. How could they get inside? The cars were too high off the ground to be boarded by girls in skirts, girls with luggage. Not one girl could figure out how to clamber aboard, and not one girl wanted to. They balked at the idea.

The guards began cursing and screaming. "You Jewish whores, you!"

The youngest of three sisters, Regina Schwartz, naively asked the guards, "Where are you taking us?"

"To the front, so the German soldiers can have a good time with you!" the Hlinka Guards said as they laughed.

These were cold men who didn't care when the girls began crying. Whips were on order for tears.

"Like an animal," Margie Becker says an SS man glared at her. "I still remember his blue eyes, piercing blue eyes. He pulled out his tongue," and panting at her said in German. "'Now your tongues are going to be hanging out, too.'" It was a curse and a threat; soon they were going to be hungry and thirsty. "It was very horrible."

Although the first transport slipped secretly away into the night, one week later, by the time the third transport was leaving Poprad, a number of parents had hired cars, "to be with their daughters, desperate at having to part with their children. The girls were loaded into cattle wagons—each with a sign reading 'eight horses' or 'forty persons.' That was the last their desperate parents saw of them," Ivan Rauchwerger recalls. "The girls were confused and distraught, many in tears." It is unlikely that the girls of the third transport were beaten and forced into the cattle cars, as the others had been on the first transport, because by that point there were witnesses: Many people, gentiles and Jews, were coming to Poprad to see the girls taken away.

"We were trying to be ladylike, but there was no way to get into the train in our skirts and dresses," Edith says. To avoid a stick across their back, they had to help each other into the cattle cars and hoist their own luggage with no assistance from the men. More mature young women struggled to maintain their composure and self-respect. Teenagers wept hysterically. They were good girls. Girls whose fathers paid taxes and obeyed the law. Girls who had obediently registered to work because their government told them they must, even though many had never been away from home for even one day in their young lives. What were nice girls doing in wagons used to haul livestock to slaughter, wagons that still smelled of manure, urine, and fear?

Edith and her sister clung to each other, but Edith remembers little of the train ride. The brain can only cope so much, and after so many indignities, her young mind simply stopped processing the horror. Reality had become a nightmare from which she could not wake.

DESPITE BEING RELIEVED OF DUTY, Dr. Weiszlovits did not leave the Poprad station immediately. Instead, he watched in horror as the columns of young women carrying their luggage were pushed and shoved into cattle cars. Afterward, he raced home and told his wife that Slovakia was "not for a child." They had to get their twelve-year-old son, Yehuda, out before it was too late. Yehuda was smuggled into Hungary, where he hid for the rest of the war. Yehuda survived the Holocaust. His father and mother did not.

AS EVENING DESCENDED and the last of the girls were boarded, the guards walked down the line, checking that the metal bars on the doors were securely latched. From inside came wails and pleading, high-pitched voices. The guards thumped the doors and walked on, waving as each car was cleared to go. The conductor blew the whistle. The signal light shifted from red to green. The engine revved. The stationmaster threw the switch, and the transport creaked forward onto the main track. As cars swayed left, then right, the weight of their cargo too insubstantial to keep the transport balanced and sturdy, the stationmaster wrote *Departure time: 20:20* in the station register.

Chapter Ten

They had come—almost as children—from the arms of their mothers, in a state of naïveté and ignorance of their future destiny.

—Dr. Manci Schwalbova

ALONG WITH KONKA'S TELEGRAM, a few of the promised exceptions arrived in Prešov on the afternoon of March 25, 1942. The moment Adolf Amster heard the news, he called his driver to bring the car to the house and rushed to the governor's office to pick up the document that would free his beloved daughter. They left for Poprad at once. If everything went according to plan, Magda would be safely home in a few hours.

Today, the distance between Prešov and Poprad can be driven in an hour on smoothly paved, four-lane toll roads. Even the old, narrow, two-lane route is paved, though one can still see donkeys and sometimes people pulling carts along the median. In 1942, the road still only had one lane, and parts of it would have been gravel or tarmacadam. The harshest winter on record had also taken a toll, creating miles of washboard surface and dangerous ditches.

Adolf Amster was not the only father racing fate. The Hartmann cousins had also received their family's exception and borrowed a friend's truck to drive to Poprad and rescue Madgduska and Nusi. There were probably other men of industry and commerce, responsible for everything from lumber mills to banks to farms, who had received exceptions, trying to rescue their daughters, as well.

Other families did not get the necessary paperwork for another few weeks. Such was the case for the Friedman and Gross families. The mayor of Humenné himself had assured Edith's father that the exceptions were on their way, but they did not arrive in time. This was government at its most inefficient.

The sun was setting over the High Tatras as the Amster car hastened toward Poprad. Adolf Amster's impatient hands worried the official paper with its government seal. Not seeing his daughter's sweet face at the breakfast table for the past few days or hearing her witty chatter with her mother, not feeling her endearing kiss on his cheek, had sent him into turmoil. Her mother had paced the house, fretting by the window curtains, peering out at a world gone mad. When the day turned to rain, she had cried because she longed to wash Magda's hair with the rainwater. All she wanted to do was brush her daughter's hair in front of the fire until it was smooth.

A confident and successful businessman, Adolf Amster had no doubt that he could secure Magda's release. When he did, he would make it up to her and allow her to go to Palestine to join her elder sister and brother and her best friend, Sara Shpira.

The sky was a twist of scarlet and orange above the icy peaks of the mountain range that defined Slovakia's northern border as Amster urged his driver to push the accelerator to the floor. In minutes, the landscape sobered into a gray dusk. The car lurched between grassy verges. A dog-fox stalked a hare in the fallow fields.

———————

IN THE FETID cattle car, girls sought each other in the dark. Through the wooden slats, they could see the light shift from pale yellow to soft pink, lavender to gray to black. The train lurched. Its cargo was so much lighter than the cattle it normally carried to the slaughterhouse that the cars swayed from side to side. Motion-sick girls retched into buckets until there was nothing left in their stomachs but bile. After being starved for five days, there wasn't much to begin with. As the train increased its speed, the cold night air whistled through the cracks. They shivered in the dark. Teeth chattered. Weeping was as communal as terror.

"And we still didn't know where we are going." Edith's voice is still shrill and indignant, seventy-five years later.

IT WAS DARK by the time Adolf Amster arrived at the Poprad barracks, only to find the building empty. The guards left behind, probably local boys, had seen the chaos around the girls' departure and told him the girls had been taken to Žilina. Amster hurried back to his driver, and together they headed west to that last major transfer station between the Slovak, Czech, and Polish borders.

The eastern railway track skirted a vast plateau before it splintered off in different directions. There were no railroad crossing gates on the plateau. The rail line did not even have warning signs where it crossed the roadways. The green glow of eyes floated in the dark night, as deer raised their heads from grazing. The car's lights bored holes in the blackness as it left behind farm fields and began a long slow ascent through pine forests, snow snakes and black ice. The highway to Žilina crisscrossed the tracks so that sometimes the train was on the driver's side and sometimes it was on the passenger's, sometimes it was below the car and sometimes it was higher. If he had been close enough in the murky night, Adolf Amster might have spotted the caboose light hugging the rocky banks of the Váh River.

Fog rose up from the gorge below. Wending its way through foothills and virgin forests, the train decelerated at sharp bends and slowly ascended and descended the mountain passes, until, just past the town of Vrútky, the tracks and road rose together into the treacherous passes of the Malá Fatra mountains. Then the train cheated the distance by ducking into the mountain, its caboose light swallowed by the tunnel. As they navigated the hairpin turns, time ticked against Adolf Amster and the other drivers. The tunnel cut at least half an hour off the journey and brought the train within twenty minutes of the main railway junction of Žilina—well ahead of the desperate fathers.

A normal passenger train would have taken less time than driving, but the cattle car's speed was markedly slower, giving the fathers a fighting chance of rescue. However, the train did not have to stop and pick up passengers. It simply slowed as it reached the depots of Štrba, Liptovský svätý Mikuláš, and Vrútky and lumbered over railway crossings, until it reached Žilina. And stopped.

A VAST JUNCTION station, Žilina was then, and still is, the intersection of lines going east to Poprad and beyond, west to the Czech Republic and Germany, south to Bratislava and Budapest, and north to Poland. Here cargo and passenger trains can have their cars connected or separated and trains can be switched back and forth from local branches to main lines.

As the Final Solution got underway, Žilina would become very busy—the central transit hub for all Slovak deportations (and later Hungarian). This was where the transports would arrive and the switch would be thrown to send the trains northward.

Switching tracks is not a quick process, especially for long, cumbersome freight hauls. The train performs a sidestep dance between tracks, moving slowly backward off one line, then waiting for the switch to be thrown before wobbling forward onto a new line, heading in a different direction. Depending on how many tracks it must shift across to reach its intended line, it repeats this zigzag dance.

From inside the train the girls peered between the slats and watched as the train clanked and swayed along the turnouts across the diamond-shaped crossing switches—destination unknown.

WITHOUT THE GERMAN and Polish railways, the Holocaust could never have been so lethal. It required the use of only two thousand trains to liquidate two-thirds of the Jews in Europe. In 1944, just 147 trains would transport 450,000 Hungarian Jews. The railway station for the town of Oświęcim and the Auschwitz death camp would become one of the busiest of the railways, with 619 trains working the deportation routes across Europe. Not one bureaucrat in the German railway system refused to authorize a single transport. In fact, the SS was required to pay the *Deutsche Reichsbahn* (the German Railway) for each Jew deported, and extra charges were levied against them for cleaning the cars once they were emptied. The cost for adults and children over ten years old was four *pfennig* (pennies) per kilometer; children under the age of four went free. It is roughly 106 kilometers from the border of Slovakia at Čadca to Oświęcim, Poland, costing roughly $4.24 per person after the border crossing.

In a few weeks, when more transports from Slovakia and the transports from France began filling the tracks, Jews would be considered the absolute lowest priority in terms of travel. They came after troop trains, supply trains, medical trains, and paying customers; even empty trains would have priority over Jewish "freight." That is most probably why the train carrying Edith and the others did not leave Poprad until 20:20. Night was the best time to move freight, and darkness provided a clandestine cloak of secrecy.

The girls were already suffering significant trauma from being uprooted, treated like criminals, and starved. Living in the barracks in Poprad had been the first step in a psychological process of "deculturation." But being locked into the cattle cars and treated as cargo was about more than cultural identity. It was about their place in humanity. No one knew what to believe anymore. All of their expectations were being crushed under the wheels of the transport.

RACING DOWN THE STATION PLATFORM at Žilina, Adolf Amster yelled at God. The transport had already pulled out of the station. Filled with anger and anguish, he stood on the empty platform unable to be the father he was meant to be—a man who protected his daughter and could rescue her. What would he do without his little Magda?

FORTY MINUTES AFTER THE TRAIN DEPARTED from Žilina, it creaked to a halt again. Woken abruptly by harsh German voices outside the train, Linda Reich peered through the cracks in the car and saw the lights of the border crossing. She weighed a little more than one hundred pounds, so she suggested the taller girls lift her up to the ventilation window so she could look out. Outside, she saw the Hlinka Guards hand paperwork to the SS. She read the signs in Polish to the girls below as everyone tried to make sense of the direction of the train. Rena Kornreich was doing the same thing for the girls in her cattle car.

"Maybe from Poland we go to Germany to work?" Linda suggested.

What she did not know was that the Slovaks had just handed the entire transport over to the Germans. The border crossing gate rose, and the train rolled forward. With the lowering of the barrier behind them, the fate of the girls was sealed.

THE TRAIN LUMBERED through the endless night, grinding away at what was left of their morale. There was no direct route to where they were going. Even today, a regular passenger train from Poprad to Oświęcim can take upwards of six hours. As the girls slept fitfully, the train lurched past a changing landscape. Mountains diminished into windswept steppes flattened by war and poverty. It was a foreign wind that now chilled the girls' already shivering bodies. Nestled up against their friends, sisters, cousins, seeking warmth and comfort, they stared into the black ink of the car. The train slowed when it passed through small towns they had never heard of—Zwardoń, Żywiec, Bielsko-Biała, Czechowice-Dziedzice—moving ever more slowly as it passed forests of silver birch, spruce, and thigh-high snow. When dawn came, its watery light barely touched the girls' pale faces.

Like Africans packed into the bellies of slave ships headed for the Americas, our girls were part of a new burgeoning slave trade. All of the major countries of Europe and Britain had outlawed the ownership of human beings and eradicated the transatlantic slave trade in the early 1800s. Now, more than one hundred years later, Germany was flouting its own antislavery laws and violating the human rights of these girls. Of course, like Africans, Jews were considered less than human—humanitarian concerns could be ignored. By the end of the war, this diabolical slave trade would generate about 60 million *Reichsmark* (the equivalent of $125 million today) for the German economy from Auschwitz alone. Yet they had no intrinsic value, so no one bothered buying or selling Jewish prisoners.

IT WAS AROUND eleven in the morning when the engine ground to a halt at another town only a few of the girls would have ever heard of, the Polish town of Oświęcim. Located on the meandering Soła River, beneath a picturesque medieval castle, Oświęcim was a pretty little town that had allowed its Great

Synagogue and the Sanctuary of the Blessed Virgin Mary Cathedral to be built overlooking the river's banks together. Surrounded by white buildings, the town square had no defining sculpture or fountain in the center, but there was a second cathedral and at least one other synagogue—worship was not in short supply. Gentile and Jewish inhabitants of the town worked together in the community, and acts of resistance were common. Residents were already being held in the local prison camp, while others had been forced to work there by the occupying German force.

A few miles outside of town were hectares of flat land for crops and grazing. This was not a poor community. It had industry and barracks for the Polish Army. After the German invasion, political prisoners and POWs needed to be imprisoned, and the Germans decided that Oświęcim's former army barracks, a few miles outside of town, would make the perfect prison camp. In 1942, to make room for an expansion of the prison camp, residents in neighboring villages were forced to relocate. Their homes were about to be demolished.

THE TRAIN HAD STOPPED in what appeared to be the middle of nowhere. There was no famous death gate. That infamous symbol had not even been designed yet, let alone erected. Birkenau was nothing but stables and swampland.

When the doors of the cattle cars opened, it was to a panorama of gray sky and flat, beige earth. A strip of snow stretched across the horizon. Bands of dark gray. Light gray. Brown gray. Black gray. Vistas as abstract as Mark Rothko's art, Edith and the girls looked out at a real version of his paintings and were swallowed up by the landscape. A nothingness beyond imagination.

The pupils of the girls' eyes contracted. Pain and light. Light and pain.

"There was nothing," Edith says. "Nothing!"

There is a semiprecious Polish flint that is created through such extreme pressure that it hardens the limestone crystals common in that country until they become invisible to the human eye. Under this forceful compression, the stones form tiny abstract landscapes—bands of gray and off-white—that, once polished into cabochons, look like minuscule works of abstract expressionist art. Spiritualists say these stones heal those haunted by the past, but Edith and the other girls had to survive first. They were about to be compressed and hardened by forced labor that was designed to pulverize them into stone.

The SS ordered male prisoners to get the girls out of the cattle cars. Men yelled. Dogs barked. Whips cracked.

"Raus! Raus!"

Hollow-eyed men in striped pajama-like uniforms peered into the cars. These were Polish prisoners arrested for crimes as petty as handing out leaflets or as serious as sabotage. None of them had seen a woman since their incarceration, almost two years for some. Now, hundreds of girls peered out at them, well-dressed, their hair less coiffed but still presentable. The girls stood blinking from inside of the cattle cars. Fumbling with their luggage, uncertain what to do next, they stood in the doorway, unmoving.

The initial response of the shocked male inmates was to hold out their hands and help the girls, but the SS beat men who moved too slowly or acted too kindly. The train was high up off the ground, and a ditch ran under the tracks. Dressed in tight fitting skirts or dresses, the girls did not know whether to clamber down or jump. They froze on the lip edge of the cars. SS shouts increased. Finally, one girl, then another, tossed her suitcase and reluctantly jumped a meter to the ground. Like lambs, the rest followed. Standing unsteadily on the ground, they smoothed the seams of their dresses and skirts. Older town girls checked their stockings for ladders. Soon, the field was filled with girls speaking Slovakian to the men, who whispered urgent warnings in Polish. The few Polish girls had the immediate advantage of language.

German orders fell on their collective heads.

INTO THIS CHAOS, Dr. Izak Kaufmann jumped off the train and demanded answers of the SS in charge. Where were they? Why hadn't there been any blankets on the train for the girls? Or food? Or water? Questions one would expect any physician to ask.

As the SS laughed at him, he became more irate.

Linda Reich watched as the distraught doctor ran back and forth trying to stop the SS from hitting the girls, and bellowing at the guards that the conditions were horrible. He wanted to know who was responsible and how President Tiso could have approved of such a travesty.

The SS taunted him, then cracked a whip against his back, his leg, his face. He tried to defend himself. It was no contest. Crippled by a blow, the doctor slumped to the ground, where the SS kicked him to death. Dr. Kaufmann was never registered in camp. His name does not appear in the historical death records of Auschwitz, but he appears to have been the first victim of the first Jewish transport. Or was he the second?

"WE KNOW THAT one of the women died on the transport," says the foremost historian on the first transport, Professor Pavol Mešťan. We are sitting in his office at the Museum of Jewish Culture in Bratislava after spending the weekend at anniversary events honoring the young women of the first transport. Since 2001, Dr. Mešťan has dedicated much of his time to preserving their history. It is due to his efforts that the Slovak government hung plaques at the railway station in Poprad recognizing the young women of the first transport and at the former barracks (now a school) where the girls were first held. On the table in front of us are rare documents that he has found over the years:

the food protocol, the bill from the SS that the Slovak govern-ment paid for deporting its Jews...documents he has unearthed in musty old file boxes in the Slovak National Ar-chives. Through his assistant and my interpreter, Dr. Stanislava Šikulová, I ask if we know the name of the girl who died.

He shakes his head.

There were rumors that a girl jumped off the train when it passed through Hungary (which at that point was possible be-cause the borders were quite different then). She could not have escaped after Poprad on the way to Auschwitz, though. Edith is certain of that, as am I. The same girls who left Poprad on March 25 arrived in Auschwitz on March 26—there are two lists that confirm that, a Slovak list and a German list.

In the archives at Yad Vashem, there is a Slovak document that mentions a woman dying on the transport, but no name is given. There is a comment at the bottom of a list of just ninety-nine girls from a dis¬parate assortment of towns. Three girls are from Poland (one from Krakow!) and two from Budapest, though on the original list they are recorded as being from Slo-vakia. All of the girls in this obscure document were on the first transport, their names on the original list of March 24, 1942. This shorter list appears to be dated March 25, 1942, but it turns out to have been compiled later by "an amateur historian, who helped to organize the first memorial events in Poprad" in 2003. Jozef Šebesta "worked for the Czech Society in Slovakia and spent a huge amount of time in archives and talking to sur-vivors" to gather information about the transport, Dr. Šikulová and Prof. Mešťan explain. So is this a list of survivors that Še-besta collected after the war, or was Šebesta trying to create a list of girls deported before the original list was discovered in the German archives? They assure me that "there is no reason to doubt that one woman died during the transport, because it was mentioned so many times by survivors, and Šebesta, as well, had to have [heard] it from somebody."

While so many of the women's death records seem to have vanished, there is one name in the *Sterbebücher*—the Auschwitz "Death Books"—that stands out. Jolana Sara Grünwald was born on 14 June 1917, and there is a death certificate for Jolana dated 27 March 1942, the day after the girls arrived in camp. She was twenty-five years old.

At the bottom of the six-page list that Jozef Šebesta compiled he writes:

> A thousand women were deported from Poprad. But only 999 arrived to Auschwitz. One died on the way. In the camp, women were given numbers from 1000 to 1998. Under the number 1000, the only doctor was deported, Dr. Izak Kaufmann, born February 4 1892 in Beloveza...
>
> Signed, Jozef Šebesta

There is another disparity—997 girls left the station in Poprad. A second list, typed by the Germans on March 28, 1942, that puts the girls' names into alphabetical order, has the same 997 girls on it. Would they have typed a girl's name on the receiving list in Auschwitz if she were dead?

Chapter Eleven

When danger is at its greatest, God is at his closest.
—ETA ZIMMERSPITZ (#1756)'S FATHER

ACROSS THIS EMPTY EXPANSE OF Polish steppe, the girls were forcibly marched through the fog and heavy weather toward what Linda Reich described as "flickering lights and boxes." As they got closer, they could see two-story brick barracks surrounded by barbed-wire fences. It was bitter cold. Gale-force winds whipped the plain, creating sharply carved snowdrifts. The temperature was near zero degrees Celsius. Edith shivered and stayed close to her sister. If their parents knew...if only their parents knew.

Along a dirt road, the girls shuffled uncertainly into this apocalypse. Detached in body and mind, they trudged across the frozen ground of a foreign country. Above their frail forms, a red-and-white striped border crossing gate rose and they trundled under the cast-iron lie that arched over every prisoner entering Auschwitz: *Arbeit Macht Frei*, "Work Will Make You Free." None of the girls at the time noticed the upside-down *B* that Polish prisoners had welded into the sign in 1940—one of the first acts of resistance in the place that would soon swallow their lives.

At the sight of a large brick building with a huge chimney, Linda whispered to a friend, "That must be the factory where we are going to work." In actuality it was a gas chamber that was not yet functioning.

The four Zimmerspitz sisters and three of their cousins walked uncertainly into the compound. Frida, the eldest of the sisters, mumbled to the rest, "We aren't staying."

NOT ALL OF THE 997 GIRLS were foreigners. Ironically, the girls who had fled Poland for the safety in Slovakia were now back home as unwitting prisoners. As the Polish girls passed their fellow Poles, they thought the men staring at them looked like madmen from an asylum. In fact, these men were part of the first line of resistance fighters captured after the fall of Poland in 1939. Many of them would do anything they could to help the new female prisoners, especially the Polish ones. There were no Slovak men in camp yet.

Marching up the *lagerstrasse*, or camp road, between rows of two-story brick barracks, the girls reached another gate—this one, attached to a brick wall with barbed-wire coils on top. As the gate swung open and the girls passed through this smaller guard post, they saw other women. For Regina Schwartz and her sisters, who had been told they were being sent to the front to be defiled by German soldiers, seeing women must have brought some sense of relief. At least they weren't at the front working as sex slaves.

These women would not provide much comfort, though. They themselves had arrived just a couple of hours before the Jewish girls. They were Himmler's first 999, commandeered from the most notorious women's prison in Germany, Ravensbrück, they were an eclectic mix of murderesses, con women, political prisoners (communists or anti-Nazis), "Bible thumpers" (many were Jehovah's Witnesses), prostitutes, and "asocials" (lesbians, actually referred to as "Poof Mamas" by prisoners). While some of these crimes may sound ludicrous today, under German law such "misdeeds" were rigorously prosecuted and those who committed them were found guilty. Our Jewish girls were guilty merely of being born.

One of the political prisoners transferred from Ravensbrück to Auschwitz, Bertel Teege, had hoped that serving her prison sentence in Auschwitz would be easier with better conditions than in Ravensbrück. She would be sorely disappointed. With a somber asymmetry to her face, her eyes, and even her mouth were slightly askew. But it was a righteous face—austere, and at the same time lost, a face that could not hide the things it had seen and was about to see, things most people could never comprehend.

Her closest confidante and friend was fellow communist Luise Mauer. Thirty-six years old, Mauer had a thin-lipped smile and a truth-seeking gaze. Little frightened her, even after five years in Ravensbrück.

Upon arriving in Auschwitz, Teege had felt hopeful at the sight of "six stone houses, with a capacity of one thousand persons per house." There would be plenty of room for prisoners with so much space available to them. A few hours later, she was shocked to see hundreds of young Jewish women, "all well dressed, with suitcases full of expensive clothes, money and jewelry, diamonds and food. They had been told they would be here for three months and therefore had to bring with them everything they needed for survival. They were thus equipped, having believed the Nazis' lies."

Looking at these well-brought-up, previously well-fed young women, healthy despite their tearstained cheeks, filled some of the new guards from Ravensbrück with pity and others with sadistic hatred. Flint-eyed convicts watched the girls like foxes stalking lambs. Ignorant of their plight, our girls had no idea what was in store for them. The Ravensbrück prisoners did. Only now, they would be able to dish out the cruelty rather than being the victims of it. Defiling innocence carries a certain delight for the perverse personality, which was not uncommon among the Ravensbrück crew, and they were about to be given *carte blanche* to punish, work, hit, and kill the young Jewish girls and women. They had certainly not been brought to Auschwitz to do office work.

Of the new recruits, Commandant Rudolph Höss wrote, "I believe that Ravensbrück was combed through to find the 'best' for Auschwitz. They far surpassed their male equivalents in toughness, squalor, vindictiveness, and depravity. Most were prostitutes with many convictions, and some were truly repulsive creatures. Needless to say, these dreadful women gave full vent to their evil desires on the prisoners under them…They were soulless and had no feelings whatsoever." Of course, Höss never wrote about his own soullessness, nor that of his SS.

PRIOR TO THE 1990s, the transport of the 999 Jewish women was referred to by former prisoners and Slovaks as the "first transport" to Auschwitz. Then, in an ironic twist, historians recalculated that classification and removed the girls from their category, replacing them with a single train car of forty Jewish men who had been arrested for petty crimes by the Gestapo and were experimentally "killed with Zyklon B" on February 15, 1942. The girls were also denied historical recognition as being on the "first women's transport to Auschwitz" because that nomenclature was given to the train carrying the 999 female *reichsdeutsche*, ethnic German prisoners from Ravensbrück. Why were German guards, who were also often the murderers of our girls, given the status of the "first women's transport to Auschwitz"?

While the standard definition of the noun "transport" does imply the movement of goods or people via a transit system, in Nazi Germany it meant something much more. It meant the Final Solution. And it was on this date, March 26, 1942, that the term "transport" should have taken on a new definition.

"Goods" now meant Jews; "transport" meant death. However, few Holocaust history books, and even fewer websites, include the girls or the first transport in their Holocaust time lines; rarely do our 999 girls even make a footnote.

In Slovakia, the girls maintain their place in history, where they are acknowledged and revered for their place on the first transport to Auschwitz. Auschwitz historians themselves refer to the girls' arrival as the First Mass Registered Jewish Transport. In 1942, the IVB4—the Department of Jewish Evacuation Affairs—identified the girls as being on the first "official" Jewish transport of Eichmann's Final Solution. Without debate, that is how the girls should be remembered.

As THE YOUNG WOMEN MARCHED down the camp road and into a separate compound from the men, secured with a locked gate, brick wall, and barbed wire, they wondered why there were so many safety precautions. Was the wire there to protect them from the insane asylum residents on the other side of the wall? It never occurred to them that it was to prevent their own escape. They were just coming to work here for a few months, after all.

On the other side of the gate, the girls were told to put their luggage in a pile. The protocol in Ravensbrück was to confiscate prisoners' possessions, search them, and then return the items to the prisoners. So even the new Ravensbrück guards were confused. How would the Jewish girls find their things in the huge pile being amassed? Some of the Jewish girls asked the same question, only to have their lives threatened. Those who still had any food were forced to set their food aside, as well. This was especially cruel, as they had not been fed since the previous day and there was little concern about feeding them now. But these were law-abiding girls, good girls, and they obediently did as they were told, putting their food with their luggage.

In a normal world, after a long and dirty train journey, you would hope for a bathroom, a change of clothes, a warm bowl of soup, a shower. Instead, our girls were forced to stand outside in the cold and snow for hours, while the new commandant of the women's camp, SS Johanna Langefeld, and her SS women tried to make sense of the situation. No one seemed to know what they were doing, and their inefficacy was probably enhanced by the fact that the list that had accompanied the girls from Poprad was misnumbered. Over and over the girls were counted, and the result was always the same: 997. Not 999. They could not account for the missing numbers. Had a girl escaped? At some point, someone must have noticed the errors on the pages and scribbled across the cover of the list from Poprad in red pencil: "*wäre zu nummerieren und alph. zuordnen.*" (Translation: "number and assign alphabetically.") That list was typed on March 28, and confirms that the exact number of women who boarded the train in Poprad, arrived in Auschwitz the next day. There were 997 Jewish women now in camp, not 999.

When the girls were finally released, the kapos, which is what the new Ravensbrück guards were now called, opened the doors to Block 5, and the SS ordered the girls inside. Frozen and desperate, the girls ran for the doors, forcing themselves between the frames and getting jammed against each other as the kapos beat them back.

"Everybody pushed. Everybody screamed. It was bitter cold," Linda recalls. Pushing and shoving friends and strangers, they stepped on each other's toes as they crowded into the building. "We were thirsty. We had to go to the bathroom." Everyone wanted to get inside where it was warm, but inside there were no lights, no cots, no heat. Filthy straw was strewn on the floor. There were ten toilets for more than nine hundred girls. The only available water was discovered dripping from a water pipe in the basement, so the girls had to lick the drops from dirty pipes. Dehydrated and exhausted, they were at their wits' end.

As Irena Fein and her friend Gizzy Grummer went to sit on one of the few benches, other girls went to sit on the tables. They were all tired and wanted to rest, but "the kapos made us lie on the dirty straw floor." No sooner were the girls forced to lie down in the blood-strewn straw than "millions of fleas covered us from our feet to our head. And that alone could have made us crazy. We were tired, and all we wanted to do was to rest."

Bedbugs climbed their legs. The girls who had collapsed to the floor leapt back up, screaming and slapping themselves as biting, bloodsucking bugs covered their legs and faces. It was as if the all the plagues that God sent down upon the heads of the pharaoh in Egypt had been perpetrated upon them—"ten plagues in one day," Helena Citron says.

One girl became so hysterical she ran up to an SS man, who was standing dispassionately at the door watching the bedlam. "I don't want to live even another minute more," she yelled in his face. "I can already see what will happen to us!" As the SS man looked down at the young woman, the terrorized cries of the others subsided. Even the most hysterical girls backed away from the girl yelling at the SS. He motioned for her to follow him. She backed away.

He pointed to the now-open door.

"Anyone who had a brain knew where they took her," Helena Citron says, "a better place, definitely not. She was the first to be taken." She could have been Jolana Grünwald or Marta Korn, the only female prisoners recorded in the Death Books in March 1942. Whoever she was, they never saw her again.

They were too terrified to sleep. "We were afraid that the kapos and the men would come and kill us," Edith says. "Nobody would say what was going to happen to us." Not knowing pushed everyone to the edge of sanity.

The only thing Edith clearly remembers is that she hid her menstrual napkins up on a brick above the stove to retrieve later. Other than that, her young mind skipped over that night as one might skip over a muddy puddle to avoid staining one's clothes or, in Edith's case, her mind. When they finally fell asleep, it was in spite of crying.

Chapter Twelve

We should never say everybody is the same. No, I think there is always an exception. In every misery, there is some kindness. There has to be. From every hell, somebody has to come back.

—MARTHA MANGEL (#1741)

AT FOUR IN THE MORNING, a hollow thumping drummed any dreams away as the kapos burst into the block and began beating anyone still asleep on the floor. "*Zählappell! Zählappell!* Roll call! Roll call! *Raus! Raus!*" It was a haphazard race outside to the *lagerstrasse*. There they were ordered to form rows of five, in a ritual that was about to define their sole means of existence—being counted. It would take hours. Standing in the predawn haze, Edith felt her teeth chatter with fear, her body shiver with exhaustion. Finally at daybreak, fifty of the girls in the front rows were told to march into a building. The rest formed a line outside and waited.

Inside, their processing began. First, they were told to take off their clothes. All of their clothes. Even their underwear and their bras were placed in a pile. Then came a table, where their jewelry was collected.

One of the guards came by and said, "Take off your earrings, watches, pendants, and rings. You will not need those anymore."

The girls put them on the table. "We still thought that it's fun," Laura Ritterova recalls. "So what. We will earn some money, and we will buy new jewelry. The world belonged to us. We told each other, 'So what? I can work.'"

The fun soon stopped when some of the girls whose ears had been pierced as young children couldn't get their earrings out. Edith was one of those girls who was unable to wriggle them free. One of the kapos reached over, grabbed Edith's earlobes, and yanked the earrings out, tearing the flesh. Blood streamed down Edith's neck. Lea lunged to protect her sister, but what power does a naked teenage girl have against armed adults? There was barely time to comfort her little sister before they heard a girl screaming.

"And so the nightmare began," Edith says.

For young virgins mostly raised in Conservative or Orthodox Jewish homes, being nude in front of other women was shocking in and of itself. In front of men, many for the second time that week? Unheard of. It was about to get even worse. Typical processing for Ravensbrück prisoners included more than being strip-searched. The first two hundred girls were now forced to undergo rough gynecological examinations, conducted with the sensitivity of a butcher disemboweling a chicken. Sixteen-year-old Bertha Berkowitz was number forty-eight. When she speaks of that moment it is with a sad shrug—nothing more is said. Others among the early numbers avoid ever mentioning the assault.

"I never told it because I was too embarrassed," Joan Rosner (#1188) confides more than fifty years later. "When we were examined internally and the SS put their hand into our private parts and they raped us like," she pauses. "We were bleeding, and they did it to the hundred that morning and the hundred before, and after that they stopped because they were looking for jewelry. And they didn't find any jewelry so they stopped doing it." Like most women, Joan kept the experience a secret. "I was too embarrassed. Now I'm an old lady, I am realizing, why should I be embarrassed? That's what *they* did. We were bleeding and ripped from the rings they had on their fingers."

Reports vary as to whether it was one male doctor or several of the Ravensbrück female guards thrusting their hands into the girls' vaginas to see if they had hidden valuables inside. Perhaps it was both. Blood streamed down the insides of the violated girls' thighs. The gynecological examinations stopped after the so-called doctor chortled, "Why bother? They're all virgins!"

Raucous laughter erupted among the Ravensbrück guards. The deflowered girls limped forward in line to the next phase of processing.

They were all crying. "We wept with them," Irena Fein says.

As if being manhandled by female guards were not horror enough, the girls were now forced to stand naked in front of male prisoners who were assigned to act as barbers. The Polish men were also horrified but, familiar with being beaten into submission, they did what they were told: clip heads first, then underarm hair, pubic hair, and leg hair. Forced to step up on stools so the men could shave them more easily, the girls were easy targets for vile ogling by SS guards, who laughed lecherously at the vulnerable girls. Meanwhile, the male prisoners were eye to eye with each girl's pubis.

As Adela Gross stepped into the room, heads turned. Her gorgeous red hair with its thick curls spiraled down her cheeks. Margie Becker remembers, "A friend of mine, a sister of mine really, she had red hair, beautiful hair, too, and they were searching in her hair for blades or for knives or for things like that." As the SS stuck a pick into Adela's tresses, she kept her chin up despite the humiliation. When he finished, he directed a brutal gaze at her red pubic hair.

He ordered her to stand up on a stool, so that her crotch was now eye level with the man who had to shave her. Within moments, Adela was shorn of her power and unique beauty. Bald, she looked just like all the other teenagers around her. There was not a shred of her hallmark red hair left. Only freckles remained.

The girls were now pushed outside of the processing building and forced to stand naked in knee-deep snow to await disinfection. Shivering in the March winds, they wrapped their arms around their bare breasts. Their shorn skin dimpled into gooseflesh. Without any underwear or hygienic pads, there was no hiding menstrual flows. "All the girls seemed to have their periods," Edith says. "There was blood in the snow under our feet." Those in front trampled down the pink snow with their bare feet as the line moved slowly forward to a huge vat of disinfectant.

Why did they need to be disinfected? the girls mumbled.

"You Jews brought lice into the camp," an SS man retorted.

"We never had lice!" Irena Fein exclaims. "How could we? We had only just arrived." Trying to argue that point was useless. The term "dirty" Jew was the only stereotype the SS believed.

How long did they stand in the snow? Too long. The warmth of their bare feet turned the snow they stood on to slush, which froze into ice. When they were ordered to climb into the vat of frigid water, they went fifty at a time, bleeding or not. Disinfectant burned their newly shaved flesh. By the time the first hundred had been doused for lice, the water was filthy. It was never refreshed.

Climbing out of the vat, the girls ran across the snow to the final building, where Russian uniforms had been left in piles for them to wear. The wool was stiff with dried blood and feces, and riddled with bullet holes. There were no undergarments to protect the girls' delicate skin. The Russian insignias of the dead soldiers were still visible on some of the clothes. Linda was given a man's blouse that "was so big, it dragged on the ground" and a pair of riding jodhpurs that went up to her head. There was "nothing to tie them up." Only the last thirty girls got a different uniform. Edith, Lea, Helena, and Adela got striped dresses. The dresses were not warm and there were no leggings or woolen stockings to cover their legs and no underwear.

A pile of footwear awaited them now. Some prisoners would refer to these as clogs, but that is a polite term for the "clappers," flat slabs of wood with leather straps over the top that were nailed onto the sides. Think Dr. Scholl's with no arch support or buckle to adjust for tightness, and no matching pairs. They had been made by male prisoners who most likely had no idea they would be used for young women, so not much thought had been given to accommodating smaller, more delicate feet. In this only were the girls at the beginning of the line lucky. They fumbled through the pile trying to find a fit. Those at the end of the line were left with what had not been taken.

Finally, white rectangles of cloth with numbers on them and yellow stars were handed to each girl, to be sewn onto their uniforms later. The first strip of white cloth handed out had the numbers 1-0-0-0 printed on it. The next girl was given 1-0-0-1, 1-0-0-2, and so on. A scribe wrote down the registration numbers next to the girls' names. Witnesses believe that the sisters Frida and Helena Benovicova from Modra nad Cirochou, not far from Humenné, were among those first few girls. Peggy, who had walked two hours to get to the bus stop in Stropkov, was number 1-0-1-9, and sixteen-year-old Bertha Berkowitz was 1-0-4-8. Their first job would be to sew their numbers on the front of their uniforms so their photographs could be taken.

Finally registered and dressed for "work," each girl was equipped with a red bowl and soupspoon, then released back into the cold, where they were told to stand in line and wait. Rows of five. Five in rows. Wrenched from the unordered routine of civilian life, the girls were quickly becoming regimented mannequins.

#1474, name unknown. Only known photo of a girl from the first transport, taken immediately after processing, circa March 28, 1942. PHOTO COURTESY AUSCHWITZ MUSEUM ARCHIVE.

Exiting the last building, the girls at the front of the line could now see their friends still standing outside the processing buildings, dressed in their best clothes, sensible boots, coats, gloves, hats. They shouted warnings.

"Throw away your jewelry!"

Those who had not yet been shaved did not recognize the poor bald wretches standing in the snow in dead soldiers' uniforms and shod in open-toed sandals shouting at them. No one recognized each other. Names dropped from the air until the girls still waiting to be processed understood—they were soon to be bald wretches themselves.

Rena Kornreich tore off her watch and stepped it into the mud, promising herself not to let the Nazis get anything else she owned.

Hanging back toward the end of the line were most of the girls from Humenné: Sara Bleich, 1-9-6-6, was just three girls away from Lea and Edith: 1-9-6-9 and 1-9-7-0. Helena Citron was 1-9-7-1. When the last thirty girls came out onto the *lagerstrasse*, it was dusk. And they still had to stand and be counted. It was the only time they would ever be in numerical order again. It was also the last time that they would all be alive.

As night descended, they were directed to Block 10 at the far end of the women's camp. The girls stumbled over one another to get into the relative warmth of the block and out of the cold. As they pushed and shoved each other in desperation to get inside, common human decency was already dissolving. Politeness was a thing of the past, or reserved only for friends and family. "I have good elbows," Linda Reich (#1173) says again and again in her testimony.

Inside the block, away from the guards and the dogs, the girls looked for each other and shouted their friends' names:

—Adela! Magda! Lea! Edith! Gizzy!

Shaved heads. Men's uniforms. Nobody looked as they should have. "We didn't recognize each other," Helena Citron says. "And then, instead of crying, we started to laugh. We laughed hysterically because there was nothing else we could do. We laughed because tears were not enough."

HOURS LATER, AFTER the degradation of processing, Edith sneaked back into Block 5 to retrieve the menstrual pads she had hidden in the brick door of the big oven in the center of the block. Someone had taken her pads. "Not that I needed them. I never got my period again until after the war."

This was common for all of the girls. It takes a certain amount of body fat for a woman to menstruate, and on a diet of less than 1,000 calories per day, there is no fat left to support a female body. Add to the equation a healthy dose of sedative-laced tea every morning to make the girls more pliable and confused. "You feel like a zombie. They were giving us bromide, so our brains wouldn't work. We didn't have to think," Edie (#1949) says. Bromide also helped stem sexual desire and inhibit menstruation.

A smattering of women in their early twenties continued to menstruate for a few months, but the only way to get a napkin was to go to the hospital and show the doctor you were bleeding. Rena Kornreich avoided that humiliation by using scraps of newspaper she found in camp. They weren't hygienic, but they enabled her to keep her secret. Robbed of that rite of passage into womanhood—menstruation—some younger women began to question their own identities. What were they if they were not women anymore? Not even human beings? "It was good not to have [our periods] hygienically," Edith admits. "There was no hygiene in Auschwitz, and without the possibility of keeping clean and of washing every day, you didn't want to have your period. But we felt like we weren't women without it." Of course, the last thing the SS wanted was for them to feel like women. It was probably why they dressed them in dead Russian POWs' uniforms.

THE BRICK TWO-STORY building of Block 10 butted up against a courtyard with a brick wall at one end. Across the courtyard was Block 11, referred to by the male prisoners as Block *Smierci*—the Block of Death. This was where political prisoners, POWs, resistance fighters, and spies were held in solitary confinement and tortured; they were then taken outside to be shot in the courtyard. It was not easy to witness these executions. Rena (#1716) slept beside the boarded-up windows along that side of the block. Peering through the slats at night, she watched Russian POWs being executed. One of the male prisoners later informed her that the girls were wearing the dead POWs' uniforms.

In the front of the top floor of Block 10 were windows that the girls would use to speak with the Polish male prisoners on the second floor of the men's block on the other side of the wall. Calling out to the new arrivals, anxious for news of the outside world and the softer voices of women, the Polish gentiles eagerly helped their countrywomen. Longing for shared language and human connection, the Polish men—some of whom had been in camp since 1940—tossed the Polish girls spare portions of bread, ropes to tie up baggy pants, and love notes. The Slovak girls did not receive the same kind of admiration.

AT 4:00 A.M. on the second day, the girls were served tea. It is also referred to as coffee by some survivors. It tasted so bad no one could be sure. This liquid "breakfast" was all the girls were served in the morning. Not long after arriving, Edith and Lea figured out that they could use the tea to brush their teeth. There was no spitting out the "very, very valuable" liquid, despite its horrid taste. "Hunger hurts very much, very, very much [but] lack of water is even worse. The thirst was unbearable," Edith says. Despite that, she and Lea "used a little bit to wash our hands and faces." After a few minutes of tea and toilet, the girls lined up in rows of five. Standing. Standing. Never moving. The ritual was becoming embedded into their brains.

Dawn broke across the rooftops, barbed-wire fences, and watchtowers surrounding them as the SS and kapos counted. After roll call, 996 girls were instructed to clean their barrack, and a few of the older women were chosen for positions overseeing the blocks. As Jews they were still underlings, but the women who had those first positions of power immediately sprang up the ranks, from the dregs to something a bit more important. Given the task of maintaining order, they woke up the block in the morning, served the food, and decided who got to stay inside and clean, who went outside to work, who got more bread. The first Jewish block elder in Block 10 was a young woman called Elza. No one seems to recall her last name. She was strict, and within a few days she became known for hitting the girls who were late to roll call or in her way. When she was told to pick an assistant, she gave her sister a position beside her. Can we blame her? Whom else would she choose?

TODAY, BLOCK 10 IS NOT OPEN to the public, but special permission is granted to survivors, children of survivors, and

researchers who enter the side door with reverent footsteps. The
first floor is cement and has a hallway with rooms on either side
where girls originally slept on bunks. At the front of the block
are a few broken and filthy toilets on one side of the hallway across from a room with a long trough for washing, though there
was no soap for prisoners. In the center of the building sits a
chimney, which would have served wood-burning stoves on
both floors.

Wending its way up to a large landing is a wide staircase. At
the top of the stairs are two small rooms, where the room elders
and her assistants slept. The rest of the space is open, with only
one wall dividing the open space. In 1942 it was filled with
bunk beds that had thin, straw-filled mattresses and even
thinner wool blankets.

The girls chose to sleep close to their friends and formed
small supportive cliques. Almost everyone knew or recognized
girls from their province. At night, from their bunk beds, some
girls talked about food, home, and their parents. Others spoke
of nothing. Most simply cried themselves to sleep.

The newly married Ruzena Gräber Knieža (#1649) was
crying bitterly on her bunk when Annie Binder, one of the
kapos, approached her and said in Czech, "Don't cry. My child,
you mustn't cry. You must be strong. You must try and survive."
Historically, the Ravensbrück prisoners have a terrible reputation, but Ruzena says, "Among them were wonderful women."
Annie Binder was one; two other kapos, one a prostitute,
Emma, and the other a communist by the name of Orli Reichert, who would be called "the Angel of Auschwitz," appear
in multiple testimonies and are credited with saving many,
many lives.

Since the new kapos were themselves prisoners, they understood prison life under the Nazi regime, and some tried to
forewarn the girls. "Many of the German kapos helped us
through an indirect whispering campaign [and warning] if you

don't work, they won't keep you." No one understood what was at stake or what it meant to not be "kept." Some thought it meant they would get to go home sooner if they didn't work. At this point, they did not understand that the real purpose of Auschwitz was to destroy them. Despite the foul conditions and treatment, they still believed they would be sent home in a few months' time.

Edith's face is solemn. "And then the girls began to die."

Part Two

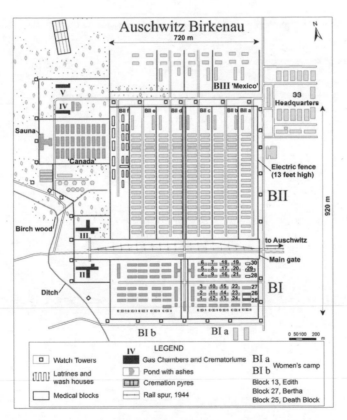

Map of Birkenau (Auschwitz II). *Much of the camp was yet to be built when the women were relocated in August 1942. There was no death gate entrance until mid 1943, and there was no train track leading into or unloading ramp in camp until 1944. Birkenau was still under construction in 1945.*
© HEATHER DUNE MACADAM; DRAWN BY VARVARA VEDUKHINA.

Chapter Thirteen

March 28, 1942

'I'he headquarter; Dr Konka, Bratislava
Liptovský svätý Mikuláš

I am asking to cancel temporarily the order for the
chief accountant of the liqueur factory in Liptovský
svätý Mikuláš, Alzbeta Sternova. She has permission
to work for our company due to the fact that there
is no Aryan workforce to replace her.

As HAD HAPPENED WITH THE telegram to release Magdalena
Braunova, the telegram to release Alzbeta Sternova arrived too
late to save her. Already in Auschwitz, Magdalena Braunova
should have been celebrating her sixteenth birthday with her
family; instead she was watching Alzbeta and 768 more teenage girls and young women arriving in Auschwitz on the
second transport.

Like the girls of the first transport, these young women had
been placed in a holding station, where they, too, had been
systematically starved on the food regime devised by the government. When this transport stopped in Žilina, two additional

cattle cars carrying one hundred additional young women from the eastern region were added to the convoy. Among them were Manci Schwalbova (#2675) and Madge Hellinger (#2318).

Manci Schwalbova was a kindhearted, no-nonsense sort of woman. She was also engaged to be married and hoped to be exempt. Fortunately for Edith and many others, she was not. Manci was the young woman who had not been allowed to finish the last medical exam to make her a licensed doctor, but Auschwitz didn't require a degree to be a working physician. She was almost immediately allowed to practice and became known by everyone as Dr. Manci Schwalbova.

Madge Hellinger had been a kindergarten teacher and was also supposed to have been exempt. When she turned down a sexual pass made by one of the local policemen, he sold her exception to another Jew, pocketed the money, and sent her to Auschwitz. A stalwart young woman, Madge would eventually be promoted to a block elder and do her moral best to treat everyone fairly from that position of power.

Rena Kornreich's sister Danka (#2779) was also on this transport, as were many other cousins and sisters of the first girls. It was not a family reunion that anyone wanted to celebrate. Girls like Rena waited in dread as they kept watch for their siblings and cousins to arrive. However, when the new arrivals entered the camp, they thought the young women with bald heads and crazed looks were part of an insane asylum. No one immediately recognized anyone else. "We thought, 'Maybe our jobs are to care for these patients,'" Madge Hellinger says.

After standing for their welcoming roll call, the girls and young women of the second transport were thrown into Block 5 with its bloodstained straw in what appears to have been part of "orientation" to the women's camp. The girls panicked and cried hysterically, swatting at the fleas, bedbugs, and lice biting their tender flesh. As if that weren't bad enough, the

Ravensbrück kapos decided to have some "fun" at the expense of the new prisoners, taunting the girls by telling them the soup and tea they were fed "will kill you if you drink it."

Perhaps because she had been a teacher and was older than most of the young women around her, Madge Hellinger took it upon herself to taste the food. "It was vile, but I recommended that everyone have some, warning the younger ones among us that they were dehydrated and needed liquid to survive." Unfortunately, the only liquid other than bromide-laced tea was a soup made out of "rotten vegetables" harvested from fields that were still deep under the snow and the meat of dead horses shipped from the Russian front.

"The soup was so bad, nobody could eat it," Edith confirms.

Many of the Orthodox girls refused to eat the unkosher soup. Margie Becker (#1955) "couldn't swallow it." Girls tried to help her by holding her nose so she wouldn't retch as she forced the tepid, foul-smelling "broth" down her gullet, to no avail. "I was so envious that they could [drink the soup] and I couldn't." She was just too sensitive to the smell, and during those first weeks, no matter how hungry she was, she ended up giving her soup away.

There was another reason to avoid the soup, though. Everyone got sour stomachs and diarrhea from it. The only thing that helped settle their stomachs was bread, but there was not enough of it to go around. After almost five days of virtual starvation in Poprad, girls were wasting away.

When the new girls looked through the windows of Block 5 they saw insane girls waving at them and shouting, "If you have some scarves or socks, hide them for us!"

"They said they would find our things when they came to clean the barracks." Scarves? Socks? "We thought they were crazy." Why did they need to hide their own clothing? It was a ridiculous thought—until the next day, when the girls of the second transport had all of their belongings confiscated and they, too, were longing for socks to keep their feet warm and scarves to protect their newly shorn heads from the cold.

Only after the girls of the second transport had been stripped, shaved, and deloused were they allowed to join the prison population. Only then did they discover their sisters and cousins among those they had thought were mad and enter what Dr. Manci Schwalbova called the "drat-maimed world" of Auschwitz.

IS THERE A SIGNIFICANT DIFFERENCE between the first and second transports? Edith is adamant that there was, "because we didn't know what would happen. The girls from the other transports had us. We could speak to them. But we didn't have anything. We came to nothing. The girls who came in after us had us to speak to. We showed them what we had learned so they didn't have to be as afraid as we were. So it was scary for them, but not as scary as it had been for us. We knew nothing. Just the horror of one thing after another. And now just a few days on, we were the old-timers." But, she adds, "help is a funny word because there wasn't much help for it. What could we do but tell the new girls be careful, keep your head down, don't do this or that? It wasn't like we were sitting around having meetings and sharing advice. We weren't chatting. That never happened. We were working, working. Tired, tired. We didn't talk about music or literature or our school studies. We spoke about, What do we think will happen to us? How do we think this can help us? How can we steal some bread? How can we steal a blanket? We were nice girls from good families trying to learn how to steal from other nice girls from good families. This was not human. They dehumanized us. Made us turn against our own people for survival."

BEING CREATED *b'tzelem Elokim* (in the image of God), Jews traditionally avoid any permanent mark on the body, because the body is not owned by a person—it belongs to God. In Auschwitz, that last dignity of belonging to the Almighty and to your parents who named you was stolen without ceremony.

Auschwitz was the only camp to ink its prisoners. This unique, permanent numbering system was the equivalent of being registered, which is one of the reasons modern historians began referring to the first official Jewish transport as the "first mass *registered* Jewish transport." The tattooing did not happen on the first day the girls arrived, but reports vary as to when it did. Some girls say it happened the day after they were processed, some say it was after the second transport arrived. Rose (#1371) remembers a Slovak friend of her father tattooing her, which would have meant they were tattooed weeks later. What we do know is that once they sewed their numbers onto their uniforms, that number became their name, and they were tattooed with the same number. If the uniform number did not match the tattoo on their arm, they would be shot.

Entering a room full of tables, the girls were shoved into chairs and had their left arms yanked forward and held down by strong men. SS shouted at them, "Hurry!" There was no time for vanity. Rough and tumble, these were not attractive numbers with artistic flourishes. Ones looked like sevens. Mistakes were crossed out with a line and re-inked below. The numbers were placed just below the elbow's bend on the forearm. The pain of the tattooist's needle piercing the delicate skin repeatedly caused tears in the eyes of even the bravest. Each prick of ink burned as the word of God was defiled.

While being tattooed was a truly dehumanizing experience, being tattooed carried more meaning than any incoming prisoner could fathom—it meant a life sentence. Life might be fleeting but it was still life.

If you can call slave labor life.

ONE MORNING, NOT long after the second transport arrived, a young woman jumped out in front of the labor squads and shouted, "Don't work for the Nazis. We shall be killed anyway. Let them rather shoot us!"

A gunshot cracked through the ranks of the women. The girl fell to the ground.

Carried to the makeshift hospital ward, where Dr. Manci Schwalbova was already working, the girl was laid on a table. "The bullet passed through her lungs and abdomen," Manci writes. The SS doctor refused the girl any palliative care. Manci was forced to watch her bleed to death. She never knew her name.

Early attempts at resistance came in many forms, but were never effective. A girl from the second transport by the name of Lia decided to go on a hunger strike to protest the conditions and lack of food. In normal circumstances, this act might have been noticed, but in Auschwitz it was simple convenience. The girls were already on a starvation diet. Besides, Jews were supposed to die anyway; it was of little matter to their captors how they perished. Protests rarely received notice in the historic record, but they remained in the consciousness of witnesses who saw the "personal protest of girls who, being on the border of hopelessness, did not care at all for such a life and had ceased to believe in a new one." There was little else to believe in.

Neither Lia's death nor the deaths of Jolana Grünwald and Marta Korn are formally noted in the *Auschwitz Chronicle*, which records the day-to-day deaths, murders, gassings and goings-on in Auschwitz, from its opening to the day it closed. In fact, not a single woman's death was logged by the SS into any surviving historic record until May 12, 1942, when a female prisoner was found hanging on the electric fences—a suicide. One month later, on June 17, another woman was reported found on the wires. If either of these women had been male prisoners, a number and name would have been logged. As women, they remained anonymous.

We know almost nothing about women's deaths before August 1942, except for what has been reported by witnesses and survivors. And while men's deaths were calculated every day and totaled at the end of the month, women's deaths were neither noted nor tallied—at least not in any documentation that survived the war. From March to August 1942, we know exactly what the male inmate population was and how many men died each month. For women, we have only the number of those registered in camp and the assurance from survivors that, whether or not their deaths were recorded, girls were definitely dying.

Marta Korn's death is remarkable, not only because she was the first woman recorded as dying in Auschwitz, but because she was also the only young woman from those first months whose death is recorded. Was she the girl who Helena Citron claims got hysterical and was removed by the SS that first night? Or did she die in some other manner? We may never know for sure.

Researchers believe that the death records for women were destroyed in the conflagration of documents in January 1945, as the Russian front closed in on the death camp. However, since the women's camp in Auschwitz was under the jurisdiction of Ravensbrück, the number of deaths should have been filed in its administrative offices. The fact is that complete records regarding women in Auschwitz (early 1942) have never been found in Ravensbrück either. All we have are Jolana Grünwald's and Marta Korn's names listed in the *Sterbebücher*—the "Death Books" database. They are the only deaths on record linked to the first transport in those first few weeks of the girls' arrival; no cause of their deaths are documented. In the vast archives of genocide, Jolana Grünwald, 25, and Marta Korn, 21, may be mere statistics, but they were also the first female victims of Auschwitz.

THE DESTRUCTION OF the women's camp documents speaks volumes, because there is no doubt that women died. At the end of February 1942, prior to the arrival of any women prisoners,

11,472 men were listed as occupying the camp; that month, 1,515 men had died. In March, 2,740 men were added to the prison population, along with 1,767 women. But although a total of 4,507 prisoners had been added, the occupancy level of the men's camp decreased to 10,629; 2,977 prisoners died in March. Prior to the arrival of the 999, the average monthly death toll in Auschwitz for men ranged between 1,500 to almost 1,800. Now in March, the number almost doubled. Could that spike be attributed to deaths among our girls?

By April, the total camp population had increased to 14,642 prisoners—5,640 of whom were women—yet the death toll dropped back to its average rate. In the chaos around women arriving into camp, had women's deaths been included with men's, then removed from the monthly death tallies in April and thereafter?

"Data is lacking concerning the female prisoners," writes historian and chronicler of Auschwitz, Danuta Czech. But then in a brilliant move, she provides a clue by looking at the records of men that *were* preserved.

On April 17, 1942, the sixth Slovak transport included 973 Jews, mostly young men. In the footnotes, Czech begins a series of notations: as of "August 15, 1942, only eighty-eight of these deportees are still alive; i.e. within seventeen weeks, 885 people die." Two days later, when the seventh Slovak transport arrived carrying 464 young men and 536 young women, Czech notes, "by August 15, 1942, only ten of these men are still alive."

Time and again, Czech reiterates that we have no death tally of Jewish women in early 1942; if their survival rate was anything like that of the Jewish men, they were dying in droves. It is important to remember that all deaths at this point were caused by disease, starvation, or outright murder—there were no mass gassings of prisoners yet. Only by using Czech's calculations of Jewish men's deaths throughout the spring and summer of 1942, can we hope to unveil these early women's shrouded history.

Chapter Fourteen

[The Exodus narrative] taught the great lesson of human solidarity, that we cannot enjoy the food of affluence, while others eat the bread of oppression.
—JONATHAN SACKS, *The Jonathan Sacks Haggada*

ON THURSDAY, APRIL 2, the third transport arrived in Auschwitz carrying 965 unmarried Jewish young women. Like the girls of the first transport, this group had been gathered from the eastern part of Slovakia and held in Poprad, many related to, or friends of, girls on the first transport. Among them was Edith's soon-to-be best friend, sixteen-year-old Elsa Rosenthal.

As the sun sank below the horizon and the guard towers loomed up dark and threatening, Block 5 was once again full of girls being attacked by fleas and bedbugs. It was the one-week anniversary of the first transport and the first night of Passover. In honor of the holiday, the SS sent everyone out to work in a "damp hole like you never saw before," Margie Becker says. The swamp detail entailed clearing refuse from the ponds and streams around the compound. Eventually, it would become a punishment detail, but on Passover it was yet another means of deculturalization. "There was that one girl, Ruzena Gross...she was all drenched. We came home and lay down, and there's no blanket, no nothing. We were shivering something awful."

Soaking wet, twenty-six-year old Klary Atles, the daughter of one of Humenné's rabbis, got up off her bunk and spoke fervently to the girls as they shivered and wept. "At home, everybody would get pneumonia," she told them, trying to raise their spirits, just as she had the day the train had taken them from home. "You will see, God will help us. Nobody will get sick." Speaking as passionately as her father, she told them how God would free them, just as he had freed the Jews from Egypt. God had protected them from the plagues, and He would protect them now. God had slain their ancestors' slavers, and He would slay them now. All they had to do was invite Elijah into their hearts. If only they had enough cups to leave one for the prophet. If only they could open the door without getting killed. Klary's conviction spread through the block, and soon some of the girls were holding tiny Seders on their bunks. Others simply fell into sleep.

Somehow, Bertha Berkowitz (#1048) had gotten hold of a Hebrew prayer book. There was no kosher wine to drink and no need of bitter herbs—the sour taste of slavery was already sharp on their tongues. Bertha whispered the text of the Haggadah to Peshy Steiner and a few of their friends from home who had gathered together on bunk beds. Without fathers or brothers to conduct the ceremonies, the girls had to step in and say the Kaddish blessing memorialized in their hearts through the time-honored tradition. In the dark, some of them raised their empty red bowls over their heads and whispered, "*Bivhilu yatzanu mimitzrayim, halahma anya b'nei horin.* In haste we went out of Egypt [with our] bread of affliction, [now we are] free people."

—Why is this night different from all other nights?

It is hard to imagine how they could answer. Their tears were shed in the darkness.

Without matzo to break, without matzo to eat, their Passover limped, but devout girls like Bertha avoided eating leavened bread for the entire week. "I did it out of respect for my parents. This was my defiance—it was the only thing I was able to do for them." She did give in and eat the vile, unkosher horsemeat soup, but she prayed that God would forgive her.

One part of the Passover ritual asks questions that teach the laws, ethics, and history of the Jewish people. The questions are asked of four sons of Israel. But there were only daughters of Israel in their block in Auschwitz, so the first question, "What are the statutes, the testimonies, and the laws that God has commanded you to do?" had to be asked of the wise daughter instead of the wise son. Then the wicked daughter is asked, "What is this service to you?" And here we pause, because in this saga there were no wicked girls, yet. That was still to come. This instruction reminded Bertha, Peshy and their friends of the importance of not standing aside from those they loved, not acting with detachment and antipathy, and not isolating themselves from each other. To deserve freedom, one needs to participate in one's community and help others. Abiding by these statutes would help them survive Auschwitz.

The last two questions remind participants that there are some who lack intelligence and need help finding answers through God and family in order to be freed of bondage. If only it were still that simple.

In 1942, there had been no Shoah yet. It was only after World War II that Seders began to add a fifth child to represent all of the Jewish children who did not survive and a final, fifth, question to ponder.

On the eve of the Holocaust, many of the girls holding secret Seders with Bertha and elsewhere in the blocks were about to become that fifth child...and already asking the question with no answer.

"Why?"

EXHAUSTED FROM CLEANING SWAMPS, demolishing buildings, clearing snow, carrying manure, and digging ditches, most of the first 997 girls sank into sleep long before the Pesach prayers were finished. This is not unusual at any Seder. Children are always falling asleep in their chairs; even adults occasionally nod. A few soft voices recited the ten plagues, dipping their fingers into a thimbleful of water in their red bowls or simply imagining water spilling, a ritual drop for each plague and for those who still suffer in the world. Was anyone suffering more than they were at that moment? Helena Citron's statement that "Auschwitz was like ten plagues in one day" resonated in the dark as a few tired voices sang "*Dayenu*" without gusto or joy, the meaning of the word—"it would have been enough" or "sufficient"—no salve for the spiritual wounds of the newly enslaved.

In traditional Seders, the participants are so hungry (and sometimes so drunk) by the time the prayers are finished that everyone dives into the food laid out on the table with gusto. In Auschwitz, prayers were met with more hunger and an empty longing for their families. "We were ready to give our lives to see our parents one more time," Bertha says.

There was no door to open and invite Elijah into their lives. What prophet would enter Auschwitz, anyway? With what little conscious energy they had left, a few may have meditated on the future arrival of the messiah, but most fell into a hard, exhausted sleep. Remembering her father's blessing, Bertha's soft voice whispered the psalms over those slumbering around her:

> *I love the Lord, for he heard my voice;*
> *He heard my cry for mercy.*
> *Because he turned his ear to me,*
> *I will call on him as long as I live.*
>
> *The cords of death entangled me,*

the anguish of the grave came over me;
I was overcome by distress and sorrow.
Then I called on the name of the Lord:
"Lord, save me!"

The solemn silence of Block 10 was shattered by gunshots ringing through the night as eleven Polish prisoners were shot against the execution wall outside. The next morning—Good Friday—the fourth transport of 997 unmarried Jewish girls and young women arrived in camp. "On Easter Sunday, eighty-nine prisoners and thirty-one Russian POWs" died. We do not know how many, if any, of those eighty-nine prisoners were female, but it was becoming clear that the Nazis had no qualms about defiling either Christian or Jewish religions.

Chapter Fifteen

I want to be the last girl in the world with a story like mine.

—NADIA MURAD, *The Last Girl*

BACK AT HOME, parents were increasingly worried. Not only had they not heard from their daughters, but a few days after the first train left Poprad for regions unknown, one of the local railwaymen returned with a scrap of cardboard from one of the girls. How she got the note to the engineer no one knows, but he clearly knew who she was and cared enough to risk smuggling the note back to her family:

> Whatever you do, don't get caught and deported.
> Here we are being killed.

Her signature was beneath the warning.

Shocked by the news, some righteous gentiles immediately took action to help their neighbors. In Poprad, nineteen-year-old Valika Ernejová was taken into a family friend's home, where they were able to forge an identification certificate for her. Jan Kadlecik and his family successfully hid "Stefánia Gregusová, born 24 March 1923" for the rest of the war.

As news of the smuggled note radiated out from Poprad to neighboring villages, other families took action to hide their girls or send them to Hungary. For those beyond the reach of the news a sense of foreboding lurked. All they could do was hope their daughters were safe working at the shoe factory.

Then postcards began to arrive.

It was Shabbat when the girls were first forced to write home. Bertha Berkowitz refused to write to her parents because it was Shabbat. A friend wrote the lies for her. The words were scripted and false, designed to assuage fears and assure future victims, the girls' families, that everything was fine, they had plenty to eat. *Hope to see you soon…*

By now, all of the girls knew what that last line meant—their families were going to be brought to Auschwitz, too. It was the last thing any of them wanted. In the margins, many of the girls sneaked in warnings in Slovak, Polish, Hungarian, or Yiddish—anything to warn their families about being deported that could not be deciphered by the Germans.

Not every family got postcards. Kapo Bertel Teege was told to throw out hundreds of postcards after she collected them. Among those that she destroyed must have been Magduska's and Nusi's—the Hartmanns never received any cards from their daughters.

A few weeks later, when the girls were forced to write cards again, they were given several to write at once and told to post-date them in advance: three months, six months, nine months. It was a ruse to ensure that families still in Slovakia would get cards at home and think their girls were alive and well. And if they heard anything to the contrary, they would say, "How is that possible? We just heard from her!'"

Parents who did get cards wondered about the postmarks. How had their daughters ended up in Poland? Why didn't they sound like their normal effusive selves? Where was Oświęcim, anyway?

Despite the paper assurances, many mothers must have begun to feel a deep sense of unease, anguish, and desperation. There is scientific evidence that a mother's brain carries her child's DNA in her brain after the child is born. Who hasn't had that experience of their mother knowing when they are in danger, upset, or doing something naughty? Moments after you've gotten bad news, been in an accident, or had your heart broken, your mom texts or calls. *I was just thinking about you. Are you okay?*

This seems like a coincidental phenomenon, but as science discovers more and more about the brain and DNA, one wonders if this invisible, conscious link might someday be explained. Take the bamboo plant. Bamboo blooms rarely, maybe every sixty to one hundred years, but when the parent plant flowers, its offspring—no matter where in the world they are— also bloom. Perhaps a mother's intuition is like bamboo. No matter where you are in the world, she is still somehow connected to you.

As mothers across Slovakia prayed for their daughters on that first Shabbat after their departure, did those prayers somehow reach their daughters through the microchimeric cells from the mothers' brains and, like bamboo, flower into strength and courage?

The girls needed all the fortitude and determination they could acquire because the real rigors of camp life—work— were about to begin. This was "not work with meaning." It was work meant to destroy body, mind, and spirit. The girls did not know that at first, though. Lining up to be assigned for labor details, they were told they could do agricultural, cooking, building, or cleaning work. Madge Hellinger (#2318) thought working in the agricultural detail would be pleasant and rushed to join it, but one of the German kapos, who had taken a shine to Madge, grabbed her out of the detail, giving her a firm slap on the face and announcing, "I need this one here."

Shocked by the slap, Madge immediately distrusted the kapo who promptly promoted her to being a room helper, cleaning the blocks, serving tea and bread. Only when the girls returned at the end of their first day of work did Madge realize how lucky she had been to stay inside.

Linda Reich (#1173) describes the agricultural detail as filthy, degrading, and exhausting. Forced to spread manure with their bare hands, the girls carried armfuls of cow droppings across frozen fields thick with snow while wearing nothing but their open-toed "clappers." Edith and Lea found newspaper scraps in camp with which to wrap their feet in hopes that the newsprint would help keep their toes warm, but "it was snowing," and the wet paper disintegrated rapidly. It was disgusting work. There was also no way to get clean afterward.

The main detail the girls were forced to work in was the "construction" detail. Their job? To demolish houses with nothing but their bare hands. Literally.

These were the houses that had been confiscated from local Poles in order to expand the Auschwitz complex. "We were the machines that had to dismantle the buildings to their foundations," Helena Citron (#1971) explains.

After male prisoners weakened the structures with explosives, the young women "were supposed to raze [the bombed houses] to the ground...hitting walls with long and very heavy iron rods," Bertel Teege confirms. It took fifty girls to wield these very long, very heavy metal rods, which had metal circles welded onto them to serve as handles. Grabbing hold of these "handles," the girls would "hammer the wall," says Helena Citron. "The minute the wall would collapse, the first row of girls were squashed and buried, and died."

Sometimes, the girls were divided into two groups: those who climbed up to the second floor of the weakened houses to throw shingles and bricks down to the ground and those on the ground, who picked up the debris while simultaneously trying to avoid being hit by falling bricks. "If you were too careful about throwing bricks down below [and tried to avoid hurting the girls below], the kapo might very likely change your place, so you worked under the hail of bricks coming from the top of the buildings."

Hauling the bricks away was another part of this work. Loading the bricks onto trucks, the girls had to push cumbersome wagonloads to a wasteland a few miles away, where a few surviving Russian POWs were being held in wooden shacks. What the women did not know was that the bricks they were unloading were being used to build new prison blocks for women, in an open expanse on the edge of a birch forest—Birkenau.

The work of these demolition teams should have been for hardened, strong men—not women and girls, many of whom weighed no more than one hundred pounds and were as short as four feet, ten inches. In the evening, the girls from the demolition work details returned to the blocks bruised and bleeding from cuts. Those at the front of the roll call in the morning were the most likely to be chosen for the demolition details. "Each morning, we would push our best friends into the front," Helena admits, "since we wanted to live. We very quickly turned into animals. Everyone looked after themselves. It was very sad."

The other choices of work were not much better.

Bertha Berkowitz (#1048) remembers marching five kilometers to an area where they had to dig ditches. "I have no idea what they used them for but this was our work, day in and day out." The worst part was their superiors' absolute refusal to allow the girls to take even the slightest break. Even standing up to straighten their backs after shoveling the heavy clay that made up the Polish earth was cause for an SS whip, or worse.

SS woman Juana Bormann delighted in setting her German shepherd on girls who paused for even a moment. "It was harsh work. It was continuous digging," Linda Reich says.

There was still so much snow on the roads that the SS assigned some girls to snow removal. After working in the fields, Edith and Lea ended up on that detail. "No brooms. No shovels. Everything was by hand," Edith recalls. "We used our bare hands to pile snow onto cardboard and old newspapers, and then carried those to the side of the road." At night, she and her sister fell onto their straw mattresses, disheartened and "so frozen and so tired that we didn't want to go to pick up the bread." Hardier than Edith, Lea made her little sister get up and stand in line to get her bread ration. Without food, they would never survive, and Edith was tiny to begin with. Lea had to keep her sister going even if the bread was dry and tasteless, made, as many prisoners surmised, with sawdust as well as flour.

The staple of their diet, the bread ration was no larger than the palm of a small woman's hand, about three inches across. Since just one portion was doled out once a day to the women— men received two portions—some girls devised a way to make it last longer by eating half at night and saving the rest for morning. Having something solid in their stomach before drinking the tea and going to work helped stretch the meager meals.

Working on snow removal allowed Edith and her sister access to one small pleasure: They would pick up cigarette butts left behind by the SS, scrounge old scraps of newspaper, and reroll the reclaimed bits of tobacco in the newsprint. At night, they lit these makeshift smokes from the fire in the woodstoves. Smoking was not a luxury; it had a practical purpose. "It helped stem the hunger."

Early on, the solidly built Joan Rosner (#1188) was assigned to work in the kitchen. She could not help but feel a little pleased at the opportunity and hoped that extra food would be easy to pilfer. It was not. The SS watched the girls carefully and beat anyone caught nibbling on even a carrot peel. The hours were brutal, as well. The kitchen shift had to wake up at one o'clock in the morning to make the tea. The cauldrons where the soup and tea were made were mammoth. Two or three girls had to climb ladders to reach the vats, and from these precarious positions one girl filled the kettle, while the other two steadied it. Holding the cast-iron kettles steady on the wooden platforms was difficult, and as they wielded giant ladles to fill the kettles, the girls kept burning themselves on the hot metal. Once the kettles were full, the girls had to reverse and maneuver the full kettles back down the ladders to the ground. It was a Sisyphean task, and it did not take long for catastrophe to strike. One of the girls at the top of a ladder lost her grip when she was burned by the side of a swaying kettle; the cauldron toppled and spilled over a girl below. The screams as she was scalded to death must have disturbed even the SS guards on duty because it was immediately decided that the work was too heavy for girls, and "the boys started working there."

On the construction site, there were even more accidents. Standing on top of one of the buildings, one of the Polish girls, Sara Bleich (#1966), slipped on a loose brick and fell two stories to the ground. Lying in the rubble of bricks and mortar, she stared up at the sky and wondered if this was the end. She was paralyzed. She had also broken her right hand. She knew better than to moan or cry and waited for a death blow from one of the SS or a dog to tear her apart. Fortunately, one of the kinder kapos ordered Sara to be carried to the newly set up revier, or hospital block. There, Dr. Manci Schwalbova set Sara's arm in a cast and treated her back with fifteen minutes of ice, followed by fifteen minutes of hot compresses. It would take Sara six weeks to be able to walk again. By that time, thousands of Jewish girls and women would be in Auschwitz, and young Jewish men had started to arrive, as well. Despite her injuries, Sarah was reassigned to the demolition and construction detail.

It was a "heavy-duty task, meant for men. For a young woman like me, it was [inhumane]."

Within a few weeks, girls falling from the tops of the buildings were no longer receiving any treatment. As the SS yelled for them to move faster and work more quickly, two more girls slipped and fell off one of the rooftops. As their twisted bodies writhed in pain, an SS walked purposefully up to them and raised his gun.

"We will have a vacation for having shot them," he said. He shot one. His colleague shot the other.

Chapter Sixteen

The prolonged slavery of women is the darkest page of human history.

— Elizabeth Cady Stanton

THEY CAME ON FINE STATIONERY and business letterhead, handwritten cards and typed letters. Some came with references from gentile business partners, neighbors, clergy. Rabbis wrote to state that certain members of the Jewish community were vital to the economic well-being of Slovakia, then had to write the government and request their own exemptions. Ever since the proclamation about young, unmarried Jewish women registering for work had been announced in that thunderous blizzard at the end of February, the Ministry of the Interior had been inundated with requests from Jewish families seeking government exceptions, called *výnimka*. These exceptions provided entire families with exemptions from "work service" and from "rehoming."

As the reality of the departure of thousands of Jewish girls sank in, and as young men started to be called up for work, rumors that entire families were going to be relocated increased. And as that new rumor spread, more and more applications for exceptions arrived at the Ministry of the Interior. Even government officials were writing references now. The Minister of Education and National Culture, J. Sivak, was noted for helping his Jewish friends and colleagues. The Slovak National Archives has file boxes of these requests. Thousands of them. Pleas for recognition and justice, but mostly pleas for life.

There was a price to pay for freedom, even if you were lucky enough to be recommended for an exception. The irony that Jews had to buy themselves out of slavery cannot be ignored. This was a new economy, and the men reaping the rewards were the same fascists who were deporting Jews and confiscating Jewish businesses and properties.

The first transport had not gone according to Konka's plan. Neither had the second or the third, or even the fourth. It had been harder than he thought to round up thousands of girls, especially in rural communities. Alexander Mach had been furious when Konka failed to deliver five thousand Jews in five days. He hadn't even delivered five thousand on five transports. What would the Germans think of them? Konka was fired.

The new Chief of Department 14, Anton Vašek, was soon dubbed the Slovak "King of the Jews." A tubby, beady-eyed bureaucrat with a lust for money and power, he was about to get plenty of both. With stacks of requests for exceptions arriving each day, his decision was a commodity worth paying financial inducements for. Processing the entreaties for exceptions was no longer carried out on a first-come, first-served basis, or solely dependent on regional governors or mayors; it was based upon who paid the most money the quickest. Vašek was amassing a small fortune selling exemptions—yet often avoided providing the required documentation that would protect the family that had paid him.

Although vitally important to Jewish families, the requests were not a priority for the ministers in Tiso's government. The process was not quick, and without financial enticement, it took much longer. Is that why the wealthier Amster family got their exception before the Friedmans? Not that it mattered in the end; neither received the documents in time to keep their daughters home.

Emmanuel Friedman did not seem to realize that slipping money under the table was an option or that his daughters' safety was for sale. Perhaps in early March, bribing government officials was not yet mandatory. By May, under Vašek, the cost of getting an exception was a reality.

They were strange-looking documents. Plentiful dashes, like inked Morse code, ran the width of the page to prevent any alterations. At the top of the page in all caps, the document states it is a legitimate document from the Minister of the Interior, the district and town, and finally a department number. Fourteen was the Jewish Department. Listed next were the head of the family's name, profession, residence, and birth date, followed by a reference to the statute §22, which legally allowed the bearer of the document to remain in Slovakia. Then came the current date, followed by the Slovak version of *Heil Hitler*, a hyperbolic reference to the Hlinka regime used for all government salutations at the time—"*Na straz!* To the Guards!"—and, finally, a hand-stamped ink authentication from the Minister of the Interior's office and the minister's signature. In later exceptions, Anton Vašek's name would appear on that line. Gejza Konka's was on the ones created in early March.

The next crucial part of the exception was the list of family members who would be protected by the document, their relationship to the head of the household, and their birth dates. This was followed by an additional reference number, and another *Na Straz!* salutation. After that section was validated once more by a representative of the Minister of the Interior, it was sent to a regional representative, the mayor or governor of the district, who then had to approve the paperwork. So there are three important dates on every document: the date on the upper portion of the document with the Minister of the Interior's name is the date the document was in Bratislava. On the lower part of the document, where the mayor of the district is named, is another date. Over a government-issued paper stamp, a legal statement has been hand stamped with a final date, the squiggle of signature and the region's seal.

One *výnimka* took at least a week to process in July 1942, but it could be processed only after a formal request had been approved and references from gentiles had been gathered to confirm the Jewish family's position and importance to the state. In March 1942, delays were more probable because the process was still untried, which might explain why the mayor of Humenné told Emmanuel Friedman not to worry, his family's exceptions were on their way.

What is most confusing is the length of time between the date next to the mayor's signature and the date by the regional seal, which should have been available in the same government building, if not the same office. It is also a mystery why the Amster and Hartmann families received their families' exceptions just a few days after the girls had been taken from their homes, hours before the transport left Poprad, while the Friedman and Gross families received theirs two to three weeks later. Of the many Jews in Humenné, about four hundred would eventually be theoretically protected by presidential exceptions due to economic importance or their having converted to Catholicism prior to 1941.

Emmanuel Friedman's glazier business, like the businesses of other Jewish professionals, had been Aryanized. It was now run by a kindly gentile by the name of Mr. Baldovsky, who did not know how to perform the tasks of a certified glazier. For those duties, the German and Slovak governments still needed Emmanuel Friedman. These were top-secret jobs, which may sound odd. What business could have been so important that it required Emmanuel Friedman to be blindfolded before being driven to work by a government-appointed chauffeur? The fact was, he was regularly taken to a secret airfield in the countryside, where he spent his days repairing the windshields on bombers. Back in town, Mr. Baldovsky handled more standard duties.

It was after Passover when the Friedman family's promised *výnimka* finally arrived. Emmanuel Friedman had been able to find out where Edith and Lea had been taken, either through a postmark on their postcard or through his government contacts. Then he did something that Mr. Amster and the Hartmann brothers had not considered. He asked Mr. Baldovsky to go to Oświęcim and free his daughters.

Like most people, Emmanuel Friedman still believed his daughters were working for the Slovak government and would be freed in three months, but he and his wife were miserable without Edith and Lea. Why not go to the administrative offices of the work center and present their government exceptions to the proper officials so that the girls could be released? Maybe they could release Adela Gross, as well.

Mr. Baldovsky and Emmanuel Friedman were not so completely naive as to neglect a contingency plan. If there was any trouble getting the girls released, Mr. Baldovsky would make contact with them and help them escape. Once they were on a passenger train, they would be safe because they had exemptions and were traveling with a gentile. That was the plan.

Mr. Baldovsky promptly boarded a passenger train for Žilina, then changed trains and headed for the Polish border.

WATCHTOWERS ROSE LIKE solemn giants in the blizzard. Clusters of snow clung to the barbs on the wire fences. The dark shapes of SS moved through the bright halos around the searchlights of the guard towers. A curtain of snow fell in the dark, clinging to the girls' eyelashes as they hesitantly stepped onto the *lagerstrasse* for morning roll call. No one wanted to be out in this sudden April storm: not the SS, not the guard dogs, not the kapos. The new prisoners even less so. Wearing nothing but their slipshod clappers, their feet sank into ankle-deep snow. The wind crept through the bullet holes in their uniforms or up their bare legs under dresses. Ice burned the skin on their cheeks and shaved scalps. Lining up as best they could, blinking back the snow in their eyes, the girls tried to stand without shivering. Arrogant and superior, Commandant Rudolf Höss tramped past the prisoners in one of his rare appearances in the women's camp. His boots were high enough that the snow did not fall inside his cuffs and as he stomped through the snow, he glared at the unhappy kapos counting the miserable girls. It was a dark dawn, and as "they were still counting us, I heard the SS woman [Johanna Langefeld] tell him, 'In this weather we cannot send them out to work.'

"Höss stomped his boot and yelled at her, 'For Jews, there is no weather!'"

That said it all. Edith glared into the fury of the storm. Why couldn't they clean the blocks or something? How could anyone be so cruel? Or was it simply since the wardress had suggested it that he rejected her idea? The fight over who was in charge of the new women's camp had only just started. Langefeld had not only lost, so had her prisoners. The girls marched out to work as the snow piled up around them.

To further drive home the commandant's point, the SS man in charge of raising the gate yelled at the girls to take off their "clappers" because the sound of the backs of the sandals hitting their feet bothered his ears. That he could hear anything above the howling wind was hard to believe. But it was his prerogative to do what he pleased. If Commandant Höss could make Jews work, his staff could make them go barefoot. It was all about power. And Jews had none. The girls took off their so-called shoes and marched silently under the archway's backwards motto: *ierF thcaM tiebrA.*

Soon after the order that the girls had to take off their shoes whenever they exited and entered the camp, the snow began melting; at least they weren't walking barefoot in snow anymore. Now it was icy mud. For the girls working in the fields and spreading manure, a new problem arose. The wet clay soil sucked the sandals right off their feet. To lose your "shoe" was equivalent to receiving a death sentence. Linda lost hers in the first days of the thaw. The rest of the girls in the detail, fearing the loss of their own shoes, began removing them before they slogged barefoot through the cold, thick mud carrying manure.

MR. BALDOVSKY ARRIVED at the train station of Oświęcim, asked directions for the work camp, and walked directly up to the gates of Auschwitz. When the guards stopped him, he asked to speak with whoever was in charge. They looked at him incredulously.

—And who are you?

He introduced himself and brandished the exceptions.

—I have come to liberate Lea and Edith Friedman, from Humenné, who were mistakenly taken for government work service. These are the official documents that relieve them of duty.

The guards laughed.

—What language is this in?

—Slovak.

—We are German.

Mr. Baldovsky explained what the documents said.

—They are exempt from work! he exclaimed.

—In Slovakia, maybe. But we are in Greater Germany now.

They did not know whom he was talking about, anyway. Edith? Lea? Friedman? He had to be kidding.

—What are their numbers?

—They have numbers?

—Everyone has numbers!

Growing irritable, the SS cocked their guns and told the businessman to leave or they would shoot him. Mr. Baldovsky backed away. It was time to enact the contingency plan. He knew the Friedman girls well enough to recognize them, and Adela would be easy to spot with her mane of red hair. Wherever Adela was, Lea and Edith would surely be nearby.

Walking down the road, he made a wide circle around the barbed-wire fences surrounding the rows of brick barracks that comprised Auschwitz. Out in the fields, he could see befuddled creatures walking through snow and mud in their bare feet, carrying muck in their bare hands. Because they were dressed in ill-fitting clothes that blew open in the cold wind, he could see that they wore no undergarments. They had no scarves covering their almost-bald heads. They were certainly female, but they looked more like the golems of Jewish myth than like women.

Mr. Baldovsky shuddered at the sight of them. These certainly weren't the well-brought-up Jewish girls he knew from Humenné. Scanning the pale gray and beige horizon, he saw nothing and no one else. Auschwitz must be an insane asylum. He concluded that Emmanuel Friedman's information had been incorrect. There was no way that Edith and Lea were here in this hell. Having failed in his mission, he returned to Humenné and told Mr. Friedman and his wife, "Edith and Lea must have been taken somewhere else. There is no way they were in Auschwitz. That place is not a work camp, it is for the mentally ill." What would he have thought if he had witnessed the girls in the demolition details throwing bricks down on the heads of other girls?

Edith sighs. "You can imagine, a normal person comes and looks around and sees those girls without hair walking around half dressed. He sees us without stockings, with naked legs in the snow. What impression do we make? Not the impression that we are normal human beings."

BALDOVSKY'S ASSESSMENT THAT Auschwitz was housing for the insane was quickly becoming true. Many girls were losing their minds. The trauma caused by their abrupt removal from the kind and caring homes of their parents and being catapulted into such brutality caused severe disassociation. Stripped of their identities, emotionally shattered, exhausted, and dehumanized by physical and verbal cruelty, even strong-minded girls had trouble holding on to their sanity. Perhaps they had died and were no longer in the land of the living? Perhaps there was nothing beyond the fog rising from the swamps.

Madge Hellinger took on the task of sleeping next to the most fragile girls who talked out of their heads at night. Like a big sister or mother, she comforted them as they tossed and turned, plagued by nightmares. When they woke to the real nightmare of Auschwitz, she spoke to them gently and encouragingly. Comfort and connection were essential for girls who had no sisters or cousins with them. Being cared for by young women just a few years older helped calm the terror and shock of those first weeks.

The trauma of their circumstances carried with it an ethical disassociation as well. Girls who had been deeply religious found their morals weakening as the stakes for survival rose. Auschwitz was a kind of cruel game played for the amusement of the SS and kapos, many of whom delighted in pitting prisoner against prisoner. The girls tried to help one another, but as cliques based on family and friendship formed, some were excluded. This was survival not just of the fittest but of the luckiest, with fierce competition for the most limited resource— food. All of the girls in camp came with a strict religious code of ethics, but within a few weeks, they were stealing from each other: food, blankets, "anything that wasn't tied to your body."

"They made us turn against each other. It was so horrible," Edith says. "You were always in danger not just of losing your life but of losing your soul. And the longer we were there, the closer the shave to the soul. Morals are something that if they are embedded in you, they cannot be gotten rid of, no matter how

depraved the life you are forced to live. I think some girls chose
to die, rather than act mean to others." Others were just mean.

Edie (#1949)—who had arrived with her sister, Ella—admits freely, "I stole everything." In fact, when the Red Cross
delivered food packages to prisoners in camp, Edie (who had
the same first and last name as our Edith) was given the responsibility of handing the packages out and decided that since
there were two with her name on them, she should get both.
Our Edith got none.

"You have no idea what you will do to survive until you are
forced to choose between starving or eating, freezing or being
warm, praying or stealing. You can pray before you steal. 'God
forgive me for taking this girl's blanket because someone took
mine. God forgive the girl who stole my Red Cross package, so
she could eat and I couldn't.'" At ninety-four years of age,
Edith offers a rare perspective on this incident: "All these years
later, I still hold a grudge against that girl. She ate. I did not. We
were both seventeen. We both survived. You know, when you
get old you don't forget the wrongs done you, but I am glad to
say I am old enough now not to care anymore.... You don't
know a girl until you live with her or, like we were, are imprisoned with her. That is when you discover not only who she is,
but who you are. This is the thing, though. We were teenagers.
We weren't adults. We were still young enough to want to throw
temper tantrums, to be lazy, to shirk a duty or sleep late. Only
a month ago, we were giggling and gossiping about the latest
bit of news in our community, and now we were seeing girls
dying, girls our age who should live to become old ladies like I
am now, already dead before their time. And then there is the
question, will that be me too? Will I be dead soon, too?"

There is another thing Edith does not forgive. When the
block elders began their jobs, they probably served bread and
soup equally to their fellow prisoners. But as the days wore on
and their own bellies hollowed with hunger, many began to

steal food for themselves and their friends or families. "*Block-ältesters* [block elders] were supposed to cut the bread in four pieces," Edith explains. "But they started cutting out the middle of the bread. So if there were a hundred pieces for us, the block elders got an extra hundred middle slices. This they ate themselves or gave to their sisters or cousins while the rest of us starved for a little bit more."

Can we really blame them? Would we be any better? If you have cousins who are starving, how can you care about strangers? Even with the extra portions, everyone was still hungry. "No Jew ever had a full belly in Auschwitz," Edith says. "Until you have actually experienced starvation, you don't know what you are capable of doing to another human being."

THE MORE STRENUOUS the work detail, the more quickly girls became weakened from the lack of food. Cold also burns fat and calories, and those first few weeks working outside led to critical weight loss. Survival depended on getting inside work, or less rigorous outside work, but the only inside work was cleaning the barracks, and that task fell to the block and room elders. For the rest of the girls, there were only demolition teams, spreading manure, cleaning streets. "In a very short time, we looked like noodles. I probably weighed about sixty-five pounds," Edith says.

Since food was the key to survival, getting in the line of a server who stirred the soup so the vegetables and horsemeat came up to the top—even if both were rotten—was a godsend. One survivor remembers girls shouting, "I have meat in my soup!" whenever they were lucky enough to get something to chew. Linda Reich (#1173) prided herself on stirring the soup whenever she served it, but many servers skimmed the top and served only broth, saving the bottom "best" for themselves. Sometimes it helped to stand in the back of the line, but if the soup kettle was emptied too soon and you were too far back in the line, you could end up with no soup at all.

Linda recalls racing to get soup at the so-called "lunch" break because the SS would shoot anyone falling into line too slowly. Death had no rhyme or reason—it came in an instant, often without warning. This was not a dystopian society created by some novelist. Auschwitz was a real-life Hunger Games.

At dusk, when they were finally done working, the girls were forced to line up before marching back to camp. "The last in the row had to drag the corpses back to the camp because they had to be counted, too." No one ever wanted to be last in the row, especially in the demolition details, which always had a number of dead girls. Add to that the sheer exhaustion of working all day, and the girls forced to carry corpses barely had any strength left. Often a dead girl was dragged along the ground until she "didn't have skin on her back anymore," Linda says, sadly. "There was always blood on the road."

After evening roll call, Linda and others began to notice that some of the injured girls never returned to the blocks. Ever. "It was very strange," Edith says. "If someone was sick, if they had a small wound on their leg, they were separated, collected, and we didn't see them anymore." Where did they go? In the beginning, it did not occur to them that the missing girls were being killed.

In her testimony at the Ravensbrück trials in 1945, the political prisoner and kapo Luise Mauer reported that "the murder machine now ran on full steam. Anyone deemed not fit for work or discovered hiding in the blocks by the supervisor [Johanna Langefeld] was killed." Mauer and Bertel Teege were ordered to select anyone not capable of working anymore and send her to the "sanatorium." The sanatorium, of course, was now a fully functional gas chamber. The two kapos decided they "would rather die ourselves than help these fascist murderers" and went to their boss, SS Langefeld. A strict Lutheran, Langefeld was often torn between her religious values and the violent demands of her job, and she respected Teege and

Mauer for their own moral judgment. In a rare moment of compassion, Langefeld did not report them for insubordination, which probably saved their lives.

With the job of selecting women for the "sanatorium" assigned to someone else, Mauer and Teege began a "whisper campaign" to quietly warn and encourage block elders to send everyone out to work or give ill girls work duties inside. They did not dare explain why the block elders should send ill girls to work. They could not confide in anyone that being sent to the "sanatorium" meant being killed, or they themselves would have been killed. The result was that many ill prisoners thought the block elders were being cruel by not allowing them to go to the sanatorium and insisted they be allowed to go. Those girls were taken away while the details were outside working and never seen again.

By the end of April, over 6,277 young, mostly Jewish women had been registered in Auschwitz—197 were Czech, a small number were Poles who had been hiding in Slovakia, and the rest were Slovakian. The total was more than the entire prisoner population of Ravensbrück. Yet how many women were still alive and part of the prison population at Auschwitz is unknown.

About the time a new work detail was created, Erna Dranger's sister, Fela, arrived on April 23 on the eighth Slovak transport. Her number was 6030. Erna and Fela were among the first group of girls, made up mostly of "old-timers," who were chosen to work in the new detail sorting clothes. Among those sorters was evidently Magda Amster, whose father had driven through the night in an attempt to rescue her.

Ever since Linda Reich had lost her shoe, she had been hiding in the back of the lines at roll call, trying to avoid being sent out to work. Given the opportunity to move into the clothes-sorting detail, she promptly stole a pair of shoes to put on her feet. Few of the girls in the new sorting detail would forget their friends and quickly figured out how to pilfer items and smuggle them back in to the general population. They called it "organizing."

Shoes were the most essential items girls needed. Like Linda, others had lost their clappers in the mud, and being barefoot was a sure route to an early grave. Other items, like underwear, bras, scarves, and socks, also made their way into the blocks and began to improve the women's lives by helping them feel like women again. For the girls sorting the clothes, smuggling these things out was a quiet rebellion against the authorities. It was also a way to honor their cultural identity—keeping Jewish clothing to clothe Jews instead of watching it be sent off to clothe Germans. No one charged for these gifts, not in the beginning. Everyone just wanted to help each other anyway they could.

"There was a girl from our transport who would bring us something from the kitchen, something cooked, like a potato," Edith remembers. "She knew how to bring it through so the guards would not find it because they checked everyone, especially the girls working with food or with clothing." Every single survivor tells a similar story of having vitally important clothing items or food smuggled to them by their friends. Like the Polish flint hidden in the earth beneath their feet, aiding one another hardened their resolve to survive and compressed the girls into semiprecious gems of mutual support.

The sorting detail was a fairly small operation at this point, but it would help save many lives in those early days. Going to work under a roof to sort clothing became one of the most desired work details. Not only was the job relatively easy, but the girls were out of the cold, and if no guards were looking they could eat bits of food found in pockets. Of course, getting caught meant twenty lashes with a whip and being sent back to hard labor outside. Organizing was worth those risks, though.

The clothing was kept in one block, where Linda and others folded blouses, skirts, coats, and trousers, ten to a package.

Then those packages were moved to another block, where they were stacked, ready to be put into empty cattle cars and shipped back to Germany. Rather than return empty, the cars that brought in Jews were filled with Jews' belongings. Stamped on the outside of the freight cars was the message, "For the Families Who Have Their Sons on the Front."

Still naive about their circumstances, some of the girls wrote messages on scraps of paper, in the hopes that the German families who received the clothes would alert the authorities and help the girls: "*Achtung!* Jewish clothing from concentration camp." They did not realize the authorities already knew.

WITH THE ADVANCE OF SPRING, the fields where the girls had spread manure were now being hoed for crops and planted with potato eyes. Edith and Lea were assigned to a new detail: cleaning the streams and ponds around the perimeter of Auschwitz, which were filthy with refuse and sometimes human bones buried deep in the muck. Forced to wade into the water, they pulled out the garbage and set it on the banks to be collected. "In the summer, this was not such a bad detail, but in the early spring and late fall, we froze. We went to bed wet and woke up wet. We never dried out."

By now, some of the girls had been moved into different blocks. Irena Fein was in Block 8, where it seems Edie's sister, Ella (#1950), may have been the block or room elder. Ella never states that she served in either position, but her sister worked as the block's scribe, a position that would have given the sisters more power and helped their position in camp. By this point, their youngest sister, Lila, had also arrived in camp on the third transport. If Ella had been promoted to block or room elder, it was an important promotion. At twenty-one years of age, Ella was not only more mature than many of the other girls, but she had gone to secretarial school and learned skills that would eventually single her out for a much more important position in camp. Functionaries like block and room elders no longer had to have their heads shaved.

Delousing and shaving took place every four weeks on a Sunday. Some girls now faced their own fathers or brothers naked. Forced to hurry, the men couldn't help but nick the girls' flesh with the unwieldy electric shears, especially as they tried to hurry past private parts. The disinfectant "bath" always came after the shaving. The girls stood naked in long lines waiting to jump into the vat for a few minutes—the only access to water they had during the month, but the disinfectant didn't clean their flesh. It just burned.

Chapter Seventeen

History, despite its wrenching pain, cannot be unlived,
but if faced with courage, need not be lived again.
—MAYA ANGELOU

BACK IN SLOVAKIA, BOTH GENTILES and Jews were increasingly disturbed by the deportations. On April 26, 1942, a crowd of Slovak gentiles organized outside the Žilina transit camp, where young Jewish men and women were being held for the next transport. They "began to curse the fact that the Jews were being concentrated [there] and deported. It almost came to a real demonstration. The [Hlinka] Guards, who were to have guarded the Jews, did not know what to do with the mob." It was one of the few acts of public resistance by gentiles on behalf of Jews. Other actions were smaller, more personal, and less likely to capture the attention of the Hlinka Guard or the police.

Ivan Rauchwerger's father had found his son work in a leather factory that had been owned by an old friend from school and then Aryanized by a Lutheran who was friendly to Jews. With a job that was important to the war effort, Ivan was not at risk of being deported, but "we were systematically being dehumanized by both the state and the Catholic Church."

There was an emotional cost to receiving an exception. At sixteen, Ivan had already seen his girlfriend board the train for "work." Now he was watching his childhood chums leave town in cattle cars. "We who remained behind carried on with our joyless lives as virtual nobodies."

His friend Suzie Hegy berated the Hlinka Guards when she was forced onto one of the April transports. "I have not done anything wrong!" she screamed. "I have not yet lived, and you are going to kill me?" Ivan never saw Suzie again.

By April 29, 1942, ten Slovak transports had illegally removed 3,749 young Jewish men and 6,051 young women to Auschwitz. No families had been deported yet.

For Polish Jews, things were quite different.

During morning roll call early in May, Edith and Lea noticed that a huge canvas tent had been set up in the center of the *lagerstrasse*. They were standing at the edge of the lines when one of the male kapos walked past. "I remember he had the green triangle of a criminal, and he said, 'You know what this tent is? There are children's shoes. And you know where the children are? You see the smoke? Those are the children.'"

"Why would he say something so crazy?" Edith whispered to her sister. "There weren't any children in camp. It was such a strange thing to say. A normal brain doesn't catch on." They simply could not believe him.

The shutters on the windows of Block 10 had been nailed closed to prevent the girls from looking into the courtyard of Block 11 and the execution wall. However, the knots in the wood of the shutters had been pushed out, so they could see what was happening down below. One day, when the girls were at work, the kapo Luise Mauer was approached by Elza, the block elder from Block 10, who had seen something she wanted to show Luise. On the other side of the shutters, on the bloodied ground between Blocks 10 and 11, SS were shooting "without mercy on women and children who were already dead, and those that were still alive."

This was not the only incident that Luise Mauer and her colleague Bertha Teege witnessed. One day, after emptying the *lagerstrasse* of prisoners as they had been ordered to do, the two women returned to Johanna Langefeld's office and peeked through the blinds of the window. "About three hundred women, children and men, young, old, healthy, and sick, some on crutches, walked along the camp road. Then they were driven into an underground passageway, which looked like a giant potato peeler with air ducts. Then we saw two SS men wearing gas masks empty canisters of what we later came to realize was the notorious Zyklon B, which was responsible for the deaths of millions, into the air ducts. Horrific screams filled the air—the children screamed longest—then all we could hear was whimpering. That, too, dissipated after fifteen minutes. And thus we knew that three hundred people had been murdered." In fact, there were many more.

Between May 5 and 12, Polish transports carrying 6,700 Jewish men, women, and children were sent directly to the newly functioning gas chambers in the first mass executions in Auschwitz. There were no crematoriums yet, so the bodies had to be buried in large pits.

When Langefeld returned to her office "looking pale and disturbed," Mauer and Teege confided that they had seen what had happened. Langefeld told them that "she had no idea that people would be killed here. And that we should on no account tell anyone what we had seen, on pain of death." The irony of that statement alone speaks to the double paradox that murder in Auschwitz required.

MEANWHILE, IN SLOVAKIA, outrage had arisen not only because unmarried young women were being removed from the protection of their parents' homes but because families were being separated. The April protests in Žilina had slowed the deportations long enough for President Tiso to reassure the country that he would act as a "good and humane person and stop the deportations of single girls." He reiterated his assurances on every radio broadcast, in every newspaper, and at every public event, "It is the basic principle of the Christian faith that families should not be separated. That principle will be observed when the Jews are sent to their new settlements." Everyone, even the Vatican, believed (or perhaps just wanted to believe) his lies. In reality, Tiso was just waiting for the Slovak Assembly to pass the legislation that would make "rehoming" Jews legal. That decision was made on May 15, 1942, when the Slovak Assembly debated the question of whether deporting Jews should be legal.

The atmosphere in the assembly's gallery was described as "oppressive" as Hlinka Guards positioned themselves opposite the "voting deputies" in order to intimidate those concerned about the moral and religious implications of the bill. By the time the vote was called, most of the assembly had left, having chosen not to cast their vote. The bill passed. Instantly, it was legal for Jews to be deported and, once deported, stripped of their citizenship and their property. Slovak Jews no longer needed to be referred to as "donating servants." Only those with exceptions would be safe now. A new surge of requests flooded the Ministry of the Interior.

With the deportations now legal, Adolf Eichmann himself arrived in Bratislava to assure the government that "Slovak Jews worked happily in their new homes." Over the next few months, twenty thousand Slovak Jews would be sent to Auschwitz. Just as Tiso had promised, families would be deported together. It was only when they got to Auschwitz or Lublin that they were separated—by death.

As the three-month mark of their supposed government service "contract" passed, the girls watched transports arriving from Slovakia with a sickening sense of despair. Something very different from what anyone had supposed was now happening. Young women were no longer the sole targets. Some of the girls were stunned to find themselves no longer bereft of their mothers, but doomed to watch their mothers suffer with them. "We were overpowered by hopelessness," writes Dr. Manci Schwalbova. "Daughters supporting their mothers had to witness how they were beaten and how they went down under the burden of heavy labor and inhuman conditions."

In HUMENNÉ, LOU GROSS rushed out to help his friend's grandmother with her suitcase, only to be dragged away by his nanny, crying. In the few short months since Adela had left home, he had grown up beyond his four years of age.

Giora Shpira was lucky enough to have a government exception through his father's work at the lumberyard, but at fourteen, he witnessed not only entire streets in Prešov being deported, but families who had remained behind being herded into a square and gunned down. "That was the fate of most of the residents on K. Street," Giora writes. Even with their exemptions, his father worried that the boys would soon be targets, so he smuggled them to Hungary. Giora's brother hid in an orphanage, while Giora worked as an electrician's apprentice.

In Rožkovany, the Hartmann family worked their dairy and agricultural fields, trying to continue life as usual. Eugene worked double duty, caring for his invalid mother and helping his father. They had still heard no word from Magduska. Her father fretted that his promise to send her a care package remained unfulfilled, but he had no idea where to send one.

Since the Hartmanns had exceptions for running a farm vital to the country's food supply, other members of their extended family came to live on the farm with them. Their cousin Lenka Hertzka had stayed in Prešov, however, and was abruptly deported in June. Fortunately, Lenka's sister, Lilly, her nephew, and mother (Magduska's aunt) were already safe on the farm.

No one in Auschwitz was safe, but Lenka had secured work as an assistant to one of the top members of the Gestapo. One of her privileges was mail. That July, a postcard arrived from Lenka, in Auschwitz. The Hartmanns finally had an address to send things to Magduska and Nusi, and immediately sent a postcard back to Lenka asking the questions that nagged the family.

Why could Lenka write, but not Magduska and Nusi? Clearly, Lenka was older and more mature, but Magduska had always acted responsibly. Was she so busy that she couldn't write to her family? What was wrong with her? Postcards were also arriving from other girls who had been deported with Magduska and Nusi. Why was it that everyone but their daugthers had found time to write?

The Hartmanns were a microcosm of innocence, suggesting what many other families also must have believed: that their daughters were living in some a kind of dormitory, saw each other regularly, had meals together, and could receive packages of food, money, clothes, bedding, and of course, news from home. They had no idea that almost everything they sent to Auschwitz was confiscated by the SS.

IN THE ENCLOSED space of a locked cattle car on in its way to Lublin, Rudolf Vrba, who would eventually become famous for escaping from Auschwitz, was listening to his neighbors talk about the postcards they had received from the girls in Auschwitz. Zachar, who ran a small vegetable stand, was sitting next to his teenage daughter, who was busily buffing her nails. Looking up from her manicure, Zachar's daughter said, "My cousin went on the first transport and she wrote to me the other day, saying everything was fine. The food was good and they weren't working too hard." A shadow crossed her freckled face. "There was only one thing I couldn't understand. She said her mother sent me her love. And her mother died three years ago."

A woman nursing her infant looked up. "There was something funny in the letter I got from my sister, too," she said. "She told me old Jakob Rakow was in fine form. But Jakob was killed in a car crash ages ago."

"A gossamer web of doubt descended on the conversation," writes Vrba.

The passengers began to open their bags and shuffle through cards that had been sent from girls performing work service in some camp in Poland. Sure enough, there were other odd comments, "references to people who were dead or to events which could not possibly have happened." Why would their daughters, sisters, or cousins write such nonsense? To a single family, the postscripts were simple oddities, but now that other families were producing cards with similar comments, a sense of foreboding descended. As the postcards were read out loud, people began to reconsider the coded messages. Then, just as quickly, they assured themselves that there was nothing to be alarmed about.

The families who had been warned were doomed to fall prey to the covert warnings the girls couldn't give clearly. It was easier to believe President Tiso's assurances and trust that they were being resettled than to believe that they were going to die, like Jakob Rakow in his crashed car. Tiso was keeping his promise, after all, to deport the Slovak Jews as entire families—instead of separating them from their daughters, as he had done in March.

As the family transports began in earnest, the young Ivan Rauchwerger drove to Poprad again to help the families newly incarcerated in the military barracks. "I saw heart-wrenching misery and desperation in a large mass of dehumanized beings. The ladies' makeup had melted, there were only a couple of taps dispensing water, a lot of the toilets were out of order, the men were unshaved, nervous, the children crying; there were not enough bunks to sleep on. I was besieged with women begging me: 'Please go into my study, I left my university degree on the desk, I am a doctor and they may need me.'

"Another said, 'I need my glasses. I am half blind and left my glasses on my bedside table, please bring them.'

"'I am a diabetic and left my insulin behind—I am not able exist without it'

"'I left sanitary pads in the bathroom. Please, I must have them now.'

"'I ran back, but their homes were locked up. All we could do was bring them some food, toilet paper, and sanitary napkins.'"

The Hlinka Guard had taken over possession of the homes and everything inside. "We observed how the guardists happily entered the homes and flats of our friends and came out with arms full of bed linens, tablecloths, clothing, and other items. Later they came out with paintings, artworks, and rugs, and toward the evening they came with horse carts for the furniture. A month later, they received titles to those properties."

When a postcard from Auschwitz arrived in Ivan's town, it appeared to report facts identical to the others: "the Germans treat us fairly. Yes we work, but not too hard. We get enough food and sleep in hygienic barracks. Our family is almost complete, only Uncle Malach Hamowet is missing. We hope he will join us soon." In Hebrew, Malach ha-Mawet is the Angel of Death. Susie Hegy had been right.

On May 28, 1942, Ivan watched as one of his school friends, Budi Stein, and his father were marched through town, carrying what worldly belongings they were allowed. Budi's father was a German-Jewish architect who had fled Germany in 1934 as the Third Reich and the Nazi party were rising to power. The Steins had built a beautiful home in Spišská Nová Ves near Ivan's family home. Now black-garbed Hlinka Guardists pointed guns at Budi and his father. The community gathered to watch people traipsing down the gravel streets carrying suitcases for the new "homes." President Tiso had promised.

"I will never forget the way Budi looked at me: 'How come I am being deported and you are free?' His face still haunts me," ninety-three-year-old Ivan Rauchwerger says solemnly. Budi was seventeen years old, the same age as Ivan at that time. None of the Stein family survived. Their large transport left Slovakia for Lublin, Poland. The next stop after Lublin was Auschwitz.

Chapter Eighteen

To lift such a heavy weight,
Sisyphus, you will need all your courage.
I do not lack the courage to complete the task
But the end is far and time is short.
  —CHARLES BAUDELAIRE, *Les Fleurs du mal*,
    quoted in *Suite Française* by Irene
    Nemirovsky

ON THE FOURTH OF JULY—America's Independence Day—the first selection of Jews was carried out "on the unloading platform while the SS Standby Squad surrounds the train." The total number of Slovak Jews on this transport is not recorded, but only 108 women and 264 men were chosen to be registered for "work." Separated by gender, the new deportees were forced to walk past an SS doctor and other camp administrators, whose job it was to decide which prisoners were able-bodied and young enough to work. "Old people, children, mothers with children, and pregnant women are told that they are to be driven to the camp." Thus separated from their families, they clambered into trucks and waved to those chosen for work. They were then driven "to the bunker in Birkenau and killed in the gas chambers." The rest were processed: shaved, deloused, and tattooed.

Selections at the train platform universally showed a preference for male prisoners over female. The reason was obvious. Not only were women more likely to want to stay with their children, but the SS were looking for physical strength. Women were not ideal slave laborers. However, there was another factor in the decision-making process: overcrowding in the women's camp.

Despite the fact that there were no formal calculations to reveal the exact number of women in camp—nor the exact number who had died—as of May 12, 1942, more than eight thousand women (Jews and gentiles) had been registered in Auschwitz, and another five thousand were about to arrive. But there were only five barracks, with bunks for one thousand prisoners in each building. To handle the additional population, domed Nissen huts of corrugated metal were erected in between the two-story brick blocks. No additional toilet facilities were added to the camp, and hygiene, which had always been a difficulty, now became a major problem.

The girls were battling not only to get the best jobs and extra food, but against an invisible enemy that could strike quicker than an SS whip—typhus. Except for monthly disinfections, there was no protection against the lice and fleas carrying the deadly disease. It spread rampantly through the men's and women's camps, killing indiscriminately, even striking down the camp doctor, SS Captain Dr. Siegfried Schwela, and at least two Ravensbrück kapos, Gertrude Franke and Helene Ott. Records indicate that approximately 77 percent of the Jewish men died of typhus in these first months. We have no record of how many women succumbed to the disease; we only know that typhus raged through the women's camp.

"Once the Jewish transports from Slovakia began to arrive, [the women's camp] was crammed to the roof within a matter of days," Commandant Höss wrote in his diary. "Conditions in the women's camp were atrocious and far worse than the men's camp." The prisoners were "piled high to the ceiling. Everything was black with lice."

"Women," he wrote, "deteriorated far more rapidly then the men. Everything was much more difficult, harsher and more depressing for the women, since general living conditions in the women's camp were incomparably worse. They were far more tightly packed in, and the sanitary and hygienic conditions were notably inferior. The women's camp, tightly crammed from the very beginning, meant psychological destruction for the mass of female prisoners, and this led sooner or later to their physical collapse.

"The disastrous overcrowding and its consequences, which existed from the very beginning, prevented any proper order being established in the women's camp."

Of course, for the lack of "proper" order, Höss blamed the Chief Supervisor of the women's camp, SS Johanna Langefeld, not himself. There was a clear patriarchy in the camp administration, which Langefeld complained about to both her superiors and her staff. Höss may have admitted that "the general congestion was far greater than in the men's camp," but he refused to take any responsibility for the overcrowding and inhumane conditions that the girls suffered. In fact, he blamed the women prisoners themselves: "When the women had reached the bottom, they would let themselves go completely."

What irony that the man responsible for the conditions women suffered should blame the women themselves for not looking better before they succumbed to death. Holding female prisoners responsible for their own misery speaks volumes about the camp's misogynistic system and its overall contempt for women. But then Jews were not even considered human; being a Jewish woman was the lowest of the low.

Nazi Germany's patriarchal ideology worked against women in particular, as Höss delighted in finding fault with the female SS and kapos in charge of the women's camp as well as the female prisoners. His criticism does reveal one possible explanation for the inadequate death-toll records for women: "Hardly a day passed without discrepancies appearing in the numbers of inmates shown on the strength-returns. The supervisors ran hither and thither in all this confusion like a lot of flustered hens, and had no idea what to do."

Chapter Nineteen

A new soldier came into the barracks and was very
sad and very afraid; sitting and shivering, he saw that
the other soldiers were singing and in a good mood. He
looked at them and asked them, "Aren't you afraid?"
"Of course we are afraid."
"So how can you be in a good mood and singing?"
"Because we are already used to being afraid."
— ILYA EHRENBURG, as told by Edith

NOW FAMILIAR WITH LIVING IN these "crazy conditions," the prisoners began to feel like being at the camp was some kind of life. They even referred to their blocks as "home." "We knew when to go to the bathroom when no one was there, and when the bathroom was being cleaned. We knew not to do more than we could, not more than we had to; we knew to show them that we were working but how to save our energy," Edith says. "We were used to being afraid, and we knew how to live being afraid." Newcomers did not.

It was so hot that summer that the women's shaved heads had blisters from sunburn. Their feet were swollen and full of blisters and cuts from wearing the open-toed clappers. Dust was amplified by the lack of rain. Sweat created brown rivulets in the crevices of their skin as they shoveled dirt, tore down buildings, and picked the ever-present lice from their bodies.

As the family transports began to arrive, there could no longer be any doubt that something was happening, because no children ever appeared in camp. Women and children vanished shortly after they arrived.

The prisoner news network was quick and efficient, and through that grapevine, Helena Citron (#1971) heard that her brother was in camp. "Wait by the window of your block after work, and he will come to the window on the other side of the fence," one of the male prisoners told her as he passed by. After evening roll call, Helena waited by the window until she saw her brother appear in the upstairs window of the block on the other side of the wall. Even from a distance, she could tell he was shocked by her appearance. Had she really aged so quickly in such a short amount of time?

"Why didn't you stay in hiding?" she asked him.

—I thought I might be able to come here and rescue you.

He told her that he and their parents had been deported to Lublin. Their older sister, Ruzinka, was living under Aryan papers with her husband, who was an engineer in Bratislava. The snippets of news hung in the air above the barbed wire.

On the morning of July 25, Edith and Lea stepped outside for roll call and saw Aron, Helena's brother, hanging on the electrical wires that surrounded the camp. He had been shot for trying to escape. The sisters looked nervously around, worried about what Helena would do if she saw her poor brother's body. As the gray dawn faded into daylight, his forlorn form glowed in a tangle of black wire. "They left his body on the wire until roll call was done," Edith recalls. It was a message no Jew could ignore.

Afraid that the news would make Helena suicidal, the Friedman sisters decided to keep the secret to themselves. However, when the girls marched out to work, Slovaks from the men's camp yelled to Helena, "Your brother is no longer alive!"

Transports filled with families deported to Lublin were now beginning to to arrive. Helena and the other girls listened desperately to the reports from male prisoners hauling luggage and belongings to the sorting depot. The men warned the girls that some of their parents were coming into camp. What about those who didn't? Dread electrified the girls.

There was "one loud scream that nearly opened the heavens. My parents and younger siblings were on the way to the crematorium," Helena says. But at least "in another hour or two they would no longer be suffering. Sometimes, in these situations, death is the best thing." All she had left now were her sister Ruzinka and her niece Aviva, hiding somewhere in Slovakia.

ON JULY 17, 1942, SS-Reichsführer Heinrich Himmler arrived at his killing fields in order to inspect the facilities and hear reports on the plans for expansion. At forty-two years old, he had chipmunk cheeks, and his chin was beginning to soften and sag. Round pince-nez balanced on his nose above a trim moustache; he looked more like an egotistical schoolboy, the type used to getting straight As and being pummeled by after-school bullies, than a mass murderer. Now he was the bully, goose-stepping his way around Germany's newly acquired countries and concentration camps—of which there were already many. Auschwitz and Birkenau were the largest.

Just prior to his arrival, Johanna Langefeld told five of her favorite Ravensbrück prisoners that she was going to ask Himmler to commute their sentences. There was a reason for this request. Langefeld was planning to ask Himmler to reassign her to Ravensbrück. Without her there to promote and protect them, she knew their status would fall, especially with a new overseer, who would have her own favorites. It was an action that would later save her life. Emmy Thoma, Tilly

Lehmann, Luise Mauer, and Bertel Teege would come to Langefeld's defense during the Ravensbrück tribunals in 1947.

On the same day that Himmler visited the camp, two transports from Holland, carrying 1,303 men and boys and 697 women and girls arrived. In a meeting with four other officials, Höss gave an overview of the current complex, then turned over the presentation to SS Major General Hans Kammler, who used both models and blueprints to illustrate the new plans for buildings, waste facilities, and gas chambers. Then they took Himmler on a tour of the farming zones, kitchens, and infirmaries, where victims of the typhus epidemic were supposedly cared for, and the train depot, where the Jews from Holland had already disembarked and were standing in long chaotic lines with their belongings.

Himmler and his cronies monitored the selection process resulting in 1,251 men and 300 women being accepted into camp. The rest of the transport—399 women and girls and 50 men and boys—were then gassed in Bunker 2. Since the crematoriums were not yet functional, Himmler was especially interested in seeing how the bodies were cleared out of the gas chamber and hauled to mass graves to be buried. It was a very full day.

In the evening, a reception was held in Himmler's honor so that SS officers could meet their *Reichsführer* and toast his health. Next came a formal dinner held at SS Brigadier General Gauleiter Bracht's house in Katowice, thirty-six kilometers north of Oświęcim. There they dined with their wives. As was customary, the time came for the women to be excused, so the men could discuss the day's events and the next day's agenda over cigars and whiskey. The women's camp was top of the program.

Under the heat-hardened sky, the girls were standing at roll call the next morning when the gates to the women's camp opened and Himmler himself marched inside. At this point, the women's section was so overcrowded that "you had to step over people who were sitting outside," Linda Reich recalls. Hundreds of new female prisoners were sleeping on the ground. Typhus raged.

SS Langefeld was not the kind of woman to spend time curling her hair with an iron. Her hair was in a bun under a hat, but her boots were polished onyx black, glinting below her skirt. It may have been hot already, but Langefeld did not sweat. It was not her fault that Commandant Höss was allowing so many women into the cramped camp space that should have held only five thousand. Now Himmler would see for himself the problems she was facing.

The Jewish girls watched as the kapos they normally feared nervously lined up in neat rows of five. Shoulders back, chins high, eyes straight forward, the kapos stood at attention, aware that while they were superior to the Jews, they were inferior in the eyes of everyone else—criminals who could be disposed of as quickly and easily as their Jewish female counterparts. As Himmler walked along the ranks of the Ravensbrück prisoners, inspecting them, Langefeld explained their prisoner categories, pointing out the prostitutes, murderers, communists. Then they stopped at the front row of kapos, where Langefeld's favorites stood.

As they passed Bertel Teege, Luise Mauer, and the three others, Langefeld paused and addressed her *Reichsführer*.

—Herr Himmler, I have a request to make.

The other men may have been taken aback by her boldness. But the two SS were the same age, and Himmler had long approved of Langefeld's organizational abilities.

Pointing to her five assistants, she said, "These women are the most senior prisoners here. They have worked hard, and I believe they have served their prison terms with honor and dignity. I depend on them and have never had any issues with them. I beg you to recognize their prison terms completed."

Luise Mauer could not believe Langefeld was making good on her promise. Having been in prison since 1935, she had never allowed herself to imagine freedom under the Third Reich. She was considered a traitor to her country because she was a communist. Himmler turned his owl eyes toward Mauer and addressed her directly. "Why are you in prison?"

Mauer thrust out her chest and spoke directly and honestly. "I was first arrested in 1933. My husband was a council member of the KPD (Kommunistische Partei Deutschlands—The Communist Party of Germany) in Hessen. In 1935, I was arrested again and sentenced to four years for treason. At the end of the trial, I was taken to Ravensbrück, then in spring this year came to Auschwitz."

"You were a communist," Himmler said, looking disgusted. "Are you still one?"

Despite the possible repercussions of her response, Mauer bravely answered, "Yes!"

Nearby, SS Maximilian Grabner was stunned by her answer, but Himmler continued his interrogation. "And what is your view now of the National Socialist state?"

"Since 1933 I have only known prison and concentration camp, so I can only feel negatively toward the National Socialist state."

"I will therefore give you the opportunity to get to know our new state. I release you!" Mauer looked doubtfully at Langefeld and the SS superiors around her.

"But Herr Himmler!" SS Grabner blurted. "She is irredeemable and politically untrustworthy!"

Himmler squinted through the pince-nez on his nose and cleaned the lenses. "Despite that, I am releasing her. But before I do, she will have to work in the house of the Waffen-SS." He turned to Langefeld and asked her a few additional questions about Mauer, then turned back to the prisoner. "The supervisor says you are a cook. You can serve there as a cook." It was a probationary position. In fact, four of the five kapos would not be released for another year or two. Only Bertel Teege was freed immediately.

As Teege left under the iron gates inscribed with the motto *Arbeit Macht Frei*, she could not have helped but be aware that she was one of the lucky few to actually work her way to freedom.

THE INSPECTION OF the women's camp was paramount for Himmler's visit, but this was no normal roll call. Released from their own inspection, the kapos joined the SS women in shouting at the girls to strip naked before the *Reichsführer* of the *Schutz-staffel (SS)*. Hesitation was addressed with whips. Pulling off their filthy Russian uniforms, the girls were ordered to "Move out! March!" past Himmler, Höss, and the other male inspectors.

—Hold out your left arm! Straight in front of you!

They were too scared to be embarrassed. Eyes forward, teeth clenched, the girls held their left arms straight out in front of them, palms facing Himmler. "If they had made us hold out our right hand, I would have been selected to die," Joan (#1188) says. She "had a big sore" on her right hand.

In the end, the only female prisoners who did die that day were twenty Jehovah's Witnesses who were used in a flogging technique demonstration. After they had been beaten to death, Himmler approved the flogging of women in camp.

Having succeeded in her request to have her favorite kapos released, Langefeld took an opportunity to ask Himmler to re-assign her to Ravensbrück, citing not only differences of opinion between Höss and herself, but also the lack of respect she was being shown by the male SS guards. In his own diaries, Höss repeatedly complained about Langefeld, and it is likely he had already voiced his displeasure with her to Himmler. Himmler denied her petition and further undermined her position as supervisor by instructing Höss that the female kapos should be allowed to "vent their evil on prisoners."

A number of these kapos were already in prison for murder, and Himmler now gave them license to kill—Jews. What little control Langefeld had had over those malevolent kapos was now lost, but it was the Jewish women who truly would suffer.

AT THE END of the day, the SS-Reichsführer concluded his business with Höss in a private meeting where he told the commandant that under no circumstances should Sipo (Security Police) operations be stopped, least of all because of lack of accommodations. He ordered Höss to complete the construction of the Birkenau camp and to kill all Jewish prisoners unfit for work. Finally, in recognition of his work and performance, Höss was promoted to SS Lt. Colonel.

The 999 girls Bertel Teege had seen arriving on March 26—or those who were left—would not be so lucky as to leave Auschwitz. With the Russian POWs almost entirely extinguished and the construction on the brick blocks nearly finished, Lt. Colonel Rudolph Höss made good on his promotion. Three weeks after Himmler's visit, Höss determined that Birkenau was ready to receive female prisoners.

Chapter Twenty

August 1, 1942: At morning roll call, the occupancy level of Auschwitz-Birkenau is 21,421 male prisoners, including 153 Russian POWs. The occupancy of the women's camp is not known; since the relevant documents are missing, it cannot be established.
—DANUTA CZECH, Auschwitz
Chronicle, 1939–1945

WHEN THE SUN ROSE over the women's bald heads on August 8, it was already hot. Flies buzzed amid the filthy prisoners' bodies packed against one another at morning roll call. There was nothing unusual about the day. Somnambulists in Russian uniforms, the girls broke into their work details as usual, but on the other side of the guard gate, an entire section of girls was diverted. With trepidation, the girls in the remaining work details turned to watch their friends and family march away down a long dirt road. They had no idea if they would see each other again.

Those marching away from the regular routine were suddenly on high alert. Trudging past fields of potatoes and over train tracks, they walked for almost thirty minutes before the shadows of fencing appeared in the distance, and their destination became clear. Ravens croaked and flapped overhead.

TODAY, THE WALK between Auschwitz and Birkenau has a highway overpass that looks down on a switchback of functioning train tracks, part of the Oświęcim station, not far from what is now the State Museum of Auschwitz-Birkenau. Buses and taxis transport crowds of visitors in a few minutes between the two camps so that visitors do not have to endure the forty-minute walk. To cross Birkenau itself takes almost as long. For many prisoners, this was a trek they had to make twice a day, to and from work after upwards of ten to twelve hours of heavy labor. They had no water bottles, no energy bars. They were sustained by nothing but a crust of bread, putrid tea, and mostly rotten vegetable and horsemeat soup.

From the highway overpass, it is hard to imagine the emptiness of the countryside back in 1942. Today, the fields of potatoes and other crops, which probably existed then, too, still surround the complex, but there are also housing developments. Commuter traffic whizzes by the ominous death gate, which looms like a historic shadow across the flat, monochromatic landscape. In 1942, when the girls marched across the fields to Birkenau, that brick structure, so commonly identified with Auschwitz-Birkenau did not even exist yet. As they entered through the wire fenced gate, a wind swept across the steppe. There was no *Arbeit Macht Frei* sign. Only a few wooden watchtowers had recently been built. This vast space contained hardly anything but fifteen brick buildings in three rows and kilometers of barbed-wire fences. A few single-story office buildings had been built to serve the SS and their functionaries, but mostly there were low rectangular brick and wood buildings for housing and a few offices.

Over the next two years Birkenau would expand to become the largest death camp of all time. The equivalent of 319 football fields, the size of Birkenau is unfathomable, even today. From a bird's-eye view, Birkenau looks more like a giant Monopoly game board of brown plastic houses in orderly rows than a death camp. Walking from one end of it to the other is exhausting, yet Edith and the other girls had to cross their section of it many times a day—to go to the toilet, to scrounge for food, eventually to sneak over to the still-to-be-created hospital ward.

The women's section, which Himmler had urged Höss to complete in a timely fashion, was on the left of the main entrance. The section on the right of the main camp road were green wooden barracks that would house the overflow from the men's camp, now to be referred to as Auschwitz I.

BACK IN AUSCHWITZ I, the girls who had been left behind worried about those who had disappeared. Where had the others been taken? Were they ever going to return? A whisper campaign by the few humane kapos assured them that the missing female prisoners had been transferred to a new camp. The next morning, when another large group of work details headed in the same direction, those still heading to work stayed calm, albeit wary. It took four days for the entire women's camp to be moved from Auschwitz I to Birkenau. Linda remembers that girls who were too ill to walk to the new location were offered transportation in the back of trucks. "Those were the first girls who were [formally] gassed in August 1942." Their deaths were not recorded.

During the transfer, a problem arose with the numbering system. Women arriving on the Slovak transports were being immediately processed and registered in Birkenau. However, there were still women from the July transports being numbered and registered in Auschwitz I, and the numbers of the female prisoners had been mistakenly duplicated. It took a few days to bring the numbers back into a consecutive sequence and to fix the replicated numbers—how is not clear. Perhaps the old number was crossed out and a new number tattooed below, but there is no record of that happening. It is more likely that the duplicate number bearers were simply removed from the prison system—meaning they were killed.

BIRKENAU WAS TRUE nothingness. "It was bare," Linda says. "No roads—lots of dust. You didn't see a green leaf—nothing." The Russian POWs who had been there had eaten the grass. Not long after they arrived, the girls began eating the grass, as well.

The soil in Birkenau was clay, and under the hot sun it hardened like cement. When it rained, the clay softened and sucked the feet of prisoners into it, twisting muscles, rotting flesh, and worse. In their wooden clappers, the Dutch girls would go scrounging for food near the kitchen, but the mud was treacherous. Margie Becker says, "They drowned in the mud. Nobody lifted a finger. They just drowned in the mud there. They were too delicate, too beautiful" to survive Auschwitz-Birkenau.

Block 13 stabled many of the girls from Humenné, including Edith, her sister Lea, Helena Citron (#1971) and Irena Fein (#1564). A few blocks away, Bertha Berkowitz (#1048) would end up in Block 27 with her best friend from home, Peshy Steiner. She probably did not yet know Margie Becker (#1955) from Humenné, or Elena Zuckermenn (#1735) from Poprad, but they were about to become good friends and coworkers.

Inside their new "homes," Edith found dirt floors and "boards with a little straw on them. In the summer, we would take off a little bit of our clothes and use them as pillows." Who would have thought they would miss the thin and uncomfortable straw mattresses of Auschwitz? Or the threadbare blankets? Now, Edith and the others had nothing but rags, probably left over from the Russian soldiers who had died building these brick tombs.

A brick dividing wall ran down the center of the block. Three tiers of wooden shelves, or *koyas*, were fitted into each horse stall–size section, lining the brick walls on both sides of dirt-floor aisles. The blocks had the same layout as the stables that had once served the Polish cavalry, where the Russian POWs had been held. Originally, each stable was supposed to accommodate eighteen horses. At the entrance were two larger rooms: one for tack and one for grooming and mucking-out equipment. This layout would now accomodate human beings. The front rooms housed block and room elders, who were in charge of doling out food in the morning and evening and assigning petty jobs, like cleaning the blocks. They were also responsible for keeping accurate records of the girls living—and dying—in the block. Initially, each block housed about five hundred girls, but it was only a matter of time before overcrowding would alter the sleeping arrangements from six girls per *koya* to ten, and the blocks would hold one thousand women or more. Sleeping near one of the cast-iron stoves was essential in the cold, dank blocks, where temperatures in the winter months regularly fell to minus thirty degrees Celsius.

As bad as Auschwitz I had been, it had felt more communal and even looked like a small town. Birkenau felt like, and was, a wasteland. The only thing growing nearby was the birch forest at the far end of the *lagerstrasse* from which the camp took its name. There were other things to miss about Auschwitz I, too. There had been water dripping in the basements and a few sinks and toilets inside the building. Now the girls had to cross the camp to reach the so-called lavatory, which was made of wooden slabs with fifty-eight holes placed over an open sewer. "Can you imagine thousands of girls going to the latrine and [being given] only five minutes, not even [to go]? Everybody wanted to go!"

Sinks consisted of a metal trough with ninety spigots, but the water was contaminated and anyone drinking it got dysentery. Eventually, there would be ten toilet and sink barracks, but in the first few months, those were still under construction. The overcrowding at Auschwitz I had been temporarily solved—the poor hygiene had not. Girls were not allowed to go to the latrines at night, so in emergencies they had to use their red bowls and then try to scrub them clean with dirt the next morning before they were served tea. To make it to the latrine before roll call, you had to get up before dawn ahead of thousands of others. "It was just horrible, no facilities, no toilet paper, no nothing. Sometimes we tore off from the shirt a piece of cloth. It was just unreal."

New arrivals suffering the same stomach problems from the rancid soup were wearing dresses now, and without toilets readily at hand and no underwear, they "had diarrhea running down their legs." Fouling yourself was reason to be killed, but there was no hiding accidents. When a transport arrived and a few hundred new girls were taken into camp, it meant a few hundred more girls all running to the toilets at the same time. In the rush, girls sometimes fell through the holes in the latrine and drowned in the sewage below. Of all the possible ways to die in Auschwitz, falling into the latrine was the death Bertha feared the most.

For many of the girls, Birkenau was the final blow. As bad as Auschwitz had been, a gossamer film of hope had covered their experience, supported by religious faith. Now hope was gone. In Auschwitz I, girls had jumped to their deaths from the second-floor windows to commit suicide. With that option taken from them, there was only one way out. Edith says, "Many committed suicide going to the high voltage [fences]. In the morning, it was like a Christmas tree. People, you know, charred, dark" hanging on the wires.

Auschwitz I was purgatory to Birkenau's hell.

Chapter Twenty-one

Do men learn from women? Often. Do they admit it
publicly? Rarely, even today.

— ELENA FERRANTE

THE TOWN OF HOLÍČ IS the site of the easternmost continental European excavation of Neolithic *menhirs* to date—a Slovak Stonehenge. In the 1940s, it had a small Jewish community of 360 people who must all have been "rehomed" by the time the harvest festival celebrations were getting underway on August 15, 1942. Why else would President Tiso have decided to commemorate the occasion in this midsize border town, eighty kilometers from Bratislava?

With his thick bulldog neck and priest's collar tucked beneath a double chin wattle, Tiso was both ferocious and charismatic. Outside a church, farmers carried maize and sheaves of wheat. Girls in white lace smocks and embroidered skirts, with long braids and floral headbands, lined up along the road to welcome their president with Heil Hitler salutes. Even the men were dressed in traditional costumes. It had been a good year. Prosperity was increasing, and President Tiso wanted to make sure the Christians of his country knew why things were going so well. Stepping up to the podium, he looked down upon his adoring citizens with stern, fatherly kindness.

"People ask if what is happening now is Christian. Is it humane?" he bellowed to the gentiles of Holíč, newly freed of their Jewish neighbors. "Is it not just looting?" His microphone crackled. "But I ask: Is it not Christian when the Slovak nation wants to defeat an eternal enemy, the Jew? Is that not Christian? Loving thyself is a commandment of God, and that love commands me to remove everything that harms me, that threatens my life. And I believe nobody needs much convincing that the Slovak Jewish element has always been such a threat to our life, and I don't think I need to convince anyone of that fact!" The townsfolk cheered and waved sheaves of wheat.

"Would it not look worse if we had not cleansed ourselves of them? And we did it according to God's commandment. Slovaks, go and get rid of your worst canker!...What did the British promise the Jews before World War I, just to extract money from them? They promised them a state and got nothing in return. And you see, Hitler asked nothing from them and even so is now giving them a state!"

That "state" was Poland's death camps.

Fake news was no longer just on the rise—it was the only news available, disseminated through the Hlinka Guard's propagandist newspaper, *Gardista*. One article published in November 1942 was titled "*Ako ziju zidia v novom domove na vychode?*" or "How are Jews living in their new homes on the outskirts?" The center photo shows young Jewish women wearing crisp white pinafores and kerchiefs, smiling into the camera. "They don't look embarrassed to death," the caption reads. In the next column, "a Jewish policeman is proud to have his photograph taken." The rhetoric was so manipulative that even the less gullible seemed to swallow it, perhaps because they could not bear to believe their own good fortune was due to the misfortunes of Jewish former friends and neighbors. One gentile

pensioner so believed the *Gardista* newspaper about the successful rehoming of Jews that he sent a postcard to the Minister of
the Interior, Alexander Mach, complaining that elderly Jews
were receiving better treatment than he, an aging Slovak citizen,
was. He asked to be given the same treatment as they were.

The ability people have to believe that government policies
targeting minorities are not racist or unfair was not unique to the
1940s. Modern regimes have been equally guilty of repackaging
genocide under the guise of immigration policies, religious convictions, ethnic purity, or economics. The common factor is
always that the first victims are the most vulnerable, and least
"valuable," in the targeted culture. By August 15, 1945, thousands
of women and children had been killed in the new gas chambers.
Only the fittest and "luckiest" women were still alive.

On the same day that President Tiso was congratulating
himself on his Christian values, 2,505 men, women, and children from Poland and Holland arrived in Auschwitz—yet only
124 men and 153 women would be registered in camp. Within
ten days of being relocated to Birkenau, the women's camp
population expanded by almost two thousand. A fresh new
slave workforce was ready to replace the "old-timers," worn-
out girls who had been there for almost five months.

THERE IS NO CONCRETE DATE in the *Auschwitz Chronicle* confirming the first selection of registered female prisoners to be gassed,
but we know from survivors that it happened shortly after they
arrived in Birkenau. We also know from the Auschwitz "Death
Books" that at least twenty-two women from the first transport
died on 15 August. It is the first time that so many registered
women were documented as dying in one particular day. And
that is evidence that the first selection of female prisoners happened on August 15, immediately after morning roll call.

Whispers passed through the lines. Why weren't they being
sent out to work? What was going on? Was it good or bad? No

one knew what the word "selection" meant. Selected for what? Forced to stand under the hot sun, feeling more blisters erupt on their bare heads and necks, unable to seek shade as the hours passed, the girls shifted their feet and looked around.

Many of the girls who had been in camp since March "couldn't stand straight. Or had marks. Bruises," Linda recalls. And then they "had to undress." This is a fact that many survivors—even memoirists, like Rena Kornreich—gloss over or avoid mentioning in their testimonies. Selections were made in the nude. That way the girls could not hide open sores or wounds, skeletal figures, or rashes. Frida Benovicova had gone to school with Edith when they were girls. Now the eighteen-year-old and her twenty-three-year-old sister, Helen, moved to the front of the line. Rena Kornreich (#1716) was standing just a few rows away and saw one of the sisters being told by the SS to go to the right. The other was told to go to the left.

"Please don't separate me from my sister!" One of the sisters fell to her knees and begged for mercy. No one knew for sure what the directions meant. Whatever the circumstance, the sisters wanted to stay together. The SS man looked down at the begging girl and flicked his hand. Frida scrambled after Helena and hugged her close.

Naked, the two walked hand in hand toward flatbed trucks, where they were herded roughly aboard. Rena had no idea who the girls were, but she recognized the sisters from the first transport and believed that their numbers were 1000 and 1001. Wherever they were going, she knew "it couldn't be good."

It would take seventy-five years for me to find their family and learn their names.

Chapter Twenty-two

You hear me speak, but do you hear me feel?
—GERTRUD KOLMAR, "The Woman Poet"

ARRIVING IN BIRKENAU cemented the first girls' fears. Things were not going to get better. The only way to save themselves, and one another, was to get decent work. Of course, "decent work" could also be dangerous and unpleasant to perform.

Margie Becker had heard that they were looking for a detail of volunteers to carry corpses as part of a detail called the *leichenkommando,* and sought the advice of her friend, Hinda Kahan, the seventeen-year-old daughter of one of the Hasidic rabbis in Humenné. When Margie asked Hinda if she should take a job handling dead bodies, Hinda looked at her incredulously. "What's the matter with you? Just pretend that it's a brick. What do you care?"

Just as Margie was about to volunteer, Hinda came up with a better plan. Edita Engleman, from the first transport and also from Humenné, was working with Dr. Manci Schwalbova in the hospital and had heard the administration was about to add workers to the sewing detail. She knew Hinda's family from home and wanted to help her get a decent job. To get work as a seamstress was lifesaving. Best of all, it meant working inside and not having to face selections anymore.

—Stay home today. I'm going to try and get you into the sewing detail, Engleman told Hinda.

When there is good fortune for one, you share it with your friends, so Hinda told Margie, "Why don't you stay home with me? We can hide in the block, and we'll get into the sewing detail together." Margie told another friend of theirs.

It was a little bit like playing hooky from school, with far more disastrous consequences if they were caught, but the opportunity to get into the sewing detail seemed worth the risk.

They hid in the block, but when the count was over the kapos came looking for them. Margie and her friend got caught; Hinda did not. The two girls were forced into the very last work detail, which was overseen by one of the criminal "murderess" kapos who beat and killed girls for fun. It was "the worst detail." And because they were the last to be collected for work, they were in the end row of girls, so the SS let the guard dogs tear at their heels and their coats, and whipped them from behind as punishment for trying to hide. Throughout the twelve-hour shift, the girls were beaten and threatened by the SS and their dogs. "We were crying all day," says Margie.

After evening roll call, Margie and her friend returned to the block to find that there had been a selection. Anyone who had stayed "home" from work had been taken to the gas chambers. Hinda Kahan was gone.

"Edita Engelman tried to do her a favor because of the rabbi [Hilda's father], and she knew her from home. She wanted to be helpful, and that's what happened."

Now Hinda was dead.

"It was *bashert*," Margie says. Meant to be.

Was anything really meant to be in Auschwitz? Margie had to believe that it was; how else could she survive? Faith plays an important role in Margie's survival narrative—she was meant to survive, so she could tell the story of Hinda Kahan. It was a fatally hard lesson to learn.

The next day, Margie pinched her cheeks so that she looked healthy when she volunteered for the "privilege of carrying corpses." Among the other volunteers was another friend of Margie's, who had tied a kerchief over her head so that she looked better, "but she had swollen eyes and was a *candidate* already, so she didn't make it." Survivors use phrases like "candidate" (for the gas) and "didn't make it," again and again, as if they were in a competition seeking the finish line. In fact, that is not far from the truth—the competition for survival was won only by the fittest and the luckiest. Reaching the finish line meant life.

ONE OF THE other girls volunteering for "decent work" in the *leichenkommando* was Bertha Berkowitz (#1048). Even when she had been free, Bertha had suffered from feeling cold all the time. There was no way she would survive the winter if she did not get work that was inside most of the time. At the tender age of sixteen, she was adult enough and smart enough to scheme for her survival. She weighed the pros and cons of being on the *leichenkommando*. Was she strong enough to lift dead bodies? Could she bear to handle the flesh of girls she knew after they had died? Was doing such work worth an extra portion of bread? Was she emotionally and psychologically strong enough to handle the task?

The key to her decision to volunteer was witnessing the first mass selection of prisoners and learning that members of the *leichenkommando* would be exempt from selections. This was a job that could help her survive. "It was horrible," though. Among those volunteering with Bertha were Margie Becker (#1955), Elena Zuckermenn (#1735), and probably, Bertha's childhood friend Peshy Steiner.

The *leichenkommando* was the worst of the "decent work" details requiring manual labor. If the girls could have gotten into the laundry or sewing details, the package or mail room detail, or the farming detail, they would have tried. Caring for farm animals might have been psychologically and physically easier, but the test to get into the farming detail was brutal and potentially deadly.

With delicate feaures and a complexion as fresh as the flowers she was named for, Rose (#1371) had dark blond hair that she had often worn in long braids, when she had hair. She didn't look hardy, but she had been raised on a farm and knew how to work. Since her arrival, she had primarily worked in the farm construction detail in Harmęże, a few kilometers from both camps. This was a particularly brutal detail, overseen by an SS man who liked to wear a white suit instead of his uniform. They were all terrified of him, as his special form of entertainment was to throw an object outside of the boundary and order a girl to fetch it. It was a no-win situation: if the girl disobeyed the order he shot her for disobeying; if she obeyed the order he shot her for crossing the boundary and trying to escape. He wasn't the only SS who enjoyed this ruse—Juana Bormann "the woman with the dog," enjoyed doing the same thing, only she used her German shepherd instead of her gun to kill girls.

After the barns in Harmęże were finished, the SS created a physical test to discern which workers were fittest and deserved to work on the farm. Rose describes being forced to stand all day outside without moving. It was a particularly cold day, and periodically additional physical tests were given to the girls. At one point, they were forced to hold their arms out straight in front of them for an indeterminate amount of time; if their arms shook or they dropped them, they were taken away to be gassed. At the end of the day, they had to leap over a ditch. Those who completed all the tasks were then rewarded: they were moved into the newly built barrack and assigned farming tasks. Rose became responsible for raising rabbits and pheasants. She knew she was lucky to be there; she even worked under a kapo who was kind. Best of all, working in Harmęże meant living in a smaller, warmer barracks on-site. The food they were fed was also better. Rose describes a bright green *nässelsoppa*, nettle soup, rich in vitamins.

FOR GENERAL "FACTORY" WORKERS and girls with no special skill sets, the real life-saving work was in the sorting details, now referred to by prisoners as the red or white kerchiefs. As transports arrived from all over Europe, more and more items had to be sorted, and more and more girls were needed to do the work. The trick was getting into the detail. The "uniform" was a head scarf—either red or white. There was only one way to get one of those: steal one or trade your bread.

The best jobs in camp required a higher skill set than those of the "factory" laborers. "Functionaries" could type, take shorthand, were multilingual, or had neat cursive handwriting—skills that farm girls and most teenagers lacked. Having been in camp longer than any other Jewish women, many of the more experienced Slovak girls were savvy to positions in the SS secretarial pool and had early on claimed many of those jobs. Being older and having finished high school had its advantages, but teens like Edith, Adela, Magda Amster, and Nusi and Magduska Hartmann had been robbed of a high school education. If they didn't get into the sewing, farming, or sorting detail, their only other option was hard labor.

WE KNOW VERY LITTLE about Magduska and Nusi Hartmann's cousin, Lenka Hertzka, and her experience working for one of the top members of the Gestapo. However, because of her position, Lenka was able to write regular postcards and letters to family and friends; she received correspondence, as well. Her cards, letters, and occasional telegrams reveal often mundane

Milan Weinwürb
Prešov Slovensko
Levočska ul 31.

Liebe Lenke!

Da schon Alle Dir geschrieben haben,

versuche ich mein Glück! Wir sind ge-

sund, wenn nur unsere Tete bei

uns were. Immer denken und sprechen

wir von Dir und r Magdus. Käthe

hat mir gratuliert in Versechen. Ich

habe ihr Taschentucher geschickt. Wie

gerne mochten wir Dir etwas senden.

Schreibet mit Magdus küssen wir

Dich Alle.

Dein Milanko.

Gift of Eugene Hartmann in memory of Lenka Hertzka,
MUSEUM OF JEWISH HERITAGE, NEW YORK.

facts and requests for food, amid coded messages about family and friends. Lenka's cards were not the by-rote lies that the other prisoners were forced to write; sometimes, her cards were not even censored. Her family's correspondence back to her reveal confusion about her circumstances and constant questions that she could not answer.

The Hertzka and Hartmann correspondence continued for the next two years. One of the first people to write was Lenka's eight-year-old nephew, Milan:

> Dear Lenke: Since everybody wrote to you already,
> I try my luck. We are healthy. If only our aunt
> [Lenka herself] were with us. We are always talking
> about you and Magduska.
> How we would love to send you something.
> Write with Magduska. We all kiss you.
>
> Your Milanko

Secretarial functionaries—like the Hartmanns' cousin, Lenka Hertzka—lived outside the barbed-wire fences of Auschwitz I and Birkenau, in the basement of Stabsgebäude, the SS staff quarters. Here were real bunk beds, blankets, and even a shower. Because the secretarial girls lived and worked in close proximity to the SS, they had to be clean, well dressed, and attractive. That meant they were allowed to grow their hair. "Some even wore stockings." Although the work they performed was physically easier, they were provided with extra portions of bread. Some went so far as to become plump.

For those working hard labor, it was difficult to see some of the same girls they had arrived with in March parading around camp with an air of superiority, with their nicely coiffed hair and civilian clothing that had been taken from Jews. "We saw that there were people who were a little bit better off than we were,"

Edith says. "There were people who were repairing shoes or clothing, sitting and working in offices." They were the lucky ones, if any prisoner in Auschwitz can be considered lucky.

Some functionaries also worked within the barbed-wire fences—block elders, room elders, scribes. When "we went out to do hard work, we had to sing. We had to go to work even if we had a fever, but they stayed inside," Edith says. "All of the block elders survived. All of them."

Faced with the difficult position of pleasing the SS, the kapos and their peers, block elders were forced to discipline the girls in their blocks, many of whom they had grown up with. Edith received a "few spanks" from her block elder, who was on the first transport with her. The block elder and her sister had a terrible reputation but seventy-five years later, Edith is still hesitant to reveal their last names because she does not want to bring shame on the women's children and surviving family. The fact is, "if you survived the first transport, you most likely did something special, and that was not always nice."

Among the functionaries, "the most important thing was to obtain a position which would lift them out of the mass and give them special privileges, a job that would protect them to a certain extent from accidental and mortal hazards, and improve the physical conditions in which they lived," Höss confided in his diary. Auschwitz was already a cutthroat business, and among functionaries, it could be equally ruthless. It only took one misdeed to get reported and be instantly demoted back to Birkenau, or worse. According to Höss, the women "flinched from nothing, no matter how desperate, in their efforts to make such safe jobs fall vacant and then to acquire them for themselves. Victory usually went to the most unscrupulous man or woman. 'Necessity is the mother of invention,' and here it was an actual question of sheer survival."

Being granted a functionary position might save your life, but being powerless to save others—especially those you loved—created a complicated psychology for those in these coveted positions. And not everyone wanted these positions of importance. When Rena (#1716) turned down the chance to become a room elder, it was because she could not face the moral ambiguity of being in a position of power. "I can't take bread from others who are as hungry as me; I can't hit people suffering just like I am." No matter what position you held in Auschwitz, whether you worked hard labor, as a block or room elder, or as a secretary to the SS, a "'hard and indifferent armor' was required to survive."

"It frequently happened that persons who had acquired these safe positions would suddenly lose their grip, or would gradually fade away, when they learnt of the death of their closest relations. This would happen without any physical cause such as illness or bad living conditions." Höss specifically identified this as a Jewish weakness: "The Jews have always had very strong family feelings. The death of a near relative makes them feel that their own lives are no longer worth living, and are therefore not worth fighting for." What is surprising is that more functionaries did not give up.

Taking a functionary position meant girls might be able to help others, but it also meant they might not be well liked by the other prisoners. How could they be? They got more food, worked fewer hours, and did not have to endure selections. They also faced a moral conundrum—they were working for the very system that was liquidating their families, their culture, and their communities. Although many functionaries used their positions to help where they could, the sad truth is that a number of them did not act ethically or morally. For good reason they were ridiculed and despised by those in the general population. Survival and morality were often at cross-purposes in Auschwitz.

Of the girls from the early transports who got higher functioning positions, Dr. Manci Schwalbova writes, "they were often young girls whose whole family had been murdered, and some of them became reckless, having been infatuated by the experience in the most difficult period of camp. Some of them actually took delight in the exercise of the power which had been [given] to them. Luckily, they were few in number." She immediately adds that "in all departments you could have found women who did not hesitate to risk their own life to save other's lives."

Dr. Manci Schwalbova was one of those risk takers. It was essential that the Jewish doctors have access to medicines and extra food or they couldn't help prisoners survive. Malaria was rampant in the summer months, and quinine was needed. Typhus required rest and hydration; lemon water was the best prisoners could scrounge. An underground network was set up, which included many functionaries willing to risk their lives to help others by smuggling food and medicine into the hospital. In this respect, one of the most important of the work details was the "package room, where parcels were arriving for already dead women." From there, workers smuggled "unclaimed" food and medicines into the hospital to help the ill recover.

Block elders were also able to smuggle medicine to the girls in their blocks. Of course, they required payment, and that meant many girls went hungry to get something as simple as salve for a cut to prevent infection. Nothing was free anymore.

Those who suffered most were the girls who did not move up the ladder to better jobs and continued to do hard labor outside, demolishing buildings, making roads, digging clay to make bricks, making bricks. Standing knee deep in water, Lea and Edith continued to clean out swamps and drainage ditches, one of the worst details. As fall descended and it got colder, Edith began to feel an ache in her knee that would not go away.

Chapter Twenty-three

Birkenau really began the death camp.
—EDITH GROSMAN

ON SEPTEMBER 2, DR. JOHANN PAUL KREMER—a seriously unattractive, wild-eyed, balding monster of a man—arrived to replace one of the camp doctors who had fallen ill from typhus. On his first day of orientation, the geneticist and professor of anatomy from the University of Münster observed the disinfection of prisoners, the delousing of a block with Zyklon B gas, phenol injections that killed sick prisoners, and the gassing of 545 French men and boys and 455 women and girls. A meticulous diarist, Kremer entered on a pristine page of paper that night: "Present for the first time at a special operation, outside at three o'clock in the morning. In comparison with this, Dante's *Inferno* seems almost like a comedy. Not for nothing is Auschwitz called the camp of extermination!" It did not seem to disturb him in the least.

At noon a few days later, Dr. Kremer accompanied the Troop Doctor Master Sergeant Thilo to Block 25, where skeletal women and girls were "sitting on the ground" in the courtyard outside. Hanging off their bodies were the filthy, threadbare uniforms of Russian soldiers. Horrified by the hollow-eyed, living ghosts, Dr. Thilo turned to his colleague and said, "We are here at the *anus mundi* [anus of the world]." It was women he was referring to.

The "stumbling corpses" in the courtyard of Block 25 were known as *musselmen* (racist slang meaning Muslims), which meant a prisoner beyond hope. These ill and starved men and women were more feared than pitied. No one wanted to come close to these physical reminders of what every prisoner was in danger of becoming: a modern-day zombie, a golem, a human being becoming inhuman. Infatuated with their power to dehumanize and destroy, the SS called them a "terrible sight," "the most ghastly of the ghastly." Prisoners, equally terrified by the sight of these frail skeletons, tried to be kinder, saying the women were "not quite alive, yet not quite dead." There was a deep-seated fear among prisoners of becoming so physically frail and spiritually obliterated, becoming one of those for whom "the spirit God breathed into their souls has been utterly sucked out." They feared it was contagious. In fact, disease was largely responsible for these prisoners' deterioration.

Dr. Kremer witnessed these undead being forced onto flatbed trucks and transported outside the women's section toward the gas chambers. Here, they were not even allowed the dignity of entering the changing room, where Jews disrobed before entering the "showers." Instead, they were forced to take their clothes off outside so that their uniforms could be burned instead of disinfected. Bared to the elements, some spirit arose from within and they pleaded for their lives.

—Have pity, they cried and begged the SS men. "They were all driven into the gas chamber and gassed."

"GIRLS WERE DYING daily, by the tens and hundreds," Edith says. Even if a girl couldn't walk, she had to come out to roll call and get counted before being carted off to the gas. "I knew a girl from Humenné who was brought to the count in a wheel-barrow, the same wheelbarrow that was being used to bring bricks from buildings." She does not remember the girl's name.

When girls didn't have the strength to get up and go to roll call, they were beaten by the block and room elders. One girl had been beaten for not getting up to work and was left sitting against the wall on her *koya*. They counted her without realizing that she had died. Margie Becker says, "She was sitting with her eyes open" for a few days. Nobody noticed.

The battering-ram winds of fall swept off the stark steppe and into the barracks of Birkenau, which were less airtight than those in Auschwitz. It cut through the cracks in the mortar, bit the tender flesh of the poorly dressed girls. With no natural windbreak, howling winds haunted their exhausted sleep. Threadbare blankets—one per three girls—barely covered their frail bodies. As they huddled closely together for warmth, it only took one cough on the blanket to pass bacteria. Lice crawled from one sleeping girl to another, spreading disease without prejudice—it killed SS and prisoners alike.

Typhus is a disease that thrives on war, famine, and disaster, and Auschwitz was a perfect storm for an epidemic: it had over-crowding, a lack of hygiene, and body lice. "The battle against pests was central, and [they] became a deadly enemy," kapo Luise Mauer remembers. With no way to shower, bathe, or launder their filthy uniforms, prisoners were at their mercy. Despite monthly delousings, typhus spread undeterred, moving from rat to prisoner, from prisoner to prisoner, from prisoner to captor. "In Auschwitz, whole streets are struck down with typhus," Dr. Kremer wrote in his diary. "First Lieutenant Schwartz is sick with it."

"The girls' camp suffered the most. The poor wretches were covered with lice and fleas," Rudolf Vrba would write with Al-fréd Israel Wetzler in "The Auschwitz Report" a year and a half later. The camp was ill-fitted with sanitary installations for the number of women using the facilities. The only potable water was in "one small lavatory, to which a common prisoner did not have access."

The ill and dying were so plentiful that they were discarded outside, behind the hospital blocks. Left lying there, these unfortunate girls and women were gathered up like so much wood to stoke the crematorium. One day not long after they had arrived in Birkenau, Margie Becker heard her name being called from among the dying on the ground in the hot sun.

"Water, please…"

In their 1938–1939 class photo taken in Humenné, Zena Haber stood in the center of the back row, towering over the other girls. Slouching forward, she looks uncomfortable with her height and her body. It must not have been popular to smile in photos in those days, as almost no one did. Hands are clasped in laps or behind backs. Only Edith, standing in the back row near Zena, is open armed; her hands touch the girl sitting below her, a friend whose name she no longer remembers. Zena's light hair curls back off her face. Chin down, she appears to be glaring at the camera, but there is just enough of an upturn to her mouth to imagine a budding smile, had the camera clicked just a second later.

"She was a beautiful tall girl," Margie says. Now her friend since girlhood, a fellow teenager, was dying.

It was a hot day. The sun beat down on their bodies. Zena Haber had sores on her body and a canker on her lips. There was no water. No mercy. Just a beautiful young woman dying of thirst and disease, neglected by the world. Margie felt forlorn and guilt-ridden—she had nothing to give her friend, had no way to help. And she was afraid to touch her. What if she caught Zena's disease? Torn between her own sense of self-preservation and her desire to aid her friend, Margie apologized to Zena and scurried away.

———

TYPHUS CAME ON ABRUPTLY, often while girls were at work. Joan Rosner's joints ached so badly that she had to stop digging in order to catch her breath. Leaning on her shovel, she felt pain sear through her limbs.

"Straighten up!" one of her friends whispered.

Joan (#1188) tried to right herself, but she was too weak.

"Attack!" the SS woman ordered. They heard a scrambling of paws against dirt. Its hot, stinking breath slapped her face as the dog clamped down on her arm, which had risen spontaneously to protect her throat. The dog's teeth sank into her bicep as she tried to defend herself. For some reason, the SS woman called the dog off, and he did not kill her. Bleeding from the neck and arm, Joan resumed shoveling like mad. Head down. Digging. Digging. Nonstop. Through the pain. Blood throbbed in her temples. Feverish. Digging. At the end of the day, Joan made it through the gate without being called to one side, then collapsed onto the *koya*, where she slept without getting any bread. In the middle of the night she sat up in her bunk.

"I am going home." She crawled off the shelf.

"Joan! Where are you going?" one of her friends called after her.

"My mother is waiting for me in the carriage," she said matter-of-factly and walked out of the block.

Going outside after curfew was dangerous, but her shelf-mate woke a few other girls, and they ran after Joan, who was walking purposefully toward the electric fence and what she thought was her mother's carriage.

They grabbed her and struggled to keep her from reaching the wire. Feverish and delusional, she fought them.

—Where's my mother? she asked.

—What are you doing here?

She looked around at the camp. The watchtowers. The searchlights.

—Where am I?

Under cover of night, they sneaked Joan to the camp hospital. She needed salve and medicine for the dog bites and cool compresses to bring down the fever tormenting her mind. Selections were still a relatively new occurrence, so the girls probably did not know that Joan could be killed for convalescing. All they knew was that she would be killed if she tried to go to work in the morning.

Enter Dr. Manci Schwalbova. Manci had a soft spot in her heart for the Slovak girls and tried to do whatever she could to help them. But at that point, the only medication available for Jewish prisoners was charcoal. We "got charcoal for everything," Joan says. She was lucky to get that; by October, Jews would not be allowed any medical intervention at all.

The hospital might not have been able to offer much in the way of medicine, but at least Joan was able to rest in an actual bed and get hydrated. Her fever abated, and the puncture wounds from the dog's teeth closed up. But life was never a sure thing in Auschwitz. Just as she was beginning to recover, one of the doctors came through the ward and chose ten girls to come to his office, where he was beginning to conduct experiments. Joan was one of those girls. Fortunately, when they arrived at his office, the electricity had gone out. The doctor sent the girls back to the hospital and said, "Come back tomorrow."

Joan wasn't *that* sick! She knew her life depended on not returning to the hospital and went straight back to her block, to disappear into the anonymity of the thousands of women around her. The respite had helped her recover, but for weeks afterward, Joan's girlfriends had to help her past the SS, who hovered like vultures at the gate, eager to feed ill prisoners to the gas. She had five friends she depended on. They were always together—always helping each other. She does not report their names in her testimony.

"To have someone who watched over you was very important," Martha Mangel (#1741) says. "Everybody watched out for somebody." For Martha, that somebody would be her eldest cousin, Frances Mangel-'Tack, who had arrived on the fourth transport and gotten a position early on as a block elder, like her cousin, Frida Zimmerspitz. Both block elders were attractive, smart, and devious. Eta Zimmerspitz (#1756) says that soon after they arrived in camp, Frida complained to one of the SS men that the kapos had stolen their food and the man sneaked her some ham. "We wept," Eta recalls, but "we ate it."

Frida became block elder for Block 18 and gave all three of her sisters positions as room elders or block scribes. Their cousin, Frances, would not remain a block elder. Instead she would become one of the few Jewish kapos in Auschwitz, a position that would make her infamous among prisoners.

Rosh Hashanah, the Jewish New Year and High Holy days, arrived with the first blush of fall. Golden birch leaves flickered to the ground, covering the mass burial pits with blankets of yellow. Murmurations of starlings swooped above a sea of suffering humanity. With new arrivals coming into the camp, the first girls were able to learn when Yom Kippur started. As the sun went down behind the watchtowers, many girls, despite their gnawing hunger, began to fast.

"What did I fast from?" Bertha Berkowitz (#1048) asks. "We fasted all the year, but I fasted."

Fasting renewed their faith and spirit, gave them courage to resist the temptation of despair. Despite the daily injustices they were suffering, the SS could not take away their faith.

It was not unusual for the SS to use Jewish holidays as an opportunity to punish Jews and foul sacred traditions. A few weeks after Yom Kippur, the Jewish harvest holiday arrived. Sukkot is considered a happy celebration of harvest and plenty, so it was the perfect moment to make a harvest of Jews. Starting on the first of October and over the next three days, the women's camp did no work at all. Instead, the girls were forced to stand at attention all day long—naked—waiting to march past the selection committee, which gave the thumb to life or the thumb to death—to the left or to the right. By the end of Sukkot, 5,812 women had been sent to the gas. The hospital ward was empty.

Chapter Twenty-four

The bonds between these women were unbreakable.
They were extraordinary. They all saved each other.
　　　　　　　—ORNA TUCKMAN, daughter
　　　　　　　　　of Marta F. Gregor (#1796)

EMOTIONALLY AND PHYSICALLY, BEING IN the *leichenkommando* would be a tough assignment. Bertha's friends asked her, "Why would you want to do something like this?"

"I am afraid for winter," Bertha explained.

She was right to be afraid. At least in the *leichenkommando* she no longer had to march out and work from dawn to dusk. She got a double portion of food and was relieved of standing for hours every morning and night for roll call. Being housed in Block 27, which was next to the hospital wards, she became close with Dr. Manci Schwalbova and the other Jewish female doctors. All of them kept a close eye on the girls working in the *leichenkommando* because it was a high-risk job. Fortunately, one of the SS doctors was in love with one of the Jewish female doctors, and she got him to give the girls gloves to wear while they handled the corpses. She also convinced him that the girls needed to wash their hands with soap, so they were granted permission to go into the one washroom with potable water and wash up. After they had handled contaminated corpses all day, this was essential to maintain their health.

But those hygienic measures were not what Bertha remembers most. After handling the dead all day, feeling the greasy residue from the smoke and ash falling down from the crematorium chimneys and the dust kicked up by the trucks as they carted the dead to the crematoriums, what Bertha remembers was washing her face with clean water. "You have no idea what it means to wash your face."

Somehow, Margie Becker (#1955) was able to organize a container and fill it with water. When she brought the water "home" to the block, she hid it, thinking she would use it every day to wash her hands and face—that was how important feeling clean was to her. "But I didn't have the heart. People were dying of thirst. [I] couldn't just go waste water on washing a face." She gave the water to the less fortunate in her block.

The daily routine for those in the *leichenkommando* was vastly different than that of the rest of the details in camp. In the morning, the *stubenmädchen*—or chambermaids—would pile the dead outside their blocks before roll call so that the numbers of dead were tallied. After the work details marched out, Bertha and the others in the *leichenkommando* began to collect the bodies and carried them to the *leichenhalle,* a storage shed behind Block 25 where the bodies were kept until the men arrived with trucks to take them to the crematoriums.

The protocol for recording women's deaths had started in August, not long after the girls had been relocated to Birkenau. A scribe accompanied the *leichenkommando* on their daily rounds, recording the registration numbers of the dead so that they could be removed from the camp register. By the next roll call, the SS knew exactly how many prisoners were still living and working in the camp.

Collecting the bodies of those who had grabbed the wire in the night could only be done after the work details had marched out of camp for their day of work and the electricity could be turned off at the main switch. Once it was safe, Bertha and the others had to release the fingers, stiff with rigor mortis, from their death grasp and emancipate the charred bodies of friends and fellow prisoners from the wires.

The bodies of suicide victims were not limp—they were puppets dangling, grotesquely stiff. They did not fold neatly into wheelbarrows. Limbs stuck out at uncompromising angles. Though the Talmud states that taking one's own life is against Jewish tradition, suicides were frequent. "I lost a lot of friends on the wires," Linda Reich (#1173) says. It was hard to witness, but in the end the girls who chose that way out were not blamed by their friends. It was one of the few ways you could control your own life, by deciding your own death.

WHEN THE GAS chambers were backed up and couldn't take any more bodies, the sick were taken to Block 25, which was heavily guarded by SS. It was usually full of ill girls and women who had not made it into the hospital or had tried to hide instead of going to work. Block 25—the sick block—was really a death block.

One of the hardest parts of working in the *leichenkommando* was finding your friends' or family's corpses, or worse, finding them dying in Block 25. Factory workers in an industry where death was a by-product, Bertha and the others did their best to respect their dead friends. "We would be very careful with their bodies. I asked for forgiveness of the dead person before we threw it on the truck to be taken to the crematorium," Bertha says. In the beginning, she tried to remember the dates of friends who died, "just in case I survived, I should be able to tell [their families] what date it was, so they could honor the anniversary of death."

Not everything the girls of the *leichenkommando* did was admirable. Margie confesses that she sometimes smuggled clothing from dead girls and sold their sweaters, socks and shoes for extra bread or margarine. One day, as she was clearing out the dead in Block 25, Margie heard Klary Atles's voice among the dying.

"I don't have a blanket," Klary said as Margie walked by. She barely recognized the rabbi's daughter who had tried to feed their spirits with her fervent faith in those first days in camp. Looking up at Margie with sweet compassion, Klary whispered, "I'm so sorry I didn't know you at home."

Although the community of Humenné was close, Klary and Margie came from different social classes and had not had much opportunity to become acquainted. Not only were their ages different, but Klary's parents had sent her to a private school in Budapest. Margie had not even finished high school. "We had different worlds, you know, so I had nothing to do with her." They were now equals in nothingness. Death has no class or status.

Helpless to save Klary, Margie could only give what little she had, not a blanket to fight the chills, but the assurance that she too wished they had spent more time together in freedom and been friends, and a last comfort of human connection.

AFTER THE MORNING shift of collecting the dead from the night before, the *leichenkommando* girls had their lunch break and an extra portion of bread with their soup. At two o'clock in the afternoon, the men arrived in a truck at the back of Block 25 to empty the *leichenhalle*. As the drivers waited, the girls lifted the corpses they had collected and carried them to the back of the truck. They worked quickly. The *leichenhalle* was not the sort of place one wanted to linger, but whenever they found one of their friends among the dead, all of the girls stopped to pray. "We asked for forgiveness and said the

Kaddish in Yiddish before their bodies were taken to the crematoriums."

Their final shift was at the end of the day, when the prisoners returned in columns from their work details. Those who had died, been injured, or murdered were left outside the gate so that their numbers could be recorded. The bodies were then moved either directly to the crematorium or stored in the *leichenhalle*. Selections were "all the time" now. "Marching in and marching out, they had selections for us. You didn't have to be tall. You didn't have to be nice. Whoever they wanted, they took." The SS men often selected whole groups of healthy girls simply because they had the power to kill whomever they wished.

WORKING FOR THE *leichenkommando* may have given the girls extra food and allowed them to escape selections, but it did not protect them from typhus. Block 25 was rife with infectious disease, and though they had access to water for washing, the lice that carried the disease moved under the cover of sleep. One day, Margie walked past a glass window and caught sight of her reflection. "I looked like I was two hundred years old. I couldn't have looked older. I just couldn't believe it was me."

As she fell into the fever and nausea of typhus, the girls in her block hid her. "I gave them my bread, of course, because I was unable to eat." Fortunately, the work she did protected her so that she was able to recover. Later on, Margie reciprocated by helping those who had helped her.

Chapter Twenty-five

The barrack is nowadays overflowed with women of various nationalities, full of hubbub, din and arguments. There they are—Jewesses from Poland, Greece, Slovakia; there are Poles, swarthy Gypsies, and dark little Croatians. They don't understand one another. They fight for space, for blankets, for bowls, for a glass of water. Foreign-language shouts and curses can be heard constantly. One cannot fall asleep in here.
—SEWERYNA SZMAGLEWSKA (#22090)

IN 1942, THE SORTING DEPOT was in Auschwitz I, or the "mother camp," which had grown from one barrack to four. It was "so full of clothing from the whole of Europe," that the SS had to continually expand the area. Because the packages of clothing were shipped away from camp, the prisoners began to refer to the detail as Canada, a place far from the strife of war-torn Europe. A country still free.

After the men delivered the luggage from the transports, the girls in the white and red kerchiefs opened the bags and sorted the items inside. For the most part, the girls in the white kerchiefs sorted coats. The girls in the red kerchiefs sorted everything else.

Linda Reich (#1173) was responsible for sorting underwear and was known to smuggle up to five pairs at a time back to Birkenau so that girls wearing dresses could maintain some modesty and comfort. She doled out what she could to the girls in the block, but "you know how many things you can bring? Three—when you have thousands and thousands?" But she "gave it to whomever came." By now bread was currency, and desperate girls would willingly give up their daily meal for undergarments. Linda was one of those rare girls who did not trade necessities for bread. Others were not so generous—unless, of course, they knew each other from the same town or village. Bread may have been coinage, but friendship was life. You needed both to survive.

THE MORTALITY RATE for girls and women had escalated once they were in Birkenau, not only because the conditions were dangerously unhygienic, but because every week one or two large selections took place. "Be ready tomorrow morning in the row of white kerchiefs because one is dying," an old friend of Helena Citron's said, slipping a white kerchief into her hands. "By the morning, they will put her outside." It was the kind of news that in the normal world would bring sorrow; in Auschwitz it was good news, at least for Helena.

After roll call, Helena secured the white kerchief over her head and hurried over to where the sorting detail was lining up. A few of the girls in the white kerchiefs looked her way, but no one said anything. The girl she replaced was already a memory.

It was a three-kilometer march from Birkenau to Auschwitz I. And every morning, the girls with the white and red kerchiefs headed out the gate and marched back to the "mother camp," where they sorted clothes and other items until dark, and then marched the three kilometers back to Birkenau. Male prisoners working in Canada observed that "every day, new girls replaced those who had disappeared."

Marching out of the gate down the concrete road that led away from Birkenau, Helena stepped in time with the others. Head high, chest out, she looked just like the girls around her except for one detail—she was wearing clappers. Wearing clappers was a sure sign that she did not belong in the white kerchiefs, and the resounding clunk of wood against dirt attracted the kapo's attention.

"Who are you?" Rita, the kapo, demanded.

Helena showed her the number on her arm

—1971.

—You don't belong here! You will be reported.

Helena's nerves shredded. Every clunk of her clappers sent a shock through her bones and brought a glare from the kapo. Upon arriving at the sorting shed in Auschwitz I, the girls were counted again, and Rita ordered Helena to follow her into the office where the overseer of the detail sat at his desk. Rita informed him that prisoner #1971 had sneaked into the detail.

SS-Unterscharführer Franz Wunsch's temper flared. He blamed the kapo for not sending Helena back to Birkenau at once and accused her of not doing her job.

Listening to the two argue, "you'd think I was here in a life of pleasures," Helena says.

"I discovered her on the way!" Rita justified.

"How did you find out?"

"She's wearing flip-flops!" She pointed to Helena's ill-shod feet. Helena's stomach sank.

"Tomorrow! I want her tomorrow in the marsh!"

The marshes, where Edith and Lea were suffering, were fast becoming the punishment detail, because working in the grime and silt where bodies and ashes were being dumped made girls deathly ill.

Helena was sent back to the sorting table with Wunsch's death sentence over her head. The others took pity on her and gently showed her what to do, whispering encouragement and hope so that she would not lose herself to tears. Standing in front of a pile of clothes, Helena felt despair descend but tried to focus on the seams and folds of the coats in front of her. How could something as meaningless as a kerchief cost her her life?

All she wanted was to work under a roof, out of the wind and rain and snow. All she wanted was a job that allowed her to fold clothes, not make bricks, or dig clay, or push wagons through the mud, or wade through the marshes, doomed to a slow but certain death. Around her, girls were sneaking tidbits of food found in pockets. Did she dare to steal anything? She was already going to die. What was death twice over for an extra morsel of food?

The morning passed slowly. Helena stared a hole into the clothes she folded. Head down. Deliberate. Not daring to look up at the girls around her. At noon, the kettles of soup arrived, and the girls lined up with their red bowls. And here the story divides into two different versions. In the first version, it was Wunsch's birthday and Rita wanted someone to sing to him. However, Wunsch's birthday was on March 21, and from Helena's own testimony and that of other eyewitnesses, we know that she was in the white kerchiefs in the fall of 1942. So what really happened?

Here is a possible theory: Entertaining the SS was one of the ways kapos garnered favor, so as the girls were sipping their soup for lunch, it is possible that Rita announced she was looking for performing artists to entertain Wunsch—she needed to get back on his good side, after the verbal thrashing she had received that morning. So she announced that she needed girls who could sing and dance, and ordered them to eat quickly so that they could practice before surprising him in his office. Helena's friends knew that she had a beautiful voice and wanted to help her stay within the white kerchiefs. They announced that Helena could sing.

Rita looked critically at #1971. "You can sing?"

Helena's eyes stayed low on the ground. "No."

"Sing," the girls around her whispered encouragingly.

"You will sing!" Rita demanded. And that was that.

"Helena was very beautiful, and had a very, very nice voice. All of the Citrons did," Edith remembers. Considering Edith's own lovely voice, that is high praise indeed.

Helena had learned a romantic song from some German Jews, and that was the song she decided to sing. She waited off to one side while a few girls did their dance number, and then there was silence. Helena cleared her throat and softly began to sing the love song she had learned from the German prisoners. What was love in this place of death? What was life? Despite it all, she sang with her heart. The last note hung in the air. Blinking back a mist of tears, she tried not to quiver in front of the man who had ordered her death in the marshes.

"*Wieder singen*, sing again," Wunsch said, and then he did something unheard of. He said, "*Bitte*? Please."

Lifting her eyes from the floor, she saw the rank on his uniform, the brass buttons that were so polished they reflected her face. She had no voice to respond.

"Please, sing the song again."

She did.

At the end of the workday, Helena folded the last of the coats in her stack and sighed. That was that. Her life was over. A shadow loomed over her as the *SS-Unterscharführer* walked past. A note dropped at her fingertips.

It said *Liebe*. Love.

Then he ordered Rita to make sure that #1971 was at work in the sorting detail tomorrow.

The order clipped over Helena's head like the crack of a whip. The kapo could do nothing against the order. Helena was in the white kerchiefs, whether she still wanted to be or not.

———————

LIKE MOST SS, Wunsch was volatile and violent. Helena feared and hated him. But rejecting an SS officer could result in something far worse than accepting his advance; he could have her killed. Terrified, Helena left the work detail with another death sentence on her lovely head. And now began the real dilemma.

"I thought I would rather be dead than be involved with an SS man," Helena says. "For a long time afterwards, there was just hatred. I couldn't even look at him."

A year younger than Helena, the dashing, baby-faced Wunsch with his soulful eyes would have turned any German girl's eye. After getting shot on the Russian front, he had been reassigned to Auschwitz and was easily recognized by the girls because "he had one leg shorter than the other" and limped.

Over the next few weeks, only a word or two passed between them. He might "see me with swollen eyes because they beat me badly or told me a word in my ear that was worse than a knife in the brain, and ask 'What happened to you?'"

Afraid that if she told him who had beaten or abused her she would be blamed and sent to the gas, Helena never answered him. He was certainly not going to reprimand an SS or kapo for doing what he himself was expected to do—for what he himself *did* do to other prisoners.

One must wonder about the price girls paid if they rejected sexual advances by the SS men—and women. Those who somehow maintained their allure, despite having no hair and being painfully thin, must have been rare, but the remnants of their beauty may have brought them unwanted attention and inappropriate intentions.

The mystery is what happened to the beautiful redhead, Adela Gross. That fall, when Adela stepped in front of the SS self-proclaimed gods during one of the mass selections, one of the men's thumbs went against her. This was not a democracy—one thumb against you robbed you of life. But why did he choose Adela for the gas? She was young, still had flesh on her beautiful bones. She was healthy. "According to their mood they selected whole groups of healthy girls." Could it have been that random? Some SS did delight in selecting beautiful and healthy girls for the gas. Or is it possible that she had rebuffed an SS's advances and paid the ultimate price for taking the moral high ground?

Rena Kornreich (#1716) never forgot watching Adela walk proudly away from the side of the living to the flatbed trucks already full of girls condemned to death. She comforted some. She helped girls weak with fear and incapable of crawling onto the flatbeds to their feet. Her dignity lodged in Rena's heart and memory forever.

We do not know what Adela's number was. We do not know what day she died. "It was early" in Birkenau, Edith says, but Edith did not see Adela get selected. There were thousands of girls in camp and no way to witness everything. Survival was an all-consuming struggle. One day you noticed that you hadn't seen one of your friends in a while, and that was when you knew. She was there then she was gone. How was unbearable to ponder. Where was undeniable. It would take seventy years for Lou Gross to discover what happened to his cousin Adela.

ALTHOUGH BY THIS point many of the first girls had been lucky enough to get "decent jobs," Edith and Lea had not; they continued to work outside, clearing roads and ponds. Their feet were cold and their skin had cracked. Then Edith's clappers wore out on the bottom. "The sole was gone and I was walking on stone and having not to say, 'Ouch!' in front of the SS." Desperate for help, she asked Helena to smuggle a new pair of shoes out of the sorting detail.

"I don't know how to do it," Helena told her. "I'm too scared."

Edith suggested that Helena ask one of the men to grab some for her.

"If I do that, after the war he will ask me to marry him because of your shoes!"

"That was Helena for you," Edith says, shaking her head with mild disgust. "She was so focused on herself." She went to Margie Becker instead.

Margie not only smuggled shoes to Edith and Lea, she got them socks as well. In the real world, shoes may seem a small comfort, but in Auschwitz they could save your life. Working outside immediately became more bearable and safer. Their feet were protected from debris and cuts, and with the threat of winter around the corner, they would be protected from the snow and the frostbite sure to strike those who were still shod in clappers.

More and more, girls were being selected by the SS as they returned from work at night. Standing by the entrance of Birkenau, SS officers watched them march past and picked out girls for the slightest blemish. The increasing randomness of selections was terrifying. If SS Lagerführer Maria Mandel caught a girl even looking at her, she was dead. None of the old-timers ever looked up. No newcomer survived if she did.

Even if you made it through the gate, you weren't safe. One night, a girl from the first transport was simply walking to her block when an SS man shouted, "You!"

"She was healthy, but they didn't care," Edith remembers. "They would grab them as they were walking by so they could make their quota."

There was a quota? There was indeed.

Chapter Twenty-six

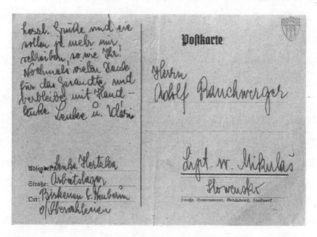

Postcard image taken from Eugene Hartmann interview,
1996. USC SHOAH FOUNDATION—THE INSTITUTE FOR VI-
SUAL HISTORY AND EDUCATION; sfi.usc.edu.

WITHIN EIGHT WEEKS of his Christian values speech in August,
President Tiso decided to slow the deportation of Jews. Of
course, over two-thirds of Slovakia's Jewish population was already either dead or working as slave laborers in any number
of Slovak or Polish camps, and the Slovak government owed
the Third Reich millions for having "rehomed" them. It was a
cost the Slovak Assembly realized "deeply interfere[d] with
state finances" and future economic development.

The end of the deportations brought relief for those who had not been removed from their homes, and who were under the conviction that the Presidential exemptions would protect them. Safe on the family farm, the Hartmann family continued to correspond with Lenka Hertzka. One of her earliest postcards is written in pencil and has a purple German postage stamp of the *Führer*. It is postmarked in red ink: *Auschwitz Oberschlesien* (Upper Silesia), the region in Poland where Auschwitz is located.

November 28, 1942

My Dears,

    First of all I want to send you birthday wishes, even if they are a bit too early but good wishes get even better with time. I also wish you good health and joy and that the good Lord gives you strength to continue working. Here, the winter is upon us and I think it will soon be the same at home with you. In the evening I travel in my thoughts to the town and remember the old familiar places.

Lenka

The writing is so faded the salutation is almost indecipherable, but the postcard is addressed to Ivan Rauschwerger's uncle, Adolf. Ivan does not know how Lenka Hertzka knew his uncle.

WORKING IN CANADA did not make a prisoner exempt from illness or death, but it did offer ways to hide sick friends. Sometimes a short respite was all one needed to recover. Ida Eigerman (#1930) was working in one of the kerchief details when she came down with typhus.

    The trick to getting past the guards when you were very ill was to be sandwiched between two other prisoners who helped you walk upright. In this way, prisoners were able to slip past the eyes of the SS seeking to make their gassing quotas by removing the ill and infirm from the ranks of laborers and replacing them with new slave laborers from Jewish ghettos in France, Belgium, Greece, Holland....

Once in the sorting barrack, Ida was hidden under piles of clothing so that she could sleep through the day and recover her strength. Throughout the day, the girls would check on her and slip her some water or a bit of food they had found in a pocket before going back to work. At the end of the day, when the SS weren't looking, they helped her out of the clothing pile and through the selection process as they entered Birkenau. If they didn't protect each other, who would? It was the only way to survive. This is what women did for each other. This is what women did for men, too.

In the fall of 1942, Rudolf Vrba was carrying luggage from the transports to the sorting barracks, where he got to know many of the young women in the white and red kerchiefs. As the typhus epidemic ripped through the men's and the women's camps, Rudi became one of its victims. It struck aggressively while he was carrying suitcases to the sorting detail. For three mornings in a row, his friends propped him up between them as they marched past the SS guards to work. Once past the SS, they snuck him over to where the Slovak girls were sorting. The girls hid him, just as they had hidden Ida, in enormous piles of clothes.

Feverish and dehydrated, he was unaware of much, but throughout the day, the girls took turns sneaking him a little lemon and sugar water. They even administered some sort of pills. Surviving typhus was a bit like Russian roulette since it took whom it wanted with little rhyme or reason. A few days later, he was placed in the sick-bay and actual medicine was administered to reduce his fever. But it was the spiritual sustenance the Slovak girls gave him that raised "what little remained of my morale."

IT BEGAN WITH A HEADACHE and muscles so stiff and aching that Edith could barely move. She was nauseated and felt chills one moment, and a burning fever the next. If the SS had made her stick her tongue out, they would have seen the telltale spots and sent her to the gas. She could not eat and fell into a stupor. Everything hurt, even her eyes. "The memory is so alive, so vivid. I feel it when I speak about it. I see myself. I see Lea pulling me to work, telling me, 'Stand straight.'" Edith could not stomach anything but liquids, so Lea gave Edith her tea and soup and ate Edith's bread in return. "I must have had a fever of forty-one degrees Celsius, and I was going to work lifting bricks for buildings."

Edith's body struggled against the infection for several weeks; then she woke up one morning and felt alive again. The fog of fever had broken. And she was ravenously hungry for solid food. Staring up at the bare wooden beams above their bunk, she wondered what month it was and felt a faint smile of relief. Turning to her sister, she whispered the good news, "Lea, I am hungry!"

Glassy-eyed and pale, Lea looked at her little sister. "But I am not."

NOW THE ROLES REVERSED. It was Edith making sure that Lea got extra portions of tea and soup, while Edith ate Lea's bread.

Typhus is not passed from one person to another; it is passed through lice. There are several strains, though. And in a place like Birkenau, it would have been easy to contract all three, because the carriers for all three infections were present: lice, rats, and mites.

For the first two weeks after Lea fell ill, Edith propped up her sister as they headed out to work. Still weak and recovering from her own illness, Edith had to pull Lea up off the wood shelves that served as their bed, help her stand through roll call, and then steer her past the SS to the marsh cleaning detail. The detail Helena had been threatened with was regular fare for Edith and Lea, and it had taken a heavy toll on the Friedman girls. As they scooped paper and bottles out of the cold water, their hands and feet cramped in the damp. When it rained and the temperature dropped, they pulled their hems up above their knees, but the water was so deep that their dresses still got wet. When they came out of the water icicles formed on their clothes. And winter was closing in.

Occasionally, it was possible to hide from work by slipping onto the top shelves and hiding under the thin blankets for the day. If you were lucky, your block and room elders allowed you to stay there unhampered. If you were unlucky, and the SS searched the blocks, you could get caught and sent to Block 25 or directly to the gas, as Hinda Kahan had been.

Lea had been ill for two weeks, but instead of recovering her strength, she was becoming weaker and less responsive to Edith's pleas to get up and go to work. Finally, one morning, she could not even lift her head. The fight had gone out of her. Anyone who has been that ill knows the feeling. Unable to move, your body as heavy as stone, you need to do nothing. You can do nothing. But rest was a luxury not available to Jews.

Frightened by her sister's refusal to rise, Edith begged, "Lea, you have to get up. Come on."

Lea could barely sway her head from side to side in refusal.

"Maybe I could have done more," Edith still frets, but she was a teenager, alone in a hostile world that was not designed for survival. She had no idea what else she could do beyond give Lea her tea. Her soup. Her prayers. In her teenage mind, Lea had to recover. Lea was the strong one. Edith was the wisp of a girl that their mother worried about.

Helena and a few other girls from the white kerchiefs were living in Block 13 with Edith and Lea. One of them must have seen how hard it was for Edith and got a white kerchief for her to wear so she could get into the sorting detail. Since Edith already had good shoes, she did not have to worry about clappers drawing the unwanted attention of the kapo, Rita.

Edith needed this lighter work to recover her own strength. She also needed to get extra food for her sister, and maybe an extra white kerchief. If she could just get Lea into the sorting detail, maybe Lea would recover her health. Time was running out. It would only take one SS guard to find Lea hiding in the block. Full of plans to rescue her sister, Edith marched out with Helena the next morning and headed back to Auschwitz I, where they sorted coats together. At least, one of them sorted coats.

Edith had heard rumors that one of the girls was having an affair with an SS man. Now, standing at a long table, emptying pockets of food and other possessions, she saw Helena making eyes at the handsome young SS officer who oversaw their detail. The looks that passed between the two were electric. When Helena disappeared from the sorting table and slipped up into the mountains of clothes around them, everyone focused on their work and pretended not to notice. A little while later, SS Wunsch made his way to a high shelf to join her. Edith was shocked, because the Citron family was strictly Orthodox. But who was she to judge? "She loved this guy," Edith says. "They were both in love."

There is a photograph of Helena in her striped prison dress, smiling broadly into the camera. Her thick dark hair falls just past her shoulders. Her face is full, unpinched, unstarved. Behind her is the backdrop of Auschwitz. It must be the only picture of a prisoner truly smiling in Auschwitz-Birkenau. She looks not only happy but in love.

AT THE END of the day, Edith had hidden a few bits of food in her pockets, but Lea needed more than food. She needed medicine. But even Dr. Manci Schwalbova was having problems getting medicine for ill Jewish prisoners.

Edith returned to the block full of ideas to help Lea. Maybe she could trade the food for a lemon or clean water to drink. Maybe she could get Lea to raise her head and eat some bread. But the bunk where Lea should have been was empty. In a panic, she rushed to the block elder, Gizzy, and her sister.

"Where is my sister? Where is Lea?"

They had taken her to Block 25.

"How could they do that? Why didn't you stop them?" she yelled.

It is the conundrum of Auschwitz. The block elders and room elders could allow girls to hide from work, but if any kapos or SS checked the blocks, they were forced to send the hiding girls to Block 25—a one-way ticket to death. Once a girl's number was registered in Block 25, she could not escape. And the only way in or out of that block was past the SS security guard and then the block elder. So how did Edith get into Block 25 to see her sister and walk back out, not just once but twice?

"We had our ways," Edith says. "But Cilka sure didn't help me!"

Cilka was the block elder for Block 25. She was only fifteen or sixteen years old and ruthless. She was one of those that Dr. Manci Schwalbova mentions, who let her power go to her head. Cilka was not the sort of person who would do a favor for anyone.

"Maybe somebody from the *leichenkommando* gave me an armband," Edith muses. If so, that person was probably Margie Becker, but all these years later it is hard to remember all the little favors girls did for each other. "Maybe because I was wearing a striped dress and had a white kerchief, I looked important enough to be let in." The truth is she does not remember.

Block 13 was just one block away from Block 25; Edith did not have far to walk to get to the courtyard entrance. Under cover of night, she slipped into Block 25. The block was a re-frigerator of death, dark and claustrophobic. Bodies were everywhere and girls moaned in the dark. Edith called her sister's name and listened for a response. She found Lea lying on the dirt floor. "I held her hand. Kissed her cheek. I know she could hear me." Lea's eyes were moist with tears as Edith wiped her brow. "I was sitting with her, looking at her beautiful face, and I felt I should be there instead of her. I had been sick and gotten well. Why couldn't she?" Inside the blackness of the unlit block rats scurried by. The air smelled of death and diarrhea. It was freezing cold. Edith tried to give Lea a little bit of food, but Lea could not eat. Curling up beside her sister, Edith tried to warm her with her body. She stayed for as long as she dared then slipped back through the shadows to her block. It was a night of hollow dreams and fitful sleep.

Chapter Twenty-seven

The fact is that when the heart is bleeding, somewhere
it doesn't realize it's bleeding.

—TSIPORAH TEHORI, NÉE
HELENA CITRON (#1971)

ON DECEMBER 1, 1942, "the occupancy level of the women's
camp in Auschwitz-Birkenau is 8,232." But on that same day
women were being tattooed with the numbers 26,273 to
26,286. Where had all the others gone? More than six thousand women and girls had been selected over three days in
October, but with no solid population tallies at month's end,
we have no idea how many women were actually in Birkenau
prior to December. If the occupancy level reported in the
Auschwitz Chronicle is correct, then what was about to happen
would have been impossible.

December 5, 1942, was Shabbat Chanukah in the Jewish
calendar—St. Nicholas Day in Christian observances, a day
of gift giving and celebrating children who have been good in
the past year. Shabbat Chanukah carries special meaning and
has a "deep Kabbalistic significance that reflects the spiritual
energies of the participants." The ritual starts with the lighting

of the Chanukah candles, because once the Sabbath begins, you can't "light" more candles or work—the Sabbath celebrates "humanity through the act of rest." Chanukah, in turn, celebrates the miracle of light, the retaking of the Temple, and God's deliverance of his chosen people from destruction. It was from destruction that Edith and Lea now needed a Chanukah miracle.

In the morning, before roll call, Edith risked her life again to sneak into Block 25. She had to go to work, but could not bear to leave her sister alone.

"Lea was on the lowest part of the shelves. Still on the floor. Lying in the dirt. Wasting away. It was so cold. She was in a coma now." Edith did not know if Lea could hear her talking to her, praying to God to save her sister. Nearby in the shadows, also dying of typhus, was Giora Shpira's dear childhood friend, Adolf Amster's daughter Magda. Alone in the dark, Magda did not have even the comfort of a kiss.

WHILE EDITH AND the privileged few in the white and red kerchiefs marched out of camp to work in Auschwitz I, the rest of the women's camp was still standing at roll call. No sooner had the sorting detail departed through the gate than the women left inside camp were ordered to remove their uniforms and stand naked in the snow. Across the frosted and forgotten world of Birkenau, the SS were about to undertake a mass typhus selection.

It was bitter cold.

"Those poor, bloody girls," Moses Sonenschein, the son of a Polish rabbi, said to Rudolf Vrba. "They'll freeze to death. They'll die of exposure in this weather."

Forty trucks waited to cart those selected away to the gas.

Among those forced to stand naked in the snow for the entire day were at least three girls from the first transport: Rena and Danka Kornreich and Dina Dranger. Despite Rena's rigorous memory and attention to detail, she never mentions the cold or that they had to stand naked all day in the snow. Did she pass over that fact to protect us and herself from embarrassment, or was it simply too unbearable to recall? At some point, the mind shuts down to all the horror.

The weather was brutal, but they stood all day until dusk, when the last girl was selected to die. As the trucks—filled with thousands of girls and women—started for the gas chambers, "a banshee wail" rose up from the doomed, "a piercing protest that only death could stop." Then one of the girls leapt off the back of a truck. And another. They were not going to go like sheep to the slaughter. They took one last stab at life and tried to escape. The SS chased after the fleeing girls, with dogs and whips.

"There is no God," Moses Sonenschein cried. "And, if there is, I curse Him, curse Him!"

STARVATION DOES NOT induce clear or focused thinking, but Edith had spent the entire day praying for a miracle to save her sister. As she sorted the pockets and linings of the coats of dead Jews, she believed in the power on this day, of all days, because Chanukah was a reminder that "there were things worth fighting for; it marked the end of a war and freedom from tyranny," while Shabbat celebrated a "world without fighting, cessation from work and redemption from slavery."

Edith clung to the messages of Shabbat and Chanukah, but those ideals were practically impossible to believe in if her sister was dying. Lea had to survive. Edith had no candles to light in this darkest hour of her young life. All she had was a thin shred of hope in a miracle.

In the fading light of that winter afternoon, Linda, Helena, Edith, and the other clothes sorters marched back to Birkenau. At the gate the SS ordered the girls to stop and disrobe. "We had to go through the gate back to the camp nude." Taking their clothes off in the bitter winter wind, barefoot in the snow, the girls marched one by one past the SS, who were dressed in long, dark, woolen coats, boots, hats, and leather gloves. Standing on both sides of the shivering girls, they looked for the telltale rash of spotted typhus on each girl's flesh. The inspection was rigorous, and anyone with the slightest spot or blemish was directed toward the administration barracks on the right. There, their numbers were written down by one of the camp scribes before they were "loaded onto the trucks and taken to the gas chamber."

To the left was the women's camp and life. "If you can call slave labor life," Linda says with a sigh. "Those who were marked or exhausted or didn't look any more like human beings" went to the right. The girls who were still strong enough screamed and yelled, railing against the injustice of the inevitable.

"Chickens meant more than people," Martha Mangel (#1741) says. Fortunately for Edith, her rash was gone, and the SS passed over her. Pulling her striped dress back on, Edith grabbed her shoes in her hands and ran barefoot down the rows of blocks to the front of camp and Block 25. In the gathering dark, something was strange. But what? She didn't pause to ponder. She had to find Lea. At Block 25, she slipped easily through the gate. No SS was there. No Cilka. The courtyard was empty. The door creaked as she opened it and stepped into the block. Not a single girl lay on the shelves or floor. Edith wheeled around and ran back outside, turned the corner, and looked up the avenues of Birkenau. They should have been full of women. Her entire body began to quiver and shake. Her teeth chattered. Cold. Fear. Where had everybody gone?

Cilka appeared in the twilight.

"Where are they?" Edith demanded.

"Gone. Everyone is gone."

As Linda entered her block, only a few faces shone in the dark, pale as ghosts. Of the one thousand girls who had been in her block that morning, just twenty were left. All over camp, girls returning from the sorting detail entered empty blocks. Linda had only nine friends left among the living. Edith had one.

Lea was gone.

Bertha Schachnerova, age twenty-seven, gone.

Lea Feldbrandova, age nineteen, gone.

Alice Weissova, age twenty-one, gone.

Our long-necked beauty, Magda Amster, age nineteen, gone.

Sara Shpira's prayer lingered in the ash: *It's simply beautiful to live. The world is so perfect.* If only they all could have embraced Sara's world instead.

DECEMBER 5, 1942, is one of the few recorded selections of women that year, but for all the meticulous detail the Nazis were known for, there is a discrepancy between the SS's administrative numbers and the survivors' reports. The historical record states that *approximately* "two thousand young, healthy and able-bodied women" were gassed. Survivors—men and women, independent of each other, and years after the fact— say that ten thousand girls and women died that day. Those witnesses include survivors Rudolf Vrba and his friend Moses Sonenschein, who watched the selection from the men's camp; women who stood all day and survived the selection; Rena and Danka Kornreich; and about three hundred clothing sorters who returned to the empty camp.

"The camp was overcrowded. And the Nazis, the SS, expected fresh arrivals. So they had to get rid of us," Linda says matter-of-factly. "The next morning, we woke up and the camp was almost empty. We heard that in the night they had burned ten thousand girls. We went out for the counting. We saw a few people we knew." Only a few.

Since the data on women was most likely destroyed, we may never have precise numbers for the Shabbat Chanukah selection. But whom should we believe? The SS records on women, which were notoriously inaccurate, or the survivors and witnesses who were there?

Whatever the ultimate truth is, nearly twenty thousand women in the prison population died in the space of about eight months, and the majority of those deaths occurred between August 15 and December 5, 1942. According to Dr. Manci Schwalbova, seven thousand women and girls had been sent to the gas from the "hospital" alone.

"After this, most of the girls who were alive from the first transport survived," Edith says, unless they died on the death march or from typhus. This was the last mass selection where girls from the first transport were sent to the gas. That is because in January 1943, the warden of the new SS overseer of the women's camp, Maria Mandel, who had replaced Johanna Langefeld, ordered that girls with four-digit numbers, especially those beginning with the numeral 1, should be passed over during selections. Unless they were seriously ill, of course. It "was nice of her to say, because from one thousand, we were three hundred left," Bertha Berkowitz states. It was probably the only nice thing Mandel ever did.

Chapter Twenty-eight

Gift of Eugene Hartmann in memory of Lenka Hertzka,
MUSEUM OF JEWISH HERITAGE, NEW YORK.

December 12, 1942

Dear Lenka. Probably you only [just] received my
cards, therefore I represent everybody, and write
weekly. Everybody joins me in this letter. There is
company here more often. We are with you in spirit,

with all of you. [From] Magduska we await lines
with impatience. Let her father know earliest. We are
all healthy and quite busy.

Best Regards, M [Mama]

STABSGEBÄUDE STAFF HEADQUARTERS was a large three-story
white brick building just outside of Auschwitz I. Behind the
building were the kitchen and the noodle factory. Both of those
forlorn and hollow edifices still stand today. Their shattered
windows stare out at a flat expanse once called the *trockenplatz*,
the drying place for the SS laundry. Today, the SS quarters
serve as a high school, full of teenagers rambling up and down
the stairs. Back then, our girls trod those same stairs under very
different circumstances.

The basement of the building had a full laundry, sewing fa-
cility, and dormitory full of bunk beds, where the girls who
worked in those details and the secretarial pool slept. It was here
that Lenka Hertzka received cards from the Hartmann farm and
read fondly about her nephew, sister, and mother. Eight-year-old
Milan wrote to say that receiving her card was the best present
of his birthday. He only wished that Magduska would write, too.
Even at eight years old, he felt the absence of the somber, dark-
eyed teen and her sunshine-faced cousin, Nusi. He had probably
heard family members discussing the girls' absence when they
gathered at the end of a long day. A holiday card from Lenka's
mother mentions that the family had sent 250 kroner to the teenagers, as well as to Lenka. Who sends money to Auschwitz? They
must have imagined that the girls could spend it in the camp
commissary, like any other regular government worker.

It is clear the family had no idea what kind of place Lenka
and their girls had gone to. The common misconception was
that everyone was together, just as President Tiso had promised.
They envisaged Lenka working closely with her cousins and see-

ing them in a cafeteria at mealtimes. Lenka's cards home could not reveal the bleak truth, and Magduska and Nusi never wrote. Meanwhile, family and friends who had heard that Lenka was corresponding from Birkenau began writing to Lenka, as well.

"[Our mother] gave me news that you are there with many of our relatives, so be very friendly and please write to me whether you have already met up with Aliska, Renka, Markus B., and other relatives," Lenka's brother, Herman wrote.

> "What are they doing? Are they healthy? Josef
> Erdie was there too but has probably already left,
> we learned this last piece of news yesterday from
> cousin Robert, who is working in the woodwork
> shop. He wrote to say that he is very well and
> would just like to know where his wife is…You
> should tell Magduska that Mark is already married.
> Lots of love and kisses.
>
> Herman Hertzka

That cousin Robert had written to Herman to tell the family that Josef Erdie had "left already" was probably code for having gone to the gas. Though, if cousin Robert was very new in the camps and didn't know the real situation, he might have actually believed that Josef Erdie had been transferred somewhere else. The fact that he was wondering about his wife may mean that he had no idea yet.

Herman's note mentions news of Mark, a boy who Magduska must have been sweet on, and was now married. In Auschwitz, she did not even have the hope of a kiss, let alone a future love. The news might have broken her heart if Lenka had shared it, but it seems Lenka had not yet seen the girls. There is no mention of Magduska or Nusi in any of Lenka's early cards. They were cetainly not in Stabsgebäude with her.

The Hartmann family was puzzled. Magduska and Nusi had been "working" in Auschwitz for months before their older cousin even arrived. Were they really so busy that they didn't have time to write their family?

January 1, 1943

Dear Lenka,

I received your congratulations cards, thank you very much. Everything goes well. We also filled Milan's boots [like a Christmas stocking]. This time I am also representing everybody. Meanwhile, you certainly received our card from Rožkovany. The girls [Magduska and Nusi] should follow your good example. Support them with it. We also sent money to Magduska. Best Regards and warm embrace to everyone.

Mama

Isolated on the family farm in the tiny village of Rožkovany, the Hartmann family seems to have settled into a safehouse of semi-naïveté, temporarily. They must have known that family transports were departing from Prešov, but deep in the countryside they were protected from the harsh scenes that those in the cities had witnessed. They must have heard about the roundups, though, especially as many of their own family members had left Prešov and were now living and helping on the farm. The Hartmanns were providing essential food for the Slovak people and army, but they still could not hire gentiles. They needed family help; in exchange, there was food on the table. Sharing their plenty, the Hartmann brothers sent packages of sheep's cheese and other nonperishables to their daughters, as well as the girls' friends, Ellie and Kornelia Mandel, who had been on the first transport with Magduska and Nusi.

IT WAS COMMON KNOWLEDGE that the only way out of Block 25 was to be carried out dead on a stretcher or in a wheelbarrow, and then tossed onto the truck heading for the gas chambers. The only prisoners allowed free access to Block 25 were the camp scribe and those in the *leichenkommando*. To make sure the block was secure, those who could go in and out wore special armbands.

Dr. Manci Schwalbova was working with others to exchange the tickets of ill girls who might recover "for the tickets of women who had already died in camp, because only the numbers had to agree." Ella (#1950) never details her participation in this kind of activity, but as a scribe she was one of the few women that Dr. Schwalbova could have worked with to alter numbers. At ninety-five years old, she has a frail constitution, but she still has moments of clarity. When questioned, she admits, "I saved a few." Irena Fein (#1564) was one of those few.

Irena had gotten frostbite in her toes and been sent to Block 25 because she was limping. Standing outside in the courtyard, to avoid the contagious ill and dying, she was trying to figure out a way to escape when Bertha, Margie, and the rest of the *leichenkommando* made their daily visit. Margie recognized Irena from Humenné and saw the plight she was in. Ella also recognized Irena because, according to Irena, Ella had been her block elder in Auschwitz I. Being on the first transport created a special bond between women. They could never have saved Irena if she had been seriously ill, but she was healthy. She just limped a bit. Since it was Ella's job to write down the new arrivals into the Block 25 ledger, she was also in the position to *not* write down numbers.

Ella "had an [extra] dead body," Irena says, "so they brought in the dead body and pulled me out."

Manipulating the file cards, Ella replaced Irena's number with the dead girl's. Now they had to get Irena out. As they were about to remove a body, Irena took hold of the stretcher and walked out with them.

"No one said a thing, of course," Bertha says. And the SS did not notice the extra girl removing the body on the stretcher.

Irena helped the others load the body onto the back of the flatbed, but now faced another predicament. She needed time to recover without being seen by the SS or reported. Ella sent her to her own block, where her sister, Edie (#1949), was the secretary. In charge of counting the girls in the block and reporting how many went out to work and how many stayed behind, Edie explains, "I had to give the report, but that was all." Nothing was that simple in Auschwitz, but at least Edie could help girls, if she wanted to. Irena had a safe place to hide until she could walk again. There was yet one more problem. Her pinkie toes were black with gangrene.

Transmetatarsal amputation is not complicated surgery, but how did Irena know what to do? Was she instructed by one of the doctors? That is unlikely because she didn't use surgical tools. Instead, under the cover of night, she slipped outside after curfew and scoured the grounds for a shard of glass. When she found one that was large enough to hold on to, she bit on a piece of cloth to prevent herself from crying out in pain, and proceeded to debride the necrosis from the gangrenous toes of her feet. She then packed the wounds with newspaper until they could heal.

A few weeks later, when Irena stepped out to work in her clappers, she still had her feet wrapped with newspaper. SS Anton Taube was a notorious brute and murderer who delighted in making prisoners do calisthenics in the mud and then killing them by stepping on their skulls. He stopped her almost immediately.

"Number 1564, what are you hiding?"

"I was itching and scratched myself, so I put a paper bandage on," Irena lied.

"If it's not healed by the next selection, you go to the chimney!" he said.

A few minutes later, SS Dreschler saw Irena with her bandage and took her stick to push Irena out of the roll call to go to the gas.

Irena held up her number, hoping the low digits would help her. "SS Taube told me that I will go next time, if I don't heal. But not now!"

Dreschler's hideous mouth curled in a snarl, but she let Irena stay in line.

One thing was sure: Irena needed one of the girls in the sorting detail to smuggle out shoes to protect her feet not just from the elements but from the prying eyes of the SS. Somehow, she was able to get a pair of boots. Even the littlest kindness could change someone's life, or more than one life. Was this also, as Margie Becker believed, *bashert*? If so, Irena's survival would help Edith to survive, too.

FOR THOSE WHO WERE ABLE to maintain a moral compass, that kind of fortitude fed their spirits in the face of horror. Girls like Bertha clung to a spiritual mandate that having a good position afforded them the grace to help other girls whenever they could. Sometimes that meant helping girls who needed salve for their wounds by giving them extra portions of bread to trade. Sometimes it meant giving extra bread to the men driving the trucks to the crematoriums because they were hungry. Sometimes it meant giving comfort and support. Sometimes it meant giving up something of yourself.

With so many desperate women in need, helping everyone was impossible. You had a nucleus of friends you focused on, but sometimes someone unknown came within your sphere unbeckoned. Then your hand became God's hand. How many functionaries did something to help someone unexpected? One can hope all of them did, but with thousands now needing help, the small deeds of a few were swallowed up in the oblivion of the many.

WITHOUT HER SISTER, Edith floundered in a swamp of despair. The questions around her sister's death haunted her and dragged her under the morass of a life without meaning. Why was she still alive but her sister not? "My sister had been able to save me, but I was not able to save her. So I lost her. I cannot describe this. It is too much to remember. I was the younger one. I was the weaker one. And yet, I am here." It made no sense, but then nothing about Auschwitz made sense.

It was hard to get up in the morning, hard to stand obediently at roll call, hard to eat, hard to live. It was so easy to die in Auschwitz. Death was always within reach—in the electrical wires, in the guards, the dogs, the whips, the lice, the gas chambers. All she had to do was step out of line to get shot. But Edith did not have a death wish. "I tell you, I loved my sister, crazy, and I went to her and was with her as much as I could [be]. But was I sorry that I was alive? No. I was happy that I was still alive. That is the truth. Sometimes you say, what spirit was there in the survivors? I don't believe that God was mixed in with the Holocaust. I don't believe that God exists as a person. But I believe in the survivors."

Some internal mechanism clicked inside and kept her going, but she needed more than willpower. She needed companionship. Elsa Rosenthal became Edith's "*lagerstrasse* sister," the term prisoners used to describe relationships that were as close and dear as blood ties—because no one survived Auschwitz on her own.

Margie Becker tells the story of one of her cousins getting selected by the SS and her cousin's sister being left to live. The Benovicova sisters had been allowed to die together, but now the "sadism was so great" that SS quite often separated family members, forcing one to the gas and the other to life. Both of

Margie's cousins were healthy, but at the whim of the SS, the youngest was selected to die "for no obvious reason but cruelty." On the other side of the fence, while her little sister was still waiting to be forced onto the flatbed trucks and carted away to the gas chambers, the older sister rushed over to Margie.

"Let's be sisters," she begged.

Losing a sister was like losing a limb or a vital organ. One's sister or sisters offered not just physical support but a deep spiritual bond, a soul connection. Coming from the same root, sisters were flowers on the same stem. You could not survive the vortex of evil that was Auschwitz without someone providing a spiritual anchor.

Margie understood this. The moment her distant cousin begged her to be her *lagerstrasse* sister, she agreed. Elsa did the same for Edith. What was the purpose of surviving without Lea? Elsa needed Edith to survive. She made Edith continue going to work in the white kerchiefs. She slept beside her and prevented the cold drafts of despair from blowing Edith away. She wiped the tears that slipped onto Edith's cheeks. She made Edith eat. Made her stand up straight at roll call. Reminded Edith that if she gave up, they would both die.

—I can't survive without you, Elsa told her. The compassion and constant reassurance worked. From somewhere deep inside herself Edith found the courage to live. Then she found another reason.

THE GIRLS IN THE SORTING DETAILS wore a kind of apron or smock now. Every morning, they slipped into their aprons, which, like their camp uniforms, had the girls' numbers and yellow stars on them. While sorting coats from a transport of Belgian Jews, Edith felt something in the hem of a black cashmere coat. She started to ignore it. Then she thought, What if it is something valuable that I can smuggle to the underground? She tore at the seam and wiggled a thin box from the lining of the coat. There were no SS nearby, so she quickly flipped up the lid and peeked inside. "Huge diamonds, already cut" gleamed up from the dark of the folds of the coat. Her heart raced. They were "worth millions, for sure." If she was even caught looking at them she could be sent to the gas, but if she could smuggle them out to the underground, perhaps she could avenge Lea's death. The box fit nicely into the pocket of her apron and did not make the slightest bulge.

It was a Saturday, the last day of the workweek. At the end of the day, Helena returned from behind the mounds of clothing where she now spent most of her days with SS Wunsch. "She did not have to work anymore," Edith says, though she did need to stand at attention and get counted before returning to Birkenau. As they were standing there, the SS ordered them to hang their aprons on the hooks and leave them there for the weekend. The new protocol stunned the prisoners, many of whom had loot in their pockets that they planned to trade in camp for bread or other necessities.

—From now on, all aprons will remain here! one of the SS men announced.

It was a measure designed to prevent theft as well as contagion.

Edith tried to steady her hand as she hung up her apron, but she was unable to retrieve the box. The underground would have to wait until Monday. She left the diamonds behind.

The next day at noon, when the men arrived with soup kettles for lunch, one of the men carrying the kettles whispered to Edith, "The SS checked your jumper and found your diamonds. They are going to question you for sure."

Edith quivered like a leaf in the wind. What was she going to do? To be caught stealing anything, even a potato, was punishable by twenty-five lashes. To be caught with diamonds? How could she have been so stupid? For all of her youthful naïveté, though, Edith had inherited her mother's cleverness;

she was shrewdly intelligent and logically minded. The man had warned her for a reason. All she needed now was a story the SS would believe.

Monday morning loomed. Marching to work, Edith's left leg dragged with a heavy sense of dread. Outside of the sorting barracks, the women were forced to line up and wait for interrogation. Even Helena had to wait. The officer questioning them was not SS Wunsch but his superior, SS Ambros. One at a time, the girls' numbers were called, and they had to step into the SS office for questioning behind a closed door. One at a time, they came out. Some went to work. Some went in the opposite direction. Edith was not the only girl who had left something in her pocket. It took all of her self-control not to let her knees knock together. By the end of the morning, she was the sole girl standing outside. Her opportunity to join Lea had arrived.

—1970!

Waved into the SS office, Edith stepped into the interrogation room and stood at attention before the stern-faced SS man.

"A box was found in your apron. Why didn't you turn it in?"

"I didn't trust the other guards to give it to."

"Why is that?"

"Because it was quite large and I thought it might be important." She paused for dramatic effect. "And if I gave it to you, I thought you might give me a little bit of sausage or something, so I saved it for you."

"If you are lying, I will send you to the gas."

She gave a perfunctory nod.

"Did you look inside?"

"I tell you the truth," Edith lied to his face, "I saved it for you to look."

"I can tell if you are lying."

She nodded again.

His piercing gaze looked through her. Then he looked her up and down. Her waif-like appearance worked in her favor. How could anyone so tiny be a threat, even if she was a dirty Jew?

"I look at her and can tell she is telling the truth," he concluded. "The little one is not guilty."

"Everyone was so surprised that I didn't go straight to the gas chamber, but I will never forget how that SS Ambros looked at me. Pure greed. He didn't want the diamonds for Germany, but for himself. The next week he took leave and went home, where he opened a factory." She never did get her piece of sausage.

THE RED AND WHITE KERCHIEF details in Canada had become so popular that everyone was organizing kerchiefs to get into them. Even Linda, who had been sorting since the beginning, got pushed out occasionally, despite her "good elbows." Edith was so tiny she was easily dislodged from her spot, and she was too depressed to try to get it back. She didn't have the energy to fight, so she returned to the frozen outdoors, clearing roads with her bare hands. Winter was dangerous. Frostbite was rampant, and the mandate that "there was no weather too bad for Jews" was adhered to.

Very few of the girls from the first transport were still working outside. Besides Edith and Elsa, those unfortunate few included Rena Kornreich and her sister Danka, their friend Dina Dranger, and Joan Rosner. "We had no socks, no coats or anything," Joan (#1188) says. "If we found a rag, we would wrap it around our body to keep warm. There were one thousand girls in one block, and we were stealing each other's blankets. [It is] humanly impossible to explain how bad it was. My legs were frozen; my toes were frozen. No head covering. We worked in the rain and went to sleep in the wet clothes."

In order to keep typhus under control, the girls' uniforms were collected for delousing on Sundays. The protocol included stripping out of their uniforms and delivering their clothes to the laundry to be boiled. Without any clothing to wear while their uniforms were washed, the girls huddled together under their thin blankets in the block, trying to stay warm. In the winter, drying the uniforms was a slow process and they usually came back frozen solid. On one of those Sundays in January, Edith woke up in excruciating pain. Her knee was as swollen as a balloon. "I couldn't step on my leg."

Because it was a Sunday, they had time to do something before any of the SS saw her. Elsa ran to the hospital block to get Dr. Manci Schwalbova.

Manci took one look at Edith's swollen leg and shook her head. "Edith, I don't know what to tell you, but it is tuberculosis." Tuberculosis was a death sentence in even the best circumstances. "You are really, really, very sick. I don't know if this can heal here with these conditions. But listen, yesterday was a selection. Now it is quiet in the hospital. I am taking you to a bed and operating. Then we'll see how long I can keep you."

In the quiet of Sunday afternoon, Manci punctured the flesh in order to relieve the pressure on the knee. With no anesthetic available, Elsa and a nurse had to pin Edith down to keep her from writhing with pain. Putrid pus drained out of Edith's knee. With the infection lanced, Manci applied a poultice to the wound to keep it open and draining. Edith slept the sleep of a thousand nights and ate a little extra food organized through the underground.

She had been in bed for only three days when Manci woke her up in the middle of the night and said, "You have to go out quick, quick, quick because tomorrow they will come and take people."

"How can I not limp with the pain? During the day I see stars."

"You have to do everything to walk properly. Do not limp!" Manci warned. "You have to."

Elsa came to the rescue. She supported Edith through the gates past the SS guards, whose eagle eyes were always seeking the sick and vulnerable, and somehow Edith worked without attracting any attention. Perhaps SS Mandel's mandate protected the "little one" with such a low number, but it is more likely that Edith was simply so small she stayed below the radar of her superiors. She worked for three days until Dr. Schwalbova could give her a bed again.

It was a survival seesaw. Three or four days of rest, then escape back to her block before a hospital selection. This was where the secretarial functionaries played an essential role in the survival of prisoners in the hospital. News of selections made its way from the SS offices, where the functionaries who were part of the internal network of resistance worked. When the notices arrived, Manci and the other Jewish doctors "quickly hid the most endangered patients in the ward or 'disguised' them as ward workers." More than once, Edith was hidden as a ward worker, herself.

Dr. Manci Schwalbova had her hands full. Not only did she face typhus and tuberculosis, but an outbreak of meningitis raged through the youngest of the female prisoners. As a doctor, she was in the difficult circumstance of trying to hide those she could save while being forced to leave those she could not to the clutches of Dr. Kremer, or the lesser-known Dr. Clauberger who specialized in sterilization experiments.

Part of the Final Solution's protocol included sterilization for Jews, and beginning in December 1942, Dr. Clauberg began trying out a variety of quick and inexpensive ways to sterilize young women. He was not interested in the health or recovery of his victims, and only a few would survive.

Chapter Twenty-nine

Gift of Eugene Hartmann in memory of Lenka Hertzka,
MUSEUM OF JEWISH HERITAGE, NEW YORK.

THE TWO LETTERS CROSSED PATHS. In hers, Lenka's mother expressed concern about mail delivery—not realizing that a prisoner receiving mail in Auschwitz was in and of itself extraordinary.

March 8, 1943

Dear Lenka!

We are writing you every 10 days by mail and also through the UZ [Jewish Council]. You only acknowledged two cards. We did not receive your January card, nor the letter from February 15th. We would be so happy to be able to send you something. We talk about you at meals and at every occasion…We also sent you money, also for Magduska. The parents of Magduska and Nusi are unhappy that they do not give any sign of life. If they could only add something to your letter…If it is permitted, please write always about our relatives and acquaintances. We are all healthy. We await your letters impatiently and kiss you warmly.

> Kisses, Milan.
> I kiss you, Opa.
> From me too, Mama

Lenka's letter also expressed concern about the post. Despite her position working for one of the top Gestapo and the privileges she received, she did not always get her mail.

April 2, 1943

My dears,

First I would like to wish you many happy returns dear Mama, even if it's rather late. I wish you all health and luck and that we can celebrate the next birthday together. This time the usual present, I am afraid, will be missing, but I believe that you will probably forgive me that. I got Lilly's card from 9th March. Since then I am

impatiently waiting for more post, unfortunately
in vain. Why don't you write more often? One
can also send little sausages and little packages of
cheese. Besides that nothing is new. I work as before and thank God I'm healthy. I send all my
love and hug you all.

Lenka

The first anniversary of the girls' first day in the Poprad
camp was also SS Franz Wunsch's birthday. He was twenty-
one years old. One year earlier, the girls had descended into
tears as they were herded away from their parents and families.
Now, they barely blinked when the latest transport from
Greece arrived carrying 2,800 men, women, and children—
2,191 of whom were gassed. The 192 women registered in
camp were numbered 38,721–38,912; the 417 men's numbers
started at 109,371. While sorting the Greeks' clothes and belongings, Rita—the white kerchiefs' kapo—again announced
to the girls that she needed performers. Glorious monkeys.
Slaves of entertainment and labor.

No one could say no.

Of the prisoners chosen to perform, only one would be sincere as she sang a traditional birthday song and cheered,
boisterously, "How nice that you were born, we'd have really
missed you otherwise. How nice that we're all together. We congratulate your birthday!"

Singing to Franz Wunsch out in the open with everyone else,
did Helena feel the words held secret meaning? Was she really
happy they were together and that he had been born? Could
she imagine life without him? Stockholm syndrome was not a
term yet, but the phenomenon certainly existed. To be fair,
Helena had fallen in love with the young SS man, and he had
fallen in love with her, too. He would carry the photo he had
taken of her in his wallet to his dying day. But there is no deny-

ing that it was a relationship defined by power—his. She had no choice in the matter. Not if she wanted to survive.

Of course, his infatuation with Helena gave her status and power over the others. "If I had said, he [Franz] would have saved me by a second. All the women were disgruntled. There was a reason to be disgruntled there. I could just say the word and a quarter of them would disappear.* But I did not do it." That was extraordinary power to have, let alone to admit to having, yet in the same breath she denies ever having had a physical relationship with Wunsch. In earlier testimonies, she claims they shared only a word or two in passing. But a few years later, she admits "in the end I honestly loved him."

When asked if she saw Helena at work, Edith laughs. "I didn't see her a lot. I didn't see him do a lot, either. They were up on the high shelves, above the mounds of clothes. She was very concentrated on herself and her love with this guy."

Helena's critics believed she "stayed alive" because of Wunsch, but he was not there to protect her all of the time. "I could have been killed twenty thousand times in other places," she says. And if news of the affair had gotten out to his higher-ups, he would have been severely punished. Of course, she would have lost her life. Still, among prisoners, their relationship was not the best-kept secret of the war. Many survivors mention Wunsch and Helena in their testimonies. "It angered us all," Eta Zimmerspitz (#1756) says.

As THE ONE-YEAR ANNIVERSARY of the first transport passed, Edith explains their bodies had learned better how to survive. "Not that things were better, but our bodies began to get used to certain conditions—weather conditions, living conditions. When we first came in, we didn't know anything, but now we

---

* Helena was referring to the other women working in Canada, who knew about her relationship with Wunsch.

knew" how to survive. Starvation had taken its toll on mental acuity and physical strength, but once a body had adjusted to the lack of food, it also figured out how to sustain itself, at least for a while.

The occupancy level of the women's camp was just over fifteen thousand, but women were about to be registered with numbers close to forty thousand. In one year, more than twenty-four thousand women and girls who had been registered in camp had died, most of them Jewish. Of the fifteen thousand women now registered, more than ten thousand were listed as "not used for work," and 2,369 were defined as "not able-bodied," which probably means in the hospital or in Block 25. Now that women's deaths were finally being calculated at the end of each month, a clearer picture of the women's camp arises out of the ashes of their history. The totals for the month of March 1943 reveal devastating losses: 3,391 women died in camp, 1,802 of them in gas chambers. That means 1,589 women died of disease, starvation, medical experiments, or violence.

With the typhus epidemic still raging, Commandant Höss ordered that all vehicles used to transport prisoners now had to be disinfected thoroughly. He also ordered that the prisoners' clothing be disinfected after they were moved from camp. Reading between the lines of the order, one can see that he is referencing the trucks taking prisoners to the gas chambers. How else would there be clothing to disinfect without human beings in them?

THE POLISH MEN who drove the trucks in and out of the women's camp in Birkenau and helped the girls in the *leichenkommando* were always asking for a little extra food, which Bertha and the other girls generously shared whenever they had any to spare. With these men came outside information, and as winter receded, they let Bertha and the others know that Passover was a few weeks away.

It is understandable that for some, faith was impossible. "Who needed religion there?" Edie (#1949) asks. "We could not have religion. We couldn't have nothing. Who would be bothered?"

Bertha, for one, bothered. She and her friends decided to risk holding a Seder and let the others in Block 27 know their plan so that they could begin organizing food. One of the girls smuggled raisins out of Canada, and someone else organized a lemon and some sugar from the kitchen workers. Those were all the ingredients they needed to make raisin wine, except water.

The girls of the *leichenkommando* had access to drinking water, but they needed a container. Margie's container was probably the one they used. In the middle of the night, the wine-makers set the container atop the wood-burning stove in the middle of the block and waited. A watched pot never boils; it takes even longer when your life depends on it.

In the preemptive silence of a Birkenau night, there was always a gunshot's report, a troubled dreamer's moan, a death-rattle breath, a scurrying rat. But in Block 27 that night, there was a sense of mystery in the darkness. This was God's work. It gave their lives meaning. Resistance does that for the spirit.

With the water finally boiling, they added the raisins, lemon, and sugar and covered the container with a kerchief to keep the wine clean from debris. Setting it up high in the corner of one of the *koyas* so that the rats would not get into it, they left the wine to ferment and fell asleep.

Every twenty-four hours, someone stirred the wine with her spoon. On the second day, a few bubbles had formed on the top; by the third day, the raisins had risen and were bobbing about on the surface and starting to lose their color. The liquid had turned from clear to light amber. It was working! After a week of fermenting, the wine was dark brown—not the most appetizing color, but it was wine. The girls strained it through a clean cloth into their red bowls. Then, when the container was empty, they poured the strained wine back into the container, covered it again, and let it sit quietly on the upper *koya* until Passover.

Dr. Clauberg had a different idea about how to celebrate Passover. He had chosen Peggy and "another four or five from Poland, who were also long in Auschwitz" for sterilization experiments. "They dressed us in beautiful striped dresses, a nice three-quarter coat, a beautiful kerchief. I had a little hair already." They were waiting by the door in the morning when Erna, one of the Slovak doctors who worked with Manci Schwalbova, saw them standing there.

"What are you doing here?" she asked the girls.

"I don't know what we are doing here," Peggy told her.

Erna went directly into the office to speak to Dr. Clauberg. "You don't need to make experiments on girls who are a year already in Auschwitz," she told him. "There is nothing anymore to make experiments on. They don't have their period. Nothing. You are better off taking newcomers from the new transports."

Ten minutes later, she came back out of the office and said, "Girls, go back to your block. You're going to work."

The curvaceous and beautiful Marta F. (#1796) from Prešov would not be so lucky. On April 1, 1942, Commandant Höss would designate Block 10 of the main camp, under the command of SS Brigadier General Professor Dr. Carl Clauberg, for sterilization experiments on women.

THIS YEAR'S SEDER would be different from the first year's spontaneous recitation of prayers. And that was true all over Europe; secret Seders were being held by Jews in camps, in ghettos, in hiding, and by those who were barely free. This ancient tradition connected Bertha and her friends to a larger world—an invisible, spiritual world. They were not alone in Auschwitz. They were praying with thousands of their people, many of whom were now in the same predicament as the first girls had been a year earlier, or worse off. And still they prayed. "You play with your life to do something like this," Bertha explains, "but it was worth it." If they were going to be punished for being Jewish, they might as well act Jewish.

As evening descended and the shadows outside lengthened, the girls of Block 27 organized themselves on their *koyas*. One of the women in the block was a Hebrew teacher, and she instructed them as a rabbi would have, giving meaning to the rituals and reminding them of the prayers. The homemade raisin wine was poured into their red bowls and held over their heads. One of the girls had smuggled potatoes into the block. There was no matzo, but to eat a potato! The ritual fed their souls and brought God into the misery of their lives. If God could lead their ancestors out of slavery, how could he leave them in Auschwitz? "In the darkness, we prayed for freedom."

Chapter Thirty

Postcard image taken from Eugene Hartmann interview, 1996.
USC Shoah Foundation—The Institute for Visual History
and Education; sfi.usc.edu.

May 6, 1943

Dear Lenka!

We just received your card today. We have to
take turns to write to you every week—and believe
me, it is a cause of such heartfelt love. I will also

send you something, but sadly everything is uncertain and difficult. I will send clothes and stockings. We are well. Only our great concern about you makes life bitter. Otherwise, all is well. We got something from Nusi [unreadable] but hear nothing about Magduska! We also read the cards from the Wahrmannova girls [also on first transport from Prešov], with whose parents we are often together. Please give them our most heartfelt wishes.

WE KISS YOU!
Pipapio [Grandpa], Lilly, Milan

Crossing its path in the mail was a letter from Lenka to her brother, Simon, that gives us insight into Lenka's life as a functionary. She lets him know that the post is delivered to prisoners every Friday and apologizes that she "couldn't write in December" as she had been ill "for a few weeks." That she was ill and allowed to return to work says volumes about her upper-level position in camp. "We are here with a number of Prešov girls and have had the chance to spend some free time together," she writes. "I have also made many new friends here." No wonder the family was confused. If she was seeing lots of girls from town why wasn't she also seeing her younger cousins? This was her first card to mention anything cryptic, though: "Nusi and Zola are with Zsenka, our cousin."

Almost immediately Mama and Lilly wrote back. "Magduska's mother [Irma] is very sick, Bela cries for Magduska and blames you that you do not write about her. Nusi's mother would also like to know…Who is Aunt Zsenka?"

Prisoners were often so cautious with coded messages that they were indecipherable. But we can guess that by May 1943, the sunshine-faced Nusi Hartmann was dead. The postcard the family had received from her was one of those that had been postdated and sent after she died. We have no idea under what circumstances Olga Hartmann (Nusi) died or on what date. Magduska's fate was also still a mystery.

"DRESCHLER WAS UGLY." Everyone said so. Her big buckteeth protruded from beneath her lips even when she tried to close them. Notorious for beating and otherwise abusing prisoners, she was feared and hated by everyone. You certainly did not want to hear her shouting your number angrily, as if it were a death sentence. But then Edith and Elsa did. The mere sound of Dreschler's voice screaming her number made the skin on the back of Edith's neck prickle. What now?

—1970! Is still outside?

The number hung on the hot breath of the ugliest SS in the world. Elsa looked at Edith in terror. Did they face the wardress or run? And where could they run, especially with Edith's limp? Slowly, eyes hugging the ground, Edith turned around.

Dreschler was pointing at them and almost hitting their block elder with her stick. "How do you let such prisoners go out for work, still?" She pointed at Edith's tiny frame and Elsa's terrified face. "They are here a long time. They have earned being some- place to work a little less hard, not to work so hard outside in rain, and snow, and freezing rain! Give them good jobs!"

Their block elder, Gizzy, who was also from the first trans- port and did not have a reputation for being either kind or fair, looked at the two girls with disdain.

—Now!

Dreschler yelled in the block elder's face.

—You! 1970! You are a *stubendienst*! Gizzy ordered.

Edith hesitated. Elsa didn't move.

—You too! She waved at Elsa.

—Get inside!

Edith and Elsa scampered out of roll call and back into the block before Wardress Dreschler could change her mind. Except for her short stint in the white kerchiefs, Edith had worked outside for almost a year and a half. Few people could survive working outside for so long, certainly not those from the first transport. Edith couldn't believe their luck. Suddenly, their lives had changed for the better. They would no longer be working every minute under the constant scrutiny of the SS with their dogs, and no longer be as vulnerable to SS whims. Of course, a few weeks later, Wardress Dreschler would slap Edith so hard that she flew through the air and landed centimeters from the electric fence. They weren't that safe.

Getting the job as a block cleaner "felt like a whole new era." As *stubendienste*, Edith and Elsa now rose extra early to accept the kettles of tea when they arrived on trucks. They served the girls heading out to work before roll call then cleaned the inside of the blocks and the *koyas*, emptied the ashes in the woodstove, swept the dirt floor, and served the bread when the girls came back from work at night.

That first night in their new positions, Edith and Elsa were called by one of the other room attendants into the block elder's room and handed a few pieces of extra bread. Edith watched as those in charge of their block showed her and Elsa the trick to cutting the bread into quarters that left the middle untouched, so the functionaries in the block could get extra portions. Edith had worked hard labor for so long that her loyalty was for those still suffering outside. Why should girls working less vigorously get more food?

"I don't want this!" she blurted. "It's stolen bread. Maybe because of this piece of bread, a girl died from hunger. It's not bread for me." She looked at the girl who had more weight on her bones than anyone else in the block. "And you don't need it, either."

"What? Do you think that by not eating this little piece of bread, you will stop it?" the girl yelled back indignantly. "You can't stop it!"

"That is on your conscience," Edith hissed. "You will do what you want, and we will do what we want."

Elsa nodded in solidarity with Edith. "We don't want this bread."

They stuck to their allotted slices and turned their backs on the greed of the more fortunate. To refuse extra portions may not have been easy for some, but for Edith and Elsa, it was an act of spiritual resistance. One more instance in which young women did their best to preserve their spiritual values and act humanely in the face of so much inhumanity.

When the cauldrons of soup were delivered by the men that Sunday, Edith and Elsa helped ladle the lunchtime allotment into the girls' red bowls. This was the first time either of them had been in a position to help those around them, and it did not take long for the girls to realize that Edith and Elsa were stirring the soup so that the vegetables and bits of meat rose to the top and were ladled into their bowls. Whispers began to filter down the line: "Elsa and Edith are mixing the soup. Get in Elsa and Edith's line." Girls changed lines and thanked Elsa and Edith for serving everyone equally. Starvation makes people stingy. It also makes you remember every slight. Survivors are quick to remember anyone who stole food from them, and every extra bit of food they were given.

Working as *stubendienste* may have started as a relief, but nightmares were a constant in camp. One afternoon, Edith returned from running an errand and entered Block 13 to find Elsa sobbing hysterically. One of the women had gotten through the registration processing despite being pregnant. It happened sometimes. The woman's belly wasn't so far distended that anyone had noticed, her prison clothes hid the bump, and there had been no selections to reveal it. When she went into labor, Elsa ran to get Dr. Manci Schwalbova. It was dangerous to deliver a baby in camp. The crying could attract the SS or one of their many spies. Everyone involved could go to the gas for help-

ing the mother. Such was the horror of life in a death camp—
there could be no life. Certainly no new life. There was only one
way to save the mother's life, and that was to get rid of the baby.

It was before two o'clock in the afternoon, so the trucks had
not arrived yet to remove the bodies piled outside the blocks.
Elsa was the one who had to hide the baby under the corpses
so that the SS wouldn't find it and do an inspection of women
prisoners. It was crying when she abandoned it.

Hyperventilating. Hysterical. Her eyes bloodshot from the
torrent of tears, Elsa told Edith what she had done. They held
each other and wept. The mother lay on the middle shelf, unable to move, lost without her child. Milk dripped from her
breasts, untasted.

Edith's eyes are red and brimming with tears as she recalls
the incident. Anguished and sobbing, she blurts out, "How did
I survive this thing?"

How did anyone?

TRUE TO HER word, Frida Zimmerspitz (#1548) had been
working on a plan to escape from Auschwitz since the day she
and her sisters arrived. Their younger sister Margit had come
on a later transport with four more of their cousins. "We were
a big family in the camp, and we didn't want anyone to lack
anything, so some [the Jewish kapo, Frances Mangel-Tack for
one] assumed roles in order to protect the family," Eta Zimmerspitz (#1756) says. "It is hard for me to explain..." It is not too
hard to understand though. Families helped each other, and
Frances Mangel-Tack made sure those who did not get jobs as
functionaries got into Canada.

Eta and her sister Fanny (#1755), and their other cousin,
Martha (#1741) lived in the same block as their cousins, the
Zimmerspitz sisters. This should have worked in their favor,
but the four sisters had formed a closed unit and did not allow
anyone—not even their cousins—inside. Frida ran the entire

block as if it were the Zimmerspitzes' personal fiefdom. They were working a few sidelines as well. "The sisters got too popular," says their cousin Frances Mangel-Tack. Popular with the SS maybe, but not with other prisoners. Frida was thought to be a spy for the SS.

"They were not nice," Ruzena Gräber Knieža (#1649) says. One of the sisters even stamped her foot and yelled at Ruzena, "You haven't died yet? You're still here? I thought you died ages ago."

According to Eta Zimmerspitz, the sisters didn't even share the extra bread they purloined. They were considered the worst kind of functionary, lording their rank over the less fortunate and running a black market through the sorting detail, trading bread for gold, diamonds, and jewelry.

The SS "liked that [Frida] was spying for them," Frances Mangel-Tack tries to explain in her eight-hour testimony with the USC Shoah interviewer. But "she was spying *against* them." The story Frances tells is convoluted and confusing. She talks as if we should know everyone she is talking about, and it is hard to follow the players. But comparing her testimony with those of her cousins and other survivors, we begin to get a clearer picture of what Frida and her sisters were doing. It all had to do with greed. The SS wanted to smuggle contraband out of Canada to send home; the sisters collected the valuables brought to them by the girls in the sorting details, trading gold and valuables for food. Then they bartered the prisoners' swag for special favors from the SS.

The girls in Canada risked their lives smuggling valuables out in their pockets and shoes, then made their way to the Zimmerspitz block, where they traded their valuables for food or medicine. "It was disgusting what they were doing," Ruzena Gräber Knieža says, "selling bread to starving girls." But gold is inedible, and in Auschwitz that meant it was less valuable than bread.

Eventually, some of the top SS figured out that one of the sisters was working with the underground. "There was a German woman from Ravensbrück, she was the brothel mistress, and Margit...said something to her," Frances Mangel-Tack says. Evidently, the brothel mistress then informed the SS. "It was a very big thing what was going on."

It was even bigger than the brothel mistress or the SS realized. Not only were the sisters helping the underground network, they were also planning their own escape. Before going to work on the night shift sorting clothes in Canada, Frida—the one with the "biggest mouth"—beckoned to her younger cousins, Martha, Eta, and Fanny to come into the sisters' room. The four sisters sat their younger cousins down and told them to look out for each other and take care of themselves. It was an odd moment, almost an opening of hearts. Eta and Fanny were grateful to finally feel acknowledged by their elder cousins, who were normally dismissive and often outright rude. Eta, her sister, and their cousin Marta headed to work that night feeling more positive about their ability to survive the hardships in camp.

In the morning, Frida, Ruzena, Malvina, and Margit were gone. The girls in the block woke and looked around in confusion. Where were the sisters? They filed outside and got their tea. Lined up for roll call, but nothing was as it should be. The SS were stamping back and forth and yelling at everyone. Then one of the SS pointed at her and her sister and shouted their numbers.

—Prisoners 1755 and 1756! Get out of line!

They were ordered to report immediately to Auschwitz I.

"We thought someone in our family had come to release us," Eta recalls.

With a kapo as escort, the girls were about to head out of the women's camp when their cousin, the kapo, Frances Mangel-Tack rushed up to them.

"Do not admit you are related to our cousins," she warned them in Slovak. "They are looking for anyone with that name Zimmerspitz."

"Why? What happened?" Fanny asked.

"Just keep quiet." Frances warned. "Don't say a word!" Then she was gone.

It was an order that sank into Eta's subconscious. Marching along the road from Birkenau to Auschwitz, the sisters had time to fret and worry. What did Frances mean, don't admit they are related? In silence Eta and Fanny walked the distance to Auschwitz I, where they were delivered to Gestapo headquarters in Block 11, the Block of Death, for questioning. Generally reserved for political prisoners and Russian POWs, Block 11 now had four young women in it. All that stood between the execution wall and Eta and her own sister was Frances's warning. Tortured screams came from within the belly of the prison. They sounded like a woman's.

Dressed in his black uniform and polished brass buttons, the SS interrogator assessed the young women in front of him. He asked them if they knew the Zimmerspitz sisters.

Eta opened her mouth to answer the question but nothing came out. She had lost her ability to speak.

—We were in Block 18 with them, Fanny answered.

—And?

—And nothing. They were the block and room elders. They were horrible to everyone.

—Aren't you related?

—No.

"How can you say that you are not related?" he demanded, pointing at Eta. "She looks exactly like Rosa."

It all hung on Fanny. Eta had lost her ability to speak.

"We may share the same name, but there is no family connection!" Fanny said. "There are lots of Zimmerspitzes in Auschwitz-Birkenau!" Just look at all the Friedmans in camp.

—They never even gave us extra bread or privileges. Ask anyone. They were mean to us, Fanny argued.

Eta nodded. It was all true. Not even an extra portion of bread.

Their reputation must have been known, and the truth Fanny told bore up. It was clear that she and Eta did not know anything. The two sisters were allowed to return to Birkenau. Never had hell on earth looked so welcome.

So HOW DID the Zimmerspitz sisters get caught?

Ruzena Gräber Knieža says a Polish prisoner found out about their plans and sold the story to the SS so she could get a lighter sentence. Frances says it was the brothel mistress. Eta says she met a Polish man in Israel, years after the war, who said he was their contact on the outside, who had tried to help them escape. That would have been a shrewd strategy, because the SS were notorious for taking payment and then betraying prisoners. It is an old story—to buy your freedom, you had to pay the SS or someone on the outside to help. But the reward for foiling an escape attempt or catching a prisoner trying to escape was usually a week's vacation, sometimes a promotion.

Whatever happened, none of the other girls understood that the sisters' cruelty had been a ruse to protect anyone who knew them in case they were caught. Anyone they showed kindness to would have been in danger after their escape, and a target for interrogation. So the sisters protected their cousins and everyone else in the block by being rude and nasty. The wealth the Zimmerspitz sisters accrued went to the underground. Their greed was for freedom.

We don't know why there is no mention of their escape, capture, or execution in the historic record. All we have is family and prisoners' testimonies. Did the SS decide it was too embarrassing to acknowledge? They had been tricked by four young Jewish women, after all. Very few people ever managed to escape from Auschwitz-Birkenau. Almost no Jewish women even attempted.

Men's attempts at escape, their numbers, and their names, are consistently recorderd in the *Auschwitz Chronicle*, but there is no mention of the Zimmerspitz sisters' escape attempt or execution. There is no record of them in Yad Vashem, except on a transfer list from Birkenau to New Berlin. Nothing in the Auschwitz "Death Books." The Zimmerspitz sisters seem to have been expunged from the historic record.

Within earshot of each other in the hope of breaking the other three, the sisters were "badly tortured. They cut them to pieces. It was terrible," Frances says. SS Taube evidently beat Frida and dragged her out in front of the roll call to make an example of her. But the Zimmerspitz sisters were tough. The SS got nothing out of them. Even bigmouthed Frida kept her silence. She was the last of the sisters to be executed.

Chapter Thirty-one

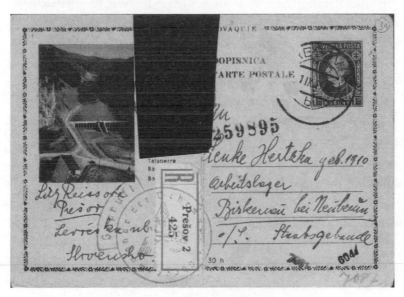

SEPTEMBER 16, 1943

As always, Lilly's card was cheery and full of bits of gossip that make little sense now. Names of people getting married, health concerns, gossip. They reveal that the Jewish community in eastern Slovakia continued despite the dark fates of many friends and family members. The Hartmann farm was hanging on, but "we are completely without help," Lenka's mother writes. The post was also having trouble getting through. Two of Lenka's letters, "the 15th of July and the 15th of August," had arrived almost simultaneously. Censoring was now much more common, as well. Blocks cut out of the middle or sides of the postcards obscure the messages. But a naive phrase, "Your return is our hope," frequently passed.

MORE THAN ONE GIRL would owe her life to Dr. Manci Schwalbova. But other Jewish doctors and nurses helped prisoners, too. The Polish prisoner Sara Bleich (#1966) had gotten relatively easy work in the red kerchiefs, though "sorting rags and clothes from the prisoners...was a nasty task since clothes were full of blood and dirt." Like Ida before her, Sara contracted typhus. Treatment in 1943 was different from 1942, though. Sara was allowed to stay in the hospital ward and had been there for about three weeks when "the devil in person," a new doctor who had arrived in Auschwitz at the end of May, walked through the ward, selecting women for the gas.

One of the doctors grabbed Sara from her cot and hid her in a barrel, then threw a blanket over the top. "And with that, she saved my life." Sara was one of the first girls to escape Dr. Josef Mengele's clutches. Without such spirited and courageous female doctors hiding them from the serial killers that stalked the hospital wards, very few girls or women would have survived at all.

"Mengele was so beautiful you would not believe that he did such bad things," Eta Zimmerspitz (#1956) says. "There was a young kid, he forced him to have sex and he just watched them." A modern-day Frankenstein who delighted in torturing and conducting experiments on innocent men, women, and twins, Mengele was someone everyone tried to avoid. But some functionaries, including Ella (#1950) and her sister Edie (#1949), had to deal with him directly and on a regular basis.

Ella's secretarial skills and neat cursive handwriting brought her to the immediate attention of Mengele, who "promoted" her to become a scribe in the sauna, as the area was called where new arrivals were processed—strip searched, disinfected, and (from 1943 on) tattooed. Her job was to record new female prisoners' names and numbers. As Dr. Mengele's scribe, Ella would face constant reminders of the tenuousness of every woman's life in Auschwitz; her neat, orderly lists documented the numbers of women selected to die or to be experimented upon. Eventually, she was promoted, becoming one of the tattooists. Ella always used "very small and neat" numbers and tried to ink only the inside of a woman's arm.

Ella does not discuss how she coped with the stress of working under Mengele. Even her sister, Edie, who was rarely at a loss for words, stammers at the memory of him. "Everyone was shaking when Mengele came in [the office]. I can't even describe [it]. If you looked at him, you could see this anger in him. You could see this dark... This dark nothing. Terrible."

Ria Hans (#1980) was among the staff working in the hospital when Mengele arrived in camp. He cursed and accosted her verbally, while forcing her to insert needles into skeletal *musselmen,* administering the phenol injections that would kill them. Edith says that Ria was caught trying to save a woman's life. "Her punishment was to be placed in a standing cell in Block 11 for six months."

Years later, when survivors had to apply for restitution from the German government, one survivor, who wished to remain anonymous, wrote about how Dr. Horst Schumann and Dr. Josef Mengele "performed test experiments on me by injecting viruses in me to see how my body was affected, which they observed by taking blood and watching me suffer. I did not get malaria, which they injected, but I contracted typhoid fever and other sicknesses of which I don't know the names. This six-month period is a blur to me because I was sick so much of the time."

As 1943 PROGRESSED, other girls from the first transport who had been working outside also found better jobs. A special laundry detail now included Ruzena Gräber Knieža, Rena and Danka Kornreich, and Dina Dranger, who had been moved to the cellar under the SS staff quarters, where Lenka Hertzka and others in the secretarial pool lived. Separated from the rest of the camp population, the girls in the laundry and sewing rooms were removed from the dangerous epidemics that plagued the general prison population. A horizon of hope appeared in their bleak lives. Getting into the laundry or sewing details was the kind of promotion that should have encouraged qualities of grace and kindness. So Ruzena Gräber was shocked when, one Sunday afternoon, the mother of one of the girls, sneaked into the cellar where the girls were resting.

The poor woman fell on her knees and reached for her twenty-two-year-old daughter's hands. "I am outside digging graves!" she wailed.

She was wretched. Worn rags hung off her body. She was covered in the festering filth of Birkenau. Revolted, the daughter, Theresa, cringed and backed away from the skeletal woman, who was not yet a *musselman* but nearing the point of no return.

She screamed at her mother. —Who am I to help you? Get out of here before you get caught and we both get killed!

And with that she threw her mother out of the block.

"I don't know if she had the courage or power to help her," Ruzena says, "but I saw how she treated her. That is a terrible picture in my mind. Under normal circumstances she was probably a perfectly nice person, so low can human beings go or be forced to go."

HELPING OTHERS COULD CARRY CONSEQUENCES. Rose (#1371) had been working on the farm in Harmęże for over a year and a half. Raising pheasants and rabbits, tending the warrens, and keeping the grounds clean for the fowl, she took pride in her work and worked hard. Her kapo even left her in charge at one point when the kapo had to go away. One day Rose visited the hospital in Birkenau, and one of the nurses asked her to take an important letter back with her to Harmęże and deliver it to another prisoner. Rose slipped the letter into her shoe, not realizing that she was being watched by one of the SS spies—a Ukrainian woman who immediately turned her in. As Rose headed out of the gate, she heard the dreaded SS shout her number.

—1371, halt!

Rose froze.

—Take off your shoe!

The note was from one member of the underground to another. Rose was immediately arrested and thrown into Block *Smierci*, Block 11, where political prisoners, resistance fighters, and escapees—like the Zimmerspitz sisters—were interrogated, tortured, and usually executed. She would spend months in detention and was not released until October 1944.

IRENA FEIN (#1564) was now working with six other girls, going from one house to another, fixing things for the wives of the SS. Sometimes the girls did laundry, sometimes they were left to clear out a house that had been recently vacated by SS families. These were the best houses to work in because while their SS guards stood outside, Irena and the others would steal the leftover food in the pantries. When you are starving, everything revolves around food, and almost every prisoner characterizes the quality of a work detail by the amount of food they organized or were given as a reward.

Irena recalls entering a home where one of the wives "was cooking curly cabbage with potatoes." While the other girls went off to do the laundry and clean the rooms, the mistress of the house asked Irena, "Could you help me hang up some curtains?"

"*Ja, gnädige Frau.* Yes, ma'am."

Irena climbed up a stepladder as the woman passed her the drapes, then hooked them onto the brackets over her head.

"How is it in camp? Are you happy there?" the woman asked.

Irena hesitated. How could this woman actually believe she was happy in Auschwitz? "Please, don't ask."

"Why not? I am curious what it is like. We are not allowed to visit."

"I can't talk about it."

"Why ever not?"

"Because you will tell your husband and I will get killed. I'm sorry."

"Why, it's so bad?"

Irena did not respond. She finished securing the last fold of the curtain and stepped down from the ladder. This was the sort of conversation that could land a girl in the gas chamber, and the German woman was too naive to know that. Their conversation was a bitter revelation. "Even the wives didn't know what's going on there." Outside of the house, just a few meters away, women and children were being gassed and burned to death. Yet this woman was raising her children and living in a world where mass murder either did not exist or was justified in such a way that it was not considered a crime. How could anyone live under the clouds of smoke billowing overhead and have no idea of the atrocities being perpetrated by her husband, his colleagues, and the whole regime? Did they not know because they were innocent or because they did not want to believe the truth before their eyes?

The woman did not need to say thank you, but she did. Irena did not trust that the gesture was sincere, but nodded with a perfunctory "*bitte.*"

———————

LENKA'S ADDRESS WAS CHANGING, and she had warned her family about the move. The new address on the cards indicated New Berlin. This may also have been an area the prisoners referred to as the New Blocks, which began to house the girls of the laundry in 1944. Lenka may have learned that her messages were being censored and somehow sent a telegram on October 15, 1943, to her aunt and uncle:

> Many thanks for your loving lines, which gave me great joy. And I am very much looking forward to the package you mentioned. You could just throw it on the train. Send something that won't break or get rotten, cheese, sausage, salami, kraut, or sardines in cans are good. Can you send sardines from Portugal through UZ post? If you write to my aunt, urge Papa to write because I have heard nothing from him. I am just sorry to say we don't work in the same place but I know that she will write to you, too. I have heard that Nusi has not visited *Herz tete.*

Lenka was still trying to give them news of Nusi's death, this time by referring to herself while using the word Herz, which also means heart in Slovak. Her message was clear.

Almost immediately, Lenka received a typed letter from Ernest Glattstein, who clearly was seeking information about his family and neighbors:

> I would be very grateful if you can let me know whether my sister, Ilone Grunwald, brother-in-law Marcel Drody, Uncle Zeig Lefkovits and son Robert, with Dr. Kraus Bela—who lived opposite you— were with Regina, Dundy, and whether all the above named, arrived together with Nusi?

His queries about whether his family members are with Nusi are the only way he can find out the fates of his loved ones. A few lines later, he mentions several of the girls from the first transport: "Please say hello to all those I know. Wachs Seri, Wahrmann Margit, Ella Friedman [#1950], Edie Friedman [#1949]."

IT WAS DECEMBER when a postcard card from Ellie and Kornelia Mandel, the sisters who had traveled with Nusi and Magduska, arrived in Rožkovany at the Hartmanns' farm. It is one of the few cards that there is no copy of, but Magduska's brother, Eugene, remembers every word:

> Dear Mr. Hartmann,
>   Thank you for your little package that I received from you. We are well off. I received mail from your daughter, Magduska, and niece, Nusi, in *gan ʿedn.** They are well off. They ask you to visit Uncle Kaddish often.

Magduska was dead. Bela was devastated, Eugene, her little brother, completely bewildered. They did not tell Magduska's mother. Everyone was racked with guilt. They had practically scolded the girls for not writing. What must Lenka think of them? Did she even know about Magduska? The card did not mention anything more, nor could it have. How long had the girls been dead? How did they die? No one knew. Their lives and their deaths are a permanent question mark that hangs over the family to this day, with no answers ever to arise from the charnel ground of Auschwitz.

---

* גַּן עֵדֶן, *heaven* in Hebrew.

Chapter Thirty-two

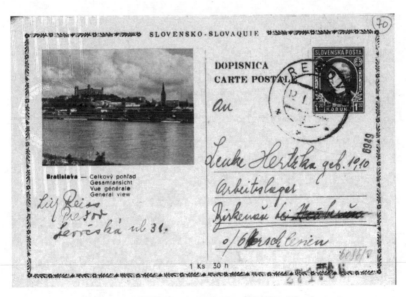

PHOTO COURTESY ARCHIVES DIVISION, YAD VASHEM
WORLD HOLOCAUST REMEMBRANCE CENTER.

December 1, 1943

Dear Lenka!

I hope you received Willi's letter and Milanko's picture. We have put aside the jacket,

salami, and medicines. Yesterday, we sent shoes and wurst—hopefully we will soon get detailed news from you whether you handed everything over to Kato [Katarina Danzinger (#1843)]. In November, we sent clothes and 500 kroner and you should have received them by now. Also, 3.5 and 2 kilos—we could hardly breathe—have you received them? Make enquiries with Kato. Willi hopes his sister-in-law has visited you. Bela is very ill, weeping for Magduska.

We are all thinking of you. Hang tough!

Kisses, Lilly

AFTER FIFTEEN MONTHS in the *leichenkommando*, Dr. Manci Schwalbova told Bertha and the others who worked with her that it was time to move to a different detail. Not all of them had made it through the fifteen months, but Peshy Steiner, Elena Zuckermenn, and Margie Becker were still there. Dr. Manci Schwalbova wielded what little power she had to arrange for the girls to work in Canada—they deserved an easier job after working so long moving corpses.

Canada was not the heaven everyone made it out to be, though. "We were able to eat during the day, but we had to go to selections," Bertha says. "And the first day, I had twisted my ankle and was brought back on a stretcher. I thought I am for the crematorium." Being one of Dr. Manci Schwalbova's pets saved her, and Bertha was allowed to continue working. Sorting clothes did not require a lot of walking, and as long as she could stand and sort, she could stay alive. However, Bertha did not "have luck in Canada!" She had made friends with a girl from France and decided to sneak a gift out for her. She had seen other girls slipping clothes on and walking out without getting caught. How hard could it be? Bertha stuffed a blouse under her uniform, just before the end of work, and headed out to roll call.

—1048! one of the SS shouted.

Bertha has one of those clear, honest faces. Her cheeks flushed bright pink. That was all the SS needed to see, to know he had guessed right.

—Take off your uniform!

Slowly, she removed her jacket and her own blouse, and the crumpled item of clothing that she was trying to smuggle fell to the ground. She was lucky not to get twenty-five lashes, as Joan Rosner had gotten when she was caught organizing. But to Bertha, a teenager still clinging to her vanity, the punishment she got was even worse. The SS man ordered her head shaved.

Up to this point, she had had her head shaved only seven times. Once she had become a member of the *leichenkommando*, her hair had been safe. Having hair was a badge of honor. A status symbol. A sign that you were special. Now, Bertha had haphazard tufts of hair sticking out like brambles from her scalp. She felt ugly. Worse, she was ugly! But this shaving did something more serious to the teen—it crushed her spirit. She "couldn't stop crying" and fell into complete despair. It was "the only time I really wanted to commit suicide."

For deeply religious girls, the shaving of their heads should have occurred as part of their marriage. On her first day in Auschwitz, Bertha had been one of the girls brutally examined gynecologically and robbed of her maidenhood. For Bertha, a newly shaved head publicly announced her shame and rape. For fifteen months, her hair had been safe; now, the horror of that first day flooded back. The pain. The blood. The screaming girls around her. Her own screams.

She had lost everything. Her family. Her home. Her virginity. Her hair was the last straw—inconsolable, she wept and wept. She considered going to the wires and ending it all. Peshy

Steiner came to her rescue. Peshy loved Bertha. Held her. Comforted her. Saved her friend from taking her own life.

In a documentary film from 1981, Bertha leans against the *koya* in Block 27, where she lived and slept next to Peshy. "This is where Peshy Steiner saved my life," she says. It is a moment of deep regret, for Bertha was not able to save Peshy's. "She was very, very ill." She does not say more.

When Peshy became deathly ill, Dr. Manci Schwalbova would certainly have been called in to help, but miracles were few and far between in Auschwitz. Not everyone could be saved from the many dread diseases—including meningitis—that lurked in every filthy corner of their lives. Peshy and Bertha had been like sisters. Without her childhood friend, Bertha faced another dark night of the soul. Like Edith, she had to look to other girls to help pull her out of the abyss of grief. Elena Zuckermenn (#1735) was one of those girls.

While Bertha "didn't have any luck" working in Canada, Margie Becker did. She was a natural contraband rustler, "an artist," she says with a mischievous twinkle in her eyes. "Once, I smuggled a bed jacket in my shoe! I nearly died, it was so tight." She began running her own little black market, trading smuggled clothing for food.

To friends, though, she gave things for free. Margie had gotten to know a girl who spoke a different kind of Yiddish, and the two became close friends while comparing the linguistic differences in their dialects. The girl asked Margie to help her get into a better work detail. Margie smuggled her a "pair of wool pants and a sweater," and the next thing she heard, the girl had been taken in by one of the SS families and was working as their maid. All because she was well dressed. "You know, that's what a difference it meant in anybody's life if you were dressed. They always liked somebody dressed decent," Margie says, shaking her head. "Those louses."

Margie even found a gold ring, which she slipped onto her toe and hid in her shoe, then using it like a savings account, bartered the ring for margarine and bread, which she shared with friends. The trinkets and valuables the girls found in the kerchief details helped them survive, as long as they were not too brazen about what they filched and didn't get caught. Joan Rosner (#1188) saw a girl get shot between the eyes after she was caught hiding some jewelry in her pocket.

DR. MANCI SCHWALBOVA heard about the difficulties Bertha was having in Canada and made her a messenger in the hospital ward, where she could keep an eye on the teen and protect her. Bertha carried documents and memos from one camp to another and spent her days at the back entrance of the ward, waiting for orders. She was also assigned to help deliver food to the bedbound prisoners and "got a little bit more food for doing" that service. Being a hospital messenger was the last job Bertha would work in Auschwitz-Birkenau. It was also the last time she would see her old friends now working in Canada.

At the start of the new year, the girls working in Canada were separated from the rest of the women's camp. Canada had already been relocated to Birkenau to accommodate the expansion from a few sorting barracks to over twenty. Now in an attempt to prevent clothing and other valuables from being smuggled into the general prison population, the SS commandeered the girls and moved them into two blocks within Canada. There were no high-voltage wires around Canada, "only barbed wire. The first two barracks were our living quarters, and the other eighteen were the working places. On the other side, the men had only one barrack. We were separated completely from the rest of the inmates. We didn't have any contact with them anymore," Linda Reich (#1173) explains.

Chapter Thirty-three

Some people say angels have wings. But my angels had feet.

—EDITH FRIEDMAN

BY THE SECOND ANNIVERSARY OF the girls' deportation from Slovakia, those assigned to Canada were working twelve-hour swing shifts, but after work they could walk around the camp road a bit. Ida Eigerman thought that since they were so close to the sauna, she might as well sneak in and have a shower. All by herself. In control of the spigots, she turned the hot water until it burned her skin. She scrubbed her flesh and inhaled the steam until her lungs felt clean of soot and oil and death. She let the water cascade over her forehead and through her hair, down her breasts and hips. She cleaned herself in places she would never have dared if the SS had been watching. She luxuriated in the quiet, the privacy, the peace of the water splashing on the cement beneath her tired feet.

The curfew bell clanged outside. There were no towels. No way to dry herself quickly. She pulled her uniform back on and ran outside.

"What are you doing?" one of the SS women yelled at her.

Ida's hair was wet. Her clothes damp. Her face clean.

Two SS men walked over to where Ida was standing. "They had hands like this. I never saw such big hands." One of the SS slapped her so hard, her teeth rattled in her mouth.

—1930 you are down for twenty-five! the SS woman ordered.

Twenty-five lashes.

Ida was terrified that the next day the commander would arrive and call her number for punishment. "Meanwhile, Ms. Schmidt, the kapo, needed some girls to go to Stabsgebäude." Ida volunteered and escaped punishment. Arriving in the base-ment of the SS headaquarters, Ida would have found an old acquaintance, Rena Kornreich (#1716). It had been four years since they had slipped across the border of Poland and hidden in their uncles' homes in Bardejov. Now their uncles and aunts were gone; their parents, gone; their cousins, mostly gone. How could they, who had come to Auschwitz in the beginning, still be alive?

THE TOWERING DEATH gate now loomed over the windswept ex-panse of Birkenau. Where two years prior there had been nothing but fields, train tracks now ran up to and under the death gate so that human cargo could be delivered directly into the mouth of hell.

The numbers being given to men were now 175,000; women were 76,000. There is no question that getting regis-tered in camp and not going straight to the gas chamber was far less likely for women. That April, 21,000 women were recorded as being in Birkenau, while 46,000 men were being held in the Auschwitz-Birkenau camp complexes.

On April 7, there would be two fewer: Alfréd Wetzler and Rudolf Vrba were about to make their famous escape from Auschwitz. They would be among the few successful escapees, but they were the most important, because their escape would bring to the world the first concrete report on the death camp's layout, the placement of gas chambers and cre-matoriums, and the approximate numbers of Jews who had been gassed. Their report would also be the first acknowledg-ment of the girls of the first transports, the horrors they had suffered in those early months and the fact that they "had dwindled to 5 percent* of their original number" or about four hundred.

Tragically, history would not only refuse to recognize the girls, but the Allied forces would fail to act on Vrba and Wetzler's information. Despite the report being sent to Switz-erland, the United States, Britain, and the Vatican, the Allies did not think bombing the tracks or the crematoriums would "achieve the salvation of the victims to any appreciable extent." They were wrong. Jews were collateral damage in a global war, and Auschwitz was now an über-killing machine capable of ex-ecuting and cremating twenty thousand people per day.

As Rudolf Vrba and Alfréd Wetzler fervently hoped that their report would save the Hungarian Jews from slaughter, the first Hungarian transport of "forty to fifty freight cars" with "approximately one hundred persons" per car arrived. The number of men, women, and children murdered from that transport was not recorded. It was, however, documented in a far more graphic way.

SS-Hauptscharführer Bernhard Walter, head of the Auschwitz photographic laboratory, and his assistant, SS-Unterscharführer Ernst Hofmann, took photographs as Hungarians Jews from Carpatho-Ruthenia disembarked from the transport. The photos they snapped of masses of people walking along the railway tracks, children standing in the birch

---

* Vrba was most likely referring to the first ten transports from Slovakia, which brought 6,051 young Slovak women and 197 Czech women to Auschwitz by the end of April 1942.

forest outside the gas chambers and crematoriums, girls laughing as they sorted goods in Canada were part of a photo essay designed to show the Red Cross that Jewish prisoners were being well taken care of and to dispel any rumors of extermination camps. It is a chilling album of mass murder, chronicled by the murderers themselves.

Leaning over a pile of pots and pans that had been collected from the new arrivals now heading to the gas, Linda Reich was dressed in a white blouse and dark trousers belted at her waist. She was horrified by the thousands of Hungarian Jews she had seen walking past the sorting piles in Canada all morning.

—Smile! SS Walter yelled at her as he focused his camera.

How did she manage to look as if she had just heard a joke, given that a gun was aimed at her head? Her teeth flash for the camera. The click preserves the image. The SS move on. Linda feels her spirit has been robbed. She is not emaciated by hunger. Her hair is pulled back. Her clothes look clean. She looks like a normal human being sorting some pots and pans, not a slave laborer going through thousands of items stolen from people being suffocated in the gas chambers just fifteen meters away, behind the photographer.

Numb, the girls of Canada watched the Hungarians walk to their deaths. Working in such close proximity to the gas chambers was devastating for them all. Some girls warned mothers with children to give their children to the older women. They did not explain why.

Many survivors who worked in Canada, like Erna and Fela Dranger from Tylicz, Poland, were never able to speak about their experience. Living and working just outside the gas chambers was just too much to speak about—ever.

"There were four crematoriums in a row, and about fifty feet away were forty sorting barracks," Linda explains. That is where she, Helena, Irena, Marta F., Erna, Fela, Peggy, Mira Gold, and the many others worked. There were no walls around the gas chambers. "It was a brick building, red, nicely landscaped around, green grass." The girls of Canada were unwitting decoys to the Jews going to their deaths. Highly visible, the well-dressed girls sorting items outside looked like "human beings," not slave laborers.

In some ways, this was an early version of the curved loading chutes that Dr. Temple Grandin designed for slaughterhouses. The idea is that cattle see other cattle walking ahead of them and remain calm as they move into the chutes. Similarly, Jews coming off the transports and heading to their ultimate demise saw the young women working in Canada and thought, *That will be us soon.*

In reality, "95 percent went straight to the gas chamber." The girls looked out "day and night, seeing the flames high in the skies…and the smell, and the clouds settled, and the ashes—black, greasy, fat on our faces."

With the onslaught of the Hungarian transports, there were masses of new items to sort through, and an additional three hundred girls were added to the sorting details. Now six hundred girls were working in Canada on swing shifts. Men hauled the luggage from the transport ramps and piled it into virtual mountains. The girls were ordered to inspect everything, because "there was lots of food. They [the Jews] were hiding their valuables. So we had to take out everything and search." The girls were not allowed to throw anything away, even broken glasses. "The good stuff, salami, cheeses, you know, durable foods, packages with sweets and so on, went on one side." Broken things, like glass and pottery, were put to the other side. The rumor was that the broken glass was ground down, put into bread, and fed to the prisoners in Birkenau.

Linda watched the comings and goings of the SS, who filched the Hungarians' riches for themselves. Canada was like a candy store for the SS. Multilingual and ever alert, Linda made mental notes of who was rummaging for furs and jewelry, and promised herself that if she survived, someday, she would make them pay.

In July 1944, Eichmann's plan to have four transports of Jews gassed each day was still unrealized, but the transports and executions had escalated. As summer temperatures rose, so did tempers. "The crowds and the heat and the lines, endless. Endless. You know, you couldn't see the end," Linda remembers "People were tired. And they were screaming in Hungarian at the girls working in Canada, 'Viz! Viz! Water! Water!'"

Water was one thing the girls in Canada had access to. "One of my coworkers couldn't take it. She went and filled up a bottle of water from the pile we were sorting and threw it over the fence. A young child ran after it."

At twenty-three, the attractive SS man, Gottfried Weise, didn't look capable of cold-blooded murder, his close-set eyes and serious nose giving him an earnest and sincere visage. He ran after the child, tore the bottle out of the child's hands, and threw it away. Then he tossed the child into the sky and thrust his bayonet into him as he fell, grabbed the boy's arm and "smashed the child's head against the wall." A woman screamed. Then silence.

"Who did it?" he bellowed at the girls. "Who threw water to those dirty Jews?" He marched into the sorting depot, trained his gun on the girls, and ordered everyone to line up. "Who did it?!" he screamed.

Nobody said a word.

"If you are not going to step out, I will shoot one girl in every ten. Their deaths will be on your head!"

Nobody moved. He shot the first girl in line.

"Who did it?" He took ten paces. Shot the next girl.

"Who threw water to those dirty Jews?"

Silence.

Ten paces. Gunshot.

Sixty girls were executed for that bottle of water. The next day, there were sixty new girls in Canada. One of those new girls was very probably a teenager by the name of Julia Birnbaum, who had just watched her parents and siblings go to the gas. Tattooed A-5796, she arrived on May 24, 1944. Her father looked at her and said, "The Poles weren't lying. This is it." Her mother told her they would always be together, but then a suave and sophisticated man, with his finger hooked around one of the brass buttons of his uniform, asked her, "How old are you?"

For some reason she lied. "Fifteen."

Dr. Mengele signaled for her to step out of the line. Julia went directly from processing into the sorting details on the first day she arrived; the fourteen-year-old was now working in Canada with Linda, Helena, and the other old-timers.

Chapter Thirty-four

*Some people end their lives long before they die, and
their extended lives are only an apparition. You took
the last step two days ago ...and now you have found
your eternal harmony.*
> —DR. MANCI SCHWALBOVA, for Alma Rosé,
> director of the Auschwitz women's orchestra,
> who died on April 5, 1944

HELENA CITRON'S FATHER APPEARED TO HER in a dream. He
told her that her sister Ruzinka had been hiding as a gentile and
had been caught. The next day at lunch, Irena and some of the
other girls from Humenné were looking out the window of the
sorting barracks when they saw Helena's sister. This seemed
odd as it was a Hungarian transport, but the girls must have
seen the white-blond hair of Aviva, and then her mother, Ruzinka, carrying a newborn infant in her arms.

"Come! Come! Helena!" her friends shouted. "Ruzinka's
coming."

The dream had been true.

Stricken with anguish and grief, Helena hid behind the
mounds of clothes. She did not want to see her sister before she

died. What was the point? An internal debate waged inside her mind and heart. How could she survive this, too? "I knew about all the people who had been exterminated, my whole family, my three brothers, my parents and my older sister with three lovely children, but this is my last sister."

Then something clicked inside, and she revolted against her own timidity. What was she hiding for? Helena did not understand her own reaction. She ran to the window. There was Aviva's white-blond head. Her elder sister, Ruzinka, was holding Aviva's hand and holding an infant in her arms. Helena was an aunt again, and she didn't even know it. A rush of emotions flooded through every cell of Helena's body. She was not an animal. She was a human being! And it was the human part of her that ran to the door of the barrack and banged on it.

"What is this?" one of the SS yelled as he opened the door. To him, she was just prisoner #1971.

Standing in front of him in overalls, she begged, "Don't shoot me. I just saw my sister, and after all these years, I want to die now with my sister."

He looked shocked, but what did he care? He waved his gun for her to go. Helena ran toward the disrobing rooms. Standing just outside the doorway were the Lager Commandant Dr. Kremer and Dr. Mengele. As Ruzinka and Aviva disappeared inside, one of the SS bellowed at Helena, "What are you doing here?"

It was obvious from her number that she was not part of the transport, and no prisoner ever reached the gas chamber's doorway and lived.

Helena stopped six steps away from them—that was mandatory. Always stay six steps away from the SS or they would shoot you. She was well trained. She was also not afraid of dying.

"I am already here many years," she told Mengele and Kremer. "I have been through a lot, and now my last sister—" She choked. "We are all going to burn here. Let me die together with them." What desire for life could she have without any family in the world?

"Are you good?" Mengele asked.

What did he mean by that? Helena had no idea and answered, "No."

"So we do not need either her or you." He and Kremer laughed at the joke, unholstered their pistols, and aimed.

Suddenly, Franz Wunsch appeared beside her and yelled at his superiors, "That's my prisoner!" He grabbed her arm. "She's been working for me for years, and we need her. There are not a lot left of these numbers, and she is a good worker."

He threw her to the ground and berated her.

—What are you doing here, you Jew? You aren't allowed in here! Get back to work!

Theatrically pummeling her, he dragged her away from her would-be executioners. Beneath the beating, he whispered, "Tell me quickly what your sister's name is, before I'm too late."

"You won't be able to. She came with two little children."

"Children, that's different. Children can't live here."

The stark truth, stated so matter-of-factly, cut her heart. "Ruzinka Grauberova," she whispered.

—Get back to work! he yelled.

Then he did what only an SS officer could do: He slipped behind Mengele and Kremer and disappeared into the disrobing area outside the gas chamber.

Had he ever witnessed this moment before? Seen the hundreds of naked women neatly folding their clothes, urging their children:

—Take off your own shoes. Hand Mama your coat. Watch the baby while I change.

"Ruzinka Grauberova!" he yelled over the heads of the women. "Ruzinka Grauberova, come forward!"

Her oval face and dark, almond-shaped eyes were the same as her sister's. He would have recognized the family resemblance anywhere. She was already naked and helping Aviva undress. The delicate little girl looked in his direction. He signaled for Ruzinka to come through the maze of women and children to him.

Of course she recoiled. What did the enemy want with her and her children? She clasped her daughter and son tightly as the handsome SS man called her back from the "showers." She stroked her daughter's blond curls. The baby cried. Shifting the baby against her full breasts and holding onto Aviva's hand, Ruzinka stepped hesitantly back through the tangled mass of women and children now heading for their shower. He spoke with dispassionate authority and told her that her sister was outside. Ruzinka looked frantic. Confused. Noise and chaos surrounded them. She was exhausted.

In a few moments, the room would be empty and the *Sonderkommando* would arrive. If he did not get Ruzinka out immediately, it would be too late to save her. And how could he ever face Helena without her sister?

—You have to come now if you wish to see your sister.

—Can't I see her later?

—No.

—Mommy, go. I will watch the baby, Aviva offered.

Nestling the two-day-old infant into her seven-year-old daughter's arms, Ruzinka assured herself that Aviva would be okay for a few moments. She asked one of the other women standing nearby to keep an eye on them. There was a perfunctory nod. Ruzinka kissed her daughter's tears.

—Be a good girl.

Wunsch covered Ruzinka with his black cape and escorted her away from her children. Aviva carried her little brother into the showers. The door shut behind them.

AFTER EXTRICATING RUZINKA from the gas chamber, Wunsch led her past Mengele and Kremer by saying, "I need this one," then delivered her to the sauna to be processed. It was an unheard-of allowance that even Helena admits "crossed a line." But Wunsch would have done anything for her, and he did.

When Wunsch arrived in the sorting hut, everyone's eyes were glued on Helena. What had begun as passionate physical attraction had now become something much more powerful—life and death hung on the curse of their love. Helena left the sorting table and moved slowly across the room. Camp noises—shuffling of cloth, stomping of feet, snuffling of noses—disappeared as they slipped behind a mound of still-to-be-sorted clothes. He pulled back a strand of Helena's hair, let his lips brush the slight curve of her ear, and whispered that her sister was being processed.

Her tears were hot and hard, a mixture of relief and sorrow. Her sister was alive. Her niece and nephew were dying. Helena leaned against him and quaked in his arms. Theirs was not a match made in heaven but in hell. Their fates and the fate of her sister were sealed with a kiss.

IN THE SAUNA, a confused and anxious Ruzinka looked for her sister but saw only SS and a few other women standing in line to be processed, disinfected, and registered. Among the women registering and tattooing new prisoners would have been Ella Friedman (#1950).

Ruzinka fretted. Where was Helena? Had she been duped? The SS man had assured her she would see Helena after she was processed into the camp. Milk dripped from her heavy breasts.

—When will my children arrive? she asked the women around her.

No one answered.

Ruzinka started to panic and run wildly around the room. She had to breastfeed. Where was Aviva? Where was the baby? Naked, pacing like a trapped animal, she demanded answers to questions that would have brought a bullet between the eyes of any other Jew. But Ruzinka was under Wunsch's personal protection now. No one could harm her.

It is not clear at what point Ruzinka was brought into Canada; normally, a new prisoner would have to undergo quarantine. When she was delivered to the block where Helena and the other girls slept at night, the others must have wondered at Helena's power to bring her sister back from death's door.

Dressed in new prison garb, bloody from her new tattoo, Ruzinka was frantic with worry and exhaustion. The minutes she had promised she would be gone had turned into hours and then into days. She had told her children she would be right back. How could she have lied to them? Like the parent bamboo dropping its flowers in mid-bloom, she must have felt it in her very being. Their DNA no longer answered hers. The connection between them had gone silent. But not knowing the truth of Auschwitz, how could she trust her instinct?

—Where is Aviva? Where's the baby?

Her sister could not bear to tell her the truth. "It was very difficult because at first, she did not know that her children were murdered, and until they transferred her to me it took a while, and I kept promising her that her children were alive," Helena admits.

Ruzinka kept talking about how big Aviva had gotten and so grown up. And wait until you meet your nephew! He's so chubby and always hungry! He must be wailing by now. Look at my milk. At the mere mention of the baby wet spots formed on her uniform. Aviva must be terrified. She hadn't eaten for days. Did Helena think she had eaten something by now? Who would nurse the baby? The other women in the block gawked at Helena. Waited for her to say something, anything.

Someone yelled, You have to tell her!

Ruzinka stared at the faces in the dark. The pale skin. Eyes glimmering in the shadows.

No woman could bear to speak the truth.

What Wunsch had done was "a great thing," Helena says.

Ruzinka's reality was far different from her little sister's. Her heavy sobs tore everyone in the block apart. Most of the girls in Canada had never been married, never had children, but they felt the horror of this mother's loss. The horror of Helena's choice. Irena grieved for her sister, but at least her sister was not grieving for her children.

Ruzinka spent the next two weeks delirious and ill. She did not speak. Barely ate. Wept without ceasing. Her breasts ached as the milk in them dried up. Helena did what she could, bringing her sister bits of food from the pockets of the Jews who had gone to the gas. She cradled her sister's head and tried to get her to eat. She prayed for her sister. She prayed for herself.

Was it selfish of Helena to save her sister? Could she have lived with herself if she had not tried? It is a dilemma no human being should ever have to face. Glassy-eyed with shock, Ruzinka stared at the bare beams of the ceiling above her head. Saw her daughter's face in the darkness. Breathed her ashes in the air. Aviva's ghost was everywhere.

Chapter Thirty-five

July 13, 1944

Dear Lenka—our daughter is now two months old.
We are well. Now we are waiting for your visit,

which we have been planning for a long time. We already have a house in Spa Vlasky, we just don't know when [we are moving]. Everyone is working on the farm. Irma [Magduska's mother] is at a hospital. Lisa often visits her there. Did you get our packages? Are you healthy? We would love to know. Write! We don't know Ella's address. Kisses...
from Lilly

IT WAS THE LAST POSTCARD Lenka would receive from her sister, dated July 13, 1944. As the summer progressed, Jewish deportations out of Slovakia began again, and even families with exceptions were now in danger. The Hartmann family was tipped off by the local policeman and fled the farm. Lenka's family—her sister, Lilly, her mother and niece and nephew—had already moved to a different town. There was no time to warn them that the Hartmanns were going into hiding. Bela and Dula split up to form two different groups. Nusi's father, Dula, her mother, and little sister were caught. They did not survive. Nusi's other two siblings, Bianca and Andrew Hartmann, were rescued by an aunt and uncle and taken into the forest, where they hid. "We lay like sardines" in an underground bunker with other members of the family, for the next three and a half months.

Bela's wife, Irma, was now in a hospital, and of everyone in the family, she seemed to be the only one *not* in danger—the SS were not searching hospital wards for Jews. Bela and Eugene (Magduksa's father and brother) fled into the mountains, where they hid. A village priest who "knew where everyone was hiding" preached to his congregation on Sundays that it was their duty to " 'feed the needy ones.' He never said Jews, but everyone knew what he meant, and everybody in that village did help the Jews," Eugene recalls.

In Humenné, Adela's cousin Lou Gross, who was now six years old was woken up in the middle of the night and carried into a hayfield to hide. Having been "born into a privileged family" and "now being on the run and hunted by some invisible enemy" was discombobulating, especially for a young child. While his father joined the partisans to fight the Nazis, his mother ushered the family to safety time and again, always just one step ahead of disaster.

As the Russian front moved closer to Slovakia and crossed the eastern Polish border, Slovakian partisans—Jews and gentiles, communists and noncommunists—continued fighting a covert war against Tiso's regime. On August 29, 1944, they revolted in what became known as the Slovak National Uprising. In response, thousands of Slovaks deserted Tiso's army and joined the partisans.

Mayhem engulfed eastern Slovakia. Violence on the Eastern Front escalated as German troops pushed the partisans back into the Tatra and Carpathian Mountains, where Ivan Rauchwerger and his friends had spent almost two years preparing caves to serve as bunkers and hideouts. Young Slovak men, and even young women like Edith's former classmate, Zuzana Sermer, were essential to the Russian invasion because they knew the mountain passes and could introduce Russian soldiers to sympathetic Slovaks who were ready to revolt.

German retribution for the Slovak Uprising immediately targeted Jews, and a law was passed stating that Jews could no longer live near the eastern border. It was a last-ditch effort on Tiso's part to relocate Jews west of Poprad and "concentrate" them in preparation for his own Final Solution.

Still living under the relative protection of the Slovak government, Emmanuel Friedman had remained a vital worker while he continued to fix the windshields of bombers. But the relocation order included everyone, and Emmanuel was not going to risk letting any more of his children fall into the hands of the Germans. Who knew where Edith and Lea were now? The Slovak Uprising had secured a free area in the middle of the country. The last remaining Jews of Humenné now fled there. On September 5, 1944, the Friedmans boarded a train with Ladislav Grosman's family and headed for Ružomberok, in the Liptov region of Slovakia.

Ladislav was still working in a military Jewish commando unit, "black uniform, no guns," and was not in Humenné when his family was forced to leave. The two families and a number of other families from Humenné arrived in Ružomberok as refugees and with no idea what to do next. There was no welcoming committee. No Red Cross.

Standing under the awning of the train station, Edith's little sister, Ruthie, tugged on her mother's sleeve. "I'm thirsty," she complained. The Friedmans headed to a café, where they could ask for advice from the locals. Minutes after the Friedman family walked away, the Germans bombed the station. Twenty-two members of Ladislav Grosman's family lay dead under the rubble. The Friedmans were saved by Ruthie's thirst.

The Friedmans spent the next few months hiding in the mountains with other Jewish families. Though barely a teenager, Edith's brother Herman began fighting with the partisans. "At night, the kids [Hilda, Ruthie, and Ishtak] went down into the villages to ask for food from the villagers, who knew the children were Jewish and wanted to help them."

AFTER GERMANY INVADED HUNGARY, Giora Shpira and his brother had returned to their family in Prešov. The Shpira family was poor and in desperate circumstances. Bereft of his daughter Magda, the aging Adolf Amster took the Shpira family under his wing. In return Giora and his brother did all they could to help the Amsters as everyone was forced to relocate into the western region of Slovakia. They would be able to avoid the last deportations that fall, but in the winter of 1945 both families—like the Hartmann and Gross families—were forced to go into hiding in a bunker in the woods.

The uprising was shortlived, and retribution by the SS and Hlinka Guard was brutal. "They went into villages accompanied by local Garda fascists looking for women who lived in their houses without husbands. Unless the wife could prove that her husband was fighting with Tiso's army, or was working as a contract laborer for Germany, she was interrogated, tortured and often killed," Ivan Rauchwerger recalls. Then he adds, caustically, "The Waffen-SS were somewhat less bloodthirsty. They usually *just* shot Jews, often whole families and, of course, partisans as well. I personally witnessed in June 1945 the exhumation of bodies, about twenty, all badly decomposed near a military airfield outside of my hometown, Spišská Nová Ves. There were about twenty women—all from the nearby villages, very distressed, and crying. I think that their husbands—the victims—had been caught either as partisans or as supporters of the uprising.

"The normal army, the Wehrmacht, went strictly by the book. They shot partisans. In the case of Jews, they jailed them and asked the Slovak fascists to take over. Hence Jews caught between October 1944 and early February 1945 could still be deported to German camps."

That is what happened to Ivan's mother, sister, and the rest of his family. Deep in the mountains fighting with the partisans, he did not know they had been caught and deported. His mother, Eugenie, would die in Ravensbrück; his sixteen-year-old sister Erika would survive.

In a last desperate attempt to rid Slovakia of its Jews, the Hlinka Guard and German security police would arrest every Jew they could find that September. Over the next two months, an estimated 12,600 Jews would be deported, "mostly to Auschwitz." As punishment for the uprising, almost no Slovak Jews

were registered in the camp. As with the Hungarian Jews, upwards of two thousand people at a time were gassed.

WATCHING THE THOUSANDS of Hungarians and people of other
nationalities moving steadily past them like a tidal surge on
their way to the gas chamber changed everyone working in Canada. Faith diminished for even the most devout. Girls who
had survived for two years did not pray as regularly as they
had in the beginning. By Rosh Hashanah, 1944, no one from
the first transport was fasting on Yom Kippur. New girls like
Julia Birnbaum did fast, and she was not alone. At sundown
on Yom Kippur, Julia folded her piece of bread into the pocket
of her apron. She would have two pieces of bread tomorrow
at sundown and hold her fast for the Lord, her parents and
her people.

With a lovely soft face and arching high cheekbones, Julia
was still a beautiful woman when she gave her Shoah testimony.
Closing her eyes, she describes a scene that is clearly playing
out as a movie in her mind. Sitting on their *koyas* that night, the
girls who had decided to fast prepared themselves with prayers,
rocking back and forth in the tradition of "davening." In the
midst of their prayers, SS Franz Wunsch burst into the block.
He went "berserk. He got hysterical."

"You idiots!" he screamed at them. "You still believe? You
believe after what you see in the fire?" He took out his whip
and began beating the girls "left and right." He grabbed the
scarves off their heads and tore them into pieces. "He was
foaming from his mouth. He was not normal." The girls fell to
the floor to avoid his thrashing, and finally he ran out.

Helena always maintained that their love had changed
Wunsch and softened his heart toward her people. Was that
transformation wishful idealism, or had he been ordered to
punish anyone caught praying on that holy night? Within

months of saving Helena's sister, he had beaten devout Jewish girls for praying and would soon perpetrate another atrocity that would come back to haunt him after the war. Whatever the backstory on Yom Kippur, Wunsch was an SS with a job to do, and being soft toward Jews was not part of his job description.

Chapter Thirty-six

It was September 30, 1944. The Slovak men working in Canada, who were responsible for emptying the cattle cars, recognized their own families arriving on the first Slovak transports in almost two years. Friends. Former neighbors. Lenka Hertzka's sister Lilly, the new baby, Lenka's two-year-old niece whom she never met, and her mother—who had written so often and encouragingly to her, sent her tins of sardines and virtual kisses—were now standing in the line for the gas. For some reason, Milan was not with his mother.

It was soul-destroying torture for the Slovak girls of Canada. The few family members they had left on the earth—the only hope they had of ever having a homecoming—were now heading for certain death, just on the other side of the fence. Irena Fein saw her sister with her children. Did Irena suddenly wish she could rescue her sister as Helena had done? Would she have dared? Irena watched as the last of her family disappeared into the brick building of no return.

It only took a moment to look up and see someone you knew or for someone to see you. Torn between wanting to hide and wanting to see people they knew and remembered, they took turns watching the lines. But these were difficult, one-sided reunions.

Lined up outside the gas chamber, Klary Atles's father and mother saw Margie Becker sorting the clothes in Canada.

"You look good, Margie!" Rabbi Atles called out to her. She was wearing a pair of blue jeans and a nice shirt. Her hair had grown out now and almost reached her shoulders. "Have you seen our daughter, Klary?"

It was a normal question to ask. They knew Margie had been on the first transport with her. Margie froze, unable to answer.

"Oh, she's not alive anymore?" Klary's father said, sadly.

"The crematorium was just two steps away." Margie looked at them and thought, In a few minutes, you won't be alive, either.

EARLY IN THE morning of October 7, 1944, as the night shift stood across from the day shift waiting to be counted and to exchange places—work for sleep—a huge explosion shattered the austerity of Canada. Smoke and particles filled the air. For once, the ash was not of human beings but of concrete. One of the gas chambers had been blown up.

How hard it was not to cheer the "boys of the Sonderkommando." The girls could not even smile, though their hearts were singing joyously as the sirens wailed.

Within minutes, hundreds of SS leapt from the backs of trucks and jeeps, and thundered into Canada. Around Canada. Past Canada. The backs of fleeing boys bobbed between tree trunks, as visible as a deer's white tail. SS bullets struck their marks.

Some of the boys ran into the sorting barracks, where they quickly buried themselves in deep piles of clothing. Several SS held the girls at gunpoint while others hunted for the culprits. Everywhere there was screaming. Yelling. Barking. Snarling. The girls were used to people dying quietly. The boys died loudly. Every shot ricocheted through the empathetic hearts of the young women. The lives of the "boys" of the Sonderkommando being snuffed out fractured the morning. There was one comfort: It was better to be shot than gassed.

In a thorough search of the sorting barracks, the SS stabbed mounds of clothes with their bayonets. SS Franz Wunsch found a boy hiding in the coats. SS Otto Graf found another. They dragged the boys outside and threw them to the ground, where they kicked and beat them until there was no breath left in their bruised and broken bodies.

"We knew now is the end of us," Linda says. "Absolutely the end." They had seen too much. It was only a matter of time before they, like the boys of the Sonderkommando, would be executed to keep the secrets of Auschwitz in the silent ash of its gray soil. There was no way they would ever be allowed to leave alive.

The next morning, the kettle of tea arrived with a whispered camp bulletin: Four young women had been caught. One of them was their coworker Roza Robota. They had not given up a single name, despite hours of torture. The underground network was safe.

The girls passed the news among themselves, sipping their tepid tea and hiding smiles behind their red bowls. The story of the girls who had smuggled the gunpowder to the Sonderkommando filled every female prisoner with pride, courage, and secret defiance. Maybe they would all die, but at least they had done something. Those young men and women had struck a blow for everyone, and everyone took it to heart. Maybe they would survive, somehow. Maybe the world would know the truth, someday.

Unfortunately, while the resistance had struck a blow, only one gas chamber was damaged beyond repair. The killing machine was barely going to limp toward the Final Solution.

Map showing the death marches from Auschwitz of male and female prisoners on foot. Detail: Map showing the routes that women from first transport were forced to take after the death marches, leading to camps in Germany and Austria, 1945. © HEATHER DUNE MACADAM; DRAWN BY VARVARA VEDUKHINA.

Part Three

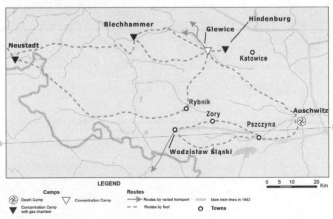

Chapter Thirty-seven

It is being honest
about my
my pain
that
makes me invincible.

—NAYYIRAH WAHEED, *Salt*

ROSE (#1371) WAS RELEASED FROM BLOCK 11 in the fall, but she was not returned to the farm in Harmęże. Instead she was commandeered into a work detail designated to clear up the rubble around the destroyed gas chamber. It was hard work, but she was lucky to be alive and out of Block *Smierci*.

As the Russian front neared, the SS moved prisoners deeper into the interior of Germany in preparation for a possible evacuation. On October 28, Bertha was transported to Bergen-Belsen with 1,038 other prisoners. Most probably on that transport was a young Dutch girl no one had yet heard of, Anne Frank. Bergen-Belsen "was the worst. We didn't have strength anymore, the food was horrible, and there was no work." Bertha did get some work; she was placed in the hospital again, "where there were piles and piles of dead bodies."

A few weeks later Joan (#1188), Ella (#1950), and Ella's sisters—Edie (#1949) and Lila (#3866)—were transferred to Reichenbach in Germany, about 200 kilometers from Auschwitz, where there was a weapons factory.

Back in Auschwitz, the only way prisoners knew what was happening in the outside world was through the prison grapevine, which came with the kettles of tea every morning. As the men carried the iron cauldrons to the blocks, they passed the latest news to the servers, who in turn gave the news to the girls standing in line with their red cups. "They were telling us that there were people in connection with the underground fighting against the Germans," Linda recalls. The most important message was, "Keep going, keep going, maybe we will be the lucky ones who will come out."

Things were definitely changing. Unbeknownst to the prisoners, Himmler had ordered the end of "killing with Zyklon B in the gas chambers of Auschwitz." The transports had also stopped, but "the killing went on in different ways. They killed the people by shooting them. They brought some people, you know, thirty, forty people, which they killed. They let some of them in. But the mass killing was over." The girls in Canada continued to work twelve-hour shifts, sorting clothing and other items. And there was a flurry of activity as the SS slipped into the sorting depot, "stealing clothing, and jewelry, and valuables. It was a bonanza." Like squirrels storing nuts for winter, the SS pilfered "everything they could" to secure their own futures.

THE WINTER OF 1944 sent another arctic blast across Europe. Facing their third winter in Auschwitz was an unbelievable feat for the girls; hope was obscured by clouds lingering on the gray horizon. "Here and there, we found pieces of newspaper. So we saw the war is coming to an end." Most of Europe was already occupied by Allied forces, and airplanes were flying overhead all the time. "They bombed quite a few times, but never the camp [itself]," Linda recalls, "and we were praying for it."

Despite the report that Rudi Vrba and Frank Wexler had written and the maps they had drawn of the camps in the spring of 1943, the only buildings destroyed by bombs were two barracks full of brownshirts, German soldiers who were not even SS. Those young men had gone so far as to flirt with the Jewish girls and give them a loaf of good German bread, the first the girls had eaten in years. Minutes after the soldiers had given the girls their bread, the soldiers' building was flattened. The prisoners' blocks were safe. The SS headquarters, the electric fences, the tracks, the crematoriums and gas chambers—all remained intact. Captive inside the camp, prisoners were terrified that the end of the war would come too late to save them.

"I swear to you," one of the SS told Linda and the others, "the only way to freedom for you is through the chimney."

MEANWHILE, EDITH HAD HEARD that "there were a few girls from Humenné working in the sewing detail, and I told Elsa we should try to get the work fixing clothing." She had good instincts. Even though they were working inside and cleaning the blocks, getting out of Birkenau was the smartest thing they could have done, as tensions and tempers escalated among the kapos and SS. The worse the war went for the Germans, the worse it got for their prisoners. With the help of one of their friends, Edith and Elsa got into the sewing detail "where we mostly just darned socks all day." In this detail Edith found two friends from Humenné, the Gelb sisters, Kornelia and Etelka. It was the last job they would have in Auschwitz.

JUST BEFORE CHRISTMAS, Linda and the other girls working on the night shift in Canada lined up across from the day shift. In front of the groups sat two nurses at a table. "The first five in the row had to go up a table," where the nurses drew blood from the girls' arms. The German blood banks were empty and now they needed their slaves' blood. The girls winced at the prick of the needle and watched as their blood filled vials to save their enemies.

After so many years of being untouchable inferiors, being called and treated as less than human by their captors, suddenly their blood was suitable to be mixed with Aryan blood and save German lives? "They squeezed out the life, inch by inch of us. They squeezed out [our] blood, too." As a reward, each girl was given a loaf of bread and some salami. The only positive thought that occurred to Linda was that the war must really be ending; why else would the Germans stoop to using Jewish blood? They were not blood "donors," Linda insists. Not one girl there would have given blood to the German army freely. The Germans called Jews bloodsuckers; now "who were the bloodsuckers?" Linda asks. "Not the Jews. They literally sucked our blood out at the end. And it was done by force."

ON CHRISTMAS EVE, an SS came into the block and announced, "We are going to have a special treat." He clapped loudly and ordered everyone to the sauna. Slowly, Linda, Peggy, and their friends moved away from the relative safety of their block in Canada toward what they believed was certain death. The sauna was where prisoners were disinfected and processed, but ever since Crematorium V had been destroyed there had been rumors that the sauna had become a secret gas chamber as well. They looked at each other with black fear in their eyes.

"This is it," Linda thought. At least she would die with Peggy (#1019), who had become one of her best friends.

Inside the large empty space of the disrobing area, a stage had been set up. "It was very nicely done." The girls looked around the room in awe and confusion. SS were sitting on chairs at the front of the makeshift theater; there were Dr. Mengele and Dr. Kremer, the infamous SS woman, Irma Grese, and Camp Supervisor Maria Mandel. Silently, the girls settled in the back of the room. At least if the SS were there, they were not going to die by gas.

Onto the platform stepped two of the Greek girls, Susie and Lucia, who worked in Canada. Dressed in evening gowns, they were almost unrecognizable,. Susie cleared her throat. Hummed a note. Lucia hummed in tune with her. Then Susie opened her mouth and began to sing.

Che bella cosa na jurnata 'e sole...

Their voices rose above the cement of the sauna and burst into the hearts of the girls of Canada. Linda and the others may not have known Italian or Neapolitan. They may not have known what the words meant. They may not have even known it was a love song. But as Susie turned her eyes to Lucia, and Lucia picked up the refrain, the girls knew the song was for them.

Ma n'atu sole
Cchiù bello, oi ne'.
'O sole mio...

Their voices lilted over the heads of SS and Jew alike. They shared the same air, the same blood, the same music, the same moment. The two sopranos serenaded their fellow prisoners, knowing full well what they were singing and what the words meant. How many years it had been since any of them had thought, *What a wonderful thing, a sunny day!* Had felt the serene air after a thunderstorm, the fresh air.

They had lost sisters, brothers, friends, mothers, fathers, uncles, aunts, cousins, daughters, and sons. The room was awash with memories of sun-filled faces, now gone. Did Ruzinka see Aviva's cherubic face in song? Did Helena cast a furtive glance at Franz Wunsch? For whom did Linda long or had she forgotten how to dream of love? Would any of them live long enough to ever see a lover's face at night?

Their voices crescendoed higher and higher, lifting the girls' hearts and hopes by octaves. Their faces became suns, their voices the girls' path to some faraway place. Where love songs were supposed to die, "O Sole Mio" lived.

THAT NEW YEAR'S EVE, the SS drank and celebrated while the prisoners of Auschwitz held their breath. If the end was near, how much longer would it take? Would 1945 be the last year of their young lives, or the beginning of a new era? To celebrate the first dawn of the New Year, one hundred Polish women, along with one hundred Polish men—all political prisoners and most likely participants in the Warsaw Uprising—were executed by gunshot outside of Crematorium V. The girls working the night shift in Canada shuddered. Those sleeping woke. The skies overhead were ominous. There would be more executions. More transfers. More losses. In the four days between New Year's Eve and January 4, the population of the women's camp in Birkenau declined by more than one thousand. They were probably transferred to other camps, but the record is not clear about where they were transferred to, and being "transferred" often meant something else entirely.

Although American bombers were doing regular reconnaissance now, flying overhead and taking aerial photographs of the complex, Auschwitz was a nightmare that would not end. In the late afternoon of January 6, the girls in the sewing and laundry details were called outside for an afternoon roll call. Among those with Edith and Elsa were Rena Kornreich, her sister, Danka, their friends, Dina, Ida Eigerman, Ruzena Gräber Knieža, and others from the first transport. Anything out of the ordinary caused alarm; marching down the road toward Auschwitz I was ample cause for worry. They were halted in front of the executioner's scaffold.

Two yawning nooses awaited their victims. The prisoners' heroes, two of the four girls who had smuggled the gunpowder to the Sonderkommando boys so that they could blow up the crematoriums were about to be executed. Edith does not recall which two of the girls from the ammunitions factory were forced up the steps of the scaffold, but it would have been Ella Gartner, Regina Safir, or Estera Wajsblum.

The SS yelled, "You have to watch because then you will know how you will be punished if you do something against us."

Anyone who looked away was threatened with death.

As the sentence was read and the nooses were tossed over their heads, SS-Obersturmführer and Schutzhaftlagerführer Franz Hössler bellowed, "All traitors will be destroyed in this manner!"

"'Long live Israel!' the girls shouted and begin to recite in unison a Hebrew prayer," Rena Kornreich (#1716) recalls. "Their voices were cut short as the chairs were pulled out from underneath them."

A few hours later, Roza Robota, who had worked in Canada, and the fourth girl were executed in front of the girls of Canada. Linda, Peggy, Margie, Helena, Erna and Fela Dranger, and the others had worked next to Roza, eaten with her, spoken with her, slept near her, and now they wept for her. Perhaps she was the lucky one. To hang was better than to burn. To hang was better than to be gassed or beaten to death or starved. To hang meant you were an individual. That young women had defied the SS and helped organize the attack on the gas chambers struck more fear in the oppressors than the prisoners.

"We had those girls before our eyes all the time," Edith says.

DEMOLITION TEAMS NOW began to disassemble the crematoriums and blow up some of the barracks in the women's camps. Guarded by SS, the secretarial functionaries were ordered to load "prisoners' documents, death certificates, and files into an auto."

The long January night skies flickered with red and orange under the bellies of clouds. Sixty kilometers away, Krakow was burning. "The war was coming so close, and the shooting—you could hear it." With the front so close, Linda and the girls still working in Canada feared they would be the last group taken over to the gas chambers and shot because they had seen too much. They were in better health than most of the other girls in camp, well fed and working under roofs. But beneath the silent sentries of the charcoal-stained chimneys, it was hard to believe in freedom. Still, the constant presence of Allied forces in the skies over the camp invigorated the prisoners' courage "to see tomorrow. Maybe tomorrow will be better."

Whisper campaigns came with the men hauling the kettles full of morning tea: "Prepare yourselves." The grapevine was abuzz with rumors of an evacuation and the SS's plans to in- cinerate the camp:

"Anyone left behind will be burned alive."

"The SS are going to pour petrol around the perimeter, turn on the wires, lock the gates, and set it alight."

As the SS made plans to use prisoners as human shields and march everyone on foot toward Germany, prisoners working in the Auschwitz underground smuggled out one last report:

> Chaos, panic among the drunken SS. We are trying with all political means to make the departure as tol- erable as possible and to protect from extermination the invalids allegedly remaining behind.

The direction of the death marches was being outlined by authorities, but with orders changing constantly, only one thing was certain. "This type of evacuation means the extermination of at least half of the prisoners."

Chapter Thirty-eight

If the oceans were ink and the skies paper,
I couldn't describe the horror of what I'm going
*   through.*

—Written by a Polish boy
in the Krakow ghetto

THE SECRETARIAL FUNCTIONARIES stopped stuffing boxes of files into automobiles and started bringing "various camp documents" out of the SS offices to be destroyed in bonfires. Among those records were the photographs of hundreds of thousands of prisoners and much of the data on the women's camp: population totals, death tallies, selection dates and totals, and execution records.

As rumors of the evacuation increased, Dr. Manci Schwalbova worked to help anyone well enough to walk. Helena was in the hospital when SS Wunsch warned her to evacuate. It was the kind of a warning the grapevine would have grabbed hold of and disseminated quickly—if Wunsch wanted Helena to leave, anyone who was capable should depart, too. A new whisper campaign began: If you can walk, save yourself. No one wanted to be locked inside when

Auschwitz was locked and set alight to become a giant crematorium.

Prisoners who had access to the clothes in Canada began smuggling items out in empty soup kettles. Rena Kornreich and friends of hers from the laundry were given boots, gloves, warm coats, and sugar. SS Wunsch made sure that Helena and her sister had warm clothes and a pair of good shoes. It was the last "good" deed he would perform for the woman he loved. "I go back to the front, and you set out. If something turns around in the world and we lose the war, will you help me as I have helped you?" he asked.

Helena promised. Her sister did not.

FOR THOSE WHO WERE TOO ILL to leave the ward, Dr. Manci Schwalbova and the other medical staff did what they could for their patients, but as Jews, the medical staff were no longer important prisoners; they were cannon fodder for the Russians, just like all the rest.

Prisoners were frantic to organize what they could to survive the last push by the SS to destroy them. Anyone wearing rags on the death march would freeze to death. The men and women of Canada did everything they could to steal clothes and shoes for others. Those in the kitchens smuggled out sugar, bread, and other nonperishables to friends.

All the while, bonfires speckled the snow-laden landscape with ash as prisoner records were tossed onto the flames of oblivion.

EDITH KNEW SHE WOULD never survive the march. "How, with tuberculosis in the leg, can I go for a march of hundreds of kilometers in the snow? I cannot make it," she told Elsa.

"If you're not going, I'm not going." Elsa was adamant.

"Please, Elsa. Go!" Edith would have fallen on her knees to beg her friend, but she couldn't bend her left leg. "Save yourself. Go! You are okay! Go!"

"Without you, I'm not going!" And so Edith lined up in the columns with Elsa and determined she would try to leave.

At one o'clock in the morning on January 18, the final roll call was conducted. Leaving behind her patients in the hospital ward, Dr. Manci Schwalbova joined the evacuation columns as a nameless number, lining up beside Edith, Elsa and Irena Fein (#1564). Other girls who had traveled with Edith on the first transport were standing nearby as well, girls who were working in the New Blocks at the time of the death march and were probably in the same group as Edith: Ruzena Gräber Knieža, Rena and Danka Kornreich, Dina Dranger, Ida Eigerman, and most likely, Lenka Hertzka.

In a separate group preparing to evacuate were the girls from Canada: Linda, Peggy, Ida, Helena, Margie, Regina Schwartz and her sisters Celia and Mimi, Elena Zuckermenn, sisters Eta and Fanny Zimmerspitz and their cousin Martha Mangel, along with many others.

"We opened and closed Auschwitz," Edith says.

THE ENSUING DEATH MARCH would be the final curtain for many, including the first girls. But for one in particular, it fell before the march even began. Ria Hans (#1980) worked in the hospital, where she often helped patients get out of the ward before the SS came and killed them. On January 18, one of those girls in the ward was Ria's little sister, Maya. "She had tuberculosis and was so ill, she couldn't walk a step." How could Ria leave her little sister behind to be burned alive in camp? She would not be allowed to remain behind and die with her, either. Ria stole a vial of morphine and injected a painless death into her little sister's vein. It was the kindest thing, the only thing, she could do.

Joining Manci and Edith in the column of girls and women, Ria could not look at them. The girls from Humenné looked around. Where was Maya? Ria could not speak.

They may still have been teenagers, but they were adults now. Women. And another one of them was gone forever. Maya had not even made it to twenty years old. The burden of her sister's death weighed on Ria's heart. How could she lift one leg after the other? How could she step over a single snowdrift given all she had lost? How could she live with what she had done?

"Everyone was mad at her," Edith says, "but she was trying to save Maya from suffering. How was she to know that the SS would not burn the camp after we marched out? And who knows if the Russians would have come in time to save her?"

It had taken all day to organize the evacuation, and by the time the women were ordered to march out, they were already exhausted from standing and waiting. The snow fell heavy and hard. What had been ankle-deep was now knee-deep. Heavily guarded by SS under the spectral watchtowers, the columns of women departed with short intervals between them. Columns of men had already marched out a few hours earlier, clearing a path through the drifts of snow.

The mandate "For Jews, there is no weather" had never been more true. The first column of women marched out into the blizzard. As "they pulled us out from the *lager*," Irena saw the SS bonfires as the threatened conflagration and thought that everyone left in camp was now burning alive. In truth, it would take several more days to empty the camp, and despite orders to "liquidate" the sick prisoners, SS Major Franz Xaver Kraus never lit the petrol-doused perimeter with a final match. A minefield had also been laid outside the fences, but the booby-trapped boundaries would not prevent the liberation of Auschwitz nine days later.

THEY COULD HEAR GUNSHOTS in the distance, but the women were moving in the opposite direction, away from the Russian advance and the hope of freedom.

The "snow was about over a meter or two meters high," Linda says. She had shoes, but they were not a pair. "It didn't matter. They were shoes," and she had warm socks on her feet. Many prisoners had nothing. Prisoners "from the camp [Birkenau] had only those very thin, summery clothing, [and] wooden clogs." There was no way those prisoners could survive the cold.

Divided into separate files, the prisoners were marched in several different directions toward the German border. As a result, the girls' stories and how many days they trod through the snow vary.

"The first who marched, they paved the road for the rest. The SS was on the sides." Some of the SS rode horses, pointing guns down at the prisoners. Whoever "was not able to walk was shot right away." Linda, Peggy, and Mira Gold (#4535) walked as far behind their *kommando* as they could manage. "We walked over corpses." Linda winces at the memory. Her voice quivers. "If the corpse still had something usable, a shoe or a sweater, we took it. But we didn't have strength to pull them up to the side. So, you know, [we] stepped [on them] in the snow. The road was paved with corpses." Linda's column would take one of the longest routes, northward through Poland into the mountains, and they would march for a week. Most of the others headed due west.

"The snow was red, like it had been when we arrived in Auschwitz," Edith remembers. "But then we were bleeding from our periods. Now we were bleeding from gunshots." As the afternoon waned, the blizzard continued and the packed snow, greased with blood, turned to ice beneath their feet. Dr. Manci Schwalbova slipped and fell. Quickly, Edith and Elsa pulled her to her feet before an SS could shoot her. Some time later, they came upon Dr. Rose, one of Manci's colleagues, who had also helped Edith. She had been shot dead. A doctor—murdered. It no longer mattered if you had once held a special position. "They had no respect for anyone."

"I could hardly lift my feet out of the snow," Ruzena Gräber Kneiža recalls. "My wet feet sank in the snow." Ria Hans was "dead tired." Every step weighed her down as she grieved for her little sister.

Marching over drifts of dead bodies, girls called out the names of those they had lost in the blizzard and the dark.

—Where are you? Can you hear me?

Their voices seemed like ghosts themselves—disembodied and invisible, howling names in the storm. "We heard about the rows of our friends…" Helena cannot finish her sentence.

"Exhaustion was also upon Ruzinka," Helena remembers. "She had no children and no husband. She sat down twice. I lost my powers as well. She had nothing to live for. She did not want to get up."

She looked up at Helena and said, "You're young. Go! There's no one to live for. Go!"

Given everything they had been through together and as deeply as she loved her sister, "at that moment I did not think. I had no thoughts. We had become something that has no explanation in our world. It was enough already."

The SS were just one row away from where Ruzinka had sunk into the snow and now awaited the sweet comfort of a bullet to her head.

Despite having only a little strength of their own left, their friends picked Ruzinka up and dragged her. As with so many others on the death march, their help gave her the few minutes her spirit needed to recover strength—and as her spirit revived, her body did as well.

How did Edith survive the death march? She cannot believe it herself. "With my leg, limping all the way, how did I survive while others who were able-bodied did not? This is a miracle I cannot explain. I think it was God."

God's power must have worked through Irena Fein, too: "I was pulling with me a girl from Humenné. She was young. She couldn't walk."

"'I can't. I can't. Don't do this to me,'" the girl said.

"You are going! I had frozen feet!" Irena yelled, reminding her that she herself had lost two toes to frostbite, two years earlier. If Irena could march, anyone could march. She pulled the girl forward, forced her to keep walking. "Otherwise, she would have been shot," Irena says.

That girl was Edith.

"THE ONLY THING we had to eat was snow. Frozen. Wet." That first night and the second, columns of young women stopped at larger farms, where they were allowed to collapse in a barn and rest for a while. The straw warmed them, but they were soaked to the skin. Those who could not fit inside the barns slept in the snow outside. "You know, you get wet, you huddle. And then everything freezes on you. Many had freezing noses, frozen toes. I didn't dare take off my wet shoes because I wouldn't be able to put them back," Linda says. "The stockings were wet. Everything was wet."

Rena Kornreich (#1716) snuck to the back door of a farmhouse. "I have a sister and we're both very hungry. We're from Tylicz. If you can spare one potato, I'll give her half. If you give me two, I'll take one." The wife of the farmer slipped Rena two warm potatoes and two hard-boiled eggs.

During the testimony of Regina Schwartz (#1064), the trauma of the death march is brutally evident. Wringing her hands, she becomes agitated and anxious. Panic rises in her eyes. Confusion descends. The interviewer keeps asking questions. But what is needed is silence. There are times, when listening to a survivor's story, that the best thing to do is shut up, take her hand, and let your own tears be her

witness. Some things are simply too hard to recall. Every survivor has moments they cannot speak of. They are not the
same for everyone, though. That is why Linda's and Edith's
memories of the death march are so important—they can tell
us what others cannot bear to remember and should not be
forced to recall.

As the snowstorm began to dissipate, Russian rockets lit up
the sky, "like a rain of bullets overhead." The front was closing
in on them, but they were being herded away, farther and
farther from freedom. No wonder so many just sat down in the
snow and refused to take another step.

The columns of women marched for anywhere from two to
seven days, depending on which route they had taken; thus the
girls' histories get quite complicated. On January 20, the first
group of women arrived in Wodzisław Śląski, near the German
border. They were forced to sleep outside near the train station.
A number of Polish gentiles were part of this group. The next
day, thousands more women arrived. "Trains of open freight
cars [were] assembled from the morning until late into the
night, into which half-dead, unconscious, and feverish female
prisoners [were] loaded."

Exhausted and starving, the girls collapsed into the black
dust of open-air coal cars. The metal sucked away their body
heat. When it began to snow again, Rena Kornreich scooped
fresh snow off the iron lip of the car for moisture. Others were
too weak to do anything. Everyone huddled together for
warmth, but there was little, given that their clothing remained
wet from snow. When the transports rolled, the weaker girls and
those leaning against the metal froze to death.

In the chaos at the station, many of the girls had lost their
friends and ended up on transports that took them away from
one other, because the trains headed in four different directions,
to four different camps: Gross-Rosen, Sachsenhausen, Ravensbrück, and Buchenwald.

The transport to Gross-Rosen with two thousand women on it was turned away by the commandant due to overcrowding, then rejected from Sachsenhausen, as well. That transport arrived at Ravensbrück on January 27 after a total of five days. The transport heading for Buchenwald was also rejected due to overcrowding and redirected to Bergen-Belsen. Irena Fein was on this transport.

The last column of women to arrive in Wodzisław Śląski stumbled into town on January 22; Rose (#1371) was in that group of prisoners. When they arrived, they were told to find houses to rest in and to meet at the train station in the morning. This was an odd request. Why wouldn't the prisoners just escape? No doubt many tried, but their uniforms were painted with crosses, and being captured and shot on the spot was more likely than freedom.

That night, Rose dreamt that the SS came and killed her, her friends, and the family who had given them shelter for the night. Terrified that with nothing but their camp uniforms to wear they would be caught, she persuaded some of her friends to go to the train station in the morning, just as the SS had ordered. Was the compulsion to obey orders stronger than their longing for freedom or was it the fear of death that kept her and her friends in bondage? Whatever the reason, they did not take the opportunity to escape; perhaps they were too tired and hungry, and simply did not know how to anymore.

Rose and four of her friends arrived at the train station and boarded an open-air coal car that was full of male prisoners. The girls were terrified, but the men were kind to them and advised them to say they had been ordered to get on the transport when it stopped. Rose could tell by the direction the train was taking that it was heading south and hoped that meant they were going to Slovakia. The transport did indeed pass through the farthest western notch of Slovakia, but it continued chugging past the border and into Austria, where it delivered the girls to Mauthausen concentration camp. Rose was devastated. Would they never be free?

Meanwhile, Linda and two to three thousand other women were still marching. "We walked for about a week" before they too ended up in Wodzisław Śląski and were loaded into open-air coal cars. Desperately dehydrated, some of the girls crawled up to where the engine was hitched to the train, where there was not only warmth but hot water dripping from a spigot. "Otherwise, there was nothing." Linda and a few others sipped the hot water greedily.

A week of trudging through the cold and snow with barely any food had left most of the girls weak and vulnerable. A hundred girls were forced into one coal car. Standing room only. "Many of the inmates died." The living couldn't care for the dead and survive. Linda and the others had no choice, but to throw them out.

It may sound coldhearted now, but the dead girls robbed the others of heat. "Naturally, [we] took everything which was usable away from them," to help keep warm. They believed the girls who had died would have wanted them to take what they could and live. "I don't know how long we traveled. I can't tell you. But the hunger—you don't know…how hunger hurts." Linda's voice cracks. Tears fill her eyes. "It's worse than a disease. Hunger hurts very much…." It takes Linda time to gather herself. Staring off to one side, swallowing hard, weeping, she says haltingly, "This…this journey on the train from Wodzisław to Ravensbrück, that was the worst experience that I ever had, freezing to death, throwing over my dead comrades, who survived three years in Auschwitz." Only to arrive in Ravensbrück—where there was no room for them. No food. Nothing.

On January 27, the same day that Linda's transport arrived in Ravensbrück, the Russians marched into Auschwitz and Birkenau camps. A few days earlier, the "30 storeroom barracks" in

Canada had been set on fire. The barracks were still smoldering, and when the Russians arrive, over a million "pieces of women's and men's outerwear...are found in the six remaining partially burned barracks." There they also found "over 600 corpses of male and female prisoners who were shot to death or died otherwise in the last few days." Of the 5,800 prisoners still alive in Birkenau, four thousand were women. It is not clear if any of those women had been on the first transport.

WHAT CAMP YOU ENDED UP IN after the death march was critical to survival, and of all of the death camps at this point, Bergen-Belsen was the most deadly. It was "a very bad *lager*," Irena says. "Everybody was sick, everybody was sleeping on the floor. Everything was on the floor. They gave us water and they gave us a piece of bread, nothing else."

Fortunately for Irena, an old friend from home who had also been on the first transport, and had probably been transferred with Bertha in October, recognized Irena and snuck her into her room. The kindness of Ruzena Borocowice, who had been nineteen years old when they were deported to Auschwitz in 1942, very likely saved Irena's life.

IVAN RAUCHWERGER'S SISTER, Erika, was death marched from Ravensbrück to Bergen-Belsen and describes eating frozen grass, which prisoners dug out from under the snow. In camp, she was rescued by two women from her hometown. One worked in the kitchen and brought her three cooked potatoes to eat. "The second, the wife of Erika's primary school teacher, managed to get Erika admitted to the children's barrack." This protected Erika from standing at early morning roll call, where SS often attacked and killed prisoners; more important, there was less disease in the children's block. Both these women died of typhus "within a week of helping Erika." Among the children in camp with Erika was Milan, Lenka Herzka's nephew.

BY THE END OF JANUARY, nine thousand women had arrived in the Ravensbrück women's concentration camp. One of those groups—very likely Linda's—marched for two weeks and about 300 kilometers before boarding the open coal cars bound for Ravensbrück, where they were left outside for twenty-four hours "because there [was] no room for them there." Linda and the few friends she had left could not even get inside a tent. "We thought that was the last minutes of our lives. No food, no nothing. And still, other inmates were pouring in." When they were finally able to squeeze into a tent, it was "full of mud," and there was no room to lie down.

Edith opens her legs in a V to show how everyone sat, like dominoes "between each other's legs on the cold ground and leaning against each other."

"In Ravensbrück, it was physically impossible to live. We were really like herrings in a barrel. We couldn't lie down. There wasn't space for us because so many people had come there from other camps in Poland that were being evacuated. There were thousands of people, more than the capacity of the camp. It was very hard. There were so many people, not washed, not kempt. I don't know if we even had food." Edith pauses. "I don't have a picture before my eyes of going for food." To survive the death march was an insurmountable task. Now, there was another to face: starvation.

The situation became increasingly desperate. When hungry death marchers rushed the kettles of soup, the kapos lost control of the crowd and the kettles toppled over, spilling the soup across the frozen camp road. Linda weeps as she describes falling on the ground to lick "the food from the ice."

There were a few brief reunions and tender moments. Among the hordes. Etelka Gelb found Ruzena Gräber Knieža's mother-in-law, "a broken, old woman." Ruzena's heart filled at the sight of the woman, whom she had thought she would never see again. "The joy was great. The grief was terribly great." She stroked and caressed Ruzena and murmured blessings. "If you survive, be happy." She was taken to the gas chamber the next day. But that moment had strengthened Ruzena's resolve. "Somehow, she blessed us."

"Listen, Elsa," Edith told her camp sister. "If they ask for volunteers, we will go. We didn't survive the death march to die a slow death of starvation."

Elsa grabbed hold of Edith in terror. "What if volunteering for work is a trip to the gas chamber?"

"Come, Elsa. I think even the gas chamber is better than this."

Trucks arrived in the camp and one thousand girls were loaded onto them. Was it for the gas? Even Elsa did not care anymore. As it turned out, several of Ravensbrück's satellite camps were able to accommodate the new prisoners. Among those camps were Retzow (where Edith and Elsa went), Malchow and Neustadt-Glewe.

Ruzena Gräber Knieža (#1649), Alice Icovic (#1221), and Ida Eigerman (#1930) ended up in Malchow, which was set up to hold one thousand women in just ten small barracks. It now had to house five thousand. Perhaps the best thing about Malchow was that the senior kapo from the women's hospital ward, Orli Reichert (#502) was also there. Having arrived in Auschwitz on the same day as the first girls, on March 26, 1942, Orli had been incarcerated since she was twenty-two years old for being a communist. Long dark lashes around deep brown eyes and pale skin made Orli a striking young woman, and she had done everything in her power to help Jewish prisoners survive. The moment the Auschwitz survivors saw the woman many referred to as the "Angel of Auschwitz," they clapped and cheered, "Our Orli is back with us!"

A number of other girls from the first transport were transferred to Neustadt-Glewe, about 120 kilometers deeper into the interior of Germany. The collection of girls onto a truck for

Neustadt-Glewe happened so fast that many friends were separated from each other. Linda Reich and Dina Dranger were among those left behind. Meanwhile, riding in the back of the open trucks were Margie Becker, Peggy, Helena and Ruzinka, Eta and Fanny Zimmerspitz, their cousin Martha Mangel, Regina Schwarz and her sisters Celia and Mimi, Julia Birnbaum (#A-5796), Magda Moskovic (#1297), and the Polish girls Sara Bleich, Rena Kornreich and her sister, Danka.

These girls did not cheer when they arrived. Not only was there no Angel of Auschwitz in camp, there was one of the devils herself. Wardress Dreschler and her buckteeth were waiting for them.

Although these satellite camps were not death camps, girls still died. Prisoners were at the bottom of the list for receiving rations, and food was limited. Violence was the other cause. One of the chief kapos at Neustadt-Glewe was a murderess who delighted in stomping girls to death if they tried to steal food. But with barely any food in camp, stealing it was worth the risk. When Rena Kornreich attempted to steal three potatoes, the murderess came after her with a board to crush her. Rena escaped into one of the blocks where probably one of the girls from the first transport hid her in her *koya* and saved her life.

WHEN LINDA WAS TRANSFERRED from Ravensbrück, she and a group of girls were taken to an unfurnished, open barrack, and locked inside. There was nothing to sit on, and the moment the door shut, the girls panicked. "We were sure it was a gas chamber." They smashed the windows and climbed out, heading for the woods.

One of the SS women from Auschwitz raced after them, shouting.

—Come back! We aren't going to kill you! You'll get shot if they find you!

They didn't know what to believe, but for some reason they trusted the SS woman and slowly returned. For once, an SS was telling the truth. The girls were not murdered. We can't be sure of the date Linda and the others revolted, but Himmler had started negotiations with the Swedish government to hand over "hostages" and had released an order, in March, "not to kill any more Jewish prisoners and to take all measures to reduce mortality among them." That order may have saved Linda and the others. They were transferred to Retzow, where Edith and Elsa had already been working for a month.

South of Ravensbrück, Retzow had an airfield not far from Berlin. As a target, the airfield was regularly bombed so that German planes could not land and refuel. The women prisoners' job was to go out onto the airfields, fill in the craters, and clear the runway of bombs. It was dangerous work, but to die by American bombs was better than to die at the hands of the SS. Besides, as soon as the SS retreated to their bunkers, the girls had free run of the camp and the kitchen. It was the first time in three years that Edith and the others got to eat something other than soup and bread. Whenever Allied bombers flew overhead and the air raid sirens wailed, the SS ran to the safety of their bunkers. The prisoners ran to the kitchen. "So we had a better life. We got food. Sometimes we even got semolina and milk, and we had clean water to wash ourselves," says Edith.

LIBERATION WOULD COME soonest to the Bergen-Belsen death camp. Typhus had become a raging epidemic and already claimed thousands of lives. On April 15, fifteen days after Anne Frank died from the disease, Bergen-Belsen was handed over to British and American troops. It was about four o'clock in the afternoon when the news came over the loudspeaker: "We're here. We're here. We've come to liberate you." The prisoners could barely believe their ears. "By seven o'clock that evening the camp was full of food." The starvation and disease were so

severe, however, that many prisoners died from gorging themselves on army rations. Bertha was lucky; she couldn't keep any
food down.

Twenty-eight thousand prisoners had died since February,
and the liberating armies designed special punishments for the
SS and kapos, forcing them to carry bodies into mass pits for
burial. They forced Dr. Fritz Klein and the commandant of the
camp, SS Josef Kramer, to crawl across the mounds of dead
bodies that had never been cremated or buried. They marched
the German townspeople through the gates, past the emaciated
corpses of thousands of human beings.

Whole blocks were incinerated to kill the disease-carrying
lice. Showers were set up for women to bathe in, and they were
doused with pesticidal powders. BBC reporter Richard Dimbleby described the camp: "Over an acre of ground lay dead
and dying people. You could not see which was which…This
day at Belsen was the most horrible of my life."

For Bertha and Irena, it was the most wonderful.

Tears fill Bertha's appreciative eyes as she recalls the soldiers
who liberated her. "They were so great to us. So much compassion, so much understanding." There is BBC footage of Bertha
wearing a skirt and a clean white blouse while leading two well-
groomed British soldiers from the crematoriums. As she walks
with the soldiers, they pass the *Lagerführer*. "He was the prisoner
now. I was a free woman." She is a classic beauty with piercing
eyes. These are not the eyes of a victim. They are the eyes of a
young woman who has witnessed the worst of humanity, has
survived, and now carries the power of that truth in her soul.

HIMMLER HAD STARTED NEGOTIATING the sale of Jewish prisoners with the Swedish government as early as March 1945.
Brokering this deal was Count Bernadotte Folke, vice-chair-
man of the Swedish Red Cross, who was also working to free
thousands of Swedish, Norwegian, and Danish prisoners.

Folke's intervention was repeatedly thwarted by Himmler's narcissism and self-delusion, but he needed the money to save his own skin. To persuade the Swedes to negotiate with him, he offered to release one thousand female hostages—he threatened to kill them if the deal fell through. Ella (#1950), Edie (#1949), Lila (#3866), Joan (#1188), and probably Erna (#1715) and Fela (#6030) Dranger and, possibly Matilda Friedman (#1890) were among those prisoners for whom freedom was being negotiated.

Joan had been working in the hollow mountain of Porta Westfalica, where she was lowered in elevators deep into a mountain to do wiring for bombs and ammunition. It was the "scariest" job she ever worked. "We thought we are never getting out of here." But Joan's biggest fear was that they could be locked inside the mountain forever, and no one would ever know where they were or what happened to them.

While Joan was working in that underground factory, Ella, Edie, and Lila were digging ditches outside of Porta Westfalica when the chipmunk-faced mass murderer himself showed up. One thousand of the female prisoners in Porta Westfalica were loaded into cattle cars and sent northward. Then the train stopped and reversed. The girls inside had no idea what was happening. No one knew where they were going, or that they were part of the extensive hostage negotiations between Himmler and the Swedish Red Cross. The constant back-and-forth on the tracks frayed their nerves. "They didn't know what to do with us," Joan says. It was a tug-of-war, with women as the rope.

Count Folke could not grant Himmler all of his demands, and Himmler kept changing his mind about what he wanted, making agreement almost impossible. When negotiations completely collapsed, the SS opened the doors to the cattle cars and began waving their machine guns and shouting, "*Raus! Raus!* Get out! Get out!"

It was 1942 all over again. The young women tumbled out of the cattle cars. They thought they were in the middle of nowhere. In fact, they were not far from Ludwiglust castle grounds.

Forced to bunch up against the train, the girls faced an impenetrable wall of SS alternately aiming their machine guns at them or returning the guns to their sides. They stood like that— the young women staring at their executioners, and the SS staring at their frightened victims—all day long. Hours passed.

"We thought this was it," Joan sobs.

In the afternoon, as the SS prepared to mow down over one thousand women in cold blood, a German soldier drove across the field honking, waving a white flag and shouting, "Halt! Don't shoot them!"

Himmler had acquiesced. Count Folke and the Swedish government had bought the young women's freedom.

Wehrmacht soldiers—also known as brownshirts—were regular army, not SS, and they now took over the transport. Holding out their hands, they helped the girls back onto the train. These were Germen men who smiled kindly at the girls, touched their hands, gave them bread, and assured them that the next time the doors opened, they would be out of Germany. Free.

It was hard to believe anyone in a uniform.

As the train paused at Hamburg station, Joan heard a newspaper hawker shouting, "*Hitler ist tot!* Hitler is dead!"

Peering through the cracks of the car, she saw a black border around the front page of the newspaper. It was true. "We couldn't believe it."

A few hours later, just as the German soldiers had promised, the train doors opened and the girls were in Denmark. "There were nuns, the Red Cross, people threw bread from the windows."

"You are free!" they shouted. "You are free!"

It took a few minutes for their eyes to adjust to the light of liberation. It took their minds much longer. Moving along the crowds on the street, they were handed "chocolate, cigars, and white bread. We were so sick from it!" Tents had been set up to receive the newly released hostages. Doctors and nurses attended to them immediately. Most important was removing any lice-infested clothing. It was the kind of protocol the young women were familiar with by now. They removed their clothing and waited for inspection.

The Red Cross workers did not mean to be callous when they poured petrol over the clothing and lit a match. But when flames leapt up the mound of clothing, the girls panicked and tried to flee. Screaming. Sobbing. They clung to each other in fear. "We were naked and thought we would be next on the fire. We didn't speak any Swedish, either, so we couldn't understand what the Swedes tried to tell us . . . We couldn't believe that [the fire] wasn't for us."

The well-intentioned Swedes led the girls away from the bonfire to showers and another eruption of terror. How could the Swedes have known that every little thing in normal life would mean death to girls who had survived three years in Auschwitz? Finally, someone explained in German that the showers had only water in them, and the steam was from the heat off the water, not gas. Still terrified and trembling, the first girls bathed. They were disinfected to kill any lice. Given fresh, clean clothes without any prison stripes on them. One of the doctors explained in German that because their stomachs had shrunk so much, if they ate too much, too fast, they could die. The lesson of Bergen-Belsen had been learned, and liberators were now cautious about what foods starving prisoners were fed and how much. The girls were given vitamins and served cereal. Hot porridge. Cream of Wheat. It was "divine."

BUT ACROSS EUROPE, freedom still hung in the balance for many others from the first transport. When the airfield in Retzow was closed and the camp disbanded, Linda was part of a group that was marched toward Berlin. Edith and Elsa were forced to march in a different direction. This time, civilians were fleeing the Russian advance, as well. Allied bombers were dropping packages of food. Of course, prisoners were not allowed to retrieve them. The SS took everything. All Linda got "was a big piece of Ivory soap. No food, no nothing."

After a long day of walking, Edith and Elsa lagged behind their column. The SS were far ahead, and the shadows lengthened as night descended. There was a little hut standing all on its own. Edith, Elsa, and nine other girls looked at the tiny refuge and quickly made a decision—they'd had enough.

It was a simple decision: "This is the last place that we are coming like prisoners. Here we will be free." They fell on the floor of the little house and slept the sleep of the dead.

Edith woke to a gentle buzzing by her ear. The breath of wings across her cheek. Tiny angels buzzed through the golden light of morning, streaming in through the windows. They had fallen asleep in an apiary.

Footsteps crunched up the path outside. The latch lifted. A broad-faced, bearded German man stepped inside, unaware that there were interlopers sleeping on the floor. Edith sat up and rubbed her eyes.

"What are you doing here?" the man asked.

"We were sleeping," she said.

"Your people are gone already," he said. "I will tell you where, so you can catch up to them!"

The girls rose slowly to their feet, so as not to upset the bees, and slipped outside. The beekeeper pointed down the road, and they headed unhurriedly in the general direction he had indicated. No sooner were they out of his sight than they slipped into a ditch to hide. All around them, gunshots fragmented the morning quiet. Were the SS shooting prisoners, or were the Russians shooting SS? The girls crouched in the ditch until the gunshots receded. Two girls, one from the first transport and one from the second, decided to scout the area while the others hid. They returned with good news.

"We found an empty horse barn, with straw." It was the perfect place to hide for the day, while they tried to scratch the red paint off their uniforms. The red crosses were so thick and bright they could be seen from far away, easy targets for SS looking for escapees. Picking the paint off the backs of their shirts and sides of their trousers took most of the day.

That night, they sneaked back to the beekeeper's house and stole a chicken. All of the houses and the farm animals had been abandoned by the German farmers fleeing the Russian advance, so the girls milked the dairy cows, foraged for eggs in the chicken coops, and had their first meager meal in freedom.

The next day, their SS officer rode past on his bicycle. He didn't stop to look inside the barn where they were hiding. He just continued on his way. In a neighboring house, two Polish men who had been working on one of the farms saw the girls pulling water from the pump and called out, "Are you hungry?"

Edith had thought she would never know a full stomach again, but the Poles brought the girls so much food they couldn't eat it all. Fortunately, because they had been able to eat porridge and other foodstuffs when they were in Retzow, their stomachs could manage the feast. Afterwards, all they could do was enjoy the luxury of a stuffed stomach.

As sunbeams filtered through the open windows, reflecting off the dust and pollen in the air, they heard a woman's voice shouting outside: "*Der Krieg ist vorbei!* The war is over!"

Running to the window, Edith saw a German woman riding a bicycle and waving the white flag of surrender.

"We are free! Free! *Kostenlos! Zadarmo! Fray!*" they shouted in three different languages, and hugged each other. Wept for joy. Then wept with sorrow.

Chapter Thirty-nine

A NOVEL WOULD END HERE. It would wrap up with everyone safe and happy and traveling home to be reunited with loved ones. Fiction can do that. Nonfiction cannot. And that is not how wars end.

These were vulnerable young women, alone in a world of male soldiers who had fought long and hard and wanted a reward. No woman was truly safe.

To hear the Russian soldiers tell the tale, sex with female prisoners was an act of brotherly love—a celebration of life. Sex with German women was revenge. But prisoner or kapo, German or Jew, Polish or Slovak, French, Dutch, or Italian—it was all rape. After Orli Reichert (#502), the "Angel of Auschwitz," fled Malchow, the entire group of women she was with was raped by the liberating Red Army.

"So now we were free, but we were not," Edith explains. "There were no trains, no cars, no bridges. Everything had been bombed and destroyed. They were soldiers with guns, and we were without anything. We were so afraid. We only had a number on our arms to show them, but they were interested in the lower parts of our body, not the upper parts."

Edith's group of girls found a flag with a swastika lying on the ground and tore it apart with their bare hands. Pulling away the swastika, they made themselves red scarves so that the Russians would respect them as communists. That evening, eleven Russian soldiers arrived, carrying buckets of food, eggs and milk that they had cooked for the girls. It was all very jovial and kind, and then it became awkward. The men sat and watched the girls eat. "When we finished eating, we did not know what to do and we were tired, so we said, 'we want to go to bed.'"

"Us too," one of the soldiers said with a chuckle, as he made what he thought was a good-natured grab at one of the girls.

She slapped him away. "No!"

"But we fed you."

"We never had a man with us. We are girls."

"But we fed you."

Such was their male logic. The soldiers tried to manipulate the girls into agreeing to sleep with them, but the girls held a unanimous front.

Finally, the officer of the men stood up. "Get out!" he ordered. "Leave them alone!"

The girls breathed a sigh a relief as the soldiers disappeared into the night. Then the officer turned, looked at them, and smiled. "So who wants to be with me?"

"You just threw the others out."

"Yes, but I have more rights because I am an officer," he explained.

"We are still girls, even if you are an officer," the eldest argued. "You have to leave, too!"

Grudgingly, he departed into the night. The girls secured the barn door and curled up as close as puppies in the straw. In the morning, they told the Polish workers what had happened.

"They will come back. If they didn't succeed last night, they will come back until they succeed on the second or third," the Poles warned them. "You can't stay here any longer." They decided to take the girls to a train depot on the border with Poland.

The Polish men brought two draft horses down from the pasture, hitched them up to a wagon, and helped the girls to get in. Sitting in the back of the wagon, Edith gazed up at blue skies emptied of bombers. Spring had erupted around them. All the colors of the world were more vibrant, more intense. Green was greener. Pink, pinker. Flowers were sweeter for the smelling of them. The earth was a miracle. Every aroma, every hue, every breath of air was an extraordinary experience. After not having had a single pleasure for three years, Edith felt every sensation until the very cells in her body woke up and sang.

In a cherry orchard, the Poles unhitched and watered the horses. The girls climbed up into the trees. Edith wedged her bottom on a branch, reached above her head, and gathered the first fruit of freedom. Her fingers and lips and teeth were stained burgundy. Juice ran down her chin. She spit the pits at the others in jest. There was laughter. They laughed. Paused. Looked at each other and then laughed all the more. Like fist-fuls of life, Edith gathered cherries into her arms and pockets and mouth, until she could hold no more.

A Russian officer trotted by on his horse and looked at the girls sitting in the back of the wagon. "Jews?" he asked.

They nodded.

"Hide them at night to avoid their being raped or killed," he cautioned the Polish men.

So that is what they did. Every night, they found a barn along the road where the girls could hide in the straw and sleep until they made it to the train depot. But now there was another problem. Without any papers or money, how could they get home?

It was a question being asked by thousands of refugees all over the continent. Another question was: Should we go home? For many Jewish survivors, that answer would be no.

"I have no family," Joan sobs, years later. "Just a second cousin. You just don't get used to it." She did have an aunt, her mother's sister, and an address in the Bronx. Joan wrote to her

Women of Poprad

Fanny and Eta Zimmerspitz (#1755 and #1756) carried injectable poisons in their shoes to use if they were ever selected to go to the gas chamber. Eta looked so much like Roza (*below*) she was nearly arrested with her cousins. They are shown here postwar, circa 1946.

This prewar photo was taken when Edith "Rose" Grauber (#1371; Goldman) was about 15 years old; she is wearing braids and standing behind her cousins, aunts, and uncles. Her mother, Hermina, is at far right. None of her immediate family survived.

A neighbor of Marta Mangel (#1741; Marek), shown here in a prewar photo, hid Marta's mother's silver candlesticks in the backyard and returned them to Marta after the war. Marta's family continues to use the candlesticks in their traditional observances.

Piri Randova-Slonovicova (#1342; Skrhová) was born in Levoča, 8 kilometers from where Ivan Rauchwerger lived. She was sixteen years old when she was deported.

Roza Zimmerspitz (#1487) was executed with her three sisters in 1943.

The Zimmerspitz cousins were caught trying to escape and were executed. From left to right: Malvina, Margit, Hector the dog, and Frida (#1548, who "had a big mouth"), circa 1926.

The Schwartz children lost
their mother when they were
young. This photo was taken
at her grave before the war.
From left to right: Magda
(Mimi), Celia, Helen, Ignatz,
Regina (sitting). Helen and
Ignatz did not survive.

Regina Schwartz (#1064;
Pretter) was sixteen
when she was deported.

Alice Iscovic (#1221;
Burianov) stands at
far right with her
family. None of her
family survived

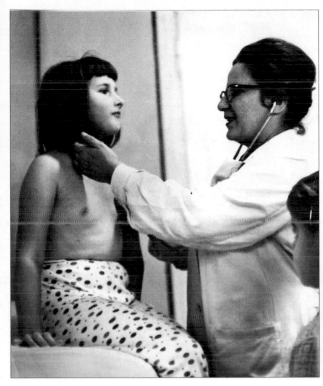

Dr. Manci (Manca) Schwalbova (#2675) did her best to care for the women in Auschwitz. Here she is shown with a young patient (her niece, Zuzana) at the Pediatric Hospital, in Bratislava, Slovakia, in the 1960s.

"The Angel of Auschwitz," Orli Reichert (#502; Wald) was arrested in 1936 and served nine years as a political prisoner. She was forced to work under Dr. Mengele. Two books have been published about her in Germany. She suffered from severe depression after the war and tried to commit suicide multiple times.

This propaganda photo shows "Prisoners in the *Aufräumungskommando* [order commandos] unload and sort the confiscated property of a transport of Jews from Subcarpathian Rus at a warehouse in Auschwitz-Birkenau." Linda Reich (#1173, shown at center) is bending over. The SS photographer insisted that she smile so that he could show the photo to the Red Cross.

In order to get them safely back to Slovakia, two Czech men in Prague, Frantischek and Bedrich, organized this group to accompany female survivors and protect them from sexual violence on the journey home. Among the women in the group are Fanny and Eta Zimmerspitz (#1755 and #1756, *far right, third and fifth row*) and their cousin, Marta Mangel (#1741, *far right, front row*). Others from the first transport may be in this photo, taken in May or June 1945.

Bergen-Belsen was liberated on April 15, 1945, the day this photo was snapped.
Bertha Berkowitz (#1048; Lautman) is the girl in the center.

At center, wearing a black dress with white collar, Ida Eigerman (#1930; Newman)
concentrates on her knitting in a displaced persons camp in Pocking, Germany, after liberation.
"Mom was always knitting," her daughters say.

Marta (last name unknown), perhaps Sara Bleich (#1966; Glancszpigel), and Elena Zuckermenn (#1735; Grunwald) after the war.

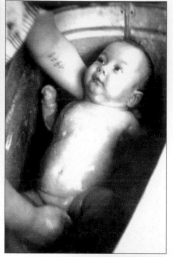

Helena Citron (Tsiporah Tehori) with her firstborn.

Like many of the surviving teenagers on the first transport, Bertha Berkowitz (#1048; Lautman) and Elena Zuckermenn (#1735; Grunwald) went back to high school after the war.

Margie Becker (#1019; Rosenberg) got married in a displaced persons camp in Braunau ("where Hitler was born, of all things," she says).

These women survivors used to get together once a month in Melbourne, Australia. *Left to right*: Magda Blau (#2318; Hellinger), Jozefa Schnabelova, Marta Friedman (#1796; Tuckman); Minka Friedman (#1174; Weiss), Vera Reich (#1967), Miriam Leitner, and Magda Reich (the last two were from the second transport).

Ruzena Gräber Knieža (#1649) with her son in Prague. She remained friends with Edith after the war.

"We were together in Auschwitz. All six of us on the first transport." *From left to right, back row:* Serena (perhaps Sternova), Roza (Lievermannova or Amselova), Margaret Friedman (#1019; Kulik). Center: bride Lily Friedman. *Front row:* Malka Tannenbaumova (Getz), an unidentified woman, and "the only child to survive the war in the town." The photo was taken in 1948.

Perel Kaufman (#1461; Fridman) with her firstborn. Perel emigrated to Israel after the war.

Margaret Friedman (#1019; Kulik) with Linda Reich (#1173; Breder) and Mira Gold (#4535) in Margaret's kitchen in Montreal, circa 1970s.

This photo, taken ten days after liberation, shows the Friedman sisters, who were among the hostages liberated by Count Folke Bernadotte and brought to Sweden. Here are Lila (*front*), Ella, and Edie Friedman (#3866, #1949, and #1950).

Among photos from the Friedman family album was this picture taken in the Swedish dormitory where they were held in quarantine for two weeks. Joan Rosner (#1188; Weintraub) is at far left, standing behind the bunk.

Edith Friedman (#1970) spent three years in a Swiss sanitarium, trying to recover from tuberculosis. After surgery made it impossible to bend her leg, Edith worried that her limp would bother Ladislav. "If your soul limped," he told her, "that would bother me." This is Edith and Ladislav Grosman's wedding photo, 1948.

The Friedman family in 1963, *left to right*: Herman, Edith (sticking out her tongue), Margita (Edith's eldest sister), Ruthie, Hilda, Ishtak. Their parents, Hanna and Emmanuel, are at center.

Edith with her great-grandsons, Elias (twelve years old) and Atlas (two months) in 2019.

Edith celebrated her ninetieth birthday with her granddaughters, Hanna and Naomi, and her son, George Grosman, in 2015.

aunt from Sweden and was one of the first of the first girls to emigrate to the United States.

The Polish girls unilaterally decided not to return home. They knew there was no one left. Rena Kornreich and her sister Danka went to Holland; their friends Erna and Fela stayed in Sweden; Dina Dranger went to France. Sara Bleich eventually emmigrated to Argentina. Margie Becker had an aunt in America, who wired one hundred dollars as soon as she heard from her niece. Margie bought a decent dress and headed east for Slovakia. On a train home she met Solomon Rosenberg, her future husband, also returning from the camps.

FOR THOSE RETURNING HOME, journeys took on the epic proportions of Ulysses' voyages as they faced one hurdle after another. They hitchhiked or caught trains, begged rides in wagons, and walked for miles. Edith had to cross a footbridge swaying over a torrent of dark floodwaters in the River Váh— spring melt from the mountains.

Some girls, like Kato (#1843), one of Lenka Hertzka's friends from Prešov, had a card from the Red Cross that gave her free passage on the trains. Others, like Edith, received nothing.

Linda sobs remembering the moment when the international commission arrived at the displaced persons camp where she and her friends were quarantined and announced that they were considered "citizens of the world." They were given papers that allowed them to go wherever they wanted. All they really wanted to do was go back to Slovakia. "I knew already that my twin brother, my sister, my other brothers, everybody was wiped out. But I wanted to go home."

Once a week, there was a train from Prague to Bratislava. To catch it, Linda and her friends walked from Berlin to Prague on foot, a 318-kilometer journey. When they arrived in Prague, the train was so full of refugees there was no room inside, so

Linda, Peggy and a few other friends clambered up the side of the train and sat on the roof.

"Why not on the top of the train? I was young." And alive.

From the top of the train, the world unfurled. Freedom was a horizon of distant green mountains, a chalk-blue sky. The desolate gray-beige bands of Auschwitz faded in the brightness of a horizon washed clean by storms. Not a single barbed-wire fence or watchtower hemmed in the distance. Freedom was the wind in their hair, the sweet spring air, and the flowering trees. The sun baked their weary bones, warmed muscles hardened by work, starvation, and fear. Tension melted into the metal top of the train. As they passed towns and villages, the refugees waved from the windows and the roof of the train. Villagers cheered and waved back. Just as they had more than three years earlier, the girls broke into song. This time, they did not sing the Slovak national anthem.

Homecomings

RIA HANS (#1980) WALKED the one thousand kilometers from Germany home to Humenné. When she arrived, in August 1945, she weighed thirty-nine kilograms, about eighty-five pounds. She had gained weight since liberation. "I was very sick. My skin, you couldn't even give me an injection. My body was completely dry, until my mom gave me oil of coconut baths." Ria was one of the lucky few whose parents had survived. Her father had a farm outside of town, and "when it started to 'stink'" in town, the family moved out to the farm. They had dressed like Slovak farmers and had taken the children to church, where the priest was a good friend. Like Lou Gross, Ria's siblings had learned how to say the "Our Father" and pretend they were Catholics. That was how the Hans family survived. Ivan Rauchwerger's sister weighed just 38 kg when Bergen-Belsen was liberated. After two months of recuperation in a British military hospital, "she came back to me still weighing only 40 kg. She had no hair and no teeth." Ivan didn't even recognize her. She suffered from ill health most of her life and "had many operations, skin grafts, and nonworking kidneys."

Very few of the girls returned to anything, though. Peggy knew that her brothers and sister had died in the gas chambers of Auschwitz, but she had hoped to find something left. She walked the two hours from Stropkov to her tiny village only to find complete desolation and her family's farm burnt to the ground. The walk back to Stropkov was even longer, weighed down by loss and memories. The last time she had walked that road, she had said good-bye to her family without knowing she would never see them again; she had been with Anna Judova (#1093) and Ruzena Kleinman (#1033). They too had survived, but where were they now? She sat on a curb in the now-empty Jewish quarter of Stropkov and wept. Peggy was penniless, homeless, and with no family—alone in the world. A young Jewish widow, whose husband had hidden her in a bunker with her twin daughters, stopped and asked Peggy what was wrong.

"I don't know what to do with my life!" Peggy sobbed.

"I have one bed and one sofa," the young widow told her. "You will sleep with one girl on the sofa, and I sleep with one girl in the bed." Adopted into this makeshift family, Peggy became the girls' nanny and slowly reentered the world of the living.

When Linda returned to her parents' house that summer, everything looked the same as it had when she left. She prayed that someone in her family was still alive and knocked on the big wooden gate. A steel-faced Ukrainian man opened it and glared at her. "What do you want?" How could anyone be so rude to a petite young woman, as frail and kind-faced as Linda?

"Well, this is our home," she stammered, unsure what else to say. "I want to come back to my house."

"It is mine. I bought it for a dollar," the Ukrainian said. "Go back where you came from!" He slammed the door in her face. "This was my welcome home....I felt like a ghost returning from my grave."

Despite all the outrages Linda had experienced in Auschwitz, the cruelty, deaths, and murders, she felt more stunned by the fact that the Hlinka Guardists had taken all of her family's furniture, all the mementos from her childhood, all her mother's heirlooms and even stolen her home. She had no family left. No inheritance. Nothing but the scraps of memory that had not been sanded away during her years in slavery.

She returned to Bratislava, where she had left some of her friends, and then discovered that her sister had survived by hiding under false papers as a Catholic. The she met Fred Breder in a bread line, and they were married in 1946. She was no longer alone in the world. It would take them twenty years to get their family home back, but Linda would fight for that house the way she had fought to survive. Of course, by the time it reverted to her family, she had emigrated to America.

ALICE ICOVIC (#1221) arrived in Slovakia on a wagon with several other girls. As they approached a farm, Alice greeted the gentile farmer with a traditional Slovak greeting: *"Dobrý deň k požehnanému Ježišovi Kristovi.* A good day to be blessed by Jesus Christ."

"Navždy!" he answered. "Forever."

It felt good to be in her home country, speaking her native language, and she smiled at his wife, who had come down to the road to see who was passing by.

"Please, could you give us a bit of a milk?" Alice asked. "We are coming from a concentration camp and are very thirsty."

Realizing that Alice and her friends must be Jews, the couple looked horrified. "Oh my God!" they said. "You were gassed and set on fire. How many of you are coming?"

"I forgot I was in Slovakia," Alice says, shaking her head. "You can't say we could be proud of those moments." She and her friends turned heel and, "shaking the dust from their feet," left.

Edith faced a similar reception in the market a few days after she arrived home when a woman recognized her and said, "There are more who came back than left."

THERE WERE SOFTER landings for some. Ida Eigerman (#1930) had ended up in a displaced persons camp in Pocking, Germany, where she was picked up by the Czechs, who had sent buses to move Czech and Slovak refugees. "I can say this was the happiest day in my life. You—you ran away from death. And the Czechs were so nice. On the way, they had kettles with milk and cakes and bread and salamis and anything you want. Who could eat so much? When you have been so hungry, you cannot eat anymore."

Eta and Fanny Zimmerspitz (#1756 and #1755) and their cousin, Martha Mangel, also made it to Prague eventually, but on foot. By then, the trains were so full that it was almost impossible to get on them, but they discovered that a group of Polish and Slovak men had decided to organize and escort female survivors home to Slovakia. It was a 300-kilometer journey and would take over a week to walk home, but the girls were safe, protected, and well cared for on the road.

Walking up the steep hill to the old town of Poprad, Martha Mangel and her cousins, Eta and Fanny Zimmerspitz, returned to empty, ruined homes, the sole survivors of their families. Martha's neighbor beckoned to her from the front gate and opened the door.

"I have something for you," she said.

She took a spade and led Martha into the backyard, where they dug up a flannel, filthy with mud. Martha's mother had come to the neighbor, just before they took her, and begged, "Keep these for Martha, if she ever returns."

"And here you are," the neighbor said, handing Martha the family heirloom. "And here *they* are."

Martha's hands trembled as she unwrapped the old flannel and saw the tarnished silver of her mother's Shabbat candlesticks. It was all Martha had left. Her daughter, Lydia, still uses them today.

Eta tells a similar story. When she and her sister returned to Poprad, a gentile reconized them and said, "I want to talk to you." Before the war, their father had loaned him 20,000 *koruna.* "I don't want this money," the man told them. He paid his debt back with the interest.

AFTER BERGEN-BELSEN was liberated, Bertha (#1048) found her sister, Fany, in a neighboring camp through one of the army chaplains. They reunited in a flurry of tears. Bertha says, "it was happy, and it was sad...We hadn't seen each other in three and a half years." Fany told her sister how the Germans were searching for Jews and had barged into the house where their elder sister, Magda, was staying. Magda hid in a cabinet. The Germans searched the cabinet and found Magda. When they came for Fany, she hid under the bed. The soldiers pushed the mattress down to see if anyone was under it, but Fany kept still and quiet, she wasn't caught until 1944. Magda went straight to the gas.

At Bergen-Belsen, the Americans had given everyone ID cards and organized a truck for survivors who wanted to travel east toward Prague. Bertha and Fany had no money to travel, but they were able to show their numbers and get on a train. On the platform, Fany saw Mike Lautman, who had lived under false ID papers during the war. She introduced Bertha to Mike, and the trio traveled back to Slovakia together. They arrived in Bratislava, where the American Jewish Joint Distribution Committee (JDC) "put us up in a hotel, not a Hilton hotel, but good enough! It even had a kosher kitchen."

Through other refugees, the girls learned that one of their brothers had worked as a partisan during the war and was still alive. They sent him a card. A few days later Emil arrived in Bratislava to take over the care of his little sisters. "He was the father, the mother, everything, and we were the little girls." For a month, Bertha and Fany did nothing but recuperate. Meanwhile, Mike Lautman kept stopping by to make sure they were okay. Bertha smiles. "A few years later, he was my husband." In their wedding photo, standing behind Bertha, is Elena Zuckermenn (#1735).

When Ruzena Gräber Knieža arrived in Bratislava, she found old friends to stay with temporarily. On the other side of the country, her husband, Emil, heard that she was alive and jumped on the night train to Bratislava. By eight o'clock the next morning he was at the Kornfields' apartment, where Ruzena was still sleeping. "I was very weak and tired. They took him to the room where I slept. He woke me, and we fell silent. Suddenly, you saw everything before your eyes, all this long time, the years. After a while, the tears came."

ON THE LAST leg of her monthlong odyssey home, Edith was thirty-five kilometers from Humenné when the train stopped in the town of Michalovce and looked like it might never move again. This was the town where Alice Icovic and Regina Schwartz and her sisters had once lived. Alice was on her way in a wagon. The Schwartz sisters were recovering in Stuttgart, Germany. Edith was alone.

Impatient, Edith paced back and forth on the platform, waiting for the all-aboard whistle. She was so close, yet so far from home, and she wondered if she should just start walking again.

"Aren't you Emmanuel Friedman's daughter?"

Edith looked down at a Jewish man—one of the few left—peering up at her face, blinking unbelievingly.

"I am."

"Your father is here! At the synagogue!"

It was Shabbat? She had not kept Shabbat or had any day of rest in so long, she had forgotten all about it.

"Please, could you go to the synagogue and tell him that I am on the train?" she begged, unwilling to leave the platform in case the train started moving.

The man hurried to the shul, where he burst through the doors and shouted over everyone's heads, "Emmanuel! Your daughter, Edith, is back from the camps!"

Emmanuel hurried out the door and up the street to the station, where the train was still waiting for the go-ahead and might continue to wait forever.

"Papa!" Edith ran toward her father's arms. She ran for the embrace that would dispel the nightmare and bring her, the lost child, home.

He couldn't touch her. Or wouldn't. The air between them hardened. He did not speak a word. Not one word. This was her homecoming?

"Papa, why are you so odd?"

He looked shy of his own child. "Do you have lice?" he asked.

The guilt of his decision to send Edith and Lea to "work" hung heavily in his heart and he could barely face his surviving daughter. The chasm of war yawned between them.

She could tell he was crying on the inside. Sorrow tangled his voice so that he didn't know how to speak to his own daughter. She was a stranger to him.

"Don't worry, Papa. Everything is okay. Come home with me. Let's find Mama and surprise her."

"It's Shabbes. I can't travel."

Edith looked at her father incredulously. "Papa, I was in hell, and I know that you can come with me. God does not care about that." She beckoned him onto the train. He stepped into the passenger car, still without touching her.

When the train rolled forward, father and daughter shifted uneasily with it. Lumbering down the tracks, it swayed too slowly. Even the engine seemed to disregard the urgency of Edith's quest. The longest part of her journey home was the shortest distance.

She had left as a child and was returning as an adult—a broken adult. Would her mother be as strange as her father?

She had no idea what to expect. A naive desire that nothing had changed remained in a secret wheelhouse of hope. But Humenné was empty now. Of the two thousand Jewish families who had once lived there, maybe one hundred remained.

In Prešov, Giora Shpira discovered that he was one of three people in his school class to have survived. His government ID card numbered him fifteen. Out of a community of four thousand only fourteen Jews had returned to Prešov before him.

AMONG THOSE RETURNING to Humenné in the weeks after armistice were Lou Gross and his family. After hiding in the mountains and pretending to be gentiles for almost two years, even six-year-old Lou understood as they walked up Štefánikova Street that it would never again be referred to as Gross Street. There were too few Grosses left. But miracle of miracles, his grandfather, Chaim, was still alive.

The story is one that is still told around the Passover table: Grandfather Chaim was sitting on the stairs outside their house when the Hlinka Guard came to cart him off to Auschwitz. He had wrapped his beautiful, hand-embroidered *tallis* or prayer shawl, with its ivory, powder blue, and silver threads around his shoulders and planted himself on the stoop outside the family home. "I'm not going anywhere," he told the guards.

They threatened to shoot him. He shrugged.

—So be it.

After much posturing bluster, the guards left Chaim sitting on the stoop alone because he wasn't "worth the cost of a bullet." His grandfather's tallis belongs to Lou now, and he still wears it on special occasions.

THE FRIEDMANS NO LONGER lived in the same flat. They had moved into the apartment building where Ladislav Grosman's sister had lived before the bomb wiped most of his family off the face of the earth. In the afternoons, Ladislav would often pause out front, grieving the loss of his parents, his sister, his cousins and aunts and uncles. He was standing there when the train whistle blew and Hanna hurried out the door.

"Mrs. Friedman, where are you running?" he yelled after her.

"I think my Edith is coming home!"

Who could believe it?

Hanna was at the station within minutes of the whistle announcing its arrival. She stumbled past the people standing on the platform, calling out Edith's name, frantically looking for her daughter's face.

As Edith exited the train, it did not seem possible that she was finally back in Hummené. Straining her neck, she caught sight of her mother and waved frantically. "Mama! Mama!"

Hanna fainted on the platform.

WHEN SHE CAME TO, Hanna couldn't stop stroking her daughter's face. Her hair. Her arm. She kissed Edith's fingers and her palms. Kissed the tears from her daughter's face. Thanked God and kissed Edith, again and again.

Arm in arm, they walked back toward Main Street. The hero of a thousand faces was a teenage girl on the verge of turning twenty. She had returned from the wars and bore scars in her mind, her soul, her leg, but she was alive. Too many of her friends and their families were not. The Jewish quarter was full of empty storefronts. Empty gardens. Empty streets. Empty homes.

There was the coffee shop where Margie Becker's parents used to sell pastries—boarded up and vacant. Margie's family was gone. There was the Moskovics' house, where Annou had lived. Never again would Annou come over for bread-making day and eat Edith's mother's warm challah. There was Anna Herskovic's house. Never again would Anna come pick up Lea to go to the movies. Never again would Adela toss her red hair in the breeze or pose for one of Irena's photographs. Zena Haber would never grow into her height. Hinda Kahan and

Klary Atles would never get married or have children or grow old. Helena's niece, Aviva, would never turn eight. The ghosts of girlhood lingered.

Limping up the road like a soldier back from war, Edith's reality was disjointed, surreal. Was this really her mother's arm around her waist? Was this really her mother's voice chatting in her ear? Outside the gate of their new apartment, Edith saw a wide-eyed Ladislav watching her, "as if he wanted to see what an actual girl looked like." There were so few girls left, it wasn't any wonder he was curious.

Looking at the handsome young man standing in the empty street, what did she foresee? Did she think, Here is my future husband? Or was it simpler than that? Was it just a greeting?

"Hi, Grosman. I know you."

"I know you, too."

And so they did.

Afterwards

If these women can tell us anything, it's to look to the future rather than the short-term solutions, and look to our children and grandchildren.
—KARA COONEY, *When Women Ruled the World*

"HE WAS THE LOVE OF my life." After three years of knowing each day could be her last, suddenly Edith was free, alive, and in love with Ladislav Grosman. "I felt so much hope. So much hope for the world, for humanity, for our future. I thought, now the messiah will come. Now the world will change for good. Everything will be different now…It did not turn out like I thought."

For one thing, she was terribly ill with tuberculosis. It would take another three years out of her young life to recover in a sanatorium in Switzerland. After surgery left her knee fused and unbendable, the doctor counseled Ladislav that her illness was so serious he should just "let her slip away quietly." But Edith has never done anything quietly.

When she asked Ladislav if it would bother him that his young wife had a limp, Ladislav assured her, "If your soul would limp, that would bother me." Her soul sings. She and Ladislav were married in 1949. After she recovered from TB, Edith finished her high school education and went on to study biology. She never became a doctor, but she did work as a researcher. Meanwhile, Ladislav got his Ph.D. in philosophy and began writing books, plays, and a screenplay. They were living in Prague when Ladislav's film won the 1965 Academy Award for Best Foreign Language Film, for *The Shop on Main Street.*

Not long after the Oscars, their good friend Rudolf Vrba announced that he was going on a "long vacation. You should go on vacation soon, too," he warned. It was a risk for both of their families, but as Ladislav told Edith, "If the Nazis couldn't keep Rudi in Auschwitz, the Soviets certainly aren't going to be able to keep him in Czechoslovakia." The Grosmans followed the Vrba family on a permanent vacation to the West and settled in Israel, where Ladislav continued to write. Just before he died, the Nobel Prize committee visited the Grosmans in Haifa, clearly considering Ladislav for the literary prize. But he had a heart attack a few days later and died without receiving the international renown he so deserved.

His literary artistry in *The Bride* helped me to better understand and capture the small-town drama of the first transport, inspiring and informing the scenes at the beginning of this book.

"My parents' Prague friends were all typical middle-European Jewish intellectuals," says George Grosman, Edith and Ladislav's son, who continues his father's artistic tradition as a jazz musician and composer. "Linguists, sociologists, writers, doctors. They would visit on weekends or we would go to their places. The contact was frequent. And invariably, over endless cups of sweet Turkish coffee and in the impenetrable haze of cheap cigarette smoke—*everyone* smoked then—talk turned to the war. It was usually my father who did the talking in our family, and his war experiences—though harrowing—were not as scary as my mother's. I learned later that during those first decades after the war my dad didn't like my mom to talk about Auschwitz. Growing up in Prague, in Communist Czechoslovakia, I never heard my mother speak about her Auschwitz experiences directly. And while I didn't know much detail, I did see the number tattooed on my mom's arm, and I knew there was this black cloud of unspeakable horror hovering over her, and over us. I'm sure it contributed in large measure to a feeling of existential anxiety that I've had all my life. A feeling that things are slightly unhinged, that the world isn't quite as straightforward as it seems, that there is a danger in the air, even if it remains unspoken. I guess we are all secondhand survivors."

DR. MANCI SCHWALBOVA (#2675) returned to Slovakia, where she continued to practice medicine after the war. She did not return to her fiancé, though. While in one of the deportation camps, her husband fell in love with a man. Evidently, Manci had also had an affair; hers was with one of the female kapos, a political prisoner. Edith laughs at the thought that Hitler may have hated homosexuals as much as he hated Jews, but "he turned Manci and her fiancé into Jewish homosexuals!"

Another little-known story about Manci that Edith tells is that in 1943, while still in Auschwitz, Manci was offered safe passage to Palestine and the opportunity to leave the camp. She told the administration in Auschwitz that she was needed and would stay. If she had made a different decision, this story would have had a very different ending.

Manci completed her medical studies at Charles University in Prague and became a licensed medical doctor in February 1947. She worked at the Children's University Hospital in Bratislava and as a professor of pediatrics. Her memoir *Vyhasnuté oči* (*Extinguished Eyes*), 1948, was the first published account of the first transport. A second memoir was titled *I Lived the Lives of Others*. Neither of her books has been translated into English. She died on December 30, 2002, in Bratislava, Slovakia.

Unfortunately, the last names of other female doctors mentioned in the survivors' testimonies are never stated, so I
cannot say more about them or how they helped girls in such
brutal circumstances.

Linda Reich Breder (#1173) testified in at least two trials
against the SS. The first was in 1969, in Vienna, against SS
Franz Wunsch and Otto Graf. The trial ignited tensions among
survivors in Israel, because Helena Citron, by then married and
living under her Hebrew name, Tsiporah Tehori, flew to Vienna
to testify on Wunsch's behalf.

"I never forgave her for that," Eta Zimmerspitz Neuman
(#1756) says. Edith says it was one of Helena's deepest fears that
she would be accused of being a collaborator and forced to leave
Israel. At the trial in Vienna, Linda almost certainly knew that
Helena came to testify, but she refrains from mentioning anything about Helena's presence at the trial in her USC testimony.

Neither Wunsch nor Graf was found guilty. "They were sa-
dists," Linda says. "Even though I told them, and other
witnesses told them. It didn't mean a thing.... They were set
free. They didn't go to jail. What millions they brought out of
Auschwitz, they took everything to Vienna—so they had ten
lawyers and they went free."

Twenty years later things would be different when Linda
was flown to Germany to testify against another former SS,
Gottfried Weise. The prisoners referred to him as Wilhelm Tell,
because he liked to place cans on the heads and shoulders of
little boys for target practice. After he shot the cans, he always
shot the child in the face. Linda had witnessed one of those
murders and had also been present when he bayoneted the
Hungarian child one of the girls from Canada had thrown
water to; Weise was also the SS who shot every tenth girl while
they stood at attention.

"It was very weird," Linda's daughter, Dasha Grafil, tells me.
"There were TV cameras and newspaper reporters and even high

school students, who had come to hear my mom's testimony." The defendant "looked like a wealthy industrialist—you would never think this was a guy who killed people."

Linda worried that this trial would be another fiasco like the Wunsch and Graf trial. As had happened in Vienna, the session started with the court grilling Linda for three or four hours. The judge and defense lawyers asked her a myriad of questions, but the fact was she knew more about Auschwitz than anyone else in the courtroom. "I remember everything what [sic] happened fifty-five years ago, but I hardly can remember what happened yesterday, what I had for lunch." She had a wry sense of humor.

Because of her position in Canada, Linda had witnessed the SS pilfering goods to enrich themselves and their homes. Like most of the Slovak girls, she also spoke German and knew what the SS were saying to each other. At one point they tried to trip her up by asking her if she saw him in the morning or at night.

"I can't tell you if it was the morning or evening because the gas was always going, but I can tell you if it was summer or the winter by the dirty smell in the ground," Linda told them.

Finally, the judge asked her if there was anything else she wanted to tell the court.

That was Linda's moment. This tiny, white-haired old lady who was our Linda Reich stood up and looked at the gallery. "Yes, I have some words to say to all of you," she said. "I have waited all my life for this. To stand here in front of you and point my finger." She walked up to Weise and pointed at him so everyone could see. "And none of you can do a damn thing about it!"

And then she walked out of the courtroom. Her daughter chokes up at the memory. "The German high school kids followed my mother out of the courtroom and started hugging her and telling her, 'Don't worry, this is never going to happen again.'"

Weise was found guilty but fled to Switzerland after he was released on bond. He was arrested twelve weeks later and served his sentence until 1997, when he was set free for health reasons. He died in 2002.

SOON AFTER ARRIVING in Israel in the 1950s, Ria Hans Elias (#1980) was denounced by a survivor who said Ria had beaten her. Ria was arrested and had to defend herself against accusations that she had abused prisoners. Edith says this was truly unfair because if anyone helped others, Ria had. "Ria was one of the good ones." The claim was serious, though. The complainant not only accused Ria of hitting a female prisoner but claimed, Ria explains, "It was impossible that I could be Jewish; only Germans got this number here." She points to the number tattooed on her arm. In fact, there were at least a few other survivors from the first transport in Israel, including Helena. But in 1944, when most of the Slovak female survivors arrived in camp, the SS had begun adding letters before prisoners' numbers, and the woman thought Ria's four-digit number starting with the numeral one meant Ria was a kapo.

Auschwitz survivors' numbers represent a strange kind of sorority or fraternity. Lower numbers command more status among survivors and garner others' respect, but low numbers can also attract suspicion. The lingering question is, What did you do to survive?

After hiring a lawyer and defending herself against the allegations, Ria was acquitted, but not before spending time in an Israeli jail—a true irony considering she had also been jailed in Auschwitz.

Forty-seven years later when she gave her testimony to the USC Shoah Foundation, she confessed to a deep confusion around the circumstances. "A week or two ago," she says, "I am certain I didn't...I'd swear I didn't beat her. Today, I don't know anymore, [because] when I start to think about how it was [in Auschwitz], I was . . . inside, I was dead."

Edith is stalwart in her defense of Ria Hans. "If she hit someone it was to protect them. New girls didn't know how to behave or where the dangers were. Ria did. I bet Ria saved that woman's life, and she didn't even know it."

PEGGY FRIEDMAN KULIK (#1019) remained friends with Linda Breder née Reich well into their golden years. Linda's daughter, Dasha, remembers hearing her mother's friends from Auschwitz and "Canada" laughing as they reminisced about sneaking things past the SS and not getting caught. Some people think survivors should never laugh. But after so many years of sorrow and horror, they deserve laughter. All of the survivors I know and have known have the most excellent senses of humor.

The photos of Peggy as a young woman reveal a girl who liked to make silly faces, despite the many hardships she suffered during and after the war. Like most of these young women, Peggy had trouble conceiving and carrying a pregnancy to term. Almost every survivor suffered miscarriages or had to have medical "interruptions"—the term for abortions at the time—to save their own lives. Peggy miscarried twins. Two boys. "I was kicked in the back by my SS man, and he damaged my uterus." She finally had one son, who was born four weeks prematurely.

For girls who had grown up in mostly large families, having only one or two children was tough. For their children, there is a different sadness.

"We were a generation that grew up without grandparents," says Sara Cohen, daughter of Danka Kornreich Brandel (#2779) and Rena's niece. "We also had very few aunts, uncles, or cousins. It wasn't until I joined my husband's family and attended gatherings with more than a dozen aunts and uncles and countless first cousins that I saw what other families experienced. When I had my own children and witnessed the unconditional love and wisdom they received from their grand-parents, I finally understood what I had missed during my own childhood."

Bertha Berkowitz Lautman (#1048) immigrated to Cleveland, Ohio, where she had one son, Jeffrey Lautman, with whom she traveled to Auschwitz several times. During her lifetime, Bertha did everything she could to educate young people about the Holocaust. "It is very important to take kids back to camps with survivors to teach them the Holocaust is not a hoax. You should study and learn as much as you can. Carry on and be active in organizations. After I am gone, it's all going to be all forgotten. Who will remember?" she asks.

You will, reader. You will.

Bertha remained friends with many of the girls she knew in Auschwitz and lived just a few blocks away from one of her best friends, Elena Grunwald Zuckermenn (#1735). Elena was the second woman I ever spoke to about the first transport and confirmed for me everything in Rena Kornreich Gelissen's account of the transport from Poprad in our book, *Rena's Promise.* At that point, I had no idea there were other survivors, as Rena's best friends Erna and Dina had already passed away.

However, Elena preferred to stay anonymous in her lifetime, and I lost touch with her over the years. Just as I was wrapping up this book, I got an email from Elena's daughter and photos of her mother with Bertha, holding schoolbooks and looking like the high schoolers they were.

"My brother and I believed that our mother was always critical of us, our choices, and our decisions," Elena's daughter says. "I occasionally referred to her as the 'Iron Lady.' Finally, I realized this was her way of shielding us and steering us to a better life and more opportunities. There is no doubt of the impact of traumatic events, which affected her practical nature, fearful world outlook, and the importance of family. At age seventeen, she was the first to be taken from her family, survived the horrors and deprivation experienced in the camps, and after liberation discovered she was the only survivor of her once-large extended family. My mother was an incessant worrier but managed to channel her anxiety into productive activity, regulating family life and maintaining a large network of friends, who were survivors and refugees. I always felt that we were different, perhaps even special, because of my parents' traumatic experiences and the loss of family. I have read about shared trauma through the generations, but I believe that strength and determination to survive can also be shared through the generations."

Post-traumatic stress disorder (PTSD) had not been defined or recognized in the 1940s and '50s, but survivors still suffered from it. Joan Rosner Weintraub (#1188) offers a poignant reminder of how it afflicted the rest of her life. "I am afraid of the shadow. If I am driving a car and a policeman is in back of me, I am shaking. I'm afraid that he is after me. I see a uniform, I am scared to death."

"We look normal, but we're not," Edith says. How could they be? "I lost my education, which was the biggest theft of my life. I lost my health. I came back with a broken body. Elsa came back healthy but was afraid of everything. The fear killed her in the end."

The fear resides in Edith, as well. She just hides it better. Usually. It only takes a small incident to trigger panic. Edith's family calls it "the mushroom story," an illustration of the kind of ongoing trauma survivors suffered.

A few days before Edith, Ladislav, and their son left to visit Edith's family in Israel, where the Friedmans emigrated in the 1950s, a newscast reported that a family had gone mushroom picking in Israel and unwittingly eaten poisonous mushrooms. The entire family had died. The names of the victims were not reported. After several days of travel from Prague, the Grosman family boarded the ferry to the Holy Land, but "when we arrived at the dock," George recalls, "there was no one there to greet us. My mother panicked. She lost it."

Edith was convinced that it was her family that had died of mushroom poisoning. Sobbing and hysterical, she could not be calmed down by George or his father. She was convinced that her entire family had died. "Then the whole Friedman clan showed up!" George says. They had gotten a flat tire on the highway. There was great rejoicing and laughter, but the moment is a refrain of the trauma Edith and all of the women suffered from, no matter how well they tried to hide it from their children and loved ones.

I AM IN TYLICZ, POLAND, with the sons of Erna and Fela Dranger (#1718 and #6030). They have flown from Israel to explore the region and are looking for any remnants of their family or Jews themselves in a village that is now dominated by ski resorts. American pop music from the 1980s blasts out of metal loudspeakers bolted onto telegraph poles that line the ski slopes.

"We are descended from very special survivors. Not anyone can survive in that place for that long." Avi is a tall and gentle man with soft, deep eyes. "I know that when I was born, she [Fela, his mother] had a breakdown." His eyes well up with tears. His older cousin reaches over and pats his leg. While they are first cousins, they are as close as brothers, because Avi spent the first two years of his life being raised by his Aunt Erna while his mother recovered her sanity. "When I was fourteen, she had a second breakdown." His voice catches. "She used to run out of the house into the lobby and scream that people are coming to hit her and murder her."

"My mother was stronger," Erna's son, Akiva, chimes in. "I have never seen her break or cry. Never." She never told anyone in the family about her experience. Children are, indeed, secondhand survivors.

"We were *all* sick," Edith confirms. "We came out of it, but the damage that was done on us, mentally, is a lot bigger than the illnesses we had physically. We will never ever, never ever get rid of the damage that they made in our hearts, changing how we look on the world and on people. This was the biggest damage that the war brought on us."

Survival brings with it a complex array of emotions, psychological explanations, and guesswork. "I never felt guilty," Rena Kornreich says. "Why should I? I didn't do anything wrong. They did! They are guilty." In contrast, Edith says, "The guilt of the survivors never goes away." Of course, Edith lost her sister, Lea. Rena did not.

"Not a day goes by when I don't think of Lea. Everything I do is for Lea. It has always been like that. You can't see her. No one knows she is there, but she is. In my mind, in my heart, she is always here." Edith taps her frail chest and shakes her head. In the light streaming in through the window, I swear I can see Lea's spirit standing behind her sister.

Guilt may be the conundrum of the survivor. As a biologist, Edith brings logic and science to the question of survival, asking, "What if I survived because of some speck in my DNA that was different from my sister? What if those of us who survived had a gene for survival that others did not?"

Many survivors seem to have made an inner contract with themselves. Rena remembered everything that happened to her so that she could tell her mother someday. When she realized her mother had been murdered in the Holocaust, she clung to her memories in order to tell someone, someday what had happened. That someone eventually became me.

"How could I remember all the little incidents?" Joan Rosner Weintraub asks. "It is humanly impossible. How many beatings? We did something they didn't like and they gave us twenty-five lashes. Can you survive twenty-five lashes? The only thing I live for now is for my daughter and my grandchildren." For many of these women, it is their children who gave meaning to their lives.

Avi's eyes fill up with tears again as he pays tribute to his mother, "It makes us really proud of our mums to see that they are survivors in a very difficult situation and to be proud of all those young women who survived and did not survive, that they did the best they could to lift up their heads. Their success is that they have lots of descendants, lots of grandchildren and great-grandchildren and great-great-grandchildren."

Ella Friedman Rutman (#1950) and her sister Edie Valo (#1949) returned to Slovakia to find five uncles who had survived, but no one else in the family. They lived in Slovakia for a time, then moved to Canada—the country—where Ella became the nanny for Edie's children. "I never wanted to have children," Ella says. "When I was in camp, I was always thinking I would be killed. In the end, I thought maybe I will be free, but I will never have children because I don't want my children to ever go through what I did." She was in her thirties when she got a surprise—a daughter. "The best surprise in my life. Without Rosette, it wouldn't be a life."

Ella and Edie's cousin—another Magda (#1087)—was Donna Steinhorn's mother. "I knew my parents were different from others at an early age," Donna says. "It always made me want to protect them. To heal the deep wounds that they tried to hide from me. To do everything in my power to make them happy." In the same way, mothers wanted to do everything in their power to make their children happy by never telling them what happened in the Holocaust. Although some survivors felt that way, one child I know was told everything too young and so often that she suffered from vicarious trauma. Genocide does not simply go away. Just as it can continue to haunt the survivors, it shapes the lives of those who live with and love those survivors.

Orna Tuckman's mother, Marta F. Gregor (#1796,) never spoke about her experience, so in 2016 Orna began a journey of self-discovery that brought her to Slovakia and Auschwitz with me. In the towns where the girls were collected, we visited the old synagogues and town halls, looking for remnants of families before retracing the train route from Poprad to Auschwitz on the seventy-fifth anniversary of the first transport. We were standing upstairs in the vast empty space of Block 10, where the girls were first held—and where, later, medical sterilization experiments were conducted on women—when Orna looked across the empty space and confided, "I think my mother was sterilized here. I was adopted." Orna did not learn she was adopted until after her mother passed away. All of the women who had survived with Marta kept her secret.

Having children may have been the greatest act of survival and healing of all. A class of psychology students at Brown University once asked Rena what she did after the war to recover, mentally. "I had babies," she said. After her first miscarriage, the birth of her daughter, Sylvia, was a miracle. Rena held her daughter and, filled with joy, looked at her husband and said, "I love you, John." Then she looked at the doctor and nurses, "I love you, doctor. I love you, nurse. I love the whole world, even with the Germans in it."

Childbirth. Creation. That was their power. Their legacy of survival.

No wonder Marta F. Gregor adopted Orna.

WHILE MARTA F.'S EXPERIENCE died with her and remains one of many stories that may never be fully uncovered, writing and art were other ways women found meaning. After emigrating to France, Dina Dranger Vajda (#1528) married a famous French resistance fighter, Emil Vajda. They raised their son in Provence. Dina kept copious notebooks, written mostly in Polish or rather poor French. Amid her musings are disturbing and macabre abstract watercolors.

Dina's son Daniel Vajda is extremely close to his cousins in Israel, but he feels largely detached from his mother's experience:

> You know that all my family was deported, and there were very few survivors. After her deportation, I found myself totally isolated. I too was an immigrant on this earth. Even the Yad Vashem site didn't bring me a lot. I have tried to rediscover names from the diverse notes I have made. It's really very short. It needs to be seen in joined-up pieces. However, I did not have the courage to do the research in my youth, and at sixty-eight years of age, I do not have the energy to do it now.

Matilda Hrabovecká née Friedman (#1890) wrote the book *Ruka s Vytetovanym Cislom* (*Arm with a Tattooed Number*) and was the subject of the documentary film and play *La Derniere femme du Premiere Train* (*The Last Woman of The First Transport*)—which, of course, she was not. Matilda passed away in 2015. To date, she is survived by at least six women who were on the first transport. There may be others.

Magda Hellinger née Blau (Madge, #2318) who was on the second transport, immigrated to Australia, where she self-published her memoir. And, of course, Rena Kornreich and I wrote *Rena's Promise* together, and now Edith and I have collaborated on this book and a documentary film. This book, Edith told me when I began the project, "should be about all of us, not just one person." And so it is.

The Slovak survivors of the first and other early transports carry a heavy yoke that is difficult to comprehend now. Ariela Neuman, the daughter of Eta Zimmerspitz (#1756), explains that "in Israel, everybody accused the Slovak women because they survived." So they tended to keep silent and not talk about it. "When they did," Ariela continues, "we were like, 'Oh no, not

Auschwitz again.' We feel guilty now that we didn't want to hear about it. And they are almost all gone, and we can't ask anymore."

That is why the Visual History Archive at the USC Shoah Foundation is such an important database. The stories are there, even if they are not perfectly captured. Older survivors tend to jump around in time, and interviewers often missed asking vital questions about important details, such as: What was her maiden name? What was her number? What was your number? In Auschwitz, your number served as a calendar, indicating the day you arrived, what transport you were on, how many people were with you, and how many went to the gas. Without a number, we cannot place survivors or nonsurvivors inside the historic record that Czech Danuta painstakingly compiled for us in the *Auschwitz Chronicle*.

POSTHUMOUS RELATIONSHIPS BRING with them a weight that is hard for most people to imagine. Andrew Hartmann's daughter, Susan Hartmann Schwartz, would have been Nusi Hartmann's niece. "Too often, the Holocaust is described in the generic term of 'six million,'" writes Susan. "Occasionally I sit back and think—that was my aunt on the first transport. Nusi was not just one of six million, or of one and a half million children, or even just one of the 999 on that first transport. She was my aunt. She was my father's sister. She was a beloved daughter. She was a person—a human being. Nusi must've had dreams, like we all do at sixteen. Her parents did not know what that first transport meant. Did she? At sixteen, how petrified was she? Was she told anything by the Germans, and if so, what? Did she bond with anyone on that transport other than her cousin Magduska? Did anyone help ease her fear just a little? I can't help but segue into the what-ifs. What if she'd been just a little older? Could she have survived? What would our relationship have been like if she had? I miss who I think Nusi would have been." So do I.

Many survivors eventually received some financial restitution from the German government. However, they had to apply to get support. That required their ID number, medical documentation, and a statement about their experience. After one survivor passed away, her children discovered a medical report that had been submitted to Germany for reimbursement. It confirmed that a psychiatrist had treated her for suicidal thoughts and depression. Her husband had kept her treatment a secret from them.

Survivors who returned to Slovakia and settled there after the war faced another difficulty: they could not file for German reparations as survivors in the west could. And in Edith's case, by the time they escaped communist Czechoslovakia, the deadline to file for reparations had passed. As a disabled survivor, she had a good case and went to court to seek an appeal. The German court agreed that she deserved reparations but said they couldn't change the law. "It's a bad law" had come back to haunt her.

When Ida Eigerman Newman's daughter filled out the forms for her mother, the German official blurted, "Nobody survived Auschwitz with that low a number [#1930]!" But they did survive, and while some got compensation, others either chose to forego the paperwork and hassle or—like Edith and Linda—were unable to apply because they were living under a communist regime. The compensation was not extravagant: It equaled about $0.32 per hour of work.

Peggy Kulik née Friedman (#1019) says, "They don't pay back what they took away. They took away everything. They cannot pay me for what my father had, what I had. There is no money for the lives they took. I was in a concentration camp for thirty-eight months. Did they pay me for my work? No. I never had a penny." And she miscarried twins.

Many survivors never wanted to return to Auschwitz or Poland. "Our mothers never wanted us to come back to Poland," Akiva Koren (Erna Dranger's son) says. Others, like Helena Citron and Bertha Berkowitz, took tours of young people back with them. There is nothing like knowing and speaking to a real survivor. Walking through camp with one is even more life changing. This was their home for almost three years. They know it well. But for some, returning was too much. There is a 1990 photo of Rena standing under the *Arbeit Macht Frei* sign in which she looks as forlorn and lost as she must have felt the day she arrived in Auschwitz. She wanted to go to Birkenau and stand in a gas chamber to say the Kaddish for her parents, but under the shadow of the death gate, she collapsed. "Take me home," she begged her husband. They caught the next plane back to America. She never went back. I took care of that wish for her, in 2017.

One of the questions that arises again and again is why did some women survive while others did not? Being in the right place at the right time, and not being in the wrong place at the wrong time, accounted for much. But there is no real explanation other than luck. And there are problems with that answer. "How can I say that I was lucky and another girl wasn't? Did God watch out for me and not her? No! I was no better than they were, so why should I survive?" Rena Kornreich asks. Some say it was *bashert*—meant to be. Fate.

"They were short!" says Lydia Marek, the daughter of Martha Mangel (#1741) and niece of the Zimmerspitz sisters and cousins. It is simultaneously humorous and shocking—could it be that simple? "My mother was four feet, eight inches, and her cousins were all under five foot," Lydia explains. Not only would their bodies have required less food, but shorter girls wouldn't have lost weight as quickly as taller women. Also, during selections, shorter girls would have been under the eyeline of guards and less likely to catch the attention of the SS selecting prisoners for the gas. The smaller the girl, the more unthreatening she would have appeared, as well.

Of course, small size could not have been the only reason for survival—there were diseases, violence, accidents, frostbite, and any number of other hazards to overcome. However, size may indeed have played an important factor. All of the children I have spoken to concur—their mothers were very short people. Rena used to joke that she was the tall one in her family; she was five foot two.

Orna has a different perspective. "The bonds between those women were unbreakable. They all saved each other." This was sisterhood in its darkest hour and at its finest. Fay Shapiro and Jeffrey Lautman concur. "I called Bertha Berkowitz and my mother [Magda Friedman] 'soul sisters'" Fay writes in an email. "They made a pact with each other that if they survived, they would be there for each other for every happy occasion— and they were. We would *schlep* to Cleveland as young children on a Greyhound bus, or they would drive down to Baltimore. [From the moment our mothers were together again,] they would almost be connected at the elbow!"

Across the world in Australia, Orna's experience was quite similar. "Mum was lucky to stay in contact with quite a few women she spent time in Auschwitz with. Seven of them lived close by in Melbourne. They met regularly, and although I was not privy to the exact content of their conversations (spoken in languages I did not understand), I remember they would often end up talking about their time in Auschwitz, and whilst there would often be tears shed, what to this day strikes me the most is how often they laughed and giggled about how they outsmarted the SS and survived. Even as a child, I was fascinated to see them laughing despite the hell they survived."

It may be that laughter about the camps was unique to the women who worked in Canada—Rena never spoke about sharing funny stories with her friends, nor does Edith. Canada was that much different, and because the girls who worked there were so accomplished at outwitting the SS and stealing necessities for other prisoners right from under SS noses, their acts of rebellion became cherished memories. How many people can boast of having stuffed a bed jacket into one's shoe, as Margie Becker did?

THE REMAINS OF CANADA burned to the ground long ago. Only rows of cement foundations remain in the field where the sorting depot once stood and where so many female survivors worked and struggled to endure. Where the ruins of Crematorium V should be there is now flat earth. Nearby stands the sauna where Ida Eigerman sneaked in to take her shower.

Standing in the flat expanse of Canada, Tammy and Sharon—Ida's children—wonder which cement slab was where their mother slept, which one was where she worked. In the sauna, they remember the shower she risked her life to take. They are looking at a memorial wall of photographs when a group of Swedish high school students descend upon us, and the room suddenly is full of young voices and faces.

"Their mother was a survivor on the first transport to Auschwitz," I tell the teachers. "It was made up of 297 teenagers, the age of your students."

Immediately, the teenagers surround the second-generation sisters. Among the blond Swedes are African refugees, who receive hugs and share tears as the sisters relate their mother's experience of escaping oppression, being a refugee after the war, and emigrating to another country.

A few hours later, we join Orna Tuckman and Ida's granddaughter, Daniela, at Block 25, where in 1942, Bertha, Elena, and Margie carted bodies away. Where Ella saved Irena. Where Edith wept for Lea. Traditionally, the Kaddish—the Jewish prayer for the dead—requires ten men. We are a *minyan* of women. Taking each other's hands, we begin the prayer. It is a prayer for Lea Friedman, for Magda Amster, for Adela Gross, for Magduska and Nusi Hartmann—for all the young women of the first transport and all of the transports who perished here in Auschwitz.

One Final Word

DEAR READER,

Please, please, you have to understand, you don't have a winner in a war. Even the winners are losing kids and losing houses and losing economy and losing everything. That's not a win! A war is the *worst* thing that can happen to humanity! This I would like to give you: to understand *through your heart* and not through your ears, so you can understand what happened in those years.

Thousands of books could be written on the disaster that was called the Holocaust, but it will never be fully described. Ever. I was there. And I have lived with it for over seventy-eight years. I *lived* it. I saw how each one of us dealt with it in a different way. Who was strong enough to hope that maybe it would get better? Who kept fighting, not physically but mentally? And spiritually, how could we survive? To tell you the truth, I did not believe that I would survive. But I said to myself, I will do what I can.

And I am still alive.

—Edith Friedman Grosman (#1970)

The Grosman and Gross families (left to right): Ladislav Grosman, Debora Gross (Adela's sister), Edith Grosman (#1970), Anna Grosman (Debora's daughter), Zuzka (Ladislav's sister), and her husband, Dr. Bela Spiegel, Juraj Grosman (Debora's son), and George Grosman (Edith's son).
PHOTO COURTESY THE GROSMAN AND GROSS FAMILIES.

List of Photographs and Illustrations

p. 1 Map of Slovakia, 1942: Redrawn from original map found in Slovak National Archives, the archival fonds Ministerstvo vnútra, 1938–1945; p. 14 Lou Gross permission; p. 14 Lou Gross permission; p. 21 Benjamin Greenman permission; p. 40 Predsedníčka ŽNO, Prešov, and Juraj Levický, Humenné archives; p. 63 Giroa Amir permission; p. 74 Ivan Jarny permission; p. 117 The Auschwitz-Birkenau State Memorial and Museum; p. 198 Museum of Jewish Heritage, collection: 2000.A.368; p. 224 USC Shoah Foundation Visual Archive, Eugene Hartmann testimony, 1996; p. 238 Museum of Jewish Heritage, collection: 2000.A.390; p. 252 Museum of Jewish Heritage, collection: 2000.A.389; p. 260 USC Shoah Foundation Visual Archive, Eugene Hartmann testimony, 1996; p. 271 Yad Vashem, document collection: Record No. O.75, File No. 770, No. 33; p. 279 Yad Vashem, document collection: Record No. O.75, File No. 770, No. 70 ; p. 296 Yad Vashem, document collection: Record No. O.75, File No. 770, No. 55; p. 376 Edith Grosman and family permission.

Photo insert:

p. 1 Friedman family photos, courtesy of Edith Grosman.

p. 2 Hartmann family photos, courtesy of Schwartz and Young family. Magda Hans image taken from Ria Elias interview, 1997, USC Shoah Foundation—The Institute for Visual History and Education; sfi.usc.edu. Annou Moscovikova and Zuzana Sermerova photo, courtesy of Juraj Levicky.

Rozalia and Therezia Ziegler photo, courtesy of family.

p. 3   Lea Friedman and Anna Herskovic photo, courtesy of Edith Grosman.
Adela Gross photo, courtesy of Lou Gross.

Image taken from the interview of Irena Ferencik, 1996, provided by the USC Shoah Foundation—The Institute for Visual History and Education; sfi.usc.edu.

Magda Amster and classmates photo, courtesy of Benjamin Greenman and Peter Chudý.

p. 4   Helena Citron image taken from the interview of Tsiporah Tehori, 1997, provided by the USC Shoah Foundation—The Institute for Visual History and Education; sfi.usc.edu.

Irena Fein image taken from the interview of Irena Ferencik, 1996, provided by the USC Shoah Foundation—The Institute for Visual History and Education; sfi.usc.edu.

Ria Hans image taken from Ria Elias interview, 1997, USC Shoah Foundation—The Institute for Visual History and Education; sfi.usc.edu.

Beth Jacob School image taken from Margaret Rosenberg interview, 1996, USC Shoah Foundation—The Institute for Visual History and Education; sfi.usc.edu.

Class of 1939 photo, courtesy of Edith Grosman.

p. 5   Dranger photos, courtesy of Koren, Ischari and Vjada families.
Ida Eigerman photo, courtesy of Sharon Neuman Ehrlich.
Kornreich photos, courtesy of Gelissen and Brandel families.
Sara Bleich photo, courtesy of Andrea Glancszpigel.

p. 6   Magda Moskovic image taken from Magda Bittermannová interview, 1996, USC Shoah Foundation—The Institute for Visual History and Education; sfi.usc.edu.

Joan Rosner image taken from Joan Weintraub interview, 1996, USC Shoah Foundation—The Institute for Visual History and Education; sfi.usc.edu.

Matilda Friedman image taken from Matilda Hrabovecká interview, 1996, USC Shoah Foundation—The Institute for Visual History and Education; sfi.usc.edu.

Ruzena Gräber Knieža image taken from Ruzena Knieža interview, 1997, USC Shoah Foundation—The Institute for Visual History and Education; sfi.usc.edu.

Perel Kaufman image taken from Perel Fridman interview, 1997, USC Shoah Foundation—The Institute for Visual History and Education; sfi.usc.edu.

Klara Lustbader photo, courtesy of Peter Chudý.

p. 7 Magda Friedman photo, courtesy of Donna Steinhorn.

Girls on bicycles photo, courtesy of Rutman family.

Minka Friedman photo, courtesy of Bernard Weiss.

Marta Friedman Gregor photo, courtesy of Orna Tuckman.

Klara Herz image taken from Klara Baumöhlava interview, 1996, USC Shoah Foundation—The Institute for Visual History and Education; sfi.usc.edu.

Katarina Danzinger image taken from Katharina Princz interview, 1996, USC Shoah Foundation—The Institute for Visual History and Education; sfi.usc.edu.

Linda Reich Breder, photo, courtesy of Dasha Grafil.

p. 8 Berkowitz family photo, courtesy of Jeffrey Lautman.

Peggy Friedman image taken from Margaret Kulik interview, 1997, USC Shoah Foundation—The Institute for Visual History and Education; sfi.usc.edu.

Regina Wald photo, courtesy of Vera Power.

Kleinmann family photo, courtesy of Peter Guttman

p. 9 Fanny and Eta Zimmerspitz photo, courtesy of Zimmerspitz family and Lydia Marek.

Edita Rose Goldman photo, courtesy of the Eva Zilberman.

Marta Mangel Marek photo, courtesy of Lydia Marek.

1997, USC Shoah Foundation—The Institute for Visual History and Education; sfi.usc.edu.

Piri Randová-Slomovicová image taken from Piri Skrhová interview, 1996, USC Shoah Foundation—The Institute for Visual History and Education; sfi.usc.edu.

p. 10 Regina Schwartz and family images taken from Regina Pretter interview, 1996, USC Shoah Foundation—The Institute for Visual History and Education; sfi.usc.edu.

Alice Ickovic image taken from Alice Burianová interview, 1996, USC Shoah Foundation—The Institute for Visual History and Education; sfi.usc.edu.

p. 11 Dr. Manci Schwalbova photos, courtesy of Zuzana Kovacik.

Orli Reichert photo, courtesy of the Auschwitz-Birkenau State Museum.

p. 12 Linda Reich working in Canada photo, courtesy of United States Holocaust Memorial Museum.

Group in Prague photo, courtesy of Ariela Neuman.

p. 13 Bertha Berkowitz in Bergen-Belsen photo, courtesy of United States Holocaust Memorial Museum.

Ida Eigerman photo, courtesy of American Jewish Joint Distribution Committee Archives.

p. 14 Elena Zuckermenn Grunwald and friends photo, courtesy of Ruth Wyse.

Arm with number and baby image taken from the interview of Tsiporah Tehori, 1997, provided by the USC Shoah Foundation—The Institute for Visual History and Education; sfi.usc.edu.

Margie Becker wedding image taken from Margaret Rosenberg interview, 1996, USC Shoah Foundation—The Institute for Visual History and Education; sfi.usc.edu.

Bertha and Elena as students photo, courtesy of Ruth Wyse.

Marta F. Gregor and friends photo, courtesy of Orna Tuckman.

p. 15 Ruzena Gräber Knieža with child image taken from Ruzena Knieža interview, 1997, USC Shoah Foundation—The Institute for Visual History and Education; sfi.usc.edu.

Wedding party and three old friends images taken from Margaret Kulik interview, 1997, USC Shoah Foundation—The Institute for Visual History and Education; sfi.usc.edu.

Perel Kaufman with baby image taken from Perel Fridman interview, 1997, USC Shoah Foundation—The Institute for Visual History and Education; sfi.usc.edu.

Photos taken in Sweden, courtesy of Rosette Rutman and estate of Regina Valo.

Dormitory in Sweden photo, courtesy of Rosette Rutman and estate of Regina Valo.

p. 16 Friedman and Grosman family photos, courtesy of Edith Grosman, Hannah Murray, and family.

Diligent efforts have been made to identify the individuals who are shown in the photos. Sadly, it has not been possible to identify all of them. If a reader recognizes any of the people who are shown, the author would welcome details, which can be sent through her website, www.renaspromise/education-form.php. She will share the information with the families and other interested parties.

TRANSCRIPTS: Heather Dune Macadam gratefully acknowledges the USC Shoah Foundation for allowing us to use transcripts of the following testimonies: Linda Breder, 1990 and 1996; Ruzena Knieža, 1997; Katharina Princz, 1996. For more information, visit sfi.usc.edu.

TRANSLATIONS: Heather Dune Macadam gratefully acknowledges the USC Shoah Foundation for allowing us to use translations of the following testimonies: Ruzena Knieža, 1997; Katharina Princz, 1996; Tsiporah Tehori, 1997. For more information, visit sfi.usc.edu.

Archives

ΛRa   Archi Mahn-und Gedenkstatte Ravensbrück
AU   Państwowe Muzeum Auschwitz-Birkenau
IWM   Imperial War Museum, London
SNA   Slovak National Archives
USHMM   United States Holocaust Memorial Museum
USC   University of Southern California Shoah Foundation Visual
            Archive (accessed at Columbia University, NY, and Royal
            Holloway University of London, UK)
WL   Wiener Library, London
YV   Yad Vashem—The World Holocaust Remembrance Center,
            Jerusalem

Source Notes

Author's Note

xix **Emil Knieža:** Author of *Šiestý prápor na stráž!* (*The Sixth Battalion on Guard!* 1964), *Kóšer rota* (The Kosher Battalion 1966), and *Mušketieri žltej hviezdy* (*Musketeers of the Yellow Star,* 1967). Knieža fought with the partisans in the war.

Chapter One

The description of Humenné was created by coalescing the writing of Ladislav Grosman, discussions with Edith Grosman, archival photographs of the town of Humenné, Lou Gross's memoir, interviews with Rena Kornreich, and my own visit to Humenné in 2016, where I was shown the town by Humenné's Jewish historian, Juraj Levický.

4   **"Shabbat Shalom!..."**: Edith Grosman, interview with the author, 20 July 2018.

6   **the town crier cried:** From Grosman, *The Bride,* p. 30.

7   **Young thugs:** Ivan Jarny, *Personal Papers.* Ivan's family name was Rauchwerger, which "is German and means a tanner of fur/skins. I did not like the association and it sounds weird when pronounced in English. I also had a bad experience caused by the name." After the war he was almost shot by the Russians, who thought with a name like Rauchwerger, he must be a German spy, not a Jewish partisan. He was rescued by some friends and changed his name to avoid future mishaps.

7   *Stuermer* **(Striker):** Ibid. and SNA.

7   **Jewish Codex:** from multiple testimonies: Amir, Friedman, and Jarny.

8   **one hundred crowns:** Jarny.

9   **"The only thing permitted…":** Ivan Jarny's mother, Eugenia Rauschwerger.

Chapter Two

Re-creating the marketplace in Humenné comes from a variety of sources, historical and personal interviews with Rena Kornreich, Edith Grosman and Ladislav Grosman's novels: *The Shop on Main Street* and *The Bride*. In order to introduce the girls who would end up on the first transport—who had grown up together—and so the reader can understand how intimate this community was I coalesced multiple sources to re-create a semi-typical day at the market in Humenné.

13   **Štefánikova Street:** Gross.

15   **Not all of the young women:** Kornreich, Interview with the Author; Bleich, family papers.

16   **The trade route:** Grosman and Šimkulič.

19   **"There must have been a shiksa…":** Rena Kornreich.

20   **all unmarried girls:** Edith Grosman.

20   **That was less than two weeks away:** On March 5 and 6, rabbis wrote to President Tiso to beg for mercy, before the announcement had even been made requiring the girls to register for "work." A letter of support from Bishop Pavol Jantausch of Trnava was also sent on the Jewish community's behalf. "Tiso refused to respond." "The response of the Interior Ministry was to interrogate some of those who signed the petitions to find out how they knew of the impending deportations." Bauer p. 65 and 267 and YV.-M-5/46(3) and M-5/136, p. 188.

20   **The largest and wealthiest town:** Amir (Giora Amir and Giora Shpira are the same person; like many people, Giora changed his name after the war) and Benjamin Greenman, who is the son of Magda Amster's older sister, Irena. Irena and Shany (Magda's elder brother) were both in Palestine in 1942 and escaped the Holocaust. Giora Shpira's sister's full name was Magdalena (Magda) Sara Shpira; in Israel she was known as Ilana Żur (Shpira). She died in 2018. In an email dated February 13, 2017, Benjamin wrote: "Magdalena (Magda) Miriam Zirl, was born in 8 Dec 1923 in Prešov to Adolf Abraham and Ethel Amster. Magda was a good-hearted, generous, and calm girl. She was a very good student.

On 20 of March, the Hlinka Guard started collecting young Jewish girls above age sixteen according to lists sent from Bratislava. Magda was hiding in the attic of the house, but when the gendarmes started hitting her father, who refused to tell them where she was, she came down and turned herself in to the Hlinka soldiers. The girls from Prešov and the surroundings were taken to the fire brigade courtyard [and sent to Poprad]. There they were kept until 25 of March, when they were taken to the train and sent to Auschwitz. Her father succeeded getting a permit to release her from the transport, but when he came to the train station, the train had already left. He followed the train by car until Žilina, but did not succeed to get there before the train.... In the camp, she worked in the Canada area sorting clothes of those sent to the crematorium. In August, a typhus plague spread in the camp. She got infected by typhus and died in 5 Dec. 1942."

23   **may have worshipped:** There was a neolog Jewish community that was socially more liberal living in Prešov at the same time. Giora Shpira's family was more active in the Neolog Synagogue on Konštantínova Street (it has not been preservered and today it is a store). However, for rites of passage, holidays, etc., Giora and many others came to the larger synagogue.

24   **Past the corset shop:** Forstater, while walking the streets of Prešov.

25   **"It's simply beautiful to live...":** Amir.

Chapter Three

This chapter utilizes multiple information sources gathered from the Slovak National Archives, historic photographs, visiting the historic buildings, walking the streets of Bratislava, conversations with Dr. Pavol Mešťan and Dr. Stanislava Siklova, Dr. Ivan Kamenec's essay "The Deportation of Jewish Citizens from Slovakia in 1942," Yehuda Bauer, the Uncovering the Shoah Conference in Žilina, Slovakia, 2015, and the personal experience of Ivan Jarny.

28   **Chief of the Jewish Department:** Dr. Pavol Mešťan, interview with the author; Kamenec; *The Wannsee Conference.*

28   **The Slovak government was paying:** "The RM 500 per deported Jew worked out at RM 45 million for the ninety thousand Slovak Jews, which was about 80 percent of all the taxes the Slovaks squeezed from them annually. From a cynically economic point of view, the Slovaks did not gain anything," Bauer p. 67.

29   **materials for Jewish resettlement:** There is a can of Zyklon B on display with the original signed order at Panastowe Memorial and Museum Auschwitz-Birkenau.

29   **In 1941, after the Slovaks:** Ibid., p. 65

29   **Koso insisted on the age:** Ibid., p. 66.

29   **Wannsee conference:** *Die Wannseekonferenz* (The Wannsee Conference), 1984.

30   **The Minister of the Interior:** Kamenec, p. 120 and Fiamová p. 66.

30   **While changing the law:** Ibid.

32   **the final economic betrayal:** Bauer, p. 66.

32   **"representatives of the German Government…":** Bauer, p. 66.

33   **"contract" laborers:** "Lists of Jews" YV.

33   **The T. & A. Baťa Shoe Company:** Dwork and Engle.

34   **Bratislava-Patrónka:** SNA.

35   **within weeks Konka all but disappeared:** The first transport did not go according to plan, and its failure led to major personnel changes at the beginning of 1942. Alexander Mach evidently fired Gejza Konak for his inability to carry out the deportations because in Bratislava, for instance, the second transport leaving from Patrónka Concentration Center included only 770 girls, not the quota of "1,000 per train" required by the Germans. Rajcan and Fiamová.

Chapter Four

38   **In Prešov, Adolf Amster:** Benjamin Greenman, email correspondence, and Giora Amir, *A Simple Life* and interview with the author.

39   **the Vatican sent another representative:** Kamenec, p. 120

39   **To counter the pressure:** Ibid. and Bauer, p. 68.

39   **"specialist and adviser in Jewish affairs":** Ibid.

39   **first "official" Jewish transport:** Helm, p.181.

39   **his "grandiose" plan:** Fiamová, p. 125

41   **When Germany annexed Slovakia:** Ibid.

41   **On the morning of March 20, 1942:** Ivan Sloboda, interview with author.

Chapter Five

42   **"very interested":** Goebbels's diary—23 Nov. 1939—cited in Kurlander, pp. 198–217.

42   "cosmobiologists" supported: Kritzinger quoted by Kurlander, p. 134.

42   "scientifically justified…": Erkmann quoted by Kurlander, p. 137.

43   "just to find out what Himmler…": Kurlander, p. 289.

43   The practice of numerology: McCord.

43   Forty-two-year-old…Langefeld: Helm, p. 181.

44   Himmler ordered her to select…999: Ibid., p. 181.

45   "wisdom tools": Kurlander.

45   In the Pythagorean system: McCord.

45   Himmler's "chart lacks emotion": McCord.

46   A dedicated devotee of astrology: Longerich, pp. 77–80; McCord.

47   Goebbels, too, was known: Kurlander, pp. 122–23.

47   "irrevocable, absolute destiny": Wilkinson.

47   the stars were best aligned: Ibid. The "Mars of the 25 March transport was close to the Jupiter of Himmler's earlier visit to Ravensbrück in 3 March, and the sun of *that* visit was in the exact location transiting Mars (the planet of war) in 10 Jul 1941 near the time."

47   the train left the station: Mešťan.

48   In astrological circles: Wilkinson.

Chapter Six

The scene inside the schoolhouse was reimagined by using Ladislav Grosman's novel, *The Bride*, which was no doubt informed by his wife's personal experience. There is little else on the experience; most personal testimonies do not discuss the situation inside. Information on girls' character traits was developed by memories shared with me by friends or family, and looking at the photographs at the USC Shoah Foundation's Visual Archive.

49   "God knows whether…": Grosman, *The Bride*, p. 102.

49   While still Chief: Kamenec, p. 123 and Bauer, p. 65.

50   Other girls thought: Testimony of Margaret Becker Rosenberg, USC Shoah.

50   The same was true of Adela: Conversation with Jurai Gross, the posthumous nephew of Adela (26 March 2017).

51   March drizzle: Grosman, *The Bride*.

52   "We are strong and young…": Ibid.

53   listed as "domestics": "Forged Certificate," YV.

59   began to sing the Slovak national anthem: Margaret Becker Rosenberg, USC Shoah.

59   **An empty two-story:** On March 25, 2017, the Prime Minister of Slovakia greeted Edith Grosman outside the former barracks and unveiled a plaque on the side of the building where she and the other 998 girls were kept just prior to being deported.

Chapter Seven

64   **"The worst disaster…":** Giora Amir, interview with the author. Most of the this chapter comes from conversations or communications with Giora and with Benjamin Greenman.

Chapter Eight

This chapter is coalesced from multiple USC Shoah Testimonies: Magda Moskovicová (Bittermanova), Linda Reich (Linda Breder), Kato (Katarina Danzinger), Peggy (Margaret Friedmanova), and Bertha Berkowitz (Lautman), as well as Giora Amir and Edith Grosman, interviews with the author.

68   **no longer even appears:** This was not unusual. There are a number of women who came from single villages, and many villages were destroyed if their residents were solely Jewish or have been swallowed up by larger villages over the years.

68   **Eta Galatin:** "Lists of Jews" YV.

68   **In the border town of Bardejov:** Amir. The list of girls who did not go to Auschwitz from Bardejov was published in the Bardejov newspaper on the 75th Anniversary in 2017. They were either hidden or escaped to Hungary. Unfortunately, we do not know about their fates. Of course, some were eventually caught or deported later, but some also escaped and survived the Holocaust. Hudek, interview with the author.

71   **Anna Judova and Ruzezna Kleinman:** In June 2019, as I was wrapping up page proofs for this book, the son of Ruzena Kleinman (#1033) contacted me and sent me a photo of his mother and her family. He also informed me that Anna Judova (#1093) had also survived the war. And who had connected us? None other than Mira Gold's daughter, who had been friends with Peggy—Margaret Friedman Kulik (you can see their photo together with Linda Reich Breder in the photo insert). The photo of Ruzena is posted on the 999 website.

72 **"And remember…":** Bertha Lautman (née Berkowitz), USC Shoah Visual Archive.

73 **"It was like a picnic!":** Margaret Rosenberg (née Becker), USC Shoah Visual Archive.

73 **They burst into song:** Ibid.

73 **150 grams of potatoes:** A copy of the food document, dated March 11, 1942, was presented to me by Dr. Pavol Mes'tan and Dr. Stanislava Šikulová, SNA, 14-D4-582/1- 1942.

76 **The Hartmann farm:** Eugene and Andrew Hartmann testimonies, USC Shoah, with additional information supplied by their daughters. Dula's name in Slovak is actually Gyula, but pronounced Diula; it was Americanized by surviving family, who spell it as Dula.

81 **Tábor Poprad:** "Lists of Jews" YV.

81 **150 grams of potatoes:** Číslo 14-D4-582/1 dated 11 March 1942, the food document was provided by Prof. Pavol Mešťan from the Bratislava Museum of Jewish Culture in Slovakia. It was translated for me by Ivan Sloboda in Sir Martin Gilbert's study in London.

Chapter Nine

86 **The telegram from Konka's office:** SNA.

87 **as defined under §255:** WL.

87 **The date on the telegram:** SNA.

89 **In fact, there was only one:** *"Pod poradovym cislom 1,000 bola deportovana jedina lekarka Izak Kaufmann nar."* Translated: "Under the order of 1,000, the only medical doctor Izak Kaufmann was deported." "Forged Certificate," YV.

90 **"You Jewish whores, you!"** Linda Breder (Reich), USC Shoah.

91 **"We were trying to be ladylike…":** Edith.

92 **Despite being relieved of duty:** Women's International Zionist Organization (WIZO), Yehuda Lahav became a world-renowned journalist and the author of *A Scarred Life*.

Chapter Ten

Benjamin Greenman and Giora Amir tell the story of how Adolf Amster raced the train; the Hartmann children remember their fathers telling a similar story about their grandfathers—this scene is re-created through those memories and my own experience driving the old road between Proprad and Žilina.

93   **"They had come—almost as children…"**: Schwalbova, p. 205.

97   **Without the German and Polish railways:** Gigliotti.

99   **60 million *reichsmark*:** Ibid.

102   **Into this chaos, Dr. Izak Kaufmann:** Hudak, Breder, and Kaufmann, YV. WIZO. Multiple testimonies. On the Yad Vashem Martyrs and Heroes Remembrance testimony form filled out in 1977, it is reported that Dr. Kaufmann was killed in the gas chamber because he refused to participate in a selection of prisoners; this report is inaccurate and was made by a relative after the war. In fact, there were no immediate selections from the trains in March 1942. Selections began upon arrival in Auschwitz in June 1942. In March 1942, the gas chambers were still being built and tested; they were not fully functional.

102   **the SS taunted him:** From Linda's USC testimony, which is only first-person account I found about what happened to Dr. Kaufmann in Auschwitz.

103   **In the archives of Yad Vashem:** YV, forged certificate with the name Stefánia Gregusová.

103   **"A thousand women were deported…"**: Ibid.

103   **Jozef Sebesta:** email from Prof. Pavol Mešťan and Dr. Stanislava Šikulová, 19 July 2019. There are definitely survivors on Šebesta's list: Edith Rose (#1371), Elena Zuckermenn (#1735), Eta and Fanny Zimmerspitz (#1756 and #1755), but the list also contains the Zimmerspitz sisters who were executed in 1943 (Frieda, Malvina, and Rosalia).

Chapter Eleven

106   **"Bible thumpers":** Höss and Helm.

106   **Poof Mamas:** Margaret Friedman Kulik, USC Shoah.

107   **"all well dressed…"**: cited in Hanna Elling.

109   **In 1942, the IVB4:** Helm, p. 181.

109   **On the other side of the gate:** Edith Grosman, Linda Breder (Linda Reich), USC Shoah No. 22979 and 53071, and Sarah Helm, p. 180.

111   **"millions of fleas…"**: Linda Breder (Linda Reich).

111   **"ten plagues in one day":** Tsiporah Tehori (Helena Citron), USC Shoah (translation by Sara Isachari).

111   **One girl became:** Ibid.

111   **"We were afraid…"**: Edith Grosman.

Chapter Twelve

113   One of the guards: Laura Špániková (née Ritterova) cited in Cuprik.

113   "We still thought that it's fun": Ibid.

114   laughed lecherously: Zilberman, p. 13.

117   "Throw away your jewelry!": Gelissen.

119   Polish male prisoners: Ibid.

121   "Don't cry. My child...": Annie Binder had been arrested for working in the foreign ministry as a secretary under President Beneš when Nazis invaded Prague and was serving time as a political prisoner in Ravensbrück when she was transferred to Auschwitz to work as a *kapo*. She survived the war and remained in contact and close friends with Ruzena Gräber Knieža after the war.

121   Many of the German kapos: Schwalbova.

Chapter Thirteen

125   March 28, 1942: SNA.

125   "the second transport": came from the Patrónka, not far from Bratislava, in the western portion of Slovakia.

127   "If you have some scarves...": Malvina Kornhauser née Gold (Mira). USC

128   "drat-maimed world": Schwalbova, p. 204.

128   "This was not human": Edith.

130   Lia decided to go on a hunger strike: Ibid.

130   "personal protest of girls...": Ibid.

131   Jolana Grünwald's and Marta Korn's names: AU "Death Books," *Sterbebücher*. We analyzed the original list and created our database comparing the death records at both Yad Vashem and Auschwitz in 2014. It is possible that additional records have been discovered since then.

131   The destruction of the women's: Despite repeated attempts to find the women's camp Auschwitz death records through Ravensbrück Archives and Museum, there do not seem to be any comprehensive record of women's deaths, as per Danuta Czech's research.

132   2,977 prisoners died in March: 580 were Russian POWs. Czech, p. 151.

132   the total camp population: 1,305 were Russian POWs. Czech, p. 131.

132   "August 15, 1942...": Czech, p. 157.

Chapter Fourteen

133 **"one girl, Ruzena Gross…":** Margaret Rosenberg (Becker), USC. Ruzena Gross was twenty-six years old and from Humenné. She died on October 18, 1942. All "Death Books" *Sterbebücher*, kept by the political department in camp, were only "partially preserved." This forty-six-volume record consists of sixty-nine thousand "prisoners who were registered in the camp and who died between July 29, 1941 and December 31, 1943." Those prisoners' names can be found on the Auschwitz prisoner digital data base on the museum website. In 2014, we typed in every girl's name from the March 25, 1942 Poprad list found at Yad Vashem into the Auschwitz and Yad Vashem databases.

134 **the daughter of one of Humenné's rabbis:** Margaret Rosenberg (Becker), USC.

136 **"I love the Lord…":** Psalm 116: 1–2.

137 **On Easter Sunday:** Czech, p. 153.

Chapter Fifteen

139 **Stefánia Gregusová:** "Forged Document," YV.

139 **Bertel Teege was told:** Helm, p. 185.

140 **There is scientific evidence:** fetal maternal microchimerism was discovered in the 2000s. Multiple sources inform this section: Martone, *Scientific America*; Zimmer, *New York Times*; and Yong, *National Geographic*.

140 **Take the bamboo plant:** Zimmer, *National Geographic*; and Biswas, *Frontiers in Plant Science*.

141 **"it was snowing":** Linda Breder (Reich), USC.

141 **It took fifty girls:** Tsiporah Tehori (Helena Citron), USC Shoah Testimony No. #33749.

142 **"If you were too careful…":** Magda Blau (Hellinger) p. 20.

145 **"We will have a vacation…":** Irena Ferenick (Fein), USC.

Chapter Sixteen

147 **There was a price to pay:** Pavol Mešťan, interviews with the author.

147 **The first transport had not:** Jarny; also: When asked at his trial why he had sacked Konka, Alexander Mach replied "for health reasons." However, Dieter Wisliceny, Eichmann's lieutenant, whose job was ad-

viser on the Jewish question in Slovakia, testified in 1946 that "as far as I know, Konka was unexpectedly removed. He was allegedly implicated in some corruption affairs, and investigations were still pending." Rajcan.

149 *výnimka*: based on the actual *výnimka* for the Stein family in Žilina, dated "25.VII.1942" and signed by Anton Vasek, Chief of the Jewish Department 14, "King of the Jews," provided by a grandson of Stein of family survivors, Peter Svitak.

149 about four hundred: Šimkulič, p. 117.

150 He asked Mr. Baldovsky: It is not confirmed, but it seems likely that the Gross family would have also asked Mr. Baldovsky to rescue Adela, as well. The families knew each other well and were very close. Edith Grosman, interview with the author, 8 Jan. 2018.

153 Edith and Lea must: Edith Grosman, interview with the author, 8 Jan. 2018.

155 "I stole everything": Edith Valo (Friedman), USC Shoah Testimony No. 17457.

157 The last in the row: Prisoners confirm that the dead women were counted. That data does not seem to have survived the war.

158 With the job of selecting women: Mauer testimony and Helm, p. 189.

158 being sent to the "sanatorium": Mauer testimony.

158 By the end of April: Czech, p. 161; Posmysz, Zofia, was #7566, a gentile from Oswiecim who was arrested for handing out pamphlets against the Nazis. She was interned in Auschwitz in June 1942. Her memoir is a powerful testament of gentile prisoners.

160 "For the Families Who…": Linda Breder (Reich), USC Shoah.

160 By now, some of the girls: Irena Ferenick (Fein), USC Shoah.

Chapter Seventeen

162 "began to curse the fact…": Bauer, cited in IFZ, MA 650/1, T75–517 German Imteligence Report, April 1942

163 Suzie Hegy: Born in 1924, and eighteen years old when she was deported on May 28, 1942 to Lublin. Source: YV, document archives No. 12013.

163 By April 29, 1942: Czech, pp. 148–60 (Please note, Czech cites 999 young women on the first "official" Jewish transport, I have amended that with the correct number of 997.)

163   **the knots in the wood:** Mauer.

164   **after fifteen minutes:** Helm, p. 189. Czech, "By the end of April
       1942, there were 14,624 men in Auschwitz: 3,479 Slovak Jews; 1,112
       French Jews; 287 Czech Jews and 186 Russian POWs—the other
       9,560 were gentile and political prisoners, for the most part," p. 161.

164   **Between May 5 and 12:** Gilbert, pp. 45–46.

164   **"looking pale and disturbed":** Helm, p. 189.

164   **Meanwhile, in Slovakia:** Jarny.

165   **"It is the basic principle…":** Vrba, p. 52

165   **The atmosphere in the…gallery:** WL and Kamenec, pp. 127–28.

165   **"Slovak Jews worked happily…":** Ibid.

165   **Over the next few months:** Dr. Pavol Mešťan, interview with the au-
       thor, and Kamenec.

168   **"There was something funny…":** All the women on that transport
       with Vrba were separated from the men at the concentration camp of
       Majdanek (Lublin, Poland) and sent on to Bełżec, where they were
       gassed with the fumes of exhaust pipes and their bodies burned in
       open trenches. "Crematoriums were still in the blueprint stage." Vrba,
       pp. 52–55.

168   **"I saw heart-wrenching misery…":** Jarny, "Tiso was hanged in
       1946, in spite of protests from the Vatican and from the U.S."

Chapter Eighteen

171   **"The Wine of Solitude":** Irène Némirovsky was a French author
       whose manuscript *Suite française* was posthumously discovered by her
       daughter, Denise Epstein, and published 64 years after her mother
       was deported to Auschwitz. On July 11, 1942, she wrote in her diary:
       "The pine trees all around me. I am sitting on my blue cardigan in the
       middle of an ocean of leaves, wet and rotting from last night's storm,
       as if I were on a raft, my legs tucked under me!…My friends the bum-
       blebees, delightful insects, seem pleased with themselves and their buz-
       zing is profound and grave…In a moment or so I will try to find the
       hidden lake." She was arrested moments later. Irène Némirovsky died
       in Birkenau on August 17, 1942.

171   **on the Fourth of July:** The Nazis loved to use important dates for their
       actions, as I have noted Jewish holidays were especially dangerous. I
       noted this because I find it ironic that the anniversary of America's in-
       dependence coincided with the first selection on the unloading platform.

Czech also notes here that "by August 15, 1942, only 69 of the men are still alive; within six weeks, more than two thirds of the men die."

171 **"Old people, children..."**: Schwalbova, p. 207, and Czech, "the women were tattooed 8389–8496; the men 44727–44990," p. 192.

172 **Gertrude Franke and Helene Ott**: Elling, p. 137 and Mauer testimony.

172 **"Once the Jewish transports..."**: Höss.

Chapter Nineteen

This chapter derives its information from survivor testimonies: Edith, Helena, the *kapos* Luise Mauer and Bertel Teege, and the excellent work of Sara Helm in her book *Ravensbrück*.

175 **"crazy conditions"**: Edith.

177 **"Your brother is no longer alive!"**: Aron Citron arrived in Auschwitz on June 30, 1942, with 400 other men who had been transferred from Lublin. Czech notes at the bottom of page 189 in Auschwitz Chronicle that by "August 15, 1942, i.e., 61/2 weeks later, only 208 of them are still alive. About half of the deportees, 192, die." Helena uses the name Moshe in her USC Shoah testimony, but in the Auschwitz death records it was her brother Aron Citron (#43934) who is listed as having died on July 25, 1942. He was eighteen years old.

178 **day that Himmler visited**: compiled from Longerich, Helm, and Czech, p. 198.

178 **at roll call the next morning**: Multiple witness testimony has been compiled from: Joan Weintrab (Rosner), Linda Breder (Reich), Edith Grosman, and the kapos Bertel Teege and Luise Mauer.

179 **Pointing to her five assistants**: Mauer testimony. Mauer was not released until the end of 1943, Czech, p. 199.

181 **twenty Jehovah's Witnesses**: Czech p. 199.

181 **Höss repeatedly complained**: Helm, p. 238.

181 **"vent their evil on prisoners"**: Ibid.

182 **At the end of the day**: cited in Czech, APMO/ Höss Trial, vol. 6, p. 85 and pp. 237–38; Höss diary, p. 199.

Chapter Twenty

184 **the equivalent of 319 football fields**: The size of Birkenau is 171 hectares (422 acres), Auschwitz Museum.

185 **green wooden barracks:** AU, Block 22B memories, testimony of Anna Tytoniak (#6866).

185 **During the transfer:** Czech, p. 211.

188 **"It was just horrible...":** Linda Breder (Reich), USC Shoah.

188 **New arrivals suffering:** Edith Grosman, interviews with the author; and Bertha Lautman (née Berkowitz), USC.

188 **"Many committed suicide...":** Edith Grosman, ibid.

Chapter Twenty-one

189 **The town of Holíč:** Holíč.

190 **"People ask if what is happening...":** Ward.

190 **"They don't look embarrassed to death":** Fialu, 7 November 1942.

190 **One gentile pensioner:** SNA.

191 **On the same day that President Tiso:** Czech, pp. 217–18.

191 **at least twenty-two women:** YV, Czechoslovakian Documents Archive No. 12013.

191 **As eighteen-year-old Frida Benovicova:** Rena Kornreich reported the first selection in her memoir *Rena's Proimse*. In 2017, Frida and Helena's posthumous niece, Eva Langer, made a connection between the story in Rena's memoir and the story that had been smuggled out of camp by someone who knew the girls and also witnessed their selection in the first prisoner selection in the women's camp.

Chapter Twenty-two

193 **"rats like large cats":** AU, Block 22B memories, testimony of Anna Tytoniak (#6866).

196 **Juana Bormann:** Gelissen.

199 **eight-year-old nephew, Milan:** Museum of Jewish Heritage, collection: 2000.A.368

199 **"Some even wore stockings":** Edith.

200 **"the most important thing...":** Höss.

200 **"flinched from nothing":** Ibid.

200 **Being granted a functionary position:** Functionaries who survived often kept their experiences in the camps and their positions a secret so they would not be ostracized after the war. Survivors who emigrated to Israel and had worked as functionaries were especially careful.

201   "hard and indifferent armor": Schwalbova, p. 206.

Chapter Twenty-three

203   **On September 2:** Czech, "Of the 1,000 men, women, and children on the transport from Drancy, France, that arrived on Sept 2, 1942, 12 men and 27 women are registered into camp." p. 232.

204   **"not quite alive":** Isabella Leitner, quoted in Shik, p. 5.

204   **"the spirit God breathed…":** Gelissen, p. 139.

204   **"They were all driven…":** Kremer, Krakow Auschwitz Trial, cited in Czech, p. 233.

205   **a perfect storm for an epidemic:** Raoult Didier, Max Maurin, M.D., Ph.D.

205   **"In Auschwitz, whole streets":** Kremer diaries quoted in Czech, pp. 230–37.

205   **"The girls' camp suffered the most…":** This section compiles information from Rudolf Vrba, p. 361, Manci Schwalbova, p. 208, and Joan Weintrab (Rosner), USC Shoah.

206   **The ill and dying:** Manci Schwalbova p. 204.

208   **by October, Jews would not be allowed:** Ibid.

210   **By the end of Sukkot:** Ibid., with Czech: Block 25 was the Jewish hospital ward.

Chapter Twenty-four

216   **Selections were "all the time":** Edith.

Chapter Twenty-five

216   **Epigraph:** Auschwitz-Birkenau Memorial Museum, Block 22b—Memories.

216   **"mother camp":** Term given by Rudolf Vrba in his memoir.

217   **every day, new girls:** Vrba.

219   **And here the story divides:** As with many of the testimonies, dates are often confused. There was no calendar for prisoners to refer to, and as the years pass, the personal narratives sometimes have mistakes in their chronology—that does not make the testimony inaccurate, it usually means the incident happened at a different time. It still happened.

221   **He had one leg shorter:** Eta Zimmerspitz Neuman (#1756), interview with the author.

221   **"According to their mood…":** Edith Grosman, interviews with the author.

Chapter Twenty-six

224   **Within eight weeks:** Dr. Pavol Mešťan, interview with the author.

225   **"deeply interfere[d] with state finances":** Kamenec and Bauer.

Chapter Twenty-seven

232   **On December 1, 1942:** Czech. On December 1, 1942 "the occupancy level of the women's camp in Auschwitz-Birkenau is 8,232," but on that same day women are being tattooed 26,273–26,286—where had they all gone? Over six thousand women and girls had been selected over the three days of selections in October, but there were no solid population tallies at month's end, and selections continued to take their toll on the population, as did the epidemics of typhus, meningitis, and murder.

232   **"deep Kabbalistic significance":** Rabbi David Adler, email correspondence.

233   **"humanity through the act of rest":** The irony is that the camps were designed to work prisoners to death under the banner of "Work Makes One Free," a lie for Jewish prisoners. Rabbi David Wirtschafter.

234   **"There is no God":** quoted in Rudolf Vrba, pp. 171–72.

234   **"world without fighting…":** Ibid.

235   **"Chickens meant more than people":** Marta Marek née Mangel, family archives.

236   **The next morning:** Linda Breder (Reich), USC.

Chapter Twenty-eight

239   **A holiday card:** The Jewish History Museum Document Archive Collections: 2000.A.371.

240   **Herman Hertzka:** YV, Image nos. 17–18.

241   **"January 1, 1943…":** Museum of Jewish Heritage, Collection No. 2000.A.382.

241 **"You certainly received our card..."**: Museum of Jewish Heritage, NY, 2000.A.382

243 **Transmetatarsal amputation**: Adam, Frankel. Irena Fein never mentions the amputation in her personal testimony. After liberation, she and Edith were on the soccer field in Humenné. They were barefoot, and Edith asked her what happened to her toes. This was the story Irena told.

Chapter Twenty-nine

A collection of testimonies from Edie F. Valo (#1949), her sister Ella F. Rutman (#1950), Joan Rosner (#1188), Sara Bleich, Ria Hans, Manci Schwalbova, and Edith (#1970).

253 **"We are writing you every 10 days..."**: Museum of Jewish Heritage, collection: 2000.A.377.

253 **"My dears, / First I would like..."**: YV, record O.75, file 770. Image: 67; text: 4.

254 **the latest transport from Greece**: Czech, p. 356.

254 **"We congratulate your birthday!"**: Edith is one of the survivors who remembers Helena being in the white kerchiefs in 1942, which means Helena's first day was not on Franz Wunsch's birthday on March 21, 1943. She was already working there and in love with him by then. Since it is likely that she sang to him on more than one occasion, I have written this scene based on her testimony that she sang to him on his birthday. The kapos and SS enjoyed forcing prisoners to perform for them, so it seems likely that she sang for him more than once. It should be noted that prisoners often felt ashamed and humiliated at being forced to perform in a place where so many people were dying and suffering. Rena Gelissen née Kornreich's experience of performing informs this perspective.

255 **"in the end I honestly loved him"**: From the documentary *Auschwitz: The Nazis and "The Final Solution"* produced by the BBC; additional information in this section was compiled from USC Shoah transcripts and personal testimonies.

255 **The occupancy level of the women's camp**: Czech, p. 361

256 **With the typhus epidemic**: Ibid., and Höss.

257 **ingredients they needed to make raisin wine**: Following a kosher recipe online, I observed the fermentation process for two weeks. Un-

fortunately, I ended up making vinegar. I tried another recipe, but got more vinegar.

257 **Dr. Clauberg had a different idea:** Margaret Kulik (née Friedman) USC Shoah Testimony.

258 **Block 10:** Czech, p. 366.

258 **This second year's Seder:** At the same time, the last Seder in Warsaw was being held in a bunker in the ghetto. It was not just the eve of Passover; it was the eve of the liquidation of Warsaw's Jewish ghetto.

Chapter Thirty

261 **crossing its path:** Because two cards covered similar news, excerpts from both have been combined for the reader. YV, record O.75, file 770. Nos. 21 and 33, letters to Simon Hertzka (Lenka's brother).

261 **"Magduska's mother...is very sick":** YV, record O.75, file 770. Photo, No. 70; text, No. 48.

262 **"Dreschler was ugly":** Edith Grosman.

265 **Zimmerspitz sisters:** Compiled from their cousins Eta Neuman, née Zimmerspitz, and her daughter, Ariela Neuman; and the USC Shoah testimonies of Ruzena Gräber Knieža and Frances Kousel-Tack.

Chapter Thirty-one

This chapter is a compilation of multiple testimonies from the USC Shoah Foundation, personal interviews with survivors, and translations of the Hertzka postcards, donated by Eugene Hartmann to the Museum of Jewish Heritage in New York.

273 **Dr. Josef Mengele:** This survivor wished to remain anonymous in regards to medical experimentation.

275 **Irena Fein (#1564) was now working:** Irena Ferenick (Fein), USC.

277 **New Blocks:** Did not survive the bombings and no longer stand at the museum complex.

277 **telegram on October 15:** Hertzka, YV. Lenka's father has died, but the family is keeping it a secret from her.

277 **a typed letter from Ernest Glattstein:** Hertzka, YV, postcard No. 48: Seri Wachs was thirty years old when she was deported from Prešov on the first transport; Margit Wahrmann was twenty-six; and Ella Rut-

man (née Friedman, #1950), Edie Valo (née Friedman, #1949). Ernest was probably a relative of Ida Eigerman's friend Gizzy Glattstein.

278   **Magduska and niece Nusi:** Eugene Hartmann, USC Shoah Testimony.

Chapter Thirty-two

279   **December 1, 1943:** YV.

280   **After fifteen months in the *leichenkommando*:** Bertha does say it was "one of the female Slovak doctors" for the purpose of narrative structure; I suggest it was Manci because she was known for helping the young Slovak women especially.

283   **"only barbed wire…":** Linda Breder (Reich), USC Shoah.

Chapter Thirty-three

285   **The numbers being given to men:** Czech, p. 604.

285   **On April 7:** Czech, p. 607.

286   **"had dwindled to 5 percent…":** Rudolf Vrba and Frank Wexler, p. 361. This is an exact quote from the Auschwitz Escapee's Report in 1944—later information reveals a different percentage, but as we have seen, women's records are inaccurate, at best. It should also be noted that this percentage refers to all of the young women on the early transports, not just the first transport—that was over six thousand young women.

286   **"achieve the salvation…":** quoted in Gilbert, p. 279.

286   **SS-Hauptscharführer:** USHMM.

289   **Eichmann's plan to have four transports:** Czech, p. 563.

290   **Tattooed A-5796:** Czech, p. 632.

290   **finger hooked around:** Schwalbova.

Chapter Thirty-four

The scene of Ruzinka's removal from the gas chamber and subsequent processing has been written using USC Shoah testimonies from Helena Citron, Margaret Odze, conversations with Edith Grosman, and the documentary filmmaker Maya Sarfaty of *The Most Beautiful Woman*. Originally, it was thought that Ruzinka and her children arrived in Auschwitz in October 1944, on one of the Slovak transports; however, source material from the Claims Conference found at the USHMM, confirms that Ruzinka (Rosa Citron)

Grauberova was deported in May 1944 on a Hungarian transport. Attempts were made to connect with Helena's and Rosa's children to confirm this.

291 **This seemed odd:** USHMM, Ornsteinova Documentation.

293 **"That's my prisoner!":** Helena does not recall what happened next. "I did not even realize what was happening to me because I wanted to be with my sister. I was somewhere else," she says in her USC Shoah Testimony. Combined narratives given by Helena Citron recorded with the USC Shoah Foundation, the BBC, and *The Most Beautiful Woman*, directed by Maya Safarty, release date: 14 Nov. 2018.

295 **In the sauna:** In 1944, a new series of numbering using the letter A was created for Hungarian Jewish Female Prisoners; however, on October 19, 1942, 113 female Jews from Sereď in Slovakia were numbered A-25528—A-25640. Czech, 735. We do not have Ruzinka's number and so cannot confirm the date of her arrival.

Chapter Thirty-five

298 **July 13, 1944:** YV, file .75, record 770 postcards 55—paraphrased translation for clarity.

300 **As the Russian front moved:** This section uses multiple sources, including conversations with Dr. Pavol Mešťan and Dr. Stanislava Šikulová; books or articles by Baeur, Gross, and Amir, the USC Shoah testimonies of Eugene and Andrew Hartmann, conversations and emails with Edith Grosman, and Ivan Jarny's personal papers and emails.

302 **His mother, Eugenie:** Ivan's mother and sister ended up in Ravensbrück in January 1945. "Mum was badly beaten and left in a barrack to recuperate. My sister tried to get some bandages or first aid kit. Without success. When she returned to the block our mum was gone, and so were quite a number of others. Erika was told that Dr. Fritz Klein had come in the night and injected phenol directly into the hearts of his victims. When phenol ran out, he used petrol." It was February 25, 1945. While Ivan was deep in the mountains fighting alongside the partisans, his family was hiding in a cave, and "found life incredibly hard, unable to light a fire, unable to wash, having to trudge through deep snow, just to find a place to use as toilet, sleeping fully dressed in their winter coats," Ivan says. "Outside it was −15 Cel-

sius or 5 degrees Fahrenheit." He found a forrester who was willing to provide his family shelter and food for three or four days and settled them into the cottage before returning to his duties as a liaison between the Russians and French. "After my shift, I took a knapsack full with my dirty clothing, which mom promised to wash for me." The forrester's back gate was open and two Germans barked at Ivan, "Show us your papers!" Ivan fled. His mother and sister were caught and promptly deported

302 **Over the next two months...12,600 Jews:** USHMM.

303 **by Rosh Hashanah, 1944:** Julia Klein (née Birnbaum), USC Shoah. The term davening come from King David and Psalms 35:10, "All of my limbs shall proclaim: Who is like You...?" "When we praise G-d, we do so with all of our being: the mind, heart, and mouth express the prayer through speech, and the rest of the body does so by moving. Every fiber of our self is involved in connecting to our Creator," writes Rabbi Rafe Konikov.

Chapter Thirty-six

This chapter is a compilation of multiple testimonies from the USC Shoah Foundation and translations of Hertzka postcards donated to Yad Vashem.

305 **It was September 30, 1944:** USC Shoah testimonies include: Margaret Rosenberg (Becker), Linda Breder (Reich), Irena Ferenick (Fein).

Chapter Thirty-seven

312 **"They were telling us...":** Linda Breder (Linda Reich), USC Shoah, and Edith Grosman.

312 **"killing with Zyklon B...":** Czech, 743.

312 **"The killing went on...":** Linda Breder (Linda Reich), USC Shoah.

312 **"stealing clothing, and jewelry...":** Ibid.

313 **the only buildings destroyed:** Rena Kornreich Gelissen, interviews with the author.

316 **one hundred Polish women:** Czech, p. 773.

317 **"All traitors will be destroyed...":** Czech, p. 775, and Gelissen, p. 223.

317 **Roza Robota:** It should be noted that even here Roza and the other three female prisoners who were executed with her do not have their prisoner numbers written into the historic record.

317 **Demolition teams now began:** Ibid.

317 **"prisoners' documents, death certificates...":** Ibid., p. 784.

318 **"This type of evacuation...":** Ibid., p. 783.

Chapter Thirty-eight

Various sources in this chapter come from USC Shoah testimonies and the factual day-to-day and sometimes hourly reports collected from Danuta Czech's research, as well as maps Rena Kornreich Gelissen gave me in 1993, from Andrzej Strezlecka's book *Marz Smeirchi*.

319 **"If the oceans were ink...":** "from a letter from a little Polish boy from a ghetto who said—just what I recall. He writes a letter to his parents because he was caught somewhere else. 'I am here in this miserable place. I have no shoes. I'm hungry. My clothes—my clothes are torn. I am hungry. The only thing I want to be with you, but I can't write so much. If the oceans were ink and the skies paper, I couldn't describe the horror of what I'm going through.' " JHM.

319 **"various camp documents":** Czech, p.784.

322 **SS Major Franz Xaver Kraus:** Czech, pp. 800–1.

328 **"over 600 corpses":** Czech, p. 805.

329 **Ruzena Borocowice:** Number unknown, she was nineteen years old when she was deported with Irena Fein in 1942; she was a friend of Lea Friedman's, as well. YV, Document Archive ID No. 12013.

329 **Loaded into open coal cars:** Ibid. See list on p. 784.

329 **One of those groups:** Czech, p. 801.

331 **It now had to house five thousand:** Czech, p. 801.

332 **Himmler had started negotiations:** Longerich, p. 724.

333 **The liberating armies designed:** Habbo Knoch.

333 **"Over an acre of ground...":** IWM.

335 **"We thought this was it":** Joan Rosner and Edith Grosman.

Chapter Thirty-nine

This narrative section has been pulled together from all of the survivors' testimonies, their families, and family photographs.

346　**A ghost returning:** Breder, *Recollection of Holocaust Part I*, p. 7.

Homecomings

347　**"shaking the dust":** Though the phrase comes from Matthew 10:14, it was an Old Testament practice for observant Jews to shake the dust from their feet after leaving cities or regions where non-Jews lived.

351　**Of the two thousand Jewish families:** Šimkulič and Edith.

351　**beautiful, hand-embroidered tallis:** Lou Gross inherited his grandfather's prayer shawl and still wears it to this day.

Afterwards

358　**Helena came to testify:** In her USC Shoah Testimony, Margaret Odze says she heard from a friend who was also called to testify at the Wunsch and Graff trial that: "They brought her to testify. He was just sitting there with his wife and son. She was a beautiful girl, and when he saw her, he started to cry."

367　**"You know that all my family…":** *"Vous savez que toute ma famille a été déportée, et les survivants étaient très peu nombreux. Après leur disparition, je me retrouve totalement isolé, immigrant sur Terre. Même le site de Yad Vashem ne m'apporte pas grand-chose. J'ai essayé de retrouver les noms à partir de diverses notes que j'avais prises. C'est vraiment très court. A voir en pièces jointes. Toutefois, je n'ai pas eu le courage d'effectuer dans ma jeunesse, et que je n'ai plus l'énergie de reprendre à 68 ans. Amitiés."* Translated by Simon Worrall.

Bibliography

Heather Dune Macadam gratefully acknowledges the USC Shoah Foundation and the Institute for Visual History and Education for allowing us to use the following testimonies: Alice Burianova, 1996; Bertha Lautman, 1996; Edita Valo, 1996; Edith Goldman, 1995; Ella Rutman, 1996; Andrew Hartmann, 1995; Eugene Hartmann, 1996; Ida Newman, 1996; Irena Ferencik, 1996; Joan Weintraub, 1996; Katharina Princz, 1996; Klara Baumöhlová, 1996; Linda Breder, 1990 and 1996; Magda Bittermannova, 1996; Margaret Kulik, 1997; Margaret Rosenberg, 1996; Matilda Hrabovecka, 1996; Perel Fridman, 1997; Piri Skrhova, 1996; Regina Pretter, 1996; Regina Tannenbaum, 1996; Ria Elias, 1997; Ruzena Knieža, 1997; Tsiporah Tehori, 1997; Frances Kousal Mangel, 1996; Samuel Zimmersptiz, 1997; Margaret Odze, 1995; Julia Klein, 1998. For more information, visit sfi.usc.edu.

Adler, David. "Two Kinds of Light: The Beauty of Shabbat Chanukah." Chabad.org. Chabad-Lubavitch Media Center. Accessed 12 October 2018. chabad.org/holidays/chanukah/article_cdo/aid/2406289/jewish/Two-Kinds-of-Light-The-Beauty-of-Shabbat-Chanukah.htm.

Amir, Giora. *A Simple Life*. Amazon Media. 8 September 2016.

———. Personal interview. Israel, 30 March 2017.

Amsel, Melody. "The Jews of Stropkov, 1942–1945: Their Names, Their Fate." Excerpted from *Between Galicia and Hungary: The Jews of Stropkov*. Avotaynu, Inc. Bergenfield, NJ.: 1999–2018, JewishGen, Inc. jewishgen.org/yizkor/stropkov1/stropkov.html.

Auschwitz: The Nazis and "The Final Solution." Directed by Laurence Rees and Catherine Tatge. Reported by Linda Ellerbee, Horst-Gunter

Marx, Klaus Mikoleit. United Kingdom: BBC-2, 2005. Television. December 2005. Accessed 12 August 2018. bbc.co.uk/programmes/ pootsl60/episodes/guide. Note: Episode 2: Corruption.

Auschwitz-Birkenau: The Death Marches. "The Death Marches." 1998. Accessed 27 September 2018. www.jewishvirtuallibrary.org/the-death-marches.

Auschwitz Death Books [*Sterbebücher*]. "Prisoner Records." Memorial and Museum Auschwitz-Birkenau. First accessed 18 May 2014. auschwitz. org/en/museum/auschwitz-prisoners.

Bauer, Yehuda. *Jews for Sale: Nazi-Jewish Negotiations 1933–1945*. New Haven, CT: Yale University Press, 1996.

Belt, P., Graham, R. A., Martini, A., Schneider, B. *Actes et documentes du Saint Seige reltifs a la seconde guerre mondiale*. Vol. 8. Liberia Editrice Vaticana, 1974.

Biswas, Prasun, Sukanya Chakraborty, Smritikana Dutta, Amita Pal, and Malay Das. "Bamboo Flowering from the Perspective of Comparative Genomics and Transcriptomics." *Frontiers in Plant Science*. December 15, 2016. Accessed 18 May 2018. www.ncbi.nlm.nih.gov/ pmc/articles/PMC5156695.

Blau, Magda (née Hellinger). *From Childhood to Auschwitz-Birkenau*. Melbourne, Australia: 1990.

———. Interview 19441. Segments 39–59. *Visual History Archive*, USC Shoah Foundation, 1996. Accessed 12 February 2018.

Breder, Linda. From talk: *Recollection of Holocaust Part I*. 1995 and 2005.

———. Interview 53071. Tape 1–4. *Visual History Archive*, USC Shoah Foundation, 1990. Accessed 12 February 2018

———. Interview 22979. Tape 1–9. *Visual History Archive*, USC Shoah Foundation, 1996. Accessed 12 February 2018.

Breitman, Richard. "Plans for the Final Solution in Early 1941." *German Studies Review*, 17, no. 3 (1994): 483–93. doi:10.2307/1431895.

Cesarani, David. *Final Solution—The Fate of the Jews 1933–1949*. London: Macmillan, 2016.

Collingham, Lizzie. *The Taste of War: World War Two and the Battle for Food*. New York: Penguin, 2012.

Conway, John S. "The Churches, the Slovak State and the Jews 1939–1945." *The Slavonic and East European Review*, 52, no. 126 (1974): 85–112. jstor.org/stable/4206836.

Cuprik, Roman. "We Were Joking Before the Trip, Women From the First Transport to Auschwitz Recall." *Slovak Spectator*. Accessed 27 March

2017. spectator.sme.sk/c/20494128/we-were-joking-before-the-trip
-women-from-the-first-transport-to-auschwitz-recall.html

Czech, Danuta. *Auschwitz Chronicle:1939–1945*. New York: Henry Holt,
1989.

Dimbleby, Richard (writer). "Liberation of Belsen" In *Home Service*. 19
April 1945. BBC News Archive. 15 April 2005. Accessed 12 August
2018. news.bbc.co.uk/2/hi/in_depth/4445811.stm.

———. "Richard Dimbleby Describes Belsen." In *Home Service*, produced
by Ian Dallas, BBC News. BBC News Archive. 19 April 1945. Accessed 12 August 2018. www.bbc.co.uk/archive/holocaust/5115.shtml.

Drali, Rezak, Philippe Brouqui, and Didier Raoult. "Typhus in World War
I." Microbiology Society. May 29, 2014. Accessed 5 August 2018.
microbiologysociety.org/publication/past-issues/world-war-i/article/
typhus-in-world-war-i.html.

Dwork, Deborah; van Pelt, Robert Jan. *Holocaust: A History*. W.W. Norton,
2002.

Eisen, Yosef. *Miraculous Journey*. Chabad-Lubavitch Media Center: Phila-
delphia. 1993–2017.

Eizenstat, Stuart. "Imperfect Justice: Looted Assets, Slave Labor, and the
Unfinished Business of World War II." *PublicAffairs*, 26 May 2004.

Elias, Ria. Interview 25023. Transcribed Sections: 94, 100–25, 150, 199. *Visual History Archive*, USC Shoah Foundation, 1997. Accessed 23 August 2019.

Elling, Hanna. *Frauen in deutschen Widerstand, 1933–1945*. Frankfurt: Roder-
berg, 1981.

Engle Schafft, Gretchen. *From Racism to Genocide: Anthropology in the Third
Reich*. University of Illinois Press, 2004.

Ferencik, Irena. Interview 14682. Tape 1–4. *Visual History Archive*, USC
Shoah Foundation, 1996. Accessed 12 February 2018.

Fialu, Fritza. "Ako Ziju Zidia v Novom Domove Na Vychode?." *Gardista*
(Bratislava, Slovakia), November 7, 1942.

Fiamová, Martina. "The President, the Government of the Slovak Republic,
and the Deportations of Jews from Slovakia in 1942." Uncovering the
Shoah: Resistance of Jews and Efforts to Inform the World on Genocide. Žilina, Slovakia, 25–26 August 2015.

"Five postcards sent by Berta Berkovits from Birkenau to Emmanuel Moskovic in Hrabovec and Salamon Einhorn in Kapišová, and a postcard
sent to Berkovits in Kosice by Nathan Weisz in Bratislava, 1946."

O.75/1749: The Document Archive. Yad Vashem: The World Holocaust Remembrance Center. Jerusalem, Israel.

"Forged Certificate with the name Stefania Gregusova issued to Vliaka Ernejová, and a list of young Jewish women deported from Poprad to Auschwitz." Yad Vashem Archives. O.7/132.

Forstater, Tammy. Personal interviews regarding her mother, Ida Eigerman. Prešov, Slovakia, and Oświęcim, Poland, 20–27 March 2017.

Frankel, Adam, MBBS, Ph.D. *Toe Amputation Techniques*. 20 September 2018. Chief Editor: Erik D Schraga, Medline.

Gelissen, Rena Kornreich, and Heather Dune Macadam. *Rena's Promise: A Story of Sisters in Auschwitz*. Boston: Beacon, 1995 and 2015.

Gigliotti, Simone. *The Train Journey: Transit, Captivity and Witnessing the Holocaust*. Oxford: Berghahn, 2009.

Gilbert, Martin. *Auschwitz and the Allies: A Devastating Account of How the Allies Responded to the News of Hitler's Mass Murder*. Rosetta, 2015.

———. *Endlosun: Die Bertreibung und Vernichtun der Juden—Ein Atlas*. (Reinbeck/Hamburg, 1982), 110–12; Czech, 165 (secondary).

Glancszpigel, Sara (née Bleich). *Family Papers*. Buenos Aires, Argentina. 30 December 1971.

Greenman, Benjamin. Email correspondence with the author (including correspondence regarding his cousin, Magda Amsterova), 2012–19.

Grosman, Edith (#1970, née Friedman). Multiple personal interviews. Slovakia and Toronto, 25 March 2017–2019.

Grosman, Ladislav. *The Bride*. Trans. by Iris Urwin. Garden City, NY: Doubleday, 1970.

———. *The Shop on Main Street*. Trans. by Iris Urwin. Garden City, NY: Doubleday, 1970.

Gross, Louis, MA-BCD. *Flight for Life: The Journey of a Child Holocaust Survivor*. USA: 2002.

Hartmann, Andrew. Interview 4916. Segments: 3, 27, 34, 59–63. *Visual History Archive*, USC Shoah Foundation, 1996. Accessed 23 August 2019.

Hartmann, Eugene. Interview 17721. Segments: 8, 59, 60, 79, 120–27. *Visual History Archive*, USC Shoah Foundation, 1996. Accessed 23 August 2019.

Helm, Sarah. *Ravensbrück: Life and Death in Hitler's Concentration Camp for Women*. New York: Nan A. Talese, 2015.

Höss, Rudolf. *Commandant of Auschwitz*. London: Phoenix, 2000.

Hoffmann, Gabriel, and Ladislav Hoffmann. *Katolícka Cirkev A Tragédia Slovenských Židov V Dokumentoch*. 16 March 2016.

Holokaust na Slovensku: Obdobie autonómie. Dokumenty. [Zv. 1–6] / [Ed.]: Nižňanský, Eduard. Bratislava: Nadácia Milana Šimečku—Židovská náboženská obec, 2001, 362 [Holocaust and Slovakia. Period of Autonomy [1938–45], Documents, Volumes 1–6. Ed. Nižňanský, Eduard. Bratislava, Milan Šimeček Foundation—Jewish religious community, 2001; 362 pages].

Hudek, Peter, Ph.D. Personal Tour of Bardejov. Slovakia, 21 March 2017.

Isenberg, Madeleine. "Poprad." *Encyclopaedia of Jewish communities, Slovakia* (Poprad, Slovakia). Jerusalem: JewishGen, Inc., and the Yizkor Book Project, 2003.

Jarny, Ivan, "To Explain the Unexplainable." Personal unpublished papers. Melbourne, Australia.

———. Personal interview and email correspondence. March 2016–March 2019.

Kamenec, Ivan. "The Deporation of Jewish Citizens from Slovakia, 1942." *The Tragedy of the Jews of Slovakia, 1938–1945: Slovakia and the "Final Solution of the Jewish Question."* Auschwitz-Birkenau State Museum and Museum of the Slovak National Uprising (Oświęcim-Bankà Bystrica, 2002), 111–38.

Kapuscinki, Ryszard. *Travels with Herodotus.* Trans. Klara Glowczewska. New York: Vintage Books, 2007.

Klein, Julia. Interview 37605. Tape 1–6. *Visual History Archive*, USC Shoah Foundation, 1998. Accessed 23 August 2019.

Knieža, Ruzena. Interview 33231. Tape 1–6. *Visual History Archive*, USC Shoah Foundation, 1997. Accessed 12 February 2018.

Knoch, Habbo, ed. *Bergen-Belsen: Wehrmacht POW Camp 1940–1945, Concentration Camp 1943–1945, Displaced Persons Camp 1945–1950.* Catalogue of the permanent exhibition. Wallstein, 2010.

Koren, Akiva, and Avi Ischari. Personal interviews regarding their mothers, Erna and Fela Drangerova. Tylicz, Poland, 21 March 2017.

Kousal Mangel, Frances. Interview 19894. Sections: 36, 37, 43, 55. *Visual History Archive*, USC Shoah Foundation, 1996. Accessed 23 August 2019.

Kulik, Margaret. Interview 36221. Tape 1–4. *Visual History Archive*, USC Shoah Foundation, 1997. Accessed 12 February 2018.

Langbein, Hermann. *Menschen in Auschwitz.* Ullstein; Auflage: 1 (1980).

Langer, Eva. Personal email correspondence. 26 March 2017–2018.

Lasker-Wallfisch, Anita. *Inherit the Truth, 1939–1945: The Documented Experiences of a Survivor of Auschwitz and Belsen.* London: Giles De La Mare, 1996.

Lautman, Bertha (née Berkowitz). *Tomorrow Came Much Later: A Journey of Conscience*. Producer: Alan R. Stephenson; narrator: Ed Asner. Lawrence, KS: Centron Films. Aired: 28 April 1981, WVIZ, Cleveland, OH. DVD.

———. Interview 22590. Tape 1–5. *Visual History Archive*, USC Shoah Foundation, 1997. Accessed 12 February 2018.

———. "Oma's Journey." April 17, 2011. Accessed 27 June 2018. www.you tube.com/watch?v=blvu2XaXr2g. Michael Naftali Unterberg.

Legal documentation from the trials held in the Slovakian State Court of Law in Bratislava against Nazi war criminals of Slovakian origin, 31/10/1946–15/05/1947. M.5/136 Yad Vashem. (created 31/10/1946–15/05/1947) p. 188.

"Letters received and written by Hertzka, Lenka, in Auschwitz regarding the welfare of friends and acquaintances and the receipt of parcels in the camp." O.75/770. Yad Vashem: The World Holocaust Remembrance Center. Jerusalem, Israel.

"Lists of Jews from Slovakia transferred via Žilina transit camp to Poland between 03–10/1942." M.5/110; 42–76. Yad Vashem: The World Holocaust Remembrance Center. Jerusalem, Israel.

Mandel, Louis. *The Tragedy of Slovak Jewry in Slovakia*. Pamphlet published by the American Committee of Jews from Czechoslovakia. Online: Jewish Virtual Library: A Project of AICE, 1998–2017. American-Israeli Cooperative Ent.

Marek, Lydia. Recorded interview, 12 October 2018.

Marta Marek. Virginia Holocaust Museum. February 22, 2016. Accessed 20 April 2018. youtube.com/watch?v=9WMKJhDHsYQ. Zimmerspitz cousin, née Mangel, Martha (#1741).

Martone, Robert. "Scientists Discover Children's Cells Living in Mothers' Brains." *Scientific American*, December 4, 2012. Accessed 13 March 2016. www.scientificamerican.com/article/scientists-discover-chil drens-cells-living-in-mothers-brain/?redirect=1.

Ministerstvo vnútra, fond 166.1942, 14. oddelenie, Box 179; ministerstvo vnútra, fond 562.1942, 14. oddelenie, Box 205; ministerstvo vnútra, fond 807.1942, 14. oddelenie, Box 214; ministerstvo vnútra, fond 807.1942, 14. oddelenie, obeznik MV z 23.3.1942, Box 214; ministerstvo vnútra, fond 876.1942, 14. oddelenie, Box 215. Slovak National Archives. Bratislava, Slovakia.

McCord, Molly. Telephone interview with author. 10 July 2018. www.con sciouscoolchic.com.

Mešťan, Pavol. Personal interview with author, 28 March 2018.

Národný súd, fond 17/46 A. Vasek, Tnlud, Boxes 110 and 111. Slovak National Archives. Bratislava, Slovakia.

Neuman, Ariela. Telephone interview with author, 28 October 2018.

Newman, Edic. Interview 23821. Tape 1–5. *Visual History Archive*, USC Shoah Foundation, 1997. Accessed 02 October 2019.

Newman Ehrlich, Sharon. Personal interviews regarding her mother, Ida Eigerman. Prešov, Slovakia, and Oświęcim, Poland, 20–27 March 2017.

Némirovsky, Irène. *Suite Francaise.* Trans. Sandra Smith. London: Vintage Books, 2007.

Nižňanský, Eduard, ed. *Holokaust na Slovensku, Obdobie autonómie* (6.10.1938–14.3.1939). Bratislava, Slovakia: Nadacia Milana Simecku, 2003.

———, and Ivan Kamenec. *Holokaust na Slovensku 2. Prezident, vláda, Senát Slovenskej republiky a Štátna rada o židovskej otázke (1939–1945).* Bratislava, Slovakia: Nadacia Milana Simecku, 2003.

Odze, Margaret. Interview 2553. Segments 49–52. *Visual History Archive*, USC Shoah Foundation, 1996. Accessed 23 August 2018.

Posmysz, Zofia. *Chrystus oświęcimski.* (The Christ from Auschwitz.) Fundacja na rzecz MDSM w Oświęcimiu. (International Youth Meeting Center Foundation.) 2014.

Pretter, Regina. Interview 19099. Tape 1–6. *Visual History Archive*, USC Shoah Foundation, 1996. Accessed 12 February 2018.

Princz, Katharina. Interview 8300. Tape 1–4. *Visual History Archive*, USC Shoah Foundation, 1996. Accessed 02 January 2019.

Rajcan, Vanda. "Anton Vašek, Head of the Interior Ministry's 14th Department, His Responsibility, and Information about the Deportees." Uncovering the Shoah: Resistance of Jews and Efforts to Inform the World on Genocide. Žilina, Slovakia, 25– 26 August 2015.

Rokytka, Roman. "The Kolbasian Tragedy: The Eternal Memento of the Nonsense of Human Hate." *Dolný Zemplín Korzár*, September 28, 2004. Accessed December 7, 2017. dolnyzemplin.korzar.sme.sk/c/4560457/kolbasovska-tragedia-vecne-memento-o-nezmyselnosti-ludskej-nenavisti.html#ixzz4z9RF7M3m.

Rosenberg, Margaret Becker. Interview 14650. Tape 1–6. *Visual History Archive*, USC Shoah Foundation, 1996. Accessed 12 February 2018.

Rotkirchen, L. *The Destruction of Slovak Jewry.* Jerusalem: Yad Vashem, 1961.

Rutman, Ella. Interview 17381. Tape 1–4. *Visual History Archive*, USC Shoah Foundation, 1996. Accessed 12 February 2018.

Safarty, Maya. Director of *Ha Yaffa BaNashim* (The Most Beautiful Woman). 2016. Facebook chat. 10 June 2018.

Scheib, Ariel. *Slovakia: Virtual Jewish History Tour.* Jewish Virtual Library: A Project of AICE 1998–2017, American-Israeli Cooperative Ent.

Shik, Naama. "In a Very Silent Screams [sic]—Jewish Women in Auschwitz-Birkenau Concentration Camp." SemanticScholar.org (2011).

Šikulová, Stanislava. Personal interviews and emails. zástupca riaditeľa, kultúrno-propagačný manažér; Múzeum židovskej kultúry v Bratislave [Museum of Jewish Culture, Bratislava], Slovakia, 2017–18.

Šimkulič, Marián, Anna Šimkuličová, and Viliam Schichman. *Zvečnené V Slzách a Pote Tváre: Návrat Rodáka Ladislava Grosmana.* Humenné: ADIN, 2016.

Sloboda, Ivan. Personal interview regarding his mother. London, UK, 15 April 2016.

Špiesz, Anton, Ladislaus J. Bolchazy, and Dušan Čaplovič. *Illustrated Slovak History: A Struggle for Sovereignty in Central Europe.* Bolchazy Carducci, 2006.

Svitak, Peter. Personal email correspondence. March–December 2018.

Strzelecki, Andrzej. *Marsz Śmierci*—przewodnik po trasie Oświęcim-Wodzisław Śląski [Death Marches: Guide to the Oświęcim-Wodzisław Route].) Katowice, 1989.

Teege, Bertel. "Hinter Gitter und Stacheldraht," ARa 647. Archiv Mahan-und-Gedensstatte, Ravensbrück.

Tehori, Tsiporah. Interview 33749. Tape 1–7. *Visual History Archive*, USC Shoah Foundation, 1997. Accessed 12 February 2018.

Tuckman, Orna. Personal interviews regarding her mother, Marta Friedman. Prešov, Slovakia, and Oświęcim, Poland, 24 and 27 March 2017.

Twenty Years of Jewish Women Association Ester. Directed by Ľuba Koľova. Slovakia: International Council of Jewish Women (ICJW), 2016. DVD.

Urad Propagandy (propaganda office) of the Hlinka Guard, including a collection of anti-Jewish propaganda proclamations, announcements, and booklets, 1938. M.5/46 Created 1938–1945. YV (images).

Vajda, Daniel. Personal interview regarding his mother, Dina Drangerova. France, 14 May 2014.

Valo, Edith. Interview 17457. Tape 1–5. *Visual History Archive*, USC Shoah

van Pelt, Robert Jan, and Deborah Dwork. *Auschwitz: 1270 to the Present.* London: Yale University Press, 1996.

Viets, Jack. "S.F. Woman's Return to the Holocaust: Testimony at Nazi Trial in Germany." *San Francisco Chronicle*, June 11, 1987.

Vrba, Rudolf. *I Escaped Auschwitz: Including the Text of the Auschwitz Protocols.* London: Robson, 2002.

The Wannsee Conference. Munich: Infafilm, 1984.

Ward, James Mace. *Priest, Politician, Collaborator: Jozef Tiso and the Making of Fascist Slovakia.* Ithaca: Cornell University Press. 2013.

Weintraub, Joan. Interview 20213. Tape 1–4. *Visual History Archive,* USC Shoah Foundation, 1996. Accessed 23 August 2019.

Wilkinson, Robert. "Astrology Class in May 2016—The Mutable T-square Is About to Become the Great Fracturing of 2016, part 2." Aquariun Papers.com. May 2016. aquariuspapers.com/astrology/2016/05/ astrology-class-in-may-2016-the-mutable-t-square-is-about-to-become -the-great-fracturing-of-2016-pt-2.html.

———. Personal email correspondence, 2018.

Wirtschafter, David Rabbi. Personal email correspondence, 14 June 2018.

WIZO Anniversary. DVD. Múzeum židovskej kultúry v Bratislave [Museum of Jewish Culture, Bratislava], Slovakia, 2012.

Yong, Ed. "Foetal Cells Hide Out in Mum's Body, but What Do They Do?" *National Geographic,* September 7, 2015. Accessed 13 September 2015. www.nationalgeographic.com/science/phenomena/2015/09/07/ foetal-cells-hide-out-in-mums-body-but-what-do-they-do.

Zilberman, Raquel. "Edith Goldman." *Hans Kimmel Competition essays: 1979–2007.* Darlington, N.S.W.: Stern, Russell, and Sophie Gelski. Australian Jewish Historical Society, 2011.

Zimmer, Carl. "A Pregnancy Souvenir: Cells That Are Not Your Own." *New York Times,* September 10, 2015. Accessed 13September 2015. www.nytimes.com/2015/09/15/science/a-pregnancy-souvenir-cells- that-are-not-your-own.html.

———. "Bamboo Mathematicians." *National Geographic,* May 15, 2015. Accessed 18 May 2015. www.nationalgeographic.com/science/phenom- ena/2015/05/15/bamboo-mathematicians.

Zimmerspitz, Samuel. Interview 35662. Tape 1–6. *Visual History Archive,* USC Shoah Foundation, 1997. Accessed 02 October 2019.

Acknowledgments

Gratitude seems a small word for such a powerful emotion and barely grasps the depth of acknowledgment I owe to the families who entrusted their mothers', cousins', and aunts' stories to me. I am sincerely grateful to them for giving me this honor. When I met Rena Kornreich Gelissen in 1992, I had no idea that twenty-five years later I would meet Adela Gross's family, discover the Benovicova sisters' names, or dare to write another Holocaust book.

This book would never have been written without Edith Grosman. Her courage to return to the past and record her account of survival on film, as well as countless personal interviews, is the force behind this research and this story. Tireless at ninety-five years of age and with a brain that is astutely sharp, Edith bore my questions and connected the dots between many of the girls that she knew in camp. I am eternally grateful to have shared so many hours of deep conversations filled with laughter, tears, and singing. Thank you for allowing me into your life and accepting me into your home and your family. While I never met Edith's husband, Ladislav Grosman, I would like to thank Laco for the novels he wrote about his hometown, which infuse the beginning of this narrative with their spirit.

It was Adela Gross's story, and the discovery of her cousin, Lou, that first started me on this journey in 2012. Thanks go to Lou's wife, Joan, for reading *Rena's Promise*, finding Adela's story, and getting in touch with me. If God's hand was in any of this, it was that moment when we connected, and Lou and the Gross family learned what happened to their beautiful red-headed cousin, seventy years after she disappeared.

My heartfelt gratitude to Ivan Jarny, who became my personal research assistant at ninety-two years of age and continued helping me for the next three years. I had hoped to find a young student, but instead found an old one who was absolutely tireless in his tenacious search for truth at his local Jewish Holocaust Center in Melbourne, Australia, which helped us unravel some of the more confusing bits of this history, especially around Dr. Gejza Konka. Ivan's personal papers and Giora Amir's memoir are important acts of witness and are among the most powerful resources I found for this book.

In 2016, I was fortunate to meet Dr. Pavol Mešťan and his assistant, the brilliant and exceedingly helpful Dr. Stanislava Šikulová of the Múzeum židovskej kultúry v Bratislave (Museum of Jewish Culture in Bratislava). Your combined knowledge and insight were essential as I untangled the web of deceit and betrayal, complicated political manuverings, government laws, codices, and of course the origins of the list. Thank you for inviting me to the anniversary events and for all you do every year in Poprad to make sure the girls are remembered, respected, and honored.

Serendipity has played a part in every corner of the creation of this book. Writing it would never have been possible if I had not met my litearary agent, Scott Mendel, at the five hundredth anniversary of the Jewish Ghetto in Venice, Italy, and he had not shown interest in the story. A few years later, my wonderful editor, Michaela Hamilton, was on board with the whole publishing family at Kensington's Citadel Press to become the champions of this story and the girls. Thank you to my foreign rights team and publicity departments for helping bring this story to the world. To Arthur Maisel, thank you for your painstaking attention to detail and help throughout the production phase of this book.

In memory of Irena Strzelecka and her work on the women's camp in Auschwitz, I am grateful for all she did in compiling the essays in *The Tragedy of the Jews of Slovakia*, and for what Rena and I were able to contribute. Dr. Ivan Kamenec may have forwarded me to the historians Jan Hlavinka and Michala Lônčiková, but I am deeply grateful to him for his early research into the first transports, which provided me a road map to the documents I needed to find in the Slovak National Archives. I am also grateful for comprehensive multivolume catalogues of the Ministry of the Interior and court documents from Tiso's government, compiled by Professor Eduard Nižňanský from Department of General History at Comenius University in Bratislava and his students, which I accessed at the Weiner Library and which lead me to the historical documents I needed to find in the Slovak National Archives. To Dr. Marek Púčik, who handed me box after box at the Archives, thank you for your patience and occasional translation assistance. I am rarely happier than when I am amid stacks of boxes and old papers. It was in those stacks that I found the elusive Gejza Konka's signature time and again.

My deepest thanks to the researchers and archivists at Auschwitz-Birkenau Państwowe Muzeum: Dr. Piotr Setkiewicz, who welcomed me into his office in 2012 and personally showed me places not on any public tour of Auschwitz that would later inform this book; to Doreta Nycz, who first brought me into Block 10; Wanda Hutny, who in 2017 brought the survivors' children I was traveling with into Block 10, where their mothers had first been kept in Auschwitz; and Magdalena Gabryś and Katarzyna Kolonko for helping us film on-site at the museum.

At the USC Shoah Foundation, I would like to thank Crispin Brooks, my first contact in 2012, who searched the database for survivors of the first transport's recorded testimonies and gave me an initial list of names, with twenty-two women on it, and photographs of them as girls. That list was the seed that germinated into this book. Thank you also to Georgiana Gomez, the access supervisor for the USC Visual Archive, who helped me wade through testimony and photograph permissions, so you, dear reader, could see the girls, as well. I am additionally grateful for all the assistance the archivists at Yad Vashem have given me over the years: Reut Golani, Marisa Fine, and to Alla Kucherenko, for showing Orna and her son, Gideon, the original list. Thanks also to Liliya Meyerovich at the U.S. Holocaust Memorial Museum for fielding my many queries and always responding quickly. I am also exceedingly appreciative to Simon Bentley, the director of Yad Vashem UK, for his abundant goodwill, support, and his wonderful staff.

None of the people involved in this project were more important than the actual survivors, their children, their witnesses, and the family members of nonsurvivors. It was through them that I uncovered many of these untold stories and am probably still uncovering them at this printing. You are a part of my family and my heart in such a deep way, I cannot suitably express my respect and love for you all.

Sitting in Sir Martin Gilbert's library with his widow, Lady Esther Gilbert, and survivor's son Ivan Sloboda, as Ivan translated the historic food document on the girls' diet, remains one of the most powerful memories I have of working on this book. Surrounded by Sir Martin's books, hearing names like Rudi Vrba's being tossed around with the familiarity of dear friends, I had a "pinch myself" moment. Who ever thought a kid from Birmingham, Michigan, who used to think history class was a good place for a nap, would be among such giants of Holocaust history? I am very touched by the support Sir Martin Gilbert gave me when I was working on the new edition of *Rena's Promise,* and that of Lady Esther Gilbert, who has been a champion of this project and encouraged me to chronicle the stories of the young women and girls of the first transport. I hope that the work I have done would make both Rudi and Martin proud.

I would like to thank Orna Tuckman, Tammy Forestater, Sharon Newman Ehrilchman, Avi Koren, Akiva Ischari, and Daniella and Jonathan Forestater for joining me on our journey through Slovakia and Poland, culminating in our visit to Auschwitz-Birkenau. To the director, cinematographer, and dear friend Stephen Hopkins—a.k.a. Hobbit—who filmed that entire journey for posterity, creating a documentary on the girls, thanks are small compensation for such stalwart work and tireless research. Next pint's on me. I am also grateful to dearest Isabel Moros for connecting me to my translator, Martina Mrazova from Levoča, who amid the academic pressures of her advanced degree work, donated her time translating massive quantities of Slovakian materials for me. Among my other translators and transcribers, thank you to Kathleen Furey, Gabriel Barrow, Esther Mathieu, Johnny Baeur, Pedro Oliveira, Shekar Gahlot and of course, Avi's wonderful wife, Sara Isachari, for her ample donation of translating Hebrew testimonies. I am also indebted to Sara Gordon for reading through an early draft and to Oliver Payne at *National Geographic,* and his marvelous wife, Cindy Leitner, for all of your support and for introducing me to Kitry Krause, my excellent copyeditor, who worked round the clock with me fixing last-minute errors.

I need to thank the many relatives of girls on the first transport who gave me stories and photographs so we can know these young women as they really were in 1942—young and innocent. Thank you, Beni Greenman (cousin to Magda Amster); Peter Chudý (son of Klara Lustbader); Andrea Glancszpigel (granddaughter of Sara Bleich); Dasha Grafil (daughter of Linda—Libusha—Reich); Ilanna Lefovitz (daughter of Serena Lefkovitz); Donna Steinhorn (daughter of Marta Friedman); Celia Pretter and Belle Liss (daughters of Regina Schwartz); Judith Gold (daughter of Perel Fridman); Jeffrey Lautman (son of Bertha Berkowitz); Naomi Ickovitz (niece of Bertha Berkowitz, daughter of Fany); Ruth Wyse (daughter of Elena Zuckermenn); Vera Power (daughter of Regina Wald); Rosette Rutman (daughter of Ella Friedman and niece of Edie and Lila); Pavol Hell (nephew of Gertrude Kleinberger); Eva Langer (niece of Frida and Helena Benovicova); Ivan Sloboda (son of Judita); Sylvia Lanier and Joseph and Robert Gelissen (children of Rena Kornreich); Susan Hartmann Schwartz (niece of Nusi Hartmann, daughter of Eugene Hartmann); Diane Young (niece of Magduska Hartmann, daughter of Andrew Hartmann); Alena Giesche (friend of Ruzena Gräber Knieža); Cheryl Metcalf (on behalf of Koplowitz and Zeigler families); also, to Maya Lee (daughter of Magda Hellinger); Sara Cohen and Norman Brandel (daughter of Danka Kornreich Brandel), and Zuzana Kovacikova (niece of Dr. Manci Schwalbova). Thank you for sharing their lives with us. I apologize that I could not include more of your stories and theirs in this book.

THE HARDEST PART of this book was writing about the girls who did not survive. When the weight of their ghosts descended, Anita Thorn sent me spiritual pick-me-ups always at the right moment. I truly wish I could have found out what happened to Magduska and Nusi Hartmann, but they are representative of hundreds of thousands—no, millions—of mysteries that will never be resolved.

To the astrologers Molly McCord and Robert Wilkinson, thank you for helping me understand the issues around Himmler's occult obsession and for taking my hunch seriously. Robert Wilkinson went beyond the dates I questioned seeking further back in time to find Goebbels's own announcement of the Final Solution and revealing a deeper nefarious astrological connection than even I had imagined. Thank you both for your dedication and service to the girls.

Writing this book was emotionally trying at times, and I am so grateful for the support of my writers' group, Suki, Felicia, and Connie, and my girlfriends, Lauren, Nicolette, and Tamara. To my brother, who was the first writer in the family, and put up with me disappearing for ten months while I hunkered down at my desk and ignored everyone, thank you for your constant encouragement and faith in me. And to my father, who does not always understood what I am doing but has been supportive nonetheless.

It was my writing partner, friend, and husband, Simon Worrall, who first insisted that I write this book. There were times when he regretted it. Thank you for translating German transcripts, speaking to archivists in Ravensbrück on my behalf, being my first reader, editor, and champion, cooking dinner, doing the dishes, bearing up with my erratic mood swings as I wrote through the grief that sometimes surrounded my desk, and most importantly for "dancing with me to the end of time."

Finally, a shout-out to my favorite teenagers of the next generation: Josie Perl, who at fourteen has just finished writing her first novel, and *ma petite* Donna Snyder, who constantly amazes me with her talent, ingenuity, and straight A's. You give my life more meaning than you know, and I am forever proud of who you are today and of who you are going to become.

Index

427